THE GROUP AS AGENT OF CHANGE

THE GROUP AS AGENT OF CHANGE

Treatment, Prevention, Personal Growth in the Family, the School, the Mental Hospital and the Community

edited by

Alfred Jacobs
Professor of Psychology and
Director of Graduate Training
in Clinical Psychology

Wilford W. Spradlin
Professor of Psychiatry and
Chairman, Department of
Behavioral Medicine and
Psychiatry

West Virginia University
Morgantown, West Virginia

Behavioral Publications
New York
1974

Library of Congress Catalog Number 73-12805
ISBN: 0-87705-128-3 (casebound)
ISBN: 0-87705-129-1 (paperback)

BEHAVIORAL PUBLICATIONS,
72 Fifth Avenue, New York, New York 10011

Printed in the United States of America
3456789 10987654321

Library of Congress Cataloging in Publication Data

Jacobs, Alfred, 1922–
The group as agent of change.

1. Small groups. 2. Group psychotherapy.
I. Spradlin, Wilford W., joint author. II. Title.
[DNLM: 1. Group processes. HM131 J17g 1973]
HM134.J33 301.18'5 73-12805

CONTENTS

LIST OF ILLUSTRATIONS AND FIGURES

LIST OF TABLES

CONTRIBUTORS

Marilyn Arnett, M.A., Research Coordinator, Behavior Research and Development Center, Department of Psychology, Western Michigan University, Kalamazoo, Michigan

Carolyn L. Attneave, Ph.D., Assistant Professor, Department of Psychiatry, Tufts School of Medicine

George R. Bach, Ph.D., Director, Institute of Group Psychotherapy, Beverly Hills, California

John D. Cone, Ph.D., Associate Professor of Psychology, Department of Psychology, West Virginia University, Morgantown, West Virginia

Albert Ellis, Ph.D., Executive Director, Institute for Advanced Study in Rational Psychotherapy, New York, New York

William Fawcett Hill, Ph.D., Group Studies Center, University of Southern California, Los Angeles, California

Ralph G. Hirschowitz, M.B., B.Ch., Lecturer on Psychiatry, Laboratory of Community Psychiatry, Harvard Medical School, Boston, Massachusetts

Alfred Jacobs, Ph.D., Professor and Director of Graduate Training in Clinical Psychology, Department of Psychology, West Virginia University, Morgantown, West Virginia

Marion K. Jacobs, Ph.D., Associate Professor, Department of Behavioral Medicine and Psychiatry, West Virginia University Medical Center, Morgantown, West Virginia

Arnold A. Lazarus, Ph.D., Visiting Professor and Director of Clinical Training, Department of Psychology, Yale University, New Haven, Connecticut

Roger F. Maley, Ph.D., Associate Professor, Department of Psychology, West Virginia University, Morgantown, West Virginia

James A. Peterson, Ph.D., Professor of Sociology, Director, Liason Office, Gerontology Center, University of Southern California, Los Angeles, California

Harold M. Proshansky, Ph.D., Professor of Psychology and Dean, University Graduate Division, The City University of New York, New York, New York

Charles Seashore, Ph.D., Director, Professional Development, NTL Institute for Applied Behavioral Science, Washington, D.C.

E. Wayne Sloop, Ph.D., Assistant Professor, Department of Behavioral Medicine and Psychiatry, West Virginia University Medical Center, Morgantown, West Virginia

C. Richard Spates, B.A., Project Director, Behavior Research and Development Center, Department of Psychology, Western Michigan University, Kalamazoo, Michigan

Ross V. Speck, M.D., Fellow, Institute for Social Change, New York, New York

Wilford W. Spradlin, M.D., Professor and Chairman, Department of Behavioral Medicine and Psychiatry, West Virginia University Medical Center, Morgantown, West Virginia

O. Lee Trick, M.D., Associate Professor and Director of Inpatient Services, Department of Behavioral Medicine and Psychiatry, West Virginia University Medical Center, Morgantown, West Virginia

Roger E. Ulrich, Ph.D., Professor and Chairman, Department of Psychology, Western Michigan University, Kalamazoo, Michigan

Maxine Wolfe, Ph.D., Assistant Professor, Department of Psychology, The City University of New York, New York, New York

Preface

Group phenomena occur naturally in many species of animal life. In the last few decades, students in the field of human behavior have begun more fully to appreciate that most of the behavioral patterns we call human are the product of group process. Human group phenomena are apparently as old as civilization; however, the harnessing of group power to alter human activities is still in its developmental stages. In many respects, the struggle against the illusion of individual autonomy is just beginning. In spite of extensive use of group process in religious, political and other defensive and offensive human interactions, the mystique of the individual has, in the past, received most of the attention of scholars and scientists. This is especially true in the fields of medicine and psychology.

Man clings desperately to his self-concept without realizing that it is a conglomeration of present and past group validations. Indeed, even experienced psychotherapists often conceptualize group therapy as a tool to educate the individual in techniques for living more autonomously. This is somewhat in opposition to social studies that indicate man is most likely to maintain emotional balance when he learns interpersonal skills in developing and belonging to flexible but cohesive groups. Recently many diverse approaches to the understanding of group phenomena have arisen; however, with our present knowledge it would be unproductive, if not dishonest, to imply that one approach is more valid or effective than all others.

In this book the editors have attempted to provide a broad basis for conceptualizing group dynamics, using a format that we hope will not place restraints on scholarly imagination. Rather than limiting themselves to a presentation of psychotherapeutic groups, the authors examine a wide array of naturally and artificially occurring groups as agents of change.

Most of the credit for compiling this material from the various distinguished contributors should go to Alfred Jacobs, who originally proposed the idea and who has worked hard in collecting and editing the manuscripts.

We would like to express our appreciation to those busy scholars who have contributed to this book and to Peggy Akers, Gail Rafter, Viola Rouse and Elizabeth Cowen, who helped us get the material into its present form.

Wilford W. Spradlin, M.D.

Introduction

Alfred Jacobs

The focus of social action has shifted from intervening solely for the purpose of curing mental illness to attempting to prevent distress and to improve the quality of social living (Ross, 1970). It has become apparent that modifying the social systems within which individuals function may be the most effective mode of intervention for producing all these varieties of social change (Korten, Cook & Lacey, 1970). Technologies derived from educational and social models of human behavior are rapidly being generated in a variety of settings to facilitate the alteration of the interactions which occur in families, classrooms, hospital wards and community systems, as will be demonstrated in the chapters to follow. The utility of these technologies is often widely applicable and has the potential for adaptation to settings other than the one of origin (Egan, 1970).

The growth of methods of group intervention has indeed been increasing at a phenomenal rate. The history of the small group movement has been adequately chronicled elsewhere (Rosenbaum & Berger, 1963; Gazda, 1968). Gazda points out, for example, that the total number of books, articles and dissertations in the group psychotherapy area in the 25-year period preceding 1931 was 34. However, MacLennan & Levy (1971) found 481 references to group psychotherapy and self-development groups in the year 1970 alone. Wolberg (1954), in his standard 800-page text, The Technique of Psychotherapy, *devoted only four pages to group therapy, commenting, "While some persons contend that the results of group therapy by itself approximate those of individual therapy, one may reasonably question the validity of this notion [P. 569]."* Egan, in 1970, begins his book Encounter *by describing the growing use of small-group methods in business, in education and in the wider community, pointing out that the overly enthusiastic are claiming that all things can be done through groups. He refers to a personal communication from Martin Lieberman, who reports the discovery of over 200 self-actualizing groups of various kinds in one city of 50,000 population.*

This book consists of a sample of varied efforts to explore the utilization of group methods of intervention for the production of change in individuals and in organizations. The editors solicited original manuscripts from social scientists and practitioners, identified by previous publications and reputation as the originators of creative approaches to the modification of systems. Contributors were selected who were engaged in using group methods of intervention for a wide variety of purposes, including the facilitation of personal growth, the treatment of mental illness, the prevention of the effects of social deprivation and the expediting of community action planning. The settings of these interventions were diverse, ranging from kindergarten to the community, and including the home, the hospital ward and the psychotherapist's office, among others.

The editors, conceptualizing group intervention as involving learning and educative processes, were biased toward the selection of contributors with similar conceptual models, or at least models which were not conceptually incompatible. Categories of potential contributors were set up to insure representation of certain particularly timely topics of general interest to those conducting groups, or doing research on groups. Among these topics were included token economy systems with mental hospital patients, milieu therapy, the use of operant methods in the school and classroom behavior rehearsal techniques, groups in community psychology work, the personal growth movement and treatment of family members. The editors contacted potential participants, identified by their work or reputation as associated with these topics, and replaced those who were unable to participate with substitutes drawn from the same category. In any case, the editors are not contending that the choice of either contributors or topics bears any resemblance to a random selection process. It follows, therefore, that any overall conclusions that the editor or readers may attempt to draw from these chapters, may not be at all applicable to other types of group leaders or group situations.

The instructions to participants requested that they address their manuscript to theoretical formulation, research or descriptions of techniques and programs. A typical excerpt from a letter to a potential contributor follows:

> We have conceived of groups and group processes in the broadest sense ranging from the climate in the family to the classroom, or the mobilization of the elements of the community, and consisting of natural groups as well as those formed artificially for the purpose of treatment and training. However, since most such endeavors go better if the participants have a central theme to which to address themselves, we think it would be helpful for contributors to focus on such group processes and variables which facilitate or impede change, and how these processes are engaged or disengaged. There are a variety of approaches to the problem including the presentation of relevant data, addressing onself to theoretical formulations in the area, and discussions of plans or ongoing research strategies, and/or proposed group programs.

The instructions were deliberately left somewhat unstructured in order to allow contributors to select those aspects of their current work they believed to be particularly important or exciting. As experimenters know too well, ambiguous instructions sometimes lead to ambiguous results. Papers were received, for example, which combined conceptualizations and descriptions of techniques. As a matter of fact, it is probably quite difficult for people trained as scientists, as our contributors are, to describe how they are doing something, and resist attempts to explain the phenomena.

Fortunately, however, the manuscripts could generally be sorted into four major categories, which make up the four major sections of the book. We have titled these four sections Perspectives and Overview, Innovative Treatment Strategies and Programs, Theory and Conceptualization and Data and Research.

SCOPE

The purpose of the first section, Perspectives and Overview, is to provide a general context for the reader. This introduction in which the reader finds himself, explains how the material for the book was collected, will go on to provide a brief description of the sections and the chapters to follow and identifies for the reader some of the common themes that reappear frequently through the text.

The first chapter, by James A. Peterson, views the amazing growth of the small-group movement from a broader social and cultural stance. Peterson identifies the group movement as a social invention designed to cope with deficits in modern social living, a reaction to the breakdown of the traditional cultural agencies that in the past have satisfied man's important personal needs.

Chapter Two, Strategies of Social Intervention, Past and Future, presents an analysis of our past and present strategies of social intervention. It is asserted in this chapter that our mental-health resources in the past have predominantly been directed towards one goal of intervention: correction or remediation of mental illness, via a dyadic interaction modality between patient and healer. There has been a widespread neglect of other meaningful goals, such as the prevention of social incompetence, and a failure to allot resources for the establishment of a variety of forms of socioemotional education that could contribute to an enrichment of social living.

Section II, Innovative Treatment Strategies and Programs, contains seven chapters, which are predominantly descriptions of treatment programs and techniques. The first two chapters are addressed to a traditional psychotherapy problem: the treatment of the patient designated as mentally ill and removed from home and community for hospitalization. First, Trick, Jacobs & Spradlin describe a milieu-therapy program based on a social-learning model in which the social aspects of the psychiatric setting are utilized as forces leading to therapeutic change. The program serves a dual purpose, since the setting also enables large numbers of students of various occupational affiliations to learn to deliver mental-health services. The second chapter, by Roger Maley, analyzes the manner in which the environment of the mental-hospital patient ordinarily maintains sick behavior. The introduction of a token-economy program into such a hospital system interrupts the subtle encouragement of symptoms by rewarding the patient for behavior more likely to facilitate adjustment in the community outside the hospital. Maley also suggests a variety of potential elicitors of such appropriate behaviors, and situations in which such behaviors might be rehearsed by patients.

The third and fourth chapters in this section represent group approaches to a second classical problem of intervention, that of the individual in the community whose adjustment is distressed but who does not require hospitalization. Arnold Lazarus, in his chapter, Understanding and Modifying Aggression in Behavioral Groups, presents a description, illustrated by case material, of learning-derived psychotherapy techniques that can be used to train group members in more constructive methods of dealing with aggressive feelings and behavior. Albert Ellis, in the following chapter, The Group as Agent of Facilitating Change Toward Rational Thinking and Appropriate Emoting, deals again with strangers who seek assistance with their lives. Ellis asserts that it is the cognitions or self-statements of individuals that exaggerate their life-difficulties. He describes how group processes may be used for the reeducation of individuals whose misused symbol-systems have created states of misery and unhappiness.

The first four chapters describe group interventions with individuals who ordinarily have little interaction with each other except for that which occurs in the time and place of intervention. The next three chapters contain descriptions of groups composed of individuals whose contractual relationships to each other involve elements additional to those deriving primarily from common social difficulties or discomforts. George Bach, in his chapter, Constructive Aggression in Growth Groups, describes in detail his technology for training husbands and wives to fight with each other in more constructive ways. Bach argues that conflict, frustration and aggression are unavoidable aspects of interdependency. He goes on to describe specific techniques of elicitation, rehearsal and evaluation that he has developed to assist pairs of individuals in more constructive resolution of their differences.

Marilyn Arnett, C. Richard Spates & Roger E. Ulrich, in the next chapter, Learning Village: Positive Control in a Group Situation, describe a truly programmed school-system aimed at longitudinal research and preventative training measures. This school, and the one described by Ellis in the earlier chapter, represent two examples in the book of deliberate attempts to use the educational structure for the very important goal of prevention. Arnett et al. hope that they may be able to assist their pupils, who have been drawn from populations of the culturally deprived, to avoid future failure in the educational and socioeconomic system by improving their educational competence through the systematic application of positive reinforcement techniques.

The final chapter in this section—Social Network Intervention in Time and Space, by Carolyn Attneave and Ross V. Speck—describes the theory and practice of building a community-support system for an individual in crisis. The chapter presents a case study of a disturbed boy treated by large group meetings involving 40 significant others in the child's life.

The next section of the book, Theory and Conceptualization, consists of four chapters that are primarily general and theoretical in nature. Charles Seashore, in the first of these, Time and Transition in the Intensive Group Experience, describes the processes that characterize growth in encounter groups designed to improve the social adjustment of the adequately functioning person. Seashore's major thesis is that the process of change itself has become so accelerated that the personal growth of most individuals requires a benevolent climate in which personal adjustments also have an opportunity to proceeed with great dispatch. He argues that the personal-growth group provides such a climate. In the second chapter, Maxine Wolfe & Harold M. Proshansky are particularly concerned with man's physical environment and the manner in which the size, location and shape of the space that surrounds an individual determine the time, amount and type of social activity that occur.

The third chapter, by Ralph G. Hirschowitz, Small Group Methods in the Promotion of Change within Interagency Networks: Leadership Models, deals primarily with the role and behavior of the leader in a group. The chapter describes typical emotional and personal reactions set in motion when a group of community representatives meet to make decisions relating to community mental-health problems. Hirschowitz contends that it is necessary for the group leader to recognize these emotional events, and to respond to them appropriately, in order for the group to achieve the goals which they have chosen. The chapter identifies the phases involved in group problem-solving and the role of the leader in each phase. The final chapter in this section, Systematic Group Development (SGD) Therapy, by William Fawcett Hill, describes research instruments developed to assess group variables. Hill explains how such instruments are useful for providing feedback to the group leader (and group members) regarding the interaction styles of the leader and participants. Hill argues that such information provides a better basis for the assignment of members and leaders to groups. In addition, the opportunity to objectively and regularly monitor the types of interactions that characterize the group process, enables the trainer to make more effective and appropriate interventions.

The last section of the book, Data and Research, contains four chapters heavily documented by current literature. The first, by John D. Cone and E. Wayne Sloop, Parents as Agents of Change, traces through history the use of parents in psychotherapy and contends that parents are the most effective potential modifiers of the behavior of their children. Parents can be trained to produce very durable modifications in the behavior of their offspring by teaching them to be better observers and more consistent reinforcers of the more desirable responses of their children. The final three chapters are review chapters by Alfred Jacobs. In the first of these, Affect in Groups, the emotions purported to occur during group interventions are described. Facts regarding the emotional characteristics of leaders and participants that are related to improvement or modified by group treatments, are also examined. The second of these review chapters, Learning-Oriented and Training-Oriented Approaches to the Modification of Emotional Behavior in Groups, describes Rogerian, Skinnerian and Systematic Desensitization approaches. The final chapter, The Use of Feedback in Groups, reviews the recent empirical literature on the use of verbal and visual feedback in groups. It concludes with a description of some recent studies of the delivery and reception of structured verbal feedback in groups, conducted by the author and colleagues.

THEMES

A number of common themes characterize the new approaches to the utilization of group methods for the modification of social behavior. The identification of these departures from the ideologies and practices characteristic of the intervention methods of the past may be of assistance to the reader, by providing a cognitive structure for the incorporation of the wide variety of contents in the chapters that follow.

THE MODEL

Perhaps the most general of these themes is the abandonment of the use of the traditional medical disease-and-healer model to generate principles and techniques for the modification of social behavior. It would be surprising if this were not the case in this volume, in view of the manner in which the editors selected contributors. However, the movement away from traditional medical models of intervention is not singular to this text. The value of medical models for social intervention has been questioned for the last decade (Szasz, 1961; Kanfer & Saslow, 1965; Sarbin, 1967), and the advocacy of psychological, social or educational models of intervention as more meaningful substitutes to the medical model is becoming widespread (Albee, 1969; Guerney, Stollak & Guerney, 1971; Goldstein, Heller & Sechrest, 1966; Bandura, 1969). The consequence of this substitution of other conceptual models for the traditional medical one is profound, since it makes available to the intervener much information about the principles of group interaction derived from social psychology, regarding the acquisition of skills derived from the field of education, and about the modification of behavior derived from psychology.

THE LEADER

The reader will also note in the chapters to follow that the role of the leader of the group is conceived of less as a variety of charismatic mystique, and more as a more knowledgeable, participant manager of the interactions within the system. (See chapters by Trick, Jacobs & Spradlin; Hirschowitz; Lazarus; and

Hill, for example.) The leader is more aware that he and other members of the sytem are models for each other, that both he and other group members beneficently or aversively attend to selected classes of each other's responses, and that this matrix of interactions generates demonstrable consequences that occur inevitably, whether the leader wills it or not, and whether he knows it or not.

The role of the group leader as trainer of trainees is also a frequent concept (see chapter by Trick, Jacobs & Spradlin; Cone and Sloop; Arnett, Spate & Ulrich), as is the function of the leader as an organizer of training experiences (see chapters by Maley and by Bach).

Another major influence on the selection and training of the group leader has been the increase in information regarding the nature of group intervention, as described in the last three review chapters by Jacobs. This information has enabled the technology of interventions to be analyzed into components of principle and technique that can be easily and rapidly taught to potential behavioral-intervention agents. The consequence has been the marked increase in employment of paraprofessionals and subprofessionals in mental-health delivery agencies (Matarazzo, 1971; Guerney, 1969). The use of paraprofessionals and subprofessionals as behavioral interveners is also illustrated frequently in the chapters to follow, and the training of nursing and medical students in methods of group intervention (Trick, Jacobs & Spradlin), as well as the training of high school and college students (Arnett, Spates & Ulrich), ministers (Peterson) and parents (Cone & Sloop).

THE INTERVENTION PROCESS

In general, the reader will observe a deemphasis, in the new approach to groups, of the necessity for participants in group interventions to engage in lengthy reviews of the antecedents to their present actions. The importance in group interventions of events in the patient's past, and of the techniques of dream analysis and free association, was characteristic of traditional psychoanalytically-oriented approaches to groups (Wolf, 1963). This historical review, and the construction and communication by the primary intervener to the other participants of inferential states of the organism that were supposedly determinants of overt behavior, was for many years the major technology for group intervention. The new group methods, on the other hand, replace the emphasis on the past by a focus on the overt and observable behavior that takes place between members during intervention, on the present and future actions of individuals, and on the visible consequences of such actions.

The preference of many contemporary group leaders to analyze interpersonal data generated by natural or simulated social interaction during the group (a process sometimes called experiential learning) contrasts sharply with the analysis of material of a more anecdotal and descriptive nature characteristic of older methods. However, advocates of a greater emphasis in intervention on experiential varieties of learning have had little influence until recently, although the recommendations and some of the necessary technology have been described in the literature for a number of years (Moreno, 1945; Perls, Hefferline & Goodman, 1951).

Along with the theme described above, the reader will note a tendency toward specific identification of the objectives of the intervention by leaders and participants: for example, groups designed to teach members to be more assertive, as contrasted with the more traditional goals of gaining insight or making the unconscious conscious, as described in Burrow (1927) and Wolf (1963). London (1972) has suggested recently that this increase in the rigor with which contemporary psychotherapists define the problem and the solution, may be the most important legacy of the struggle between behavioral and medical models.

Of particular importance, the reader will observe, is the emphasis in the chapters to follow on the importance of the individuals' environment, particularly the social environment, and both the environment of the treatment and the natural environment. (See chapters by Trick, Jacobs & Spradlin; Maley; Arnett, Spates & Ulrich; Attneave & Speck; Wolfe and Proshansky). The importance of the family, peer group and teachers as determiners of behavior, and often as maintainers of the symptoms they protest, can be amply documented (from the operant literature) (Patterson, 1969; Hawkins, Peterson, Schweid & Bijou, 1966). Patterson, for example, reports families reinforcing as many as 44 percent of the deviant responses of their children.

The authors of the chapters to follow believe that the social environment of the individual is an important determinant of his adaptive and maladaptive behavior. When the structure of the environment does not provide a viable support-system for the individual, the objectives of intervention may be more satisfactorily achieved by attemp · g to modify the interactions between the individual and the system, rather than attempting to modify only the responses of the individual. Under such circumstances, those "significant others" who interact most frequently with the "patient" become the most logical targets of intervention. It therefore becomes more plausible, as is seen in the chapters to follow, to train husbands and wives, fathers and mothers, nurses and other patients, and relatives and friends to assist the members of their system. The massive involvement in the intervention process of close associates, such as family members, is also a departure from traditional methods of treatment, as stated by Wolberg in 1954 when he advised, "when one wishes to achieve goals of personality reconstruction, simultaneous treatment is not advisable."

One will also note the brevity of the intervention period in the new approach to groups, as contrasted with the tendency toward lengthy treatment in traditional methods of intervention. Studies of the past frequently found over 50 percent of schizophrenic patients still hospitalized after five to ten years of treatment (Coleman, 1950). The oldest and most influential of psychotherapeutic approaches—standard psychoanalysis—typically requires the patient to meet with the psychotherapist five sessions a week for several years (Coleman, 1964). However, the reader of the chapters to follow will find contributors describing an average of 13 days of treatment on the psychiatric ward (Trick, Jacobs & Spradlin) or of three sessions of several hours each to assist a community system in dealing with a problem (Attneave & Speck), or raising the issue of the value of a single two-hour or four-hour session to teach college students about feedback (Jacobs, Chapter Seventeen).

Finally, the reader will become aware of the cross-fertilization of conceptualization that now characterizes group interventions.

The trend is more general than the present text and may be revealed elsewhere in the concern of psychiatrists for group cohesiveness (Yalom, 1970) or feedback (Berger, 1970), and in the interest of social psychologists in psychotherapy research (Goldstein & Simonson, 1971; Wechsler, Solomon & Kramer, 1970). The use of T-group methods to treat psychiatric patients (Morton, 1967), in factories (Blake & Mouton, 1967) or for community development (Klein, 1967) provide additional evidence for the spread of concepts to new intervention purposes and settings.

SUMMARY

Contemporary society has expanded the concept of mental health so that it now encompasses the reduction and prevention of social incompetence and discomfort, as well as the augmentation of interpersonal skillfulness and effectiveness. Intervention designed to improve the interactions between the individual and his natural social environment, or its simulation when members of the natural environment are unavailable, hold promise for the achievement of mental-health goals. The use of group methods of intervention has increased at a spectacular rate in recent years, and group methods have been used in a wide variety of settings and for a wide variety of purposes.

This book contains a broad sample of descriptions of group intervention programs and techniques, as well as the conceptual context from which they derive. Empirical information gathered with respect to some of the group techniques, processes and outcomes is also presented and evaluated.

Themes that reoccur in the chpaters to follow are identified for the reader. Such themes include the substitution of educational or psychological intervention-models for the traditional medical model, definition of the role of the group leader as manager or teacher rather than healer, and the use of subprofessionals and paraprofessionals as group leaders. The nature of the intervention process is characterized by the preference for the study of social interaction generated during intervention, rather than historical material; a more specific identification of the objectives of intervention than in the past; an emphasis on the importance of the social environment during treatment, and on including members of natural systems in the treatment process; the use of briefer treatment periods than in the past; and the cross-fertilization of concepts across disciplines and settings.

REFERENCES

Albee, G. W. The relation of conceptual models of disturbed behavior to institutional and manpower requirements. In F. N. Arnhoff, E. A. Rubenstein & J. C. Speisman (Eds.), *Manpower for mental health* Chicago: Aldine 1969, Pp. 93–112.

Bandura, A. *Principles of behavior modification.* New York: Holt, Rinehart & Winston, 1969.

Berger, M. M. (Ed.) *Videotape techniques in psychiatric training and treatment.* New York: Brunner Mazel, 1970.

Blake, R. R. & Mouton, J. S. A 9,9 approach for increasing organizational productivity. In E. H. Schein & W. G. Bennis (Eds.), *Personal and organizational change through group methods.* New York: John Wiley & Sons, 1967, Pp. 115–151.

Burrow, T. The group method of analysis. *The Psychoanalytic Review* , 1927, **14**, 268–280.

Coleman, J. C. *Abnormal psychology and modern life.* Chicago: Scott, Foresman, 1950.

Coleman, J. C. *Abnormal psychology and modern life.* Chicago: Scott, Foresman, 1964. 3rd edition.

Egan, G. *Encounter: Group processes for interpersonal growth.* Belmont, Calif.: Brooks/Cole, 1970. Pp. 1–25.

Gazda, G. M. Group psychotherapy: Its definition and history. In Gazda, G. M. (Ed.). *Innovations to group psychotherapy.* Springfield, Ill.: Charles C. Thomas, 1968. Pp. 3–14. Goldstein, A. P., Heller, K. & Sechrest, L. B. *Psychotherapy and the psychology of behavior change.* New York: John Wiley & Sons, (1966).

Goldstein, A. P., Heller, K. & Sechrest, L. B. Psychotherapy and the psychology of behavior change. New York: John Wiley & Sons, (1966).

Goldstein, A. P. & Simonson, N. R. Social psychological approaches to psychotherapy research. In A. E. Bergin, & S. L. Garfield, S. L. (Eds.). *Handbook of psychotherapy and behavior change: an empirical analysis.* New York: John Wiley & Sons,(1971), Pp. 154–195.

Guerney, B. G. (Ed.) *Psychotherapeutic agents: New roles for nonprofessionals, parents and teachers.* New York: Holt, Rinehart & Winston, 1969.

Guerney, B., Stollak, G. & Guerney, L. The practicing psychologst as educator: An alternative to the medical practitioner as model. *Professional Psychology,* 1971, **2,** 276–282.

Hawkins, R. P., Peterson, R. F., Schweid, E. & Bijou, S. W. Behavior therapy in the home: amelioration of phobic problem parent-child relations with the parent in the therapeutic role. *Journal of Experimental Child Psychology,* 1966, **4**, 99–107.

Kanfer, F. H. & Saslow, D. Behavior analysis: An alternative to diagnostic classification. *Archives of General Psychiatry,* 1965, **12**, 529–538.

Klein, D. C. Sensitivity training and community development. In E. H. Schein and W. G. Bennis (Eds.), *Personal and organizational change through group methods.* New York: John Wiley & Sons, 1967, Pp. 184-200.

Korten, F. F., Cook, S. W. and Lacey, J. I. (Eds.). *Psychology and the problems of society.* Washington, D. C.: American Psychological Association, 1970.

London, P. The end of ideology in behavior modification. *American Psychologist,* 1972, **27**, 913–920.

MacLennan, B. W. & Levy, N. The group psychotherapy literature, 1970. *International Journal of Group Psychotherapy,* 1971, **31**, 345–380.

Matarazzo, J. B. Some national developments in the utilization of nontraditional mental health power. *American Psychologist,* 1971, **26**, 363–372.

Moreno, J. D. (Ed.) *Group psychotherapy: A symposium.* New York: Beacon House, 1945.

Morton, R. B. The uses of the laboratory method in a psychiatric hospital. In E. H. Schein & W. G. Bennis (Eds.) *Personal and organizational change through group methods.* New York: John Wiley & Sons, 1967, Pp. 115–151.

Patterson, G. R. Behavioral intervention procedures in the classroom and in the home. In A. E. Bergin & S. L. Garfield, *Handbook of psychotherapy and behavior change: an empirical analysis.* New York: John Wiley & Sons, 1971, Pp. 751–775.

Perls, F. S., Hefferline, R. H. & Goodman, P. *Gestalt therapy.* New York: Julian Press, 1951.

Rosenbaum, M. & Berger, M. M. *Group psychotherapy and group function.* New York: Basic Books, 1963.

Ross, A. O. An advocate for children. *The Clinical Psychologist,* 1970, **23,** 1–2.

Sarbin, T. R. On the futility of the proposition that some people can be labelled mentally ill. *Journal of Consulting Psychology,* 1967, **31**, 447–453.

Szasz, T. S. *The myth of mental illness*. New York: Harper, 1961.

Wechsler, H., Solomon, L., & Kramer, B. M. *Social psychology and mental health*. New York: Holt, Rinehart & Winston, 1970.

Wolberg, L. R. Technique of psychotherapy. New York: Grune & Stratton, 1954.

Wolf, A. The psychoanalysis of groups. In M. Rosenbaum, & M. M. Berger, (Eds.), *Group psychotherapy and group function*. New York: Basic Books, 1963, Pp. 273–327.

Yalom, I. E. *Theory and practice of group psychotherapy*. New York: Basic Books, 1970.

Section I

Perspectives and Overview

Introduction

The first two chapters are intended to provide the reader with a context for the remainder of the book. The Introduction described the purposes and organization of the book and how the material was gathered, and underlined for the reader some general themes that characterize the remaining chapters. Considerable agreement exists among contributors, on the value of the use of principles of learning and education to generate intervention techniques, and the insistence on the importance of the environment of the individual to his adjustment. These views contrast dramatically with the medical orientation and the concern of intrapsychic equilibrium that has been characteristic of past methods of intervention.

Chapter One looks at the growth of groups from a socio-cultural vantage point. A sociologist points out that the breakdown of social institutions and the consequent alienation of individuals produces a vacuum in society. The small group movement has expanded into this vacuum, and for its members, has come to represent community. Chapter Two examines traditional and contemporary methods of social intervention. Differences in emphasis, in conceptual models, in goals and in techniques are examined. A model is proposed to facilitate decisions regarding the allotment of resources for intervention.

1. *The Interface of Institutions and Group Process*

James A. Peterson

A sociologist speculates in this introductory chapter on those dimensions of our contemporary social climate that have made the small-group movement one of the most rapidly growing social phenomena of our time. He proposes that, aside from their efficiency in modifying individuals and institutions, groups are a functional social invention to compensate for the almost total loss of social and personal meaning in a technological world.

Dr. Peterson points to the ugliness of our habitat, the disappearance from our civilization of the gratifications of creative work, our alienation from fellow and family and our loss of faith and spiritual support. These create the need for community between men that is being satisfied by the small-group movement.

The small group may indeed fulfill this hunger for intimacy and belonging in our age so effectively, asserts Dr. Peterson, that its members may become addicted or unfit to function in the general ecosystem. He supports these speculations by referring to the psychotherapy groups that continue on beyond cure, to the group gurus whose workshops are attended repeatedly and perhaps indefinitely by their devotees, to the increasing number of presidents of major corporations whose experiences with encounter groups lead them to drop out.

Dr. Peterson concludes by noting the increase in systems approaches to intervention. He remarks the increased tendency to involve families in the intervention process, and the tendency to develop inter-institutional programs of intervention. A significant number of institutions, such as the school, the church and industry, Peterson points out, now employ the methods and principles of group work to accomplish a variety of goals.

In his brilliant exegesis of "The Myth of Sisyphus," Camus dissects the plight of modern man. Sisyphus is condemned for all eternity to push his rock up the mountain, only to observe in his fatigue its tumultuous descent, and he must run down to labor it up again. For all time he alone must repeat this meaningless exercise—alone. No one during that hard pull wipes his brow or offers him a cup of water. The myth, and Camus does not challenge it, assumes that kin, friends, peers, medicine man and priest finally have little relevance to the integration or disintegration of Sisyphus. It is a lonely struggle.

THE HISTORY OF GROUP

Group psychotherapy may be described in one way as the mobilization of significant others in the struggle. Sisyphus was not aware that there were others pushing larger rocks on the other side of the mountain, or that there was a group walking beside him cheering higher his every push, or several in the group that felt how his muscles ached and his spirit sagged. It is true, that psychoanalysis, in later times, offered him a companion well equipped to help him understand why he had gotten in the predicament and why he sometimes cursed or daydreamed, but he was not permitted to cheer, to weep, to criticize or to enlist others who might help in the struggle.

This may partially account for the historical fact, at least in the United States if not in Europe, that the enlistment of a group of peers as change agents was initiated in nonpsychiatric settings. In 1905 at the Trudeau Tubercular Sanitarium, Dr. J. H. Pratt conducted a group meeting of tubercular patients (Pratt, 1922). One of his students, W. R. P. Emerson (1910), used a modified group method, somewhat a precursor of the rewarding game method now used with retardates and delinquents, in dealing with a group of undernourished children. J. L. Moreno, a pioneer in Europe, in 1911 initiated psychodrama with children's groups. L. C. Marsh in 1909, and E. W. Lazell in 1919, experimented with types of educational and inspirational group meetings with neurotics.

In the thirties, sequentially-related and idiosyncratic group movements appeared. Slavson (1950) and Redl (1942) refined work with children's groups. Pratt's work expanded in classes for patients with diabetes, peptic ulcers, hypertension and heart disease (Buck, 1937). In the middle of the decade, an Ohio physician and a New York broker established *Alcoholics Anonymous,* which was to profoundly influence group treatment of alcoholics, obese persons and drug addicts (Alcoholics Anonymous, 1955). Experiments were beginning with psychotics. Family group therapy developed out of work with children's groups and parents' groups (Ackerman, 1958). By now it was apparent that a group—be it family, friends, or peers—had power as a change agent.

The forties and sixties saw institutional appropriation of the principles evolving from group psychotherapy. Analysis of group dynamics and the impetus of group therapy made their impact on T (training) groups and sensitivity training, which began in the well-known experiment in New Britain, Connecticut, in 1946 (Benne, 1964). The early programs soon spread into university training programs for students in business and public administration, theology and psychology. From there it was inevitable that it became interfaced with these institutions. Before long, business executives, public administrators, ministers and psychologists were not only participating in groups but utilizing them in their institutions.

THE URBAN MILIEU

Carl Rogers has said that the small-group movement is one of the most rapidly growing social phenomena of our time. It is one thing to record the phenomenon of the growth of group activity, however, and another to understand certain facilitating conditions in the social milieu.

The first of these is the utter ugliness of our habitat. Most of us live in the great, gray, concrete canyons of cities where there is little sunshine and no grass, where the sirens howl and crowds mill like cattle. Our most familiar vistas are garbage on the street and in the air. There the tempo of the business world, of the social world, of the political world moves faster and faster, and man runs, anxious and driven, through the shadowy canyon.

And, although some men find some surcease in dollars or in alcohol or in heroin, still half of our hospital beds are filled with those who could not stand the smoke, the tension, the bustle, the nervous derelicts burned out by the friction of such an accelerated and unlovely life.

Of course the habitat has never been judged as important as the social environment for mental health, but the sources of support in social life are likewise trammeled. As the industrial processes move more and more to automated systems, the reward of creative work for the vast majority is occluded. Though there are a few well-publicized efforts to include all levels of personnel in planning and production control, on the whole the industrial machine becomes more and more depersonalized and computerized; the compass is the clock, the horizon is the deadline and man is an equally mechanical cog.

Man is alienated from his work and his product but even more alienated from his fellows. He lives in an alienated place which has lost any sense of community or neighboring. His friends are from his occupational strata, and they live across town but not across the street. He might of course turn to his mate or his family for his need for intimacy, but every study we have shows that after fifteen years of marriage the alienation of husband from wife is characterized by "disenchantment," by the "corrosion of time" or by "devitalization," to use the three words chosen by our family researchers to describe middle-age marriage.

If the habitat is ugly, the social environment is vacuous. The third aspect of the modern milieu is the loss of spiritual support. The focused glare of scientific inquiry and rational consideration has melted down the old idols, and they seem to exist only as vestigial monuments to a past that is not relevant to today for most persons. You may remember one of the paragraphs with which Niebuhr concluded that benchmark analysis of modern spiritual trends, *Moral Man and Immoral Society*. He wrote:

> Our age, for good or ill, is immersed in the social problem. A technological civilization makes stability impossible. It changes the circumstances of life too rapidly to incline anyone to a reverent acceptance of an ancestral order. Its rapid developments and its almost daily changes in the physical circumstances of life destroy physical symbols of

> stability and therefore make for restlessness, even if these movements were not in a direction which imperils the whole human enterprise [p. 275].

There is not "acceptance of the ancestral order," but neither is there anything to take its place, as witnessed by the somewhat ironic picture of the hippie smoking pot to the glory of Allah. And Niebuhr's reference to the "direction which imperils the whole human enterprise" reminds us of Keats, who said that "where but to think is to be full of sorrow and leaden-eyed despair." It is not only that God is dead but that his prophets, like Niebuhr, have nothing to offer in their funeral orations. To the sociologist who has documented the essential functions of religion as prophetic (social innovation) and priestly (spiritual support), the eclipse of this institution leaves a foreboding of darkness.

Man wanders then through these canyons without love and without purpose. While this text has spoken about religion in its failure to find new grounds for purpose, one could describe the other major institutions in the same way. Goldsen, Williams, Rosenberg, Williams and Suchman (1960) conclude their superb report of a study of 4,000 college-age men and women by suggesting that the major failure of our whole educational system is to give any philosophical system or spiritual foundation on which young people could adjust to a world of change.

GROUPS AND INDIVIDUALS

Institutions are characterized by their very structure by a gradual rate of change, and this is dysfunctional as they try to find cogent and relevant answers to the plight of the human spirit. It may well be that the new community in a complex and pluralistic world is the small group with its capacity for primary relationships and working through conflict and confusion. Thus the ability of small groups to help an individual face his existential anxiety, to give him courage and support in his grief work in leaving the idols of his childhood and to give him solace and comfort in this world which can never have stability, gives those groups an indispensable place in the present system. One of the latent functions of the group may be not only change in the individual because of some idiosyncratic behavior patterns but, equally important, a social structure in which he can accept change as a constant. The small, intimate and concerned group may well be the means for salvation when God is dead, and God's temple is a mausoleum instead of a place of living spirit. In this sense the social process going on in groups is validated not because of their contribution to change or to stability, but simply as community. One is reminded that when the leaders of Vietnam Summer were interviewed after their intensive summer working for peace, they all recalled the meaning of the summer not in terms of contributions to peace, but in terms of fellowship and intimacy; in much the same way some therapy groups continue long after their leader has declared them "cured," which leads one to suspect that perhaps the group was more meaningful than the cure. One wonders then if the immense expansion of small groups does not have more to do with loneliness than neurosis. What we may be experiencing is a valid adaptation to the industrial world of persons who have found that either they love or they go to the hospital.

The possibility that small groups are efforts to establish community between men does not at all diminish the importance of those groups in healing. Most of us are involved in various group processes because we have found them an efficient way to deal with a great variety of human perplexities. But in dealing with those perplexities the sociologist endeavors to discover how effective and how permanent is the predicted change and what other consequences are derivative to the group process. He is much concerned about role shock or role discontinuity as he looks at the interrelationships of group systems. It is extraordinarily important to assess not only individual's nontherapeutic group life but also what happens under the stress of the group experience.

We are going to read a remarkable story of the success of an experimental school at Western Michigan University (Chapter Nine). All reports to date authenticate the uniqueness of success of the school in achieving two things: (1) its goal for personality development and (2) the inculcation of social attitudes judged by the school to be those that will bring the Kingdom of God. There yet remains that research to determine how much capacity those personality products will have in adjusting to a nonschool world that is incongruous with them.

MECHANISMS OF CHANGE

The illustration to follow introduces the pivotal problem of change that is partial to one part of the system. You remember Whyte's careful analysis of the eight girls who worked painting toys at the Dashman Company. The girls did very well when the trouble started. Then the engineers introduced a conveyor system and prescribed its velocity, which meant telling the girls how many units they had to spray-paint. They rebelled, and production fell off. A consultant was brought in to work with the foreman. As a result the girls and the foreman became a group, and the group finally concluded it was the deadly common pace of the conveyor that disturbed them. It was agreed that the pace would vary. In three weeks the production rate went up 50 percent above what it had been. They were all happy, but other workers were not. Nor were the engineers who felt their authority threatened. So the conveyor was reset at a constant rate and production fell off. Conflict developed, and six of the eight girls and the foreman quit their jobs. Authority had subtly shifted in the system, or rather in one part of it, and the total system could not stand the inconsistency. Likewise, the foreman in becoming a change agent, doing research, conducting discussions and making group decisions, abandoned the former legalistic definition of his role, which disturbed the system.

I used to visit a school for boys which was fifteen years ago a sort of model of group work with delinquents. The superintendent would always take me with great pride to the model cottage in which lived the boys who had made great progress. It was clean, orderly and decorated with examples of creative work. He was very warm and supportive in his interaction with these nearly "normal" lads. Then I would gently ask him how soon the boys would be back. His face fell and he estimated in three months. They were socialized very well indeed in an isolated cultural island segregated from the reality of their neighborhood and family, but when they left the group to go outside, the new learning did little to enhance their changes of making it on the outside. I have done some training in family therapy with therapists at the narcotic prison at Narco in California. They have an interesting small piece of research that is not very elegant in terms of a matching sample, but I will share it with you for what it is. They compared the recidivism rate of those who were in general group therapy with those who were in family therapy. The rate was statistically significantly lower for those in family therapy. How much lower the rate might have been had the extended family system, a possible work-system group and any significant others been included, is of course not known.

As the spray-gun girls dropped out, so others in the industrial system drop out when they change in such significant ways that their role definitions no longer concur with the system. I have been observing two presidents of major corporations who first became involved in group therapy and then graduated to participate in the more intensive group experiences of an institution like Esalen. They now are proud of their beards, their casual dress and their relaxation, but they sold their businesses and dropped out. I met recently with a hundred other presidents. Many of them, and they are all in their forties or fifties, are thinking of dropping out. These men saw some discontinuity of old roles with their present definition of self, but they were eager to explore possibilities of some social utility for their future. Many of them have been sensitized by attending the best groups for change in the country. They are not sure where they will fit, if fit they can.

I want to give one other illustration of the general problem from my own field of marriage and family counseling. We regard both small groups as highly interwoven role systems, and we have learned by long experimentation, that if you do succeed in helping one member of the dyad or the family change their role-expectations for others and their own role-behavior without a concomitant change in others, you have structured the failure of the unit. I don't suppose that George Bach ever sees one member of a dyad alone because he is magnificently successful in helping persons make their anger explicit and also in handling that anger positively. But conflict is social, and a conflict situation is a system, and openness on the part of only one would seemingly be destructive. It is quite possible that his paper can give us some light on that possible outcome.

One solution to the discontinuity of role experienced by some successful group members seems to be a substitution of continuous group participation for other forms of recreation, education or work. There are some therapists scheduled at Tahoe

Institute that seem to be surrounded by devotees. Their groups are always full whether held in Los Angeles or Esalen or Tahoe Institute, and we suspect some of the same persons continue to worship. I use the word advisedly because these people speak of their experiences in reverent tones because there they come alive, discover themselves and truly exist. Other persons are more eclectic and move from one growth-group center to another and from one orientation to another. They find the contrast between the vivid and supportive and growth aspects of groups, as compared to the reality of humdrum social life, so great that they seem to have elected perpetual self-actualization.

I have been asking questions about the outcomes of group change in terms of their continuity and utility outside the experiences within the group. The question sometimes seems to be that the more successful the cohesiveness and intensity of the group, the more dysfunctional the outcome for interactions outsider the group itself. Of course this may in no way be ultimately disastrous, as dropping out of a system may ultimately be as useful for major changes as staying within it and attempting to modify it.

THE INTERFACE OF INSTITUTIONS IN GROUP PROCESS

Ralph Hirschowitz is going to discuss group process as it relates to interagency collaboration. Some exciting innovations are occurring in Southern California in this area when we can perceive them through our smog. The State Mental Hygiene clinics are taking strides to interface effectively with other institutions. The therapists are doing crisis intervention, brief psychotherapy and some group work, but they are also slowly interweaving their efforts with other groups. In the schools they are not content simply to identify children that seem to be disturbed or acting out. They study the classroom to see if they can identify either structural or interactional patterns that explain these outcomes. One method is to videotape a classroom session and then sit down with the teacher to identify sequences of classroom interaction that might be productive of the troublesome behavior. The use of the videotape record lends to the conference objectivity and the opportunity for both the consultant and the teacher to study carefully the whole interactional process. But the intervention does not stop there. Another institution is involved. If there is reason to believe that the antecedent for the behavior may be located in the family, the family is invited to participate in family conferences. From six to ten sessions are held with the family. One of my therapists from my clinic, who is on leave to work in this program, estimates that in 10 percent of the cases the family is involved in therapy. This may seem like a minor achievement, but that 10 percent is exactly 10 percent higher than would have been recorded five years ago. Interestingly enough, two aspects of change through group experience is involved. In the first case the group interaction of the classroom is studied, but in the second case the family as a group enters therapy. And, of course, if there are physical problems complicating the case, other agencies are included.

There is another area in Southern California where interagency or interinstitutional programs are developing. It is in the field of preventative marital hygiene. This is important in California because our divorce rate leads the nation. And Los Angeles County does even better than California as a whole. If you stay married in Los Angeles County you are either extraordinarily rigid or extraordinarily flexible. The Los Angeles County Health Department was given a grant to look at its overall program for family life. At about the same time the state passed legislation making premarital counseling mandatory for any couple where one of the partners was under eighteen years of age. The County Health Department decided to move in two directions: first, to serve as a catalyst to involve as many institutions in three pilot communities as possible in educational and counseling programs, and second, to fulfill needs that no other group seemed capable of meeting. It is too early to make any assessment of results, but there is no doubt that a good deal of agency collaboration has been promoted and a new focus on preventative marital hygiene has been introduced to displace somewhat the emphasis on counseling devitalized couples and moribund marriages. The collaboration of institutions and groups within those institutions that have specialized functions is an important step, about which I am sure we will read more. This movement toward interagency or interinstitutional collaboration may well be the most effective approach to community that is possible in our pluralistic and mobile society.

I suppose that there is no one represented in this volume who is not convinced that the small group is the most effective agency of change. We have a whole literature on the influence of face-to-face or primary interactions, mostly from social psychology. I will mention only one recent study which is relatively new. Ira Reiss (1968), who is now the head of the Family Study Center in Minneapolis, did a major study attempting to develop a theory that would account for changes in sexual attitudes of permissiveness. It is a very careful analysis and one worthy of some reflection. But the one conclusion from that study that I want to share with you is that individual sexual attitudes can be predicted as a vector that falls between the attitudes of two small groups: the family and the peer group. The highest point of permissiveness is somewhere between these two, generally somewhat closer to the peer group during late adolescence, but when the respondent is married and himself a parent, his permissiveness drops and comes closer to the attitudes of his own family of orientation, although it never drops to the same level. This leads Reiss to conclude that over a period of time, more and more permissiveness is inevitable. We often talk as though the therapeutic community turned to groups as an expedient because of the shortage of personnel. I suspect that before we conclude we will have documented even more fully the other alternate conclusion that we use the group method because it is more productive than other methods of intervention.

SOCIAL CONTINUITY

Whether or not it is in fact productive and whether that productivity has continuity, can only be established by some very elegant and I think longitudinal studies. If I have any alarm over the proliferation of groups, it is only that we are inventing them faster than we are measuring their effectiveness. I complained to my secretary last week because she had put on the bulletin board about thirty announcements of marathons, nude therapy groups, leaderless therapy groups, meditation groups, and on and on in such an array that no one could read all of them. We have already learned a good deal about the dynamics of change through groups, we have learned a good deal about the function of the change agent and we know something about ways of scaling movement in those groups. This book is important because out of these papers will come some even more incisive observations that may make work with groups more effective. One can appreciate innovation and progress, but I suspect that not all of group work in this country is based on a background of incisive observation or even incisive training through supervision. It may be that the reports to follow can have some influence in setting standards and promoting assessment, if only by example.

In conclusion, let me say that it grows increasingly impossible for one to distinguish between groups that are initiated primarily for therapeutic reasons and groups that, like the classroom, are focused on other goals. At least a significant number of institutions such as the school, the church and industry have adopted the methods and principles of group work. Sometimes the descriptions and labeling of these groups are very similar. The young rector at the Episcopalian Church in Palos Verdes is doing much the same thing as the young psychologist at Gateways Hospital in working with a group of dope addicts. But when he conducts a regular Sunday evening young people's group or meets with a group of young married women, the same group approach is visible. What I am suggesting is that for better or worse a great many institutional groups have learned from us that our methods are productive and popular. It is not only that there is an interface between institutions and social process: there is a marriage. It remains for us to establish training on a much broader basis so that all leaders at least have some opportunity for critical appraisal and evaluation and for us to use and facilitate the type of scientific assessment that will give us some answers to the kinds of issues that will be raised. At the least we have learned the value in intervention of the support of others as we push the rock.

REFERENCES

Ackerman, N. W. *The psychodynamics of family life.* New York: Basic Books, 1958. Chapters 1, 2, 3, 4, 5, 6, 16, 17, 18, 19.

Alcoholics Anonymous. New York: A.A. World Services. 1955.

Benne, K. D. History of the T group in the laboratory setting. *In T Group theory and laboratory method.* L. T. Bradford, J. R. Gibb, K. D. Benne, (Eds), New York: John Wiley & Sons, 1964.

Buck, R. W. Class method in treatment of essential hypertension. *Annals of Internal Medicine*, 1937, **11**, 511–18.

Emerson, W. R. P. The hygienic and dietetic treatment of delicate children in groups. *Boston Medical & Surgical Journal*, 1910, **163,** 326–328.

Goldsen, R. K., Rosenberg, M. Williams Jr., R. M., Suchman, E. A. *What College Students Think,* Princeton, New Jersey: Van Nostrand, 1960.

Niebuhr, R. *Moral Man and Immoral Society,* New York: Scribner & Sons, 1932.

Pratt, J. H. The principles of class treatment and their application to various chronic diseases. *Hospital Social Service*, 1922, **6**, 401.

Redl, F. Group Emotion and Leadership. *Psychiatry*, 1942, **5,** 573–596.

Reiss, I. The social context of premarital sexual permissiveness. New York: Holt, Rinehart & Winston, 1968.

Slavson, S. R. *Analytic group psychotherapy with children, adolescents and adults.* New York: Columbia University Press, 1950.

2. Strategies of Social Intervention, Past and Future

Alfred Jacobs

Historical accidents and cultural scientific lag have been important determinants of our past approaches to social intervention, argues this chapter. Research, training, and delivery of intervention have been dominated by conceptualizations derived from traditional medicine and university customs and strategies. The consequence has been the generation of information describing the nature of individuals by individual researchers, and the correction of medically defined social illnesses in individual patients by individual healers trained in traditional medical models of training.

New approaches to social intervention capitalize on the potential of groups for influencing the behavior of members. The modification of behavior of the system in which the individual functions, in addition to the modification of the responses of the individual, offers promise for more stable interventions. It is proposed that interventions be planned to create viable ecological systems for sets of individuals for whom social environments are absent, and where it is unlikely that such individuals will be able to produce a satisfactory matrix of social interactions without assistance.

The conceptualization of intervention as an educative rather than as primarily a medical process, extends the range of variables and informations that are germane to intervention. An opportunity is produced, as well, for the mental-health professions to reconsider how and where they will set priorities for intervention among the wide variety of human problems.

The Albee Report (Albee, 1959) and similar documents of the past decade illuminate a number of crucial parameters affecting the growth of mental-health resources and the patterns of deliveries of health services. To put it succinctly, mental-health manpower resources are falling behind the need for services at an ever increasing rate; the smallest amounts of mental-health services are furnished to the poor, and particularly to the very young and very old poor. Psychologists and other social scientists have responded to such information by becoming more self-conscious, as well as more sophisticated, regarding their professional roles and identities and the determinants thereof. We have become much more concerned with the relationships between political activity and funding, between sources of funding and types of mental-health workers developed. We analyze the manner in which mental health concepts and ideology affect one's perception of what are mental-health problems, how services are delivered and to whom.

I will address myself to some of these issues and how they relate to strategies of social intervention in the remainder of these introductory comments. Elaborations and applications of the changing concepts, and of approaches to the utilization of the group as a vehicle for change, appear in the chapters which follow. The introduction to each of the chapters attempts to identify the common themes and their translation into practice or research.

The use of a model, as in Figure 2.1, may facilitate the identification of various intervention strategies for the future, as well as the examination of allocations of resources in the past. The top face of the model identifies three of the major goals for social intervention. The side face of the cube contains types of units at which the social intervention might be aimed, and at the bottom, three of the major systems necessary for the production of social change are portrayed. The various cells in the cube therefore represent the large numbers of alternatives which can be generated for the immediate or eventual production of social change.

GOALS OF SOCIAL INTERVENTION

The major purposes of intervention consist of correction and alleviation, prevention and enrichment or improvement. Some

FIGURE 2.1
STRATEGIES OF SOCIAL INTERVENTION

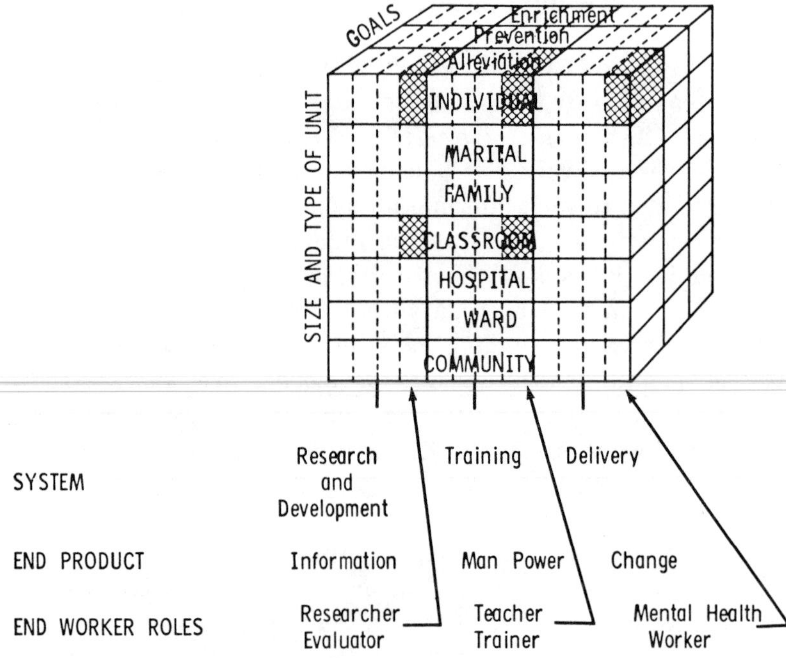

overlap exists among these goals. Improving one's skills as a parent may have implications for prevention of behavioral problems in one's children, for example. The major intervention enterprise of the past 20 or 30 years has been the production of mental-health workers trained to provide direct corrective services by means of a dyadic relationship (Lubin, 1967) to adults (Rotter, 1967) diagnosed as having some mild or severe mental illness which required treatment. Efforts at prevention[1] and enrichment were minimal, and in the past, were ordinarily regarded by those who treated the mentally ill as relatively superficial kinds of professional activity which could be performed by almost anyone. I refer to premarital counseling, for example, or those who helped high school or college students more effectively plan their educational or vocational careers. We were dubious of the value of such excursions because of the rationality oriented techniques employed, in view of our supposed knowledge that the important and powerful determinants of human behavior were irrational.

Although some psychologists like Maslow (1954) theorized and even did some research exploring human potential, little application existed. The lack of information on the nature of effective mental-health prophylaxis discouraged efforts at prevention. Our belief that the really important work was remedial and corrective may have been partly attributable to these information gaps.

The major source of the corrective concepts of intervention of the times was traditional medicine. The public and professional expectations and attitudes generated by such terms as doctor, patient, illness, cure and hospital shaped the direction of the mental-health movement. Physicians were accustomed to treating the patient rather than his family. Psychotherapists also concentrated on producing intrapsychic changes within the patient (Alexander & Ross, 1952; Wolberg, 1954; Menninger, 1958), and, as a matter of fact, were often loath to meet with the intimate others of adults undergoing treatment for fear that treatment might somehow be interfered with or damaged (Wolberg, 1954; Levine, 1958). The curative elements of behavior treatment were rooted in status and expert power of the doctor, as in physical medicine, and the desire of the patient to recover from his illness. Insight, or the understanding of the motivation and historical determinants of one's behavior, was presumably the catalyst for change, although some psychotherapists denied that they were even interested in producing behavior change.

The elaboration of the analogy between behavioral interventions and the traditional medical services of the times, generated other unquestioned implications. Common medical interventions such as the use of drugs or surgical techniques were fraught with real dangers to the existence of the patient. Mental-health professionals uncritically assumed that similar dangers also existed in social or behavior interventions. It was, therefore, altogether plausible to require the potential intervener to undergo a long and closely-monitored period of training in order to reduce the risks of intervention for the patient.

To the contrary, however, Margaret Rioch (Rioch et al., 1963), recently demonstrated that housewives could be trained in relatively short time-periods to perform insight therapy quite adequately. A flood of literature describing the training of teachers and teachers' aides to use behavior modification techniques, and other reports of the training of paraprofessionals (Guerney, 1969; Matarazzo, 1971), raise serious doubts that prolonged training is necessary. It also seems clear that the special information which often composes a substantial proportion of the prolonged training programs, such as that derived from a general medical education, for example, or knowledge of research methodologies in psychology, ordinarily has no relevance to the efficacy of treatment, or to its freedom from danger.

SOCIAL INTERVENTION SYSTEMS

Three major systems for intervention are identified at the bottom of the cube in Figure 2.1. The first of these is responsible for the generation of the information and technology for social intervention by the efforts of social and biological scientists. The second system transmits the information and technology to mental-health workers and others by means of formal and informal teaching and training programs. The third system delivers social interventions to various segments of the population through the activities of mental-health workers with a variety of professional affiliations.

Large gaps exist in the information generated regarding the production of change in large aggregates of individuals, such as hospital or community populations. Although a considerable body of knowledge already exists concerning social intervention, generally expense and magnitude, as well as the methodological problems, have inhibited such research on larger units. Hopefully, principles derived from the large literature that exists on the study of smaller groups in laboratory situations by social psychologists may apply, as has been suggested by recent theorists of group intervention (Egan, 1970).

Additionally, the research system has suffered from a number of major handicaps in the past. The first has been the retention of several medieval customs that interfere with the adequate organization of manpower to efficiently and quickly generate the large amount of data relevant to the solution of important social issues. I believe that the tradition of the single-gentleman—Ph.D.—academic scholar, assisted by his lowly, underpaid and transitory research assistant, as one of the major resources for generating information, is anachronistic as well as ludicrous, and must eventually be replaced by well-organized research teams who do not divide their time among research, teaching and other activities. These teams should consist of individuals who have experience with the types of intervention under study, and who are familiar with the relevant information that already exists. Experts on research design, analysis of data, construction and evaluation of measuring instruments, computer programming and technical writing should be included. The organization and funding of such research teams is already beginning.

A second handicap of the research and development system is the absence of inter-system specialists and technologies to communicate information rapidly (Ziman, 1971) The consequent time-lag impedes the effectiveness of mental-health workers in various professions, as well as others who may be in strategic positions to utilize mental-health information, such as teachers. Third, the production of scientists, as well as that of teacher-trainers for the mental-health movement, has been dominated by the issue of advanced training in a similar manner to that which we observed earlier in the case of mental-health workers responsible for the delivery of corrective services. An unwillingness or inability on the part of those in the research and training systems to analyze the missions of the systems, the skills required to complete the missions, and the types and amounts of manpower resources necessary and available, has resulted in bottlenecks. The historical precedent that locates the production of members of these systems in the university setting, with its red tape and resistance to innovation, has added to the problems. The training of researchers and trainers, as well as the performance of research and training roles, has been restricted to generalists who must complete large amounts of often irrelevant post baccalaureate training. The methods of producing manpower for these systems is inefficient and requires an inordinate amount of participation from a very small existing pool of very high-level personnel, which is difficult and costly to expand.

It would not be surprising if a careful scrutiny of the typical activities of these generalists uncovered many functions that could be performed quite competently by individuals with less training. Training programs are necessary to insure substantial cadre at the baccalaureate and sub baccalaureate level in order to increase the productivity of the systems for delivery of social interventions. Research technicians, teachers' aides at various levels and mental-health aides could accomplish much in unblocking all systems.

The fourth handicap of the research system and of the training and delivery systems as well, is that little attention has been devoted to the training of individuals to perform the vital support roles in each of these systems: organizers, administrators, consultants, etc. Seniority, professional visibility and promotability, rather than skill and training, have been the bases for assignment to such support positions in the past. It is not plausible that systems have benefited from such criteria for assignment to key positions. The mental-health professions could benefit by providing training programs for those who are likely to perform such roles, recruiting from other programs individuals who already possess such skills, or collaborating in inter-disciplinary programs with those who prepare individuals for such positions.

As in the research system, the manpower shortage that now exists in the delivery system is attributable to the stance taken by psychology, medicine and social work, that post baccalaureate training is an essential ingredient of adequate preparation to perform social interventions. This state of affairs is partly caused by attempts to emulate the traditional medical model on the part of other professional groups who have identified themselves as participants in the mental-health movement. It is economically desirable for nonmedically trained mental-health workers to develop a title or a degree which permits them to compete with those having a medical degree for salaried positions, or in the public market of individuals wishing to purchase mental-health services. The use of the Ph.D. and the title *doctor* is common, and permits other mental-health professionals to share in the status and positive stereotypes assigned by the general public to the physician, who is also referred to as a doctor. The transfer is facilitated by public confusion and ignorance regarding differences in training and experience among the mental-health professions (London, 1964). The degree, and the licensing or certification which follows, attempts to serve as a quality-control measure by insuring that the vendor has successfully completed a number of academic courses and experiences or their equivalents. The ingredients of such programs may differ considerably from profession to profession (Watkin, 1966), and, even within any profession, from individual to individual (Rosenhans and London, 1968), such being the state of the art. Licensing also serves to restrict the numbers of those who can perform services (Henderson and Hildreth, 1967). A scarcity of mental-health services is thereby maintained, which is clearly to the advantage of the few eligible to vend mental-health services, but not to the general population, particularly the poor. However, the rivalry and competition for economic advantage and authority among mental-health professions has perpetuated the prolongation of training for the mental-health worker.

The conceptualization of social intervention as a variety of medical procedure has also played a role in the determination of the priorities assigned to the allotment of the resources of the delivery system, the choice of delivery media and the context of the training programs of the delivery-system personnel. For example, we devote a proportionately large amount of resources to the custodial care of the relatively small number of patients who are defined as mentally ill. At the same time we virtually ignore the larger number of children in minority groups who have low self-esteem; we provide little organized assistance during the many emotional crises which occur in families when a member is seriously ill or dying; and we fail to develop institutions to deal with the stresses precipitated by divorce and separation.

The media of intervention have also been dictated by medically-oriented conceptualizations and customs. The "disease concept," with its attendant emphasis on the treatment of internal, often biologic, etiology, was translated into the psychoanalytic mental-health model for the treatment of mental illness. Workers, strongly influenced by psychoanalytic thinking (Rotter, 1967), believed that symptoms, being maintained by intense inner forces, were invulnerable to amelioration by simple information, or by training programs aimed at symptom removal. Even more forboding, practitioners asserted that symptoms directly removed might be replaced by even more disabling symptomatology because of the continued presence of the powerful inner causative agents. There is little, if any, evidence to support this last belief, by the way, and it is ignored today by many psychologists, who concentrate almost exlusively on symptom removal with almost no reports of dire consequences (Bandura, 1969).

But to continue, the generally held belief that behavior change was opposed by powerful hidden internal causes, and therefore could only be treated indirectly, and over a long period of time, by individuals, preferably M.D.'s who needed many years of post doctoral training to acquire the necessary skills, did not provide an encouraging climate in which to explore the utility of information as an intervention medium for correction or prevention. It is also the custom of scientists and M.D.'s to regard wide publicity or advertising as not quite respectable. Therefore, the tremendous potentiality for influence of TV, radio and newspapers has been, for the most part, neglected. In such rare instances where newspapers or television have been used to disseminate mental health information (Dear Abby, Dr. Joyce Brothers), I would not be surprised to discover that the effect has been more profound than that of most groups of 1,000 mental-health workers one could select.

The medical ethic requiring direct observation of the patient by the M.D. can be plausibly supported on the basis of the necessity for the physician to employ special technical assessment devices—blood tests, X-rays and other laboratory techniques ordinarily inaccessible to patients—in order to select appropriate treatment plans. However, recent evaluations of the attempts by psychologists to develop analogous laboratory-type instruments taking the form of projective and objective psychological tests (Mischel, 1968; Megargee, 1966) have raised a considerable amount of controversy regarding the effectiveness of predictions made on the basis of psychological instruments, as well as regarding the relevance of such test results to treatment plans.

In addition, behavioral-social models of intervention generate alternative strategies whose effectiveness may be empirically tested. It may indeed be possible for parents or others (see Cone and Sloop, for example) including self (Watson and Tharp, 1972), to collect the relevant information on which to base a treatment plan in the absence of direct observation by an expert if this data consists of tabulation of the frequencies of easily recognizable overt and covert responses, and clearly specified environmental events. It may be possible to adequately communicate such simple programs of instruction for assessment as well as treatment plans through the mail (Bastien and Jacobs, in press) or over the telephone,[2] including arrangements to monitor the effects of intervention. The advantages of such long-distance treatment strategies in rural areas where local mental-health resources are underrepresented, or to members of poverty groups who lack transportation, are immediately obvious.

Our utilization of the educational system as a medium for social intervention has been impaired seriously by the illness-cure, doctor-expert, contagion-isolation conceptualizations that appear to have shaped our strategies. The public school systems are a potentially magnificent instrument for preventative interventions, because the schools provide accessibility to an enormous proportion of our young for a significant period of time each day. We have failed to designate as necessary aspects of the educational process courses and experiences in the primary grades that have as their objective facilitating the ability of children to cope with stress, to identify and satisfy their social needs, to communicate with and understand others, to learn how to mobilize their influence and the influence of their peers for constructive social change, and to assist in the modification of the deviant or destructive behavior of those around them.

Instead, the tactic of the educational system is corrective and attends primarily to the child in need of assistance, particularly if he is disruptive. The teacher refers the child to the school counselor. The school counselor decides whether the child's name will be placed on the waiting list of a therapist in a child guidance center, or whether the child is to be removed from his classroom community to the isolation of the special education class with other misfits, or banished from school (Bersoff, 1971). It is rare that treatment is attempted in the classroom, or that the potential influence of a student's peers is enlisted as a treatment modality.

I do not wish to appear at this point (and later) to be placing the major responsibility for the ineffectualness of our mental-health strategy at the door of the medical profession. Clearly, communities have always more often rejected and punished deviants whose behavior has frightened or offended than tried to assist them. It is also true, and to the credit of medicine, that massive and effective preventative efforts have characterized the treatment of physical illness. Also, medical columns in newspapers, and telephone communication with patients by G.P.'s, are long-established methods. It is unfortunate, however, that those in the mental-health professions have identified with the more conservative, rather than the innovative, aspects of medicine.

The medical conceptualizations of social intervention markedly affect the content of the training programs of delivery-system personnel. As one might expect, the programs of medically-trained mental-health agents, psychiatrists and psychiatric nurses, demonstrate the influence most obviously (Brody, 1967). The psychiatrist, whose major modality of intervention is likely to be verbal and social, will ordinarily be required, like other physicians, to have completed a ratio of four years of biological and physical science to one year of social studies before even being admitted to medical school. The psychiatric nurse, whose main functions in the mental hospital appear to me to be predominantly those of ward management, would certainly become more effective if courses in the school of business administration, or in methods of group treatment, replaced some of the somewhat irrelevant training in the biological and physical sciences.

The graduate student in clinical psychology is likely to spend as long as two years in assessment courses to train him to diagnose individuals (Pumroy 1967). The diagnostic systems which he will be expected to master include those of psychiatric and psychoanalytic derivation, and often have little relevance to treatment plans. He ordinarily is trained to detect the behavioral characteristics of individuals with neurological damage, although he may encounter very few such instances in his later career. On the other hand, he ordinarily receives little or no formal training in the assessment of group processes. His training and experience in methods of individual treatment is likely to be much more extensive than in the management of groups.

Therefore, recruitment of personnel for social intervention has been dependent on training systems in which a large amount of the content is designed to prepare trainers for activities which are irrelevant to or inefficient as techniques of social intervention. The training period in such systems is irrationally and excessively lengthy and costly. Delays in the production of manpower and inflation in the cost of prevention are inevitable.

SIZE AND TYPE OF UNITS

The type and size of units at which intervention may be directed are found on the left axis of the cube in Figure 2.1. This topic is, of course, the main focus of the following chapters. I have cross-hatched small sections of the cells in the top front layers of the cube to suggest that the major thrust of all of the social-intervention systems up to now has resulted in the production of small numbers of unnecessarily highly-trained mental-health workers, trainers and scientists whose mission has been the generation of information and the delivery of mental-health services with the goal of alleviation to single individuals rather than to the various larger aggregates which exist. Training researchers and teachers was also sometimes conducted in classrooms. Very few departments of psychology, psychiatry or social work offered training in methods of group intervention before 1950; even in 1960, training programs rarely offered courses in group psychotherapy or in community psychology or psychiatry. However, mental-health professionals of various affiliations had been experimenting with interventions in groups for many years.

Gazda (1968), in his history of the group psychotherapy movement, identifies the early period of group psychotherapy as primarily a classroom-like situation. General information could be imparted more efficiently to a group than to single individuals. The convening of patients in groups also had the advantage of allowing group members to share similarities in experiences and problems, and therefore to decrease both the social stigma experienced by those labeled as mentally ill and some of the risk associated with discussing taboo behavior and thoughts. In the second period of group psychotherapy, therapists performed individual therapy with one of the patients in a group while the other patients observed, or functioned as auxiliary therapists. I believe we are now in a third era in which our concern is to try to use the group itself as an agent of change, to harness the power which seems to be inherent in groups to influence members.

I have not elaborated on the characteristics of these group units because the important dimensions have not yet been identified. Certainly size of unit is an important determinant of the numbers and types of interactions possible. The contractual agreements that exist among group members, and the implicit or explicit aspects of such contracts, are probably important group variables. Strangers may meet for a brief period of time for the specific purpose of identifying and modifying styles of relating to others, as in the encounter group. Families have complex and long-term contracts, and many mutual goals; children in a classroom meet regularly for long periods of time, and generate complicated attitudes and interrelationships. Members of all such units exert mutual influences on each other, but rarely in a systematic and effective manner, designed to contribute to the mutual benefit of all. I believe that it now is possible to teach groups the techniques for mobilizing the influence of group members on each other. Future strategies of social intervention will be profoundly influenced by the introduction of such powerful methods to modify human behavior (Nelson, 1967).

This new approach is based on information derived from several areas. Social psychologists interested in group dynamics have accumulated substantial evidence that groups, particularly cohesive groups, generate considerable influence over the behavior and attitudes of their members (Yalom, 1970). A second source of new input into systems of intervention is based on the research on social learning and human learning. The literature of the past decade demonstrates that modeling, shaping, rehearsal and reinforcement can reliably modify the responses of group members (Bandura, 1969). A byproduct of the entry of learning theory into the study of group process and functioning has been a greater emphasis on specificity, and on identifying the behavior to be changed, the behavior to be substituted and the methods to be utilized.

The National Training Laboratory movement has provided a third pool of information resources regarding the value of laboratories and exercises for experiential learning: that is, learning based on an analysis of interactions which are generated between group members. Such behaviors serve as the data for the identification of habitual classes of social responses of group members. The laboratory provides an opportunity to experiment with new alternative responses and to observe the consequences.

The Journal of Applied Behavior Science reports research of this type.

The implications of the new social change technologies generated by the movements described above find a favorable climate in the action orientation which generally characterizes the spirit of our times. Rather than the more contemplative approach of more traditional treatment orientations, which might attempt to modify aggressive behavior via the analysis of one's dreams when the content appeared appropriate, the social learning theory adherents would provide a model for the behavior to be acquired by a group, and would encourage group members to engage in behavior approximating that of the model. The elicitation exercises employed by NTL trainers (Pfeiffer and Jones, 1969) insure that group members monitor each other's behavior, rather than hoping that verbal feedback occcurs. Trainers provide such a structure by designating a time for feedback to be initiated, instructions on how it is to be delivered, and providing formal categories to assist group members in the generation of feedback (see feedback chapter by Jacobs, for example).

Existential and Gestalt psychologists (Brammer and Shostrom, 1968) have conveyed the preoccupation of contemporary society with issues of personal and social responsibility into the context of group interventions. Groups scrutinize the operations of commitment statements by members, in order to insure that action elements accompany verbal assertions of intention; attempts by members to abrogate responsibility by inaction or indecision do not escape unchallenged. The increased emphasis on action and on the assignment or responsibility in interventions is augmented by the insistence of behavior modifiers and laboratory trainers that:

(1) The behaviors to be changed or the goals of laboratories must be identified objectively and specifically.
(2) The objectives and conditions of intervention contracts must be made highly visible to clients.
(3) Adherence to contractual agreements during intervention on the part of both clients and interveners must be constantly monitored.
(4) An integral aspect of intervention is the formal evaluation of progress toward, as well as achievement of, contract objectives.

Also from the Zeitgeist comes an emphasis on social and physical ecology—that man is affected by his environment—that will be reflected over and over again in the following chapters as they discuss the construction of environmental support systems, working with family members, improving interaction in mental hospital wards, etc.

Those who work with natural groups, as in family therapy or in a laboratory attended by members of the same business organization, have been dubious of the efficacy of intervening with one member of the group or system: for example, the child, without modifying the environment provided by the other members of the system, such as the parents and other family members. Much speculation and observation exists to the effect that the effects of interventions limited to one member of the system are not durable. More recent systematic evidence reveals that deviant behaviors of a group member are often strongly encouraged and frequently reinforced by peer group or family culture (Patterson, 1969).

The disappointment of interveners with the efficacy of intrapsychic change as the sole or main vehicle of intervention, leads us to entertain the hypothesis that more stable interventions may be produced by attempting to modify the responses of the significant "others" in the system in which one individual has been nominated by the others in the system as the patient. Maximally effective intervention may be the consequence of intervening with the entire subsystem in which cohesiveness, common goals and contractual agreements already exist, and by building into the group the techniques for maintaining and stabilizing behavior congruent with the goals of the intervention contract. It is plausible that we can enhance the stability of interventions if we teach parents to reinforce the appropriate rather than the deviant behavior of their children simultaneously with teaching the children more effective and legitimate means of obtaining gratification from the family. Even more effective and stable intervention might be a consequence of also teaching children to reinforce their parents for good rather than bad family management. Recent evidence (Graubard, Rosenberg & Miller, 1971) suggests that pupils may be taught to be effective reinforcers of their teachers.

Even further, we might well benefit from turning our attention to the creation or production of subsystems, where natural opportunities are absent as in the case of the social isolate, which may increase the stabilization of the intervention. A self-perpetuating intervention for the maintenance of social interaction where a previous deficit existed might be produced in a classroom by assisting a pair of socially-isolated children to mutually generate and reinforce social responses from each other.

The freedom to entertain innovative solutions in some of our contemporary intervention systems has been hampered by our conceptualizations of illness and cure, which are dichotomous and discrete, and which may be contrasted here with those of education and training, which we more often view as continuous and perhaps even indeterminant. Is there any greater need for a personal growth group to be terminated than a poker club? The use of programmed materials that are emerging for the generation and study of social interactions (Berzon, Solomon & Reisel, 1972) could make it possible to continue indefinitely in the process of improving the skills of living without draining mental-health manpower resources. The halfway house for a mental-hospital patient who has lost his community roots and may have poor skills at reestablishing relationships may be a misnomer and a self-delusion of the mental-health movement. It may be more useful to conceptualize the halfway house as a permanent subsystem of the community. Cure, in the sense of resuming one's prehospitalization roles and relationships in the community, may be an unrealistic objective for such patients. What are the essential ingredients of community living and how might these elements be provided when hospitals are no longer necessary? The same logic applied to the population of the aged in Veterans' Administration or state mental hospitals may permit us to design a community more effective in meeting patient needs, rather than maintaining the illusion that they may some day leave. Today such institutions contain aggregates of individuals who docilely exist in a drab, unproductive, unrewarding, regimented, unisexual environment. If, on the other hand, we accepted the permanence of this quasi community, what provisions would we conceive of to satisfy its members' needs for belonging, identity, self-esteem, privacy, support, sexual activity, systems of communication, opportunity for self-government etc.?

In conclusion, I would like to comment on the relevance of

sources of funding to training. Federal and state funds provide the major support for graduate training in the area of social intervention. Student stipends, money for staff positions, or consultant funds to improve communications between university and field training agencies are derived primarily from public funds. Freeman (1972) presents data showing that almost half of graduate students in psychology are federally supported. To the extent that the donors of such funds—the Veterans' Administration, for example—contract the funds to insure training and placement of students in their agencies, constraints are placed on types of training available to students, and the populations and techniques with which students become familiar. The American Psychological Association requires students in clinical psychology to complete a year of internship as part of the fulfillment of requirements for the Ph.D. The economic support of interns by mental hospitals certainly has an influence on the development of interests and skills of psychologically-trained mental-health workers.

I am not arguing the legitimacy of public agencies' shaping the training of mental-health workers by economic means, but rather an awareness of the powerful influence of money on mental-health training, the consequences associated with its sources and its availability. Neither the generation of information, the training of mental-health workers nor the delivery of social intervention, is possible without financial support. We need to think clearly whether the constriction deriving from the present support bases hampers the maximal development of mental-health resources. If this is the case, what influence can be brought to bear on present agencies to modify the restrictions; what other less-hampering sources of support can be generated; what more flexible training contents can be developed?

REFERENCES

Albee, G.W. *Mental health manpower trends.* New York: Basic Books, 1959.

Alexander, F. & Ross, H. (Eds.) *Dynamic psychiatry.* Chicago: University of Chicago Press, 1952.

Bandura, A. *Principles of behavior modification.* New York: Holt, Rinehart, & Winston, 1969.

Bastien, S. & Jacobs, A. *Dear Sheila: An empirical study of psychotherapy by means of written communication.* In press. Journal of Consulting and Clinical Psychology.

Bersoff, D.N. School psychology as "institutionalized psychiatry." *Professional Psychology,* 1971, **2**, 266–269.

Berzon, B., lomon, L.N. & Reisel J. Audiotape programs for self-directed groups. In L.N. Solomon & B. Berzon (Eds.) *New perspectives in encounter groups.* San Francisco: Jossey-Bass, 1972.

Brammer, L.M. & Shostrom, E.L. *Therapeutic psychology: Fundamentals of actualization counseling and Psychotherapy.* Englewood Cliffs, N.J. Prentice-Hall, 1968.

Brody, E.B. Interprofessional relations of psychologists and psychiatrists are common too, only more so. In B. Lubin and E.E. Levitt (Eds.), *The clinical psychologist: background, roles an functions.* Chicago: Aldine, 1967. Pp. 247–252.

Brown, J.F. Psychodynamics of abnormal behavior. New York and London: McGraw-Hill, 1940.

Coleman, J.C. *Abnormal psychology and modern life.* Chicago: Scott, Foresman, 1950.

Egan, G. *Encounter: Group processes for interpersonal growth.* Belmont, Calif.: Brooks/Cole, 1970.

Freeman, R.B. Labor market adjustments in psychology. *American Psychologist,* 1972, **27**, 384–392.

Gazda, G.M. (Ed.). *Innovations to group psychotherapy.* Springfield, Ill.: Charles C Thomas, 1968.

Graubard, P.S., Rosenberg, H. & Miller, M.M. Student applications of behavior modification to teachers and environments or ecological approaches to social deviance. In E.A. Ramp & B.I. Hopkins (Eds.), *A new direction for education: Behavior analysis,* 1971. W. Kansas Support and Development Center for Follow Through, Lawrence, Kansas: 1971. Pp. 80–101.

Guerney, B.G., Jr. (Ed.). *Psychotherapeutic agents: New roles for nonprofessionals, parents and teachers.* New York: John Wiley and Sons, 1969.

Henderson, N.B. & Hildreth, J.D. Certification, licensing and the movement of psychologists from state to state. In B. Lubin and E.E. Levitt (Eds.) *The clinical psychologist: Background roles and functions.* Chicago:, Aldine 1967. Pp. 350–354.

Hutt, M.L. & Gibby, R.G., Patterns of abnormal behavior. Boston: Allyn & Bacon, 1957.

Klein, P.B. *Abnormal psychology.* New York: Henry Holt, 1951.

Landis, C.P. & Bolles, M.M. *Textbook of abnormal psychology.* New York: MacMillan, 1950.

Levine, M. Principles of psychiatric treatment. In Alexander, F. & Ross, H. (Eds.), *Dynamic psychiatry.* New York: Basic Books, 1958. Pp. 307–366.

London, P. *The modes and morals of psychotherapy.* New York: Holt, Rinehart & Winston, 1964.

Lubin, B. A survey of psychotherapy training and activities of psychologists. In B. Lubin & E.E. Levitt (Eds.), *The clinical psychologist: Background, roles and functions.* Chicago: Aldine, 1967. Pp. 132–135.

Maslow, A.H. *Motivation and personality.* New York: Harper, 1954.

Matarazzo, J.D. Some national developments in the utilization of nontraditional mental health power. *American Psychologist,* 1971, **26,** 363–372.

Megargee, E.I. (Ed.), *Research in clinical assessment.* New York and London: Harper and Row, 1966.

Menninger, K. *The theory of psychoanalytic techniques.* New York: Basic Books, 1958.

Mischel, W. *Personality and assessment.* New York: John Wiley and Sons, 1968.

Nelson, S. E. Training psychologists for the therapeutic community. In B. Lubin & E.E. Levitt (Eds.), *The clinical psychologist: Background, roles and functions.* Chicago: Aldine, 1967. Pp. 117–119.

O'Kelley, L.I. *Introduction to psychopathology.* New York: Prentice-Hall, 1949.

O'Kelley, L.I. & Muckler, F.A. *Introduction to psychopathology.* Englewood Cliffs: Prentice-Hall, 1955.

Patterson, G.R. Behavioral techniques based on social learnings: An additional base for developing behavior modification technologies. In C.M. Franks (Ed.), *Behavioral therapy: Appraisal and status.* New York: McGraw-Hill, 1969. Pp. 341–347.

Pfeiffer, J.W. & Jones, J.E. *A handbook of structured exercises for human relations training.* Vol. III. Iowa City: University Associates Press, 1969.

Pumroy, D.K. Current characteristics of the education of clinical psychology. In B. Lubin & E.E. Levitt (Eds.), *The clinical psychologist: Background, roles and functions.* Chicago: Aldine, 1967. Pp. 75–83.

Rioch, M.J., Elkes, E., Flint, A.A., Usdansky, B.S., Newman, R.G. & Silber, E. National Institute of Mental Health pilot study in training mental health counselors. *American Journal of Orthopsychiatry,* 1963, **33,** 678–689.

Rosenhans, D. & London, P. Therapy and remediation. In P. London & D. Rosenhans (Eds.), *Foundations of abnormal psychology.* New York: Holt, Rinehart & Winston, 1968. Pp. 557–598.

Rotter, J.B. A historical and theoretical reanalysis of some broad trends in clinical psychology. In B. Lubin & E.E. Levitt (Eds.), The clinical psychologist: Background, roles and functions. Chicago: Aldine, 1967. Pp. 23–52.

Watkin, J.G. Psychotherapy: An overview. In I.A. Berg & L.A. Pennington (Eds.), An introduction to clinical psychology. New York: Ronald Press, 1966. Pp. 457–481.

Watson, D. & Tharp, R. *Self-directed behavior: self-modification for personal adjustment.* Monterey, Calif.: Brooks/Cole, 1972.

White, R.W. *The abnormal personality.* New York: Ronald Press, 1948.

Wolberg, L.R. *The technique of psychotherapy.* New York: Grune & Stratton, 1954.

Yalom, I.D. *The theory and practice of group psychotherapy.* New York: Basic Books, 1970.

Ziman, J.M. Information, communication, knowledge. *American Psychologist,* 1971, **26,** 338–345.

Notes

[1]I examined eight college textbooks in abnormal psychology commonly used in the forties and fifties (White, 1948; Hutt and Gibby, 1957; Brown, 1940; O'Kelley, 1949; O'Kelley & Muckler, 1955; Landis & Bolles, 1950; Klein, 1951; Coleman, 1950). Only two of the eight, Coleman and O'Kelley & Muckler, had any references in their subject indexes to prevention or prophylaxis. O'Kelley and Muckler begin their section with a comment to the effect that prevention can hardly be said to exist.

[2]Unpublished data recently collected by Bastien and Jacobs support the effectiveness of telepnone psychotherapy.

Section II

Innovative Treatment Strategies and Programs

Introduction

Section II contains seven chapters describing treatment strategies and programs used in groups. The first four describe group treatment methods applied to groups of individuals who live together or meet together because their behavior is unsatisfying to themselves or frightening or annoying to society. The goal of treatment is correction or remediation of these social deficiencies. The first two chapters deal with patients hospitalized for so-called mental illness. In the first, a milieu-therapy system is described in which patients, who are conceptualized as having maladaptive ways of relating socially, and trainers meet together in groups for learning about and practicing socially-adaptive behavior. In the second chapter, a token-economy system is described in which patients earn material rewards, social approval and the opportunities to participate in enjoyable activities by engaging in more socially-acceptable and less deviant behavior.

The next two chapters also deal with treatment, but of those individuals whose behavior deviations are not so severe as to make it necessary to interrupt their ordinary activities while treatment occurs. In the first of these chapters, techniques derived from social-learning theory for modifying aggressive behavior are described and illustrated with actual case material. Techniques for assisting individuals to think more rationally and respond with more appropriate emotional behavior are discussed in the second chapter, as are the advantages of learning these new responses in a group situation.

The next three chapters describe the use of groups as intervention devices with participants among whom relationships, roles and contractual agreements already exist, and are not primarily related to the issue of treatment. The first of these chapters is concerned with enabling groups of married couples or other emotionally interdependent individuals to manage conflict more effectively. An elaborate description of the exercises and techniques for accomplishing these goals is presented, along with a scoring system for the evaluation of interactions between pairs of individuals.

The next chapter describes a programmed school where the techniques for teaching academic subjects, and social behavior as well, are derived from the principles of learning developed by B.F. Skinner. Instruction is pyramidal with parents, college students, high school students and even the pupils themselves serving as behavior modifiers and teachers. The last chapter in this section describes an aspect of community psychology called social-network intervention. The theory and techniques for stimulating family and kinship groups, friends, neighbors and work associates to assist an individual in crisis are reviewed, and actual case material is presented to illustrate the application of the principles.

All of the writers of the chapters in this section are practitioners in the delivery systems of the mental-health professions. The descriptions of the programs, as the reader will note, will differ one from another in the amount of detail the author spends on theory, technique or documentation. Many of these programs were so new at the time of writing, and even now, that little opportunity for evaluation of overall or long term effectiveness is available.

3. An Inpatient Teaching Laboratory as a Milieu Force

O. Lee Trick
Marion K. Jacobs
W.W. Spradlin

The principal responsibility for the treatment and care of hospitalized psychiatric patients is delegated to medical students, untrained in mental-health intervention. Together with students from other disciplines, the medical students employ verbal techniques to treat the patients in small group meetings and in a daily community ward meeting. A psychiatric training clerkship for third-year medical students is the context for this treatment program.

The results compare very favorably with those of other inpatient services. Average length of hospitalization is less than two weeks; there are fewer than 6 percent readmissions in a six-month period; over 95 percent of patients report that they would return if additional treatment was needed and that they would recommend the program to family or friends that needed psychiatric help.

This new approach to social intervention with the hospitalized psychiatric patient by the West Virginia University Department of Behavioral Medicine and Psychiatry is characterized by the following ingredients common to contemporary innovation in the use of groups:

1. The usefulness of traditional medically derived strategies and concepts such as doctor, patient, sickness and cure undergoes reevaluation. In the consequent role-change that ensues, doctor and patient both become students of behavior. The task of cure is transformed into the identification and modification of maladaptive behaviors in either of the participants.

2. Concurrently, the program adopts concepts and strategies derived from social psychology and human learning theories: social setting, feedback, reinforcement and modeling.

3. The program attempts to specify as clearly and openly as possible for patient and staff the maladaptive responses, the correct responses and the treatment strategy, and to assign responsibility by means of highly-visible contractual arrangements between staff and patients.

4. Treatment tactics derive from an awareness of the influence of social ecology on behavior. The power of ward members is mobilized for treatment by means of community ward meetings. Families of patients are involved in the intervention process in order to provide more favorable milieus for the patient after the conclusion of treatment.

5. Mental-health training as well as treatment agents are interdisciplinary, and often at subdoctoral levels.

Unique is the attempt of the training system to practice what it preaches. Formal and informal self-monitoring and evaluation of programs by patients, students and staff provides information on which to base system changes that may result in more effective training and treatment. Although the strategy is in the tradition of the NTL laboratory approach to experiential learning, it is rare within university-based training or treatment programs.

That the social setting in which a person finds himself has some effect on the way he behaves, seems almost too obvious to mention. It is generally accepted that one doesn't shout at a funeral, or take off all his clothes in the street. Yet for years, psychiatrists and psychologists who treated hospitalized psychiatric patients seemed to be operating on the assumption that these people were somehow exempt from being influenced by the world around them. The disordered behavior was viewed entirely as the patient's response to his own internal events, with little regard for the role of the hospital environment as a behavioral determinant.

Eventually, it became apparent that the social systems of psychiatric wards function as powerful influences on patient and staff behavior. Left to evolve unchecked, the results were frequently undesirable and untherapeutic, but properly channeled, the social aspects of a psychiatric setting represented one of the most effective forces leading to therapeutic change. Numerous programs designed to capitalize on this phenomenon have arisen, and have been labeled *therapeutic milieus* or *therapeutic communities*.

Almost anyone working in a milieu-therapy program will tell you that it is a stimulating and fascinating experience—so much so, that mental-health professionals are prone to being seduced by the excitement of day-to-day activities, while shunning the more arduous task of evaluating what they're doing and sharing this information with colleagues. There are, of course, notable exceptions. One such is the factor-analytic study by Almond, Keniston & Baltax (1968), in which they explored the value system of a milieu-therapy unit at Yale–New Haven. They identified a new factor, which they named "Social Openness and Ward Involvement," as emerging for the first time as an explicitly-stated value. Generally, however, the literature is lacking in systematic attempts to isolate the salient features of particular psychiatric milieus that seem to make them effective forces toward change. Should the inpatient community also be intended as a training facility, as is the case in most university medical centers, the problems of designing and evaluating a successful program are compounded. Besides providing high-quality service for numerous patients or clients, one would also like to be able to provide experiential training for large numbers of students concurrently, utilizing a minimum of teaching manpower.

In this paper we describe such a program, unique in some of its approaches to psychiatric treatment, and proven as an efficient way of delivering health care while at the same time training health professionals of many different disciplines. In addition, we attempt systematically to analyze the essential features of the program and relate them to social learning theory (Rotter, 1970).

A key assumption of the program currently in operation at W.V.U. Medical Center, Department of Behavioral Medicine and Psychiatry, is that training and therapy, far from being separate entities, are highly similar, *educative* processes. It then follows that the place in which this education takes place can be viewed as a school or, to use our preferred term, a teaching laboratory, and the goal for all the participants, whether they are technically "patients," "staff," "students" or "faculty," is to learn something.

In this case, the topic is human behavior—particularly one's own.

We have informally labeled several variables we believe to be important to this learning process. They are identified as: (1) Redefining patient-doctor and student-teacher relationships; (2) encouraging each individual to assume responsibility for his own behavior; (3) maintaining peer-level involvement of staff, students and patients; (4) using a large group to establish personal accountability; (5) applying social learning theory; (6) providing staff growth groups; (7) handling information honestly; and (8) changing the program continually in response to participants' evaluation. Conceptually, some of these variables overlap, and are only separated for clarity of exposition.

REDEFINING PATIENT-DOCTOR AND STUDENT-TEACHER RELATIONSHIPS

Although most programs reflect an awareness that the social milieu can be very influential in reducing deviant behavior, they seldom test the full power of the force. The retarding factor is the traditional medical model, which requires the patient to be sick, the doctor to heal, and the student to learn. These roles, as usually defined, permit each group only a narrow range of responses, thus setting an upper limit on how much any of these persons can grow. Maxwell Jones (1968) spoke pointedly on the patient's role when he said, "How far patient and staff roles can be allowed to overlap is an open question. It would seem however, that the danger in any hospital community arises if the patient is not allowed to develop his optimal potential as an individual or a leader; and this dimension of the role of the patient in the hospital has generally been neglected."

But, what about the role of the doctor? or the student? They must be allowed to grow too. When a milieu is designed to help each person develop his optimal potential as an individual, be he student, patient, or staff, then everybody benefits maximally. With this in mind, we have substantially altered the medical model of psychiatric care and all its attendant assumptions.

Replacing it is the view, mentioned earlier, that a therapeutic inpatient unit should be a laboratory in which each individual can study human behavior: his own and that of other people.

Consider first the patient. He finds it less painful to use his "sick" role than to recognize that he is a person who must learn more adaptive ways of relating to other people. If we stop seeing him as riddled with schizophrenia or in some other way sick, it becomes much more apparent that far from being the victim of uncontrollable internal impulses and overwhelming environmental forces, he is, rather, an active participant in the construction of the reinforcement contingencies (Bandura, 1969) that maintain his state of patienthood. Similarly, the doctor frequently uses his role as an expert, to protect himself from discovering his own deficits in personality functioning. If both are now forced to relate on a person-to-person level, neither can use the doctor or patient role to avoid assuming responsibility for his own behavior and learning from it.

A parallel problem often arises between faculty and students. It is a matter of speculation whether students are more awed by teachers or teachers more threatened by students, but in most medical settings both groups can be found engaging in highly ritualistic, stereotyped behavior designed to keep the other at a "safe" distance. The teacher prevents himself from discovering deficiencies in his ability to form personal and professional relationships, by retreating to his role as "the authority." This establishes the perfect counter-role for the student under pressure, who then becomes a cynical protester rather than face his own inadequacies.

In the present program, however, the teaching-laboratory approach stimulates direct encounters between people, giving each individual a chance to learn about his strengths and weaknesses by openly examining his contributions to the relationships in question. Both "teacher" and "student" thus have opportunities to increase their interpersonal skills by studying their own behavior, learning from it and practicing behavioral changes when necessary. In a program of this type, the risk to the faculty member is great as he presents his own behavior to his students for their evaluation in order that he may learn from them. If he is unsuccessful as a personal force with his students, he cannot then allow himself the luxury of blaming the students' ignorance for their lack of understanding him, but rather is faced with the repulsive task of learning from his own failures. However, the faculty's willingness for this objective review demonstrates to the students the relative safety of the process and its many dividends. The student, in turn, begins to see that there's more to being a good professional than just knowing facts and attending to patients. As he begins to appreciate the importance of using his own personality effectively, he becomes more willing to learn about himself, despite the considerable anxiety that this often arouses.

ASSUMING RESPONSIBILITY FOR ONE'S OWN BEHAVIOR

If the ward is to be a laboratory for the learning and practice of socially adaptive, self-controlled behavior, it follows that it must truly be an open ward. As it relates to patients, an open ward must mean no restraints, no seclusion rooms, no locks on the door, no confiscation of razor blades and no attempt whatsoever to assume responsibility for other people's lives. Anything less sets up an expectancy for "sick" behavior and shifts responsibility away from the patient.

From the moment a person enters this unit, the message is clear. He is expected to behave appropriately and take responsibility for himself. Patients do not walk around behaving bizarrely, and nobody, patient or staff, will knowingly reinforce inappropriate behavior on the part of anybody else. The social pressure is so strong that even when a patient arrives from the emergency room in a very distraught state, or behaving inappropriately, usually he elects to control himself in a very short period of time.

It is important to understand clearly the distinction between this type of program and the kind that is often called an open ward, but where the staff takes responsibility not just for the medical welfare of the patient, but for his behavior as well. When an individual threatens to act out, we refuse to see ouselves as his keeper. Rather, we attempt to provide a social climate in which he can have an opportunity to receive honest feedback about himself and take a hard look at the way he is behaving in his relationships with other people. Then he can make whatever changes *he* elects in order to make himself more comfortable. As pointed out elsewhere (Quarrick, Jacobs & Trick, 1971), this approach functions well, but it takes a great deal of administrative support and courage to initiate and maintain it.

PEER-LEVEL INVOLVEMENT FOR STAFF, STUDENTS AND PATIENTS

Probably a unique, and definitely one of the most exciting aspects of the program is the use of untrained therapists to do the front line work. Third-year medical students, serving their Behavioral Medicine and Psychiatry clerkships, have principal responsibility for patient care. Two fulltime faculty, a psychiatrist and a psychologist, plus four psychiatric residents, are available for consultation and guidance. The main treatment modality is group therapy with patients participating in two and one-half hours of group meetings daily.

All patients and students are divided into four small groups, each consisting of student-doctors and their own patients, plus students from other disciplines, including nursing, physical therapy and psychology, who are in training on the ward at the time. Usually this amounts to some 12–17 people per group, with students often outnumbering patients. Obviously, if each of these students considered himself "the therapist," and expected patients to discuss "their problems" while he reflected, listened or gave advice, the patients would quickly become discouraged. With this many therapists, the feeling would probably be like testifying before a jury. Instead, the students, staff and patients are charged with *exactly the same assignment*. They are all to interact together and observe their own and other behavior. As each person explains his feelings about the effect that other individuals are having on him, and accepts feedback about himself, he begins to understand the characteristic ways in which he relates to people.

Many highly-trained professionals first have to unlearn the ways in which they use their theories and techniques to distance themselves emotionally from patients, before they can engage in this type of therapy. It is fortuitous that the students' background in psychopathology and psychotherapy is elementary enough that they are spared this unlearning process. Left with little choice but to use the force of their own personalities, they more easily learn to use themselves therapeutically.

The way any individual, be he student, staff or patient, relates to the people in the group, is typical of his behavior with others outside of the hospital. The people in the hospital become temporary "significant others" in an experimental environment. By keeping the focus on behavior that is occurring in the here and now, rather than having someone discuss his "problem," each person is offered the opportunity to interact with others and learn from them the impact his behavior has on them. If this impact is not what he intended, and is not bringing the returns he wants, he is then more receptive to suggestions about what changes are necessary in his behavior in order for him to obtain the desired social rewards. For the patient, to insure generalization of newly learned behaviors to his family system, family members (including children) are expected to attend groups. It is not uncommon to make admission to the unit conditional upon family willingness to participate in the program.

The many contrasts between this model and psychodynamic ones are quite obvious. Perhaps the most significant, however, is that using this framework, even the "sickest" patient can contribute substantially to the self-understanding of the most "accomplished" therapist, or the most frightened student.

At first, most students, because they are so accustomed to more authoritarian models, are reluctant to take off their white coats and just be people. They soon learn, however, that the most inexperienced individual can observe behavior, share reactions with others, and learn to give and receive feedback.

Similarly, the patients are afraid to give up their "sick patient" roles. As patients they have learned to use their symptoms to avoid taking responsibility for their actions. Now, deprived of dependency on a health-giving expert, the patient learns that he can no longer play the "one-down" role. He is now a peer with every other person in the group. His job is to learn about himself and other people, and by so doing to change those aspects of his behavior which he decides are maladaptive for him.

This idea of expecting people to assume the role of learner rather than patient has been successfully tried before. For example, Robert Morton (1967) set up a time-limited, residential training laboratory on a psychiatric unit. The patients were labeled as delegates, and related as "students" to "teachers" rather than patients to doctors. The unique feature in our unit is that by relating as a peer, the patient is being asked to be a learner in the functional absence of a teacher or so-called expert. At any given moment in a relationship, the "patient" might be the "expert." That is, he might be the "teacher" and the student or faculty member might be the "patient."

THE USE OF A LARGE GROUP TO ESTABLISH PERSONAL ACCOUNTABILITY

In addition to the two hours of small-group meetings, all patients, students and faculty come together for a daily, half-hour, large-group meeting. Although the use of large meetings is not new (Schiff & Glassman, 1969), here again, our focus is somewhat different. Stated in its simplest terms, the large group does exactly what the small group does, except that there there are sixty people present instead of sixteen. It is not a ward meeting in the old sense of the word nor therapy for the patients. Rather, when used properly, it forces all members of the program, including the permanent staff, to engage in the dynamic, ongoing process of learning about themselves and the kind of relationships they establish with other people. The particular value of this meeting is that it can be used to work through feelings or problems between individuals who do not happen to be in the same small group. Everyone knows that any group member is free to bring up whatever is on his mind, the emphasis still being that this is a laboratory for learning about human behavior, and *all* behavior is fair grist for the mill. If, after a particular piece of behavior has been examined, the individual involved feels it did not have the effect he intended, or did not bring him desired rewards, the group will help him consider alternate ways of relating, give him a chance to practice new behaviors and provide feedback about how well these behaviors are working.

It is our impression that this meeting, more than any other single factor, removes the necessity for acting-out behavior of all sorts. Each individual knows that any and all interactions are potentially subject to scrutiny, and manipulatory efforts on the part of staff or patients are all subject to the critical question, "How well is this behavior working?" For example, if suicide is the issue, once the individual understands that his threats will be met with an open, interested but investigative attitude, which places responsibility for his actions on him, suicide becomes the *least* workable solution. The threat no longer brings unqualified, sympathetic attention for irresponsible or manipulative behavior. With such an approach, suicide attempts or gestures have, for the most part, become a thing of the past on this unit, even though so-called high-suicide-risk patients are constantly in treatment. An additional benefit of this meeting is that it provides the faculty with an opportunity to assess, on a daily basis, the general tenor of the milieu. They then can help catalyze discussion of those feelings and attitudes about which people do not seem able to talk but that are affecting the therapeutic climate. Since eight to ten medical students are assigned to thirty-two patients, this opportunity for overviewing the ward is also critical from a medical-legal standpoint.

APPLICATION OF SOCIAL LEARNING THEORY

As stated earlier, we choose to view the patient not as sick, but rather, as having learned maladaptive ways of relating socially. Actually, this is carried one step further. The patient and his immediate family are considered to constitute a social system which, at least in some aspects, is functioning maladaptively. It is not only the patient who needs to relearn. Both he and his family need to understand that the real "patient" is the interspace between the family members: that is, their relationship. The designated patient just happens to be the member in the family who was "elected" to come to the hospital. Therefore, we attempt to involve all the significant family members in as much of the group therapy sessions as possible.

This cybernetic view of the family system has been well described elsewhere (Patterson, 1969). When a family member emits deviant, as opposed to adaptive, behavior, the responses of the rest of the family are limited because of the aversive nature of the deviant behavior This is what Patterson terms the "coercion hypothesis." For example, if a member threatens suicide, he coerces the rest of the family to become attentive and sympathetic and to take extra care of him. This in effect provides strong reinforcement for his deviant behavior. There is considerable experimental evidence both with children and with nurses working with psychotic patients on psychiatric wards, that "not only did they [parents, teachers or nurses] tend to provide positive reinforcement for deviant behaviors, but the data showed that they were most likely to provide those reinforcers during periods of high-rate or high-amplitude behaviors (Patterson, 1969).

Our own experience supports the coercion hypothesis. That is, an individual, in his normal social environment, receives the most attention from others when he acts the "sickest." Clearly, then, it becomes more than a matter of relearning on the part of the patient. Those who reinforce him must learn to do so more appropriately, while the patient, in turn, must learn to reinforce, or respond to, the people in his environment more appropriately.

STAFF GROWTH GROUPS

In addition to the group therapy sessions which the patients attend, the students and staff meet for an additional hour daily in a "critique" session. It should be noted that this totals three and one-half hours of group experience each day for the students. Although patients are not present in critique, they are directly affected by the work done in these sessions. The primary purpose of the critique is to provide the students and staff with additional opportunities to work on their relationships with one another. They also explore their feelings and attitudes about themselves and their patients. When any member discovers unresolved feelings towards someone who is not in this group, he is expected to take this conflict back to the small, and/or large, group meeting and work it through with the individuals involved.

It has been our repeated experience that when the "staff" (that is, students, staff and faculty) know where they stand with each other, through having become aware of, and being able to label, their own feelings and expressing themselves openly and honestly, it is immediately reflected in the mood of the general milieu. We have learned through painful trial and error that excessive tension, anger or frustration among the patients, or between patients and staff, usually means something is wrong among the staff. They have not worked out their problems and their stress filters back to the patients. We strongly believe that patients do not learn about their feelings and behavior unless the staff is growing and learning too. Because of this emphasis on learning to label one's feelings and examining the effects of one's behavior, some of our research efforts have also been in this area.

We have developed, and are currently experimenting with, a relatively simple mood-check list that can be used while a group is in progress to (1) help members assess how well their behavior communicates what they intended, (2) train people to pay more attention to behavior and (3) help a person who is trying to change his behavior, determine if his attempts are successful (Jacobs and Gatz, 1971).

HANDLING INFORMATION HONESTLY

A final note about the specifics of the program concerns the "staffing" of new patients: each newcomer has a complete physical examination and psychiatric evaluation, which is done by the student-physician. In the presence of the patient, his family and the rest of the treatment team, this data is then read verbatim from the chart. A psychiatric resident and a faculty member are also present.

It is at this time that various communication problem areas are identified and a treatment contract is worked out. The contract is an explicit agreement entered into by the treatment team, the patient and the family. It specifies (1) the behaviors to be altered, and (2) the specific procedures by which we will attempt to produce change. It is a three-way contract in which the patient, the family and treatment-team members all accept mutual responsibility for providing one another with the feedback needed to keep all participants honest in carrying out their part of the contract. The treatment contract, like all other behavior in this teaching laboratory, is subject to continuing reevaluation and change. If feasible and desirable, the patient is also scheduled to begin in an outpatient group (for example, adolescent group or married-couples group) while he is still on the ward. This lessens the number of individuals who are lost to followup.

This staffing procedure communicates, early in the person's stay, that we will work openly and honestly together, and nothing that concerns him will be withheld. It also typifies our more general belief that patients must accept responsibility for themselves. The moment a staff member decides that there is some information about the patient that cannot be openly discussed with him, he assumes inappropriate responsibility, and automatically puts the patient in a dependent, inferior position. Such secrecy is also damaging to the program as a whole. If we sanction concealing one type of information from the individual and/or group, it becomes all too easy to use the same rationale to avoid other topics that are uncomfortable to examine.

CHANGING THE PROGRAM CONTINUALLY IN RESPONSE TO PARTICIPANTS' EVALUATION

Obviously, we are enthusiastic and excited about the program. The question still remains, however, as to whether it works. Observationally, we have seen dramatic changes in many patients during their inpatient stay. Though we are not yet able to offer much hard data to answer the question, the following information may be of some interest. The average length of stay is 13 days. This means the patient is only away from family and job for a short period and has minimal opportunity to develop the institutionalized dependency pattern so typical of people who are removed from the community for very long. Followup is planned for every patient and in many cases is carried out in our own outpatient department. In a six-month survey ending May, 1970, of 399 patients who had been admitted to the program, only 26, or 6 1/2 percent, were readmissions, 4 or 1 percent of which were third admissions. This is surprisingly low, considering that we do not regard readmission as a failure, but rather prefer recurrent short-term admissions to one long period of hospitalization and communicate this view to the patients. Although some national and state statistics about average length of stay and readmission rates are available, it is difficult, if not impossible, to make useful direct comparisons because of differences in admission procedures, demography, available finances, extent of facilities, etc.

Another form of patient evaluation is done at the time of discharge from the hospital. Patients are asked to complete a 115-item questionnaire evaluating many aspects of the program. During a four-month sampling period, 90 percent indicated that they felt more responsible for their own behavior and feelings than they used to, and over 95 percent indicated that if they ever needed help again they would come back to this hospital and would recommend this program to any family or friends that needed psychiatric help.

There is also a student program-analysis. This consists of a detailed rating and evaluation of the staff and program, completed anonymously by the medical students at the termination of their clerkship. Their response has been overwhelmingly positive, and for the last three years psychiatry has been voted the best clinical clerkship in our medical center. Student acceptance has been also verified in that the residency program has always been able to fill its quota from our own student population, a most unusual medical-school occurrence. Additionally, our students have performed above the national average on the psychiatric portion of the National Board Examinations in Medicine, demonstrating that they can and do learn content, even though they are in an experiential setting that rarely uses didactic teaching methods.

We are aware, however, that this is only preliminary evidence. More controlled, vigorous evaluation of the program and its long term effects is at present underway. One such project is a detailed telephone followup interview with patients conducted one year after discharge from the hospital. This is a new undertaking, and only 61 patients have been sampled as of this writing, so the following figures should be interpreted cautiously. Seventy-five percent of the patients did not require rehospitalization, 78 percent of those who had been advised to have outpatient followup did so and 76 percent returned to their usual home and job responsibilities. Concerning their hospitalization, 34 percent rated it very useful, 47 percent useful and 19 percent not useful. Eighty-six percent would recommend the program to a family member needing treatment again. These findings would suggest that the majority of patients, after less than two weeks in the hospital, can, when properly supported by appropriate followup treatment, return to their usual responsibilities and avoid rehospitalization and at the same time realistically credit themselves for their improvement.

In addition to formal evaluation, constant feedback has been sought from all participants as to whether this laboratory for learning about human behavior was adequately meeting their needs, and if not, what changes could be made to improve it. The utilization of this feedback to guide the program's growth, has caused the individuals involved to feel that it is truly theirs and not just the faculty's. In this regard, it should be pointed out the

the faculty remains unyielding in its insistence that constructive criticism be used to chart the course of the program's development. As it now stands, all aspects have literally grown from previously attempted structures, which for one reason or another did not adequately meet everyone's requirements. Each change has been one which has arisen from a mutual recognition of need. We feel our commitment to constant change in response to ongoing evaluation is perhaps the most significant factor in maintaining the vitality of this program.

THEORETICAL FORMULATIONS

Having described the program and some of our feelings about it, we would like to now turn attention to a few theoretical speculations as to what is happening.

We view the symptoms which bring a patient to a psychiatric hospital as representing grossly deviant behaviors which are socially learned, but maladaptive, ways of communicating and relating. The student too, though not "symptomatic," often is not maximally effective in communicating with colleagues, and is frequently far from therapeutic with patients. Like the patient, he can benefit from substituting more adaptive behaviors for previously learned, less useful ways. However, despite his deficits, the student almost always possesses a much broader repertoire of adaptive behaviors than the patient. Thus, while the student is learning to smooth out the rough edges in his own style, he is simultaneously serving as a relatively effective model for the patient.

When one considers that there is not 1 student, but 15 to 30, students of varying disciplines at any given time, it is apparent that this constitutes a massive input of "healthy" modeling and concern into the social system. Far from being a liability, the large number of trainees has proved to be one of the best features of the program. This is consistent with research that suggests that groups composed of friendly, expressive, person-oriented members are more effective than groups whose members lack such attributes (Chapter 15).

The permanent staff and faculty, having had the most experience with modifying behavior in groups, initially serve as models for both new patients and new students, while continuing to work on their own behavioral self-improvement. However, it is not long before the patients, and particularly the students, become quite proficient and serve as important sources of input to the faculty and each other.

Since so much of an individual's maladaptive or ineffective behavior is learned, principles similar to those which were involved in the original learning can be applied to the unlearning and relearning process. This program overtly attempts to utilize the body of knowledge developed by social learning theorists and researchers to bring about therapeutic change. The term social learning is used in the same sense as Patterson does to mean "changes in learning or performance which occur as a function of contingencies which characterize social interaction (1969)." It is beyond the scope of this discussion to attempt a review of the literature on modeling and reinforcement, both key social-learning concepts. The more interested reader is, however, referred to Patterson's excellent chapter.

We concur with his major point, in considering *modeling* a catalytic mechanism that increases the initial probability that some new response will occur, and *social reinforcement* as the mechanism which establishes this response in the individual's behavioral repertoire. In short, modeling elicits novel behavior, and social reinforcement sustains it. In the following section we describe the general process by which we use these techniques to alter the behavior of patients. However, much of what is discussed obviously applies to students and faculty as well.

Initially, the patient is in some type of crisis. By this we mean he is not getting feedback (reinforcement) that acceptably validates his self-image. The anxiety that results causes him to revert to old, maladaptive methods or to try new behavioral techniques intended to bring him the feedback necessary to regain or restore his desired self-concept. If these techniques do not work, he then resorts to some of the more extreme behaviors commonly known as symptoms. The main fuctions of the symptoms are to distance him from the sources of feedback, or to lessen the meaning of the disparate feedback and at the same time excuse him from responsibility for the behavior that generated that feedback. All three have been accomplished by the time the patient presents himself to the treatment sources implying, through his behavior, "I'm not responsible for what is going on, or what people think about me, because I'm too sick."

It is at this point that the individual is most likely to be admitted to an inpatient unit, expecting many of the things stereotypically associated with a place for "crazy" people. Instead, in this unit, he finds people behaving appropriately and modeling adaptive behavior. He finds a staff engaged in peer-relationships and self-evaluation. He is free to come or go at will. The setting forces him to be responsible for his actions. This communicates at the outset, and, with great force our expectancy that (1) people can, and will, behave in a socially acceptable manner and (2) this is the type of behavior that will be positively reinforced.

We assume that all of us have some aspects of ourselves that are functioning adaptively, and some that are not. Little is accomplished if we judge anyone as a person, but much is accomplished if we evaluate his behavior. It is our job to help the patient evaluate his specific behaviors and find out which ones are working for, which against him. Part of his job—and this expectation is directly communicated to him—is to help evaluate the staff's specific behaviors, as well as those of the other patients. The vehicle we use for accomplishing these goals is interaction in group sessions. These interactions generate the data which enable us to see more clearly which behaviors are maladaptive and which are working. "Working" as used here, simply means bringing the person the feedback he needs or wants from others.

After evaluating any given interaction, the next step is to give the individual feedback about our reactions to his behavior. If the behavior is adaptive, positive reinforcement is given in the form of social approval for appropriate specific behaviors. If the feedback is negative (that is, social disapproval and/or withdrawal of positive reinforcement), we always try to clearly specify the contingencies necessary for him to obtain positive reinforcement. In more common group terms, it is a mixture of confrontation with support. The support, however, is not a matter of saying something nice before clobbering a person with criticism. Rather, it comes in the form of "such and so that you just did makes me angry with you. *I don't like feeling* that way toward you. Let's take a look at what *we can both do* to change the way we are relating." Specific examination of behavior them ensues.

Since individuals are usually not accustomed to such honest, interpersonal evaluation, modeling techniques frequently must be employed to get them started. We conceptualize two types of modeling. The first we call implicit modeling. Included here is all the adaptive modeling that occurs in the milieu, but which is not necessarily specifically labeled or discussed. Frequently an individual is not even aware that he is serving as model for someone else. Much of the adaptive behavior in which the students spontaneously engage, falls in this class. Another form of implicit modeling is the staff's conscious involvement at a peer level. By behaving in a way that says, "We are interested enough in you to expose our feelings and welcome your reaction; we are willing to be open, to be peers and to receive your feedback," we communicate that this place is psychologically safe enough for the patient to do the kind of exploring and learning that we are suggesting he do.

It is not uncommon for an individual eventually to realize that what he is doing is not working well, but yet not see clearly how to change it. On these occasions implicit modeling is not enough, and it is necessary to explicitly model an appropriate way of interacting with another person. After attempting to show him how he appears at present, we verbally label what we are about to do. Then, using role-playing or other modeling procedures, we show him how he might try to do it differently and more effectively. As soon as the first appropriate behavior is elicited, it is positively reinforced (through social approval), and the individual is thereby encouraged to continue behaving in this more adaptive way. Social approval, as we are using the term does not mean, "That's very good, Mary," said in the condescending tone of voice so typical of psychiatric personnel talking to mental-hospital patients. It refers to a genuine, positive expression that connotes increased acceptance, closeness, and caring. The specific words and gestures, naturally, vary with the individuals involved.

In many ways it is easier to describe the approach than to do it. Given the complex behavioral patterns, verbal and nonverbal, emitted by any individual at any given moment, it is quite a challenge to (1) sort out specific behaviors, (2) determine which exact behaviors are bringing which feelings and reactions in ourselves, (3) help the individual see the different effects from different aspects of his behavior, (4) positively reinforce the appropriate while negatively reinforcing the maladaptive and at the same time (5) stay in touch with our own behavior, assess its effects and make changes as we receive feedback. This procedure becomes even more complex when one considers that each individual processes his external social reinforcement through his own internal system of thoughts, attitudes and values. It has been our experience however, that for the most part, feelings of personal acceptance or closeness are received as positive social reinforcers, whereas feelings of personal rejection or distance are perceived as negative social reinforcers.

As they learn to use this approach, student, teacher and patient deepen their self-understanding through the mirror of interpersonal feedback. The doctor-patient and student-teacher relationships fall by the wayside as all see, more clearly, that these separations are often designed to secure the emotional economy of the students and teachers and preserve the symptoms of the patient. One can imagine a triangle. In one corner towers the white-coated teacher with the security blanket of his professionalism wrapped rigidly around him. In another corner, cringes a hospital-gowned patient wearing his "patientmanship badge" and stoutly proclaiming, "You can't be my doctor unless you accept my responsibility for me." In the third corner stands the cynical student, grumbling about how psychiatry isn't real medicine. But, when all the wrappings are removed, one will find underneath a person (teacher, student or patient) whose insecurity has forced him into a rigid role—a role that can best be altered by another person willing to use *himself* as a means of modifying that sterotyped behavior.

SUMMARY

In an attempt to delineate the salient features that make a therapeutic milieu an effective force for change, the authors describe an inpatient psychiatric unit designed as a laboratory for learning about human behavior. All participants, whether they are faculty, patients, students, nurses or house staff, engage in the same process of examining their interpersonal relationships and learn to change those aspects of their behavior which do not bring the feedback from others that they need. Eight essential variables are identified as: (1) redefining the "doctor-patient" and "student-teacher" relationship, (2) encouraging each individual to assume responsibility for his own behavior, (3) maintaining peer-level involvement of both staff and patients, (4) using a large group to establish personal accountability, (5) applying social learning theory, (6) providing staff growth groups, (7) handling information honestly and (8) changing the program continually in response to evaluation by the participants. Finally, the application of modeling and social reinforcement techniques, as used in this group setting, to promote self-understanding and socially adaptive behavior, are described.

REFERENCES

Almond, R., Keniston, K, & Baltax, S. The value system of a milieu therapy unit. *Archives of General Psychiatry*, 1968, **19** (5), 545–561.

Bandura, A. *Principles of behavior modification*. New York: Holt, Rinehart & Winston, 1969.

Jacobs, M. & Gatz, M. The development of a mood-check list to aid in identifying and giving feedback about feelings and behavior in groups. Paper presented at West Virginia University Medical Center, January 1971.

Jones, M. *Beyond the therapeutic community: Social learning and social psychiatry*. New Haven: Yale University Press, 1968.

Morton, R. B. The uses of the labortory method in a psychiatric hospital. In E. H. Schein & W. G. Bennis (Eds.), *Personal and organization change through group methods*. New York: John Wiley & Sons, 1967, Pp. 115–151.

Patterson, G. R. Behavioral techniques based upon social learning: an additional base for developing behavior modification technologies. In C. M. Franks (Ed.), *Behavioral therapy: Appraisal and status*. New York: McGraw-Hill 1969, Pp. 341–374.

Quarrick, E., Jacobs, M. & Trick, O. L. A new role-model for psychology students in a medical setting. *American Psychologist*, 1971, **26**, 317–319.

Rotter, J. B. Some implications of a social learning theory for the practice of psychotherapy. In D. J. Levis (Ed.), *Learning approaches to therapeutic behavior change*. Chicago: Aldine, 1970, Pp. 208–242.

Schiff, S. B. & Glassman, S. M. Large and small group therapy in a state mental health center. *International Journal of Group Psychotherapy*, 1969, **19** (2), Pp. 150–157.

4. *Group Methods and Interpersonal Learning on a Token Economy Ward*

Roger F. Maley

One of the oldest goals of intervention is the reduction of the symptomatology of the mental-hospital patient. One of the newest approaches to the treatment of the "mentally ill," the learning theory–derived token-economy system, attempts to organize for the patient a hospital environment that will provide gratifications for the performance of behaviors necessary for him to survive outside the hospital.

Maley asserts that symptoms of the chronic mental-hospital inhabitant ordinarily are actually reinforced by the typical hospital environment; the "sick" behavior of the patient extinguishes efforts of staff members to get him to attempt painful change, and the patient's avoidance of other people, which often is the instigation for hospitalization, is perpetuated in the hospital environment. Neither staff members nor other paients provide reinforcements for social interaction.

The token economy system introduces more potential reinforcements into the ward environment, and also makes the dispensation of reinforcement contingent on the emission by patients of nonsymptomatic and more appropriate behavior. Token economies deal with the manpower shortage that exists in mental hospitals by providing a method of intervention comprehensible and manageable by aides and nurses. Round-the-clock programs of treatment manned by aides and nurses may therefore be substituted for the typical hour per week of psychotherapy which is ordinarily the most available to the chronic patient. The initial evaluation of the treatment effectiveness of such token economy programs has been promising.

However, Maley contends that up to now the programs have been overly narrow and simplistic. There exists little data on attempts to combine the token economy approach with other more complex tactics and techniques derived from the training laboratory approach, the psychodrama approach, or the patient self-government movement.

Maley points out the potential value of patient self-government in providing opportunities for apathetic patients to practice independent behavior and decision-making at the level of the patients' ability. Exercises can be used to elicit for examination by patients such basic conflicts as may center around the patients' fear and distrust of others. Role-playing by patients gives them opportunities to practice and be rewarded for socially more appropriate behavior. Maley's emphasis on action-oriented treatment and on the importance of the patient's environment is echoed in many other chapters. Maley concludes that the token economy efficacy will improve as a consequence of its incorporation of other sound behavioral change principles in addition to operant conditioning techniques.

INTRODUCTION

Behavior therapy is a generic term used to label the process of modifying abnormal human behavior through the use of experimentally-derived psychological principles. Although there are disagreements concerning the precise definition of behavior therapy, most would accept a definition which includes a strong emphasis on social-learning-theory principles. Consequently, the grist for the behavior therapist's mill is the relationship between changes in the environment and changes in a person's behavior. The focus is obviously upon behavior that can either be observed or measured by scientific instruments. Ullman & Krasner (1965) state that the behavior therapist asks three questions: "(a) what behavior is maladaptive, that is, what subject behaviors should be increased or decreased; (b) what environmental contingencies currently support the subject's behavior (either to maintain his undesirable behavior or to reduce the likelihood of his performing a more adaptive response); and (c) what environmental changes, usually reinforcing stimuli, may be manipulated to alter the subject's behavior [p.1]."

As a result of this therapeutic approach, more and more

practicing clinicians are concerned with behavior patterns capable of being described in objective and quantifiable terms. Such nebulous criteria as "personal growth," "self-actualization," and "increased insight," while not necessarily denied all validity are held in abeyance in favor of more observable and specific behavioral changes. The increased acceptance of the "psychological model" of maladaptive behavior along with the decline of the strict "medical model" interpretation of mental illness has allowed learning-oriented clinicians to become more credible. The concepts of learning, unlearning, relearning, discrimination learning, etc., can now be heard in practically every clinical setting and indicate the increasing acceptance of behavioral approaches in dealing with problems of deviancy.

Thus, the last decade has witnessed a sharp upsurge of interest in the application of behavior therapy techniques to psychotherapeutic situations. Procedures such as desensitization, aversion therapy, operant conditioning, implosive therapy, negative practice and counterconditioning have been attempted with many different deviant behaviors. Most of this work, however, has been done with patients exhibiting neurotic difficulties that are frequently monosymptomatic, such as phobias. All of these techniques appear quite promising and desensitization appears to be the treatment of choice for phobias (Paul, 1967).

A good deal less evidence is available with regard to the efficacy of these techniques when applied to hospitalized psychiatric patients who have long-standing psychotic difficulties (Davison, 1969). Nevertheless, since Lindsley and Skinner (1954) reported the successful use of operant conditioning procedures in controlling the behavior of regressed psychotic patients, more and more psychologists have been attempting to use the techniques and orientation of Skinnerian psychology with mental-hospital populations. Much of this work has centered around the use of "token economy systems" with "chronic mental patients."

THE CHRONIC MENTAL PATIENT

Jones and Sidebothem (1962) acknowledge the fact that since 1955 the total resident population of public mental hospitals has consistently decreased in spite of increased admissions, but stress the point that there is a large custodial population which remains constant. In essence, then, we are confronted with "two hospitals" within most public mental hospitals: one is an acute, short-term, rapid-turnover facility, and the other is a large, custodial facility with a relatively constant population. This chronic population accounts for two-thirds of the entire resident population across the country and can be expected to increase if certain trends continue (Paul, 1969).

Even though mental hospitals seem to be doing a better job with the acutely disturbed patient, seemingly because of psychoactive drugs, more community involvement and a return to "moral therapy" treatment notions such as unit decentralization, open-door policies, etc., the long-stay chronic patient is relatively unaffected by all this. As a sidelight, one of the more important reasons why psychologists have been allowed by medical staffs to see what these new "conditioning therapies" could do is the fact that a whole succession of hospital therapies from cold baths and lobotomies to electroconvulsive shock and chemotherapy have failed to improve the lot of the chronic patient (Davison, 1969).

Before considering therapeutic strategies to induce positive behavioral changes in the chronic patient, it might be well to specify some of the behaviors commonly associated with chronicity and to speculate about the environmental factors that may produce such behavior.

The chronic mental patient is usually described as being (1) apathetic, withdrawn, nonresponsive to the social milieu; (2) extremely dependent on the institution's staff; (3) lacking in responsibility; (4) afraid of other people; and (5) troublesome and/or bizarre. Let us consider each of these behavioral patterns in order to better understand the task of making therapeutic progress with chronic patients.

Apathy

Apathy, or lack of interest, or lack of motivation, all seem to be the same behavioral pattern looked at through different clinical orientations. The apathetic patient may spend the entire day sitting and staring out the window or pacing the floor or chattering away regardless of whether there is a listener or not, or whether the chatter makes sense or not. It is often said such patients never do anything. But this is clearly not true since the patient continuously emits the behaviors contained in his limited repertoire. In effect, the patient does not reinforce the responses made by therapists, and as he ignores attempts at verbal interaction he practices the most effective form of extinction imaginable (Schaefer & Martin, 1966). This gives us a clue: the patient's behavior effectively and remarkably painlessly extinguishes any attempt made by members of the staff to effect change. In a very real sense, then, apathetic behavior serves as an operant that allows the patient to avoid a painful situation. By engaging in this behavior he can escape from other people and pressures to change his behavior. Thus, apathetic behavior can be conceptualized as being, at least partially based upon avoidance learning—and we know from the experimental literature how difficult it is to extinguish a behavior based on avoidance learning. The therapeutic question then becomes: How can we "force" the patient to gradually face the anxiety associated with either other people or change?

Dependency

The typical public mental hospital literally forces patients to become very dependent upon the staff. The staff controls every aspect of their lives; what few rewards do exist are given to the good, quiet patient who "blends into the woodwork." The patient is given little, if any, responsibility and is treated as if he were a child (and sometimes even a person who has an illness)! It is no wonder then that the chronic patient who has been subjected to years of conditioning on the back wards is a very dependent person. Related to this, I think it is quite interesting that by using behavior-rating scales we have found that as chronic patients get better (ready to leave the hospital) they are rated as being *more* belligerant than previously (Maley, submitted manuscript). This may sound "bad" but is actually only a sign which shows that they have learned to be more assertive and less dependent on the staff.

Responsibility

Responsibility or the lack of it in chronic patients can be explained in much the same way as dependency. Patients do not take responsibility simply because it does not pay off in the hospital environment. For the most part they merely need to be retrained in those behaviors we label as "responsible" and reinforcers must be found which will then maintain the behavior. It seems reasonable to assume that being irresponsible is somehow easier in the sense of requiring less energy than acting in a responsible manner.

Afraid of Others

Being afraid of other people is perhaps a more complicated phenomenon. These fears seem to be related to traumatic experiences with people and/or to the realization that in a mental hospital one gets along better if one keeps to oneself. In essence, then, most mental patients have been "hurt" by other people and have learned a series of behaviors which serve to reduce contact with these feared objects. In addition, it is unusual for patients to be close friends with one another because patient friends have little, if any, reinforcement value. Much of the behavior in this area also seems to be related to avoidance learning as discussed above.

Bizarre Behavior

Bizarre and troublesome behavior is for the most part learned and frequently is unwittingly reinforced by staff. For example, Ayllon (1963) produced several studies which clearly showed how staff attention could produce and maintain many kinds of "psychotic" behavior. Practically every ward has one or two patients who emit bizarre behavior merely because the staff thinks it is "humorous" and very directly rewards it. One patient whom I ran across on the back wards of a state mental hospital entertained visitors to his unit by pulling dead insects out of his pocket and eating them. Following each of these performances, the staff laughed and joked with him and gave him a cigarette. Later, of course, this behavior was used to illustrate how "crazy" *he* was!

Frequently, the only way a patient on a crowded ward can get attention is by misbehaving, and the resultant physical contact and restraining (seclusion) is frequently quite reinforcing.

Patterson & Reid's (1969) coercion hypothesis nicely summarizes problems in this area by pointing out that much disruptive behavior forces the staff to reinforce it when the behavior is the most deviant and at its highest rate.

Indeed, there is an impressive amount of experimental literature which convincingly demonstrates the effectiveness of behavioral approaches in eliminating "psychotic" behavior. King, Armitage & Tilton (1960) used a vending-machine reinforcer to elicit more social behavior and environmental interest in withdrawn schizophrenics. Ayllon & Haughton (1962) eliminated eating problems by merely denying access to the dining hall to patients who did not enter during a brief time period. Isaacs, Thomas & Goldiamond (1960) used chewing gum to reinforce successive approximations of speech in two mute catatonic patients. Rational speech was increased in a verbose psychotic patient by manipulating the therapist's attention to the speech content, in work done by Richard, Dignan & Horner (1960). There are many more examples that could be listed, but note that time and time again psychotic behavior has been shown to be maintained by environmental contingencies.

My main point here is relatively simple: much of the behavior which is exhibited by chronic mental patients is taught to them in the hospital setting. These behaviors are *not* the unfolding of a mental disease and can be dealt with *directly* by various psychological techniques. Also, keep in mind that most, if not all, of the behavior shown by chronics is influenced by or closely related to interpersonal difficulties which can be treated by various group techniques.

In the past most mental-health specialists have assumed that the reasons for chronicity lay within the patient himself. It was part of a disease. However, this is now, at best, too limited, and the hospital's environment must be considered as a possible cause of chronicity. This type of consideration is closely related to the psychological model of disorders. In this model a person is labeled as exhibiting "deviant" behavior that results in the social action of hospitalization. The behavior is not seen as an inherent characteristic of the individual but as a behavior which has been learned according to the same principles as "nondeviant" behavior. This formulation also allows one to consider the community from which the individual comes. Obviously, the degree of distress the patient's behavior produces in significant others is an important variable both in terms of his institutionalization and of the probability he will return to his community. Consequently, the degree of distress imposed on significant others, their tolerance and support as well as the patient's behavior, are important for prognostic considerations.

At this point we seem to be faced with an inescapable conclusion: public mental hospitals frequently make patients worse! That is, most hospital environments are so constructed that they do much to create the chronic patient. In fact, there is proof that time-in-hospital is linearly related to the development of the patient's "social breakdown" (Gruenberg, 1967) and increasingly "regressive" behavior. In other words, the longer a person remains in a mental hospital, the poorer are his chances of ever being released. If a patient has been in continuous hospitalization for two or more years the probability of his being released and never being readmitted is about 6 percent (Honigfeld & Gillis, 1967).

These conditions will not be improved until mental institutions stop seeing their mission as the treatment of disease in a hospital setting and begin to conceptualize their activities as educational and their function more like that of a school than as a hospital.

TOKEN ECONOMIES

The use of learning-theory principles in the treatment of institutionalized patients is becoming more and more popular, and initial results indicate that these programs are fairly effective in dealing with chronic patients (for example, Heap, 1970; Atthowe & Krasner, 1968; Ayllon & Azrin, 1968; Maley & Feldman, 1971.) Although many questions about token economy systems have yet to be answered, this type of treatment modality is becoming increasingly popular all over the country. Despite the fact that the actual composition of these token economies varies from institution to institution, they can all be defined by the use of three elements. First, the staff specifies the behaviors they want to teach the patients, and these behaviors are considered to be adaptive, desirable, specifiable and reinforceable, Second, a medium of exchange (tokens) is established. These many be poker chips, real money, paper money, marks on a piece of paper or even stamps. Third, backup reinforcers are established which can be puchased by use of the tokens. These are the "good" things in life and range from beds, meals and cigarettes to a walk with a nurse or permission to watch television. In other words, the attempt is made to provide sufficiently different backup reinforcers so that each patient can find something he values. In this way patients learn (or relearn) behaviors that lead to reinforcement and improve on those skills necessary in ultimately living successfully outside of the institution or, at least, in assuming a more responsible social role within the hospital.

Most existing token economies deal with "hard-core" chronic schizophrenics and attempt to change those behaviors described in the preceding section of this paper. The therapeutic goals usually center around increased social responsiveness and decreased bizarre behavior. In order to accomplish these goals a highly structured environment, usually an entire hospital ward, is established in such a way as to allow the staff maximum stimulus-control. Careful records of patient behaviors are kept and close attention is paid to the environmental consequences following behavior. Operant conditioning concepts such as "shaping," "schedules of reinforcement," and "facing" are applied to the token-delivery system and internal, dynamic explanatory concepts are kept at minimal levels.

As a sidelight, anyone who has ever worked in a public mental hospital soon becomes painfully aware that there are never enough professionally trained personnel. This shortage will be a fact of life for many years to come and stresses the need to develop treatment modalities which can be effectively used by the aides, who are the only personnel having extended contact with the patients. Token economy systems are readily comprehendable by aides and thus allow therapy to become a round-the-clock activity rather than being limited to the traditional hour or two every week spent in a professional's office.

During the past three years I have been actively involved in establishing and running a token economy unit in a large state hospital. This project is currently funded by a Hospital Improvement Project grant from the National Institute of Mental Health and has 40 to 50 chronic patients on its two wards at any one time. We share much in common with other token economy systems, but as will be explained later, have tried to expand our model of effective treatment activities.

Davison (1969) discussed some of the problems with the "narrowness" of the operant model of behavioral change, and the reader is referred to his excellent article for more detailed criticisms than can be given here. Suffice it to say that my training and experiences in group work and "therapeutic community" (e.g., Jones, 1953; Kraft, 1966) convinced me that more could be done with these patients than merely teaching them to brush their teeth and make their beds. It appears to me that total reliance on the operant model and operant methodology has caused many investigators to overlook the possiblity of using other social learning principles.

Dollard & Miller (1950) presented a convincing case for regarding covert responses as behaviors which follow the same laws as overt muscular responses. Since that time increasing evidence has strongly indicated that (e.g., Jacobs & Sachs, 1971). Consequently, we are left with some sort of mediational-S-R-position (e.g., Davison, 1969; Osgood, 1953; Mowrer, 1960). This means that we can conceptualize the behavior of chronic patients on the basis of functional relationships which go beyond the immediate observables. However, one must make certain that the intervening variables are securely tied to behavior on both the antecedent and consequent ends.

Ayllon and Azrin (1965) have been a major impetus for the growing interest in operant work in institutional settings. Without their valuable work we would probably not know as much as we do. However, as Davison (1969) has pointed out, their successes may have tied them too tightly to the operation model and blinded them to the possiblity that some behavior (both overt and covert) is controlled by processes which have little to do with operant conditioning. In other words, the assumption that all psychotic behavior is a function of its environmental consequences remains to be proven. At least part of the problem lies in the wholesale application of Skinnerian techniques derived from laboratory work with animals to verbal, symbol-producing humans.

Again, I feel there is no doubt that the operantly based, traditional token economies have great treatment benefits for chronic mental patients. My concern is with the narrrowness of the model. It seems to me that there are many other social-learning principles which could be utilized in such a setting. And most of these principles are tied to the use of group methods as vehicles for producing changed interpersonal behavior. For the most part, people are put in mental hospitals because they have difficulties with others. They frighten people or behave in crazy ways when others are watching—people can hallucinate and/or be delusional as long as these behaviors are not made public. Consequently, it makes sense to ultimately place patients in situations which provide the interpersonal experiences necessary to remedy their lack of social skills.

GROUP METHODS ON TOKEN ECONOMY WARDS

The remainder of this chapter will be devoted to presenting and justifying treatment models which utilize group approaches to interpersonal learning for use in token economy systems. The theoretical orientation of such treament is a combination of operant and mediational S-R frameworks. In essence, such a treament program attempts to incorporate experimental psychology principles wherever they can be used effectively and focuses upon producing changes in interpersonal behavior.

Group approaches are not used merely because they save time and effort and are economical ways of treatment, but because they provide the ideal setting for the learning, unlearning and relearning necessary to alter many kinds of deviant behavior. Since many of our behaviors are learned in group settings (such as the family, peer groups, schools, etc.) and maintained by group reinforcements, using group treatment approaches seems to be a logical way to proceed. Although many of the techniques and strategies to be presented here overlap with more traditional group therapy approaches, the reader will hopefully have no difficulty seeing the unique contributions offered by behavioral approaches in group settings.

There are numerous ways in which group approaches may be beneficial for chronic patients in a token economy system. One can make use of Wolpe's (1958) reciprocal-inhibition paradigm for reducing phobic responses based on conditioned anxiety. In this framework a response inhibitory of anxiety, such as relaxation or assertive behavior, is made to occur in temporal contiguity with anxiety-evoking stimuli. The association of these stimuli causes the anxiety response to diminish. As Lazarus (1968) points out there are many *specific* responses which may be incompatible with anxiety, such as relaxation, assertiveness, mirth and sexual and eating behaviors. Even close rapport may provide a nonspecific anxiety-reducing stiuation. Thus a close, friendly, nonjudgmental therapeutic relationship may be a very helpful (although usually insufficient) condition of change.

When the goal of therapy is to establish new motor habits rather than overcoming maladaptive anxiety per se, the behavior therapist usually uses operant conditioning techniques involving reinforcements of one kind or another. In this form of therapy we are trying to develop or extinguish stimulus-response connections. Since the elimination of anxiety typically has reinforcing consequences, counter-conditioning and operant conditioning can be used to strengthen each other's effect (Lazarus, Davison & Poleka, 1965).

The use of behavior therapy in a group setting has several advantages over more traditional forms of group therapy: (a) it is based upon experimentally established and tested procedures; (b) the major techniques used can be clearly described and are relatively easy to reach; (c) the studies done to date lend clear support to the efficacy of behavioral approaches as compared to more traditional forms of group therapy; (d) the therapist has more control over the situation and can utilize a large number of alternative strategies of change behavior; (e) therapists can be easily interchanged if necessary because of the common conceptual system and the relative lack of importance of "transference" relationships; and (f) therapists are not required to have extensive formal education and training (Lazarus, 1968).

Patient Government

Training in assuming responsibility and learning how to make decisions can be taught by allowing the patients on a token economy ward the opportunity to make certain decisions within a patient-government framework. The exact decisions about which patients can be given responsibility is determined by the "primitiveness" of their behavior and by the general composition of the ward. However, even severely "regressed" chronic patients can be taught to make decisions if they are "involved" in the things which are under discussion. In other words, the staff has to be careful not to give the impression that the decisions left to the patient government are trivial or will be thoughtlessly vetoed.

As Peterson points out in Chapter Two, it is best if the behavioral changes expected by the staff are "culturally congruent." This is frequently a problem when middle-class staff is dealing with lower-class patients. Such things as how clean the ward should be and how much swearing will be tolerated are two examples of potential "culture-clashes" between patients and staff. Patient governments can be useful in both monitoring and successfully resolving such conflicts. Typically, institutional staff needs training in order to allow patients to be somewhat independent and to avoid forcing their value-systems upon the patients. This process is facilitated as the staff observes good patient decisions and learns that patients can act independently and responsibly if the environment encourages such behavior.

It seems likely that token economy systems could learn a good deal from therapeutic community principles (e.g., Jones, 1953; Miskimins, 1965; Kraft, 1966) which heavily rely on the use of patient government as a therapeutic modality. Whenever possible, token units should have unlocked, open wards with the staff dressed in street clothing. A relatively "flat" administrative hierarchy serves to model democratic decision-making and active involvement as well as to increase staff morale. If the unit leader makes decisions solely by administrative fiat, he will have trouble with his staff being too controlling of the patients and, consequently, it will be difficult to convince the patients that they should assume increasing responsibility for their behavior and should become involved in their own treatment program.

Patient leaders and acceptable suggestions can be reinforced by tokens as can attendance at the meetings. It is also possible for staff to increase group cohesiveness by reinforcing patient group-centered verbalizations and ignoring patient individual-centered verbalizations. For the most part, the staff's role in these meetings is to facilitate interaction, provide reinforcement for appropriate or helpful behavior and to help the group avoid "restrictive solutions" to their problems which will only lead to further difficulties (Whitaker & Lieberman, 1964).

A well-run patient government helps to control bizarre and

aggressive behavior by involving the patients with one another. If patients take pride in their ward on the ward, they will be very helpful in controlling deviant behavior by members of their own community. Many times they can be more effective than staff in calming an agitated or destructive patient. Perhaps patients respond better to each other than to staff because staff is paid and, therefore, expected to tolerate "crazy" behavior. Also, in patient-government meetings a good opportunity is provided for eliciting patient models for the behaviors which are trying to be taught. For futher infomation concerning patient government the reader is referred to Kraft (1966).

Group Contingent Reinforcement

Most chronic mental patients are extremely fearful of close personal interactions. They have learned that people are dangerous or harmful to them. Consequently, they avoid other people and prefer, as much as possible, to live within themselves. This behavior can be conceptualized as based on avoidance learning which allows the patient to evade anxiety-provoking stimuli (Mednick, 1958) and, as such, it is very difficult to extinguish. The counterconditioning process can be expedited by reinforcing contact with others in a group setting and by making the receiving of reinforcement dependent upon cooperation with others.

For example, to enter a reinforcing, high-use area such as the snack bar or TV room, a "group gate" can be installed which calls for two or more patients to simultaneously drop metal coins into slots. The slots are spaced far enough apart so that it is an impossible task for one person alone. Behaviorally, this kind of arrangement forces the patient who wishes to enter the reinforcing area to convince another patient to cooperate with him. In addition to learning to engage in cooperative behavior, the patient is being desensitized to other people and learning that human beings can be a source of reinforcement.

Another example of group contingency-contracting involves paying tokens for various group games and prosocial behavior. By having tokens available for planned interpersonal interactings, the shy and withdrawn patient can begin to obtain reinforcement for doing activities with others. Patients also can be encouraged to interact with others and to assume responsibility for others by making individual reinforcement dependent on a group "product" such as all the group members being in attendence for a group meeting before any one individual is paid his tokens.

King, Armitage & Tilton (1960) used a therapeutic strategy they called the "operant-interpersonal method" in order to elicit more interest in the environment and to promote better interpersonal skills in chronic schizophrenics. Basically, they constructed an experimental room which could provide controlled interpersonal experiences which progressed from the simple to the complex in terms of the response characteristics demanded for reinforcement. Such "programmed environments" can be used in token economy systems to help patients communicate with each other and enter into cooperative relationships in order to solve problems. This type of procedure allows for the breaking down of simple social skills into smaller units which can then be mastered by even severely regressed patients. In this way interpersonal behaviors are gradually "shaped" and progress can be systematically measured. One can safely predict that therapeutic efforts such as these increasingly will be seen in the future.

Role-Playing

Cognitive dissonance theory predicts attraction to the therapy program would increase if they could be induced to participate in overt behaviors discrepant with resistive behavior (Goldstein, Heller & Sechrest, 1966). This means that one way of dealing with chronic patients, who are almost always resistive and negatively attracted to an active treament program, would be to reinforce role-playing procedures which focus on valued attitudes and behavior. Several empirical investigations (e.g.,) Kelley, Blake & Stromberg, 1957; Krasner, 1959; Mann, 1956) suggest that favorable changes can be induced by role-playing and that role-playing increases the skill with which new roles can later be played. Inducing patients to act "as if" and then strongly reinforcing this behavior appears to be a valuable therapeutic technique.

Goldstein (1967, 1971) demonstrated the effectiveness of a

psychodrama technique called "doubling" in promoting verbal interactions in a group of severely withdrawn patients. The double in this role-playing situation provides support to the withdrawn patient and helps him express the thoughts and feelings which he finds difficult to verbalize. Thus, the double functions as a teacher who helps "label" certain phenomena and as a model of appropriate behavior. The modeling aspect helps to elicit behavior which otherwise would not occur.

It might be well to mention at this point some other techniques for dealing with "resistive" patients unskilled in introspection and fearful of close interpersonal relationships. During the beginning stages of a patient's stay on a token economy ward, the staff should not force the patient into close interpersonal contacts, but rather should utilize those behaviors in which the patient is already proficient. This strategy is based on the assumption that this type of patient has a history of punishment for affiliative behavior and the Skinnerian concept of "shaping" would be successful in working for the emergence of normal interpersonal closeness.

Small-Group Task Therapy

Patients on token wards can be placed in small (4-member to 8-member) groups whose main function centers around accomplishing certain tasks; for example, one group can serve as a "laundry group, ' another as a "cleaning group," another as a "food-serving group," etc. The types of groups actually used are, of course, determined by the institutional setting and the actual token system in operation. Besides learning to do certain types of work, interpersonal skills can be taught within these groups.

Group cohesiveness can be operationally defined as the attraction the group has for its members. This type of "resultant" cohesiveness (Schacter, 1951) can be measured by asking the group participants if they desire to remain a member of the group and how frequently they would like to meet with the group. Highly cohesive groups have certain desirable consequents for aiding the behavior-change process. For example, small-group studies have shown that members of highly cohesive groups, in contrast to members of groups in low cohesiveness, will be more influenced by other group members, find more anxiety reduction within the group, be more active group members and be absent less often from group meetings (Goldstein, Heller & Sechrest, 1966). These considerations clearly indicate that cohesive group structure is a powerful influence on individual member behavior and should be maximized in group treatment programs.

Task groups on token economy wards can easily be put in competition with one another for tokens and/or privileges. Sherif and Sherif (1953) and Myers (1962) demonstrated that intergroup competition functions to increase within-group cohesiveness and thus leads to a more beneficial climate for behavioral change. Although most of the available research indicates that even failure in competitive intergroup activities increases group cohesiveness, the findings also show a much stronger positive effect of competition when one is on the winning side (Goldstein, Heller & Sechrest, 1966). In the light of these findings, it might be advisable for the outcome of competition to be "scored" or in some way be potentially manipulable by therapists.

The point here is that there are always numerous opportunities within a token economy system to provide therapeutically meaningful experiences centering around group activities.

Small-Group Therapy

Small-group therapy can be an important part of a token economy ward's treatment program. However, in order to keep in step with the guiding philosophy of the unit—a fairly rigorous social-learning theory—and because of the behavior deficits of chronic patients, certain modifications need to be made. Basically, most of these modifications center around diminishing the amount of reliance placed on verbal interactions and reducing the role of "insight" or "understanding" as the desired treatment-outcome.

The group leader *must* focus on here and now problems. Although this strategy is becoming more popular than the "there and then" orientations with all kinds of patient populations (Egan, 1970), for chronic patients there is no other option. For most chronic patients the past is merely a dim recollection, which can not be adequately recalled or effectively dealt with. By focusing on the patients' behavior in the group, the likelihood of significant therapeutic gains is greatly enhanced as current behavior remains the target of therapeutic interventions.

By focusing on the present and here-and-now behavior, the

content of interactions in the group is both relevant and understandable to all those involved. A patient may well talk about the past, but the past must be made relevant to the present. In like fashion, he may talk about things happening outside the group, but his "there" story must also be made a "here" story. The problem with past events and things outside the group is that they are difficult to make meaningful and frequently are used as devices to avoid involvement in the real problems of here-and-now behavior and feelings. Linking behavior with past events requires very good abstract verbal skills and presupposes an "insight" level seldom found in chronic patients. In addition, all the necessary elements exist in the present to the extent that only present tensions and reinforcers actually produce behavior. Even though past experiences have established expectancies of reinforcement and have modified the meaning of current events, there is no reason to assume that present behavior is better understood by focusing on the remote past.

The attainment of the primary goals of behavior changes generally produces several secondary gains as well. For instance, self-esteen is increased as the patient's behavior becomes less disabling. As Lazarus (1968) points out, "the elimination of maladaptive habits and the acquisition of adaptive responses is not a static process, but results in a dynamic reorganization of the patients' overall intra-and interpersonal relationships [p. 152]."

Special consideration must be given to the problem of gereralizing gains derived from treatment. The group leader must take steps which extend behavior changes beyond the therapy sessions, and the token economy framework provides ample opportunity for this. For example, a patient who has learned to be more assertive with women in the group setting can be continually reinforced for this behavior on the ward. In this way a newly emergent behavior is less likely to undergo rapid extinction.

Group therapy sessions can also make use of systematic desensitization procedures as described by Wolpe (1958) and Lazarus (1968). Several individuals with the same phobia can be taken through anxiety-arousing hierarchies step by step. The group leader takes an upward step in the hierarchy only when all of the patients in the group can imagine a given scene without anxiety. Done in the standard way, chronic patients have to be somewhat "improved" before they can actively participate in forming the necessary mental images. However, one can construct a "people-phobia hierarchy" and by using actual experiences within the group guide the patients through various anxiety-arousing interpersonal situations. Because most chronic patients are afraid of other people and tend to avoid close, meaningful interpersonal relationships, a general hierarchy can be constructed which will be applicable to most, if not all, of the group members.

Small-group therapy sessions should have highly specificable goals for each patient in each group session. This forces the group leader to pay attention to small behavioral changes and keeps him accountable for his therapeutic interventions in terms of the specific behavioral objectives being sought. Thus, vague, subjective variables such as "increased insight," "stronger ego," etc. are avoided.

The group leader is very active and quite manipulative within the group. His interactions with the group are designed to elicit specific behavioral responses, whether he conceptualizes his behavior as a stimulus event or as a modeled response. In other words, the leader is not trying to have his interventions be insightful, right, honest or even loving; he is merely concerned with the consequences of his behavior in terms of getting the group or individuals within the group to behave in certain ways.

Exercises

Group exercises are used primarily to stimulate participation by reducing the verbal demands in the group setting. Exercises can be both verbal and nonverbal. When used by a skilled leader, exercises can produce therapeutic material which could not be elicited in any other way. Exercises effective with chronic patients, of course, tend to be of the nonverbal variety. On occasion, exercises can be used to highlight various aspects of the group's behaviors and conflicts, such as their lack of trust and fear of being close to one another. In some groups exercises can project missing elements into the group's experiences, such as giving patients a "safe" way to express hostility at the leader.

Group exercises can be freely used but should be coordinated with the overall goal for that particular meeting. Leaders must be very careful in how they introduce exercises to the group. Even simple, nonthreatening exercises can generate a lot of anxiety and immobilize the group if they are clumsily or hesitatingly introduced by the leader. Exercises, especially of the nonverbal type, will create much less anxiety if they are first introduced as experimental games rather than as deadly serious attempts to make the group participants behave in a certain unspecified manner.

The following is a sample list of exercises collected by Pfeiffer and Jones (1970) which we have found useful in dealing with chronic patients: Giving and receiving coins, nonverbal trust exercises, consensus-seeking, group-ranking tasks, animal names, pass-the-object, unwrapping, behavior description and "lemons." It is also necessary for the group leaders to innovate and try new approaches. One of our group leaders hit upon the idea of giving patients marshmallows which they could throw at people who made them angry. This device produced a good deal of therapeutic material because withdrawn patients who would not verbalize their anger would throw marshmallows when provoked. Consequently, the patients were helped to more accurately label their feelings and become more involved in the group process.

Videotape Feedback

The use of videotape recordings has made possible the development of growing interest in the role of "feedback" in the group setting. Feedback about self via a videotape arrangement may be able to penetrate the encapsulated chronic patient better than any other device. Seeing oneself on the TV screen has an immediate and sometimes dramatic effect, even on severely regressed patients.

Interpretation requires considerable training and extensive experience in its appropriate application before this mode of presenting people information about themselves is helpful. Most group members give inappropriate interpretations, which are difficult, if not impossible, for the recipient to utilize. On the other hand, feedback when it involves specific behaviors can be most useful. The aim of videotape feedback is to improve a person's ability to control his own behavior and see himself as others see him. It can also be used to confront resistive and denying patients who refuse to accept the fact that they behave in certain ways.

Videotape feedback should not focus exclusively on the negative aspects of a person's behavior but should also be used to reinforce adaptive behavior patterns. This type of feedback seems to have strong reinforcing qualities which tend to stabilize and strengthen effective and appropriate behavior. Chronic patients frequently verbalize great surprise when they view themselves doing something well.

Videotape feedback is too recent a technical innovation to have been the subject of much research especially on chronic patients. Nevertheless, the technique seems promising because of its objective features and its strong reinforcing properties. The reader is refered to Stoller's (1968) excellent article on the uses of this technique.

Discharging Patients in Groups

Token economy systems do produce significant behavioral changes in chronic mental patients. However, these therapeutic gains can be easily reversed if proper environmental management does not continue after the patient leaves the unit (Paul, 1969). Consequently, various strategies to maintain appropriate reinforcement contingencies have to be devised. One way is to discharge patients in groups of four or five, especially since the long-stay patient frequently has nowhere to go and no one who wants to take care of him after he leaves the hospital. In this way the patient's environment may be able to provide the continuity so important in his remaining out of the institution.

Prerelease work with groups of patients planning on living together is a must and should center around helping them learn to be "reinforcement-dispensers" to each other. Behavioral objectives and criteria should be spelled out for each patient in order to minimize confusion and maximize their effectiveness in controlling each other's behavior. For many patients artificial ways will need to be created which make the noninstitutional environment more rewarding and less anxiety-provoking than the hospital, if the patient is to be able to maintain himself in the community. In spite of the numerous problems involved in this discharge strategy, the blend of group methods and behavioral principles may prove to be an effective way to reduce readmissions.

In conclusion, I believe that the marriage of token economy systems and group treatment practices will be a happy one. Group approaches will prosper by being exposed to "hard-headed" behavioral demands and evaluations which insist on knowing the value of various treatment strategies. Token economies will be improved because they will begin to expand their theoretical horizons and to use sound behavioral change principles derived from areas of psychology other than operant conditioning. This combination of events will hopefully lead to advances in the treatment of chronic patients and be helpful in changing the "mission" of mental institutions from hospitals, where diseases are treated, to schools, where people are taught new ways of coping with their interpersonal problems.

REFERENCES

Atthowe, J.M. Jr. & Krasner, L. A preliminary report on the application of contingent reinforcement procedures (token economy) on a "chronic" psychiatric ward. *Journal of Abnormal Psychology*, 1968, **73,** 37–43.

Ayllon, T. Intensive treatment of psychotic behavior by stimulus satiation and food reinforcement. *Behavior Research and Therapy,* 1963, **1,** 53–61.

Ayllon, T. & Azrin, N.H. *The Token Economy*. New York: Appleton-Century-Crofts, 1968. Pp. 357–383.

Ayllon, T. & Haughton, E. Control of the behavior of schizophrenic patients by food. *Journal of the Experimental Analysis of Behavior,* 1962, **5,** 343–352.

Davison, G.C. Appraisal of behavior modification techniques with adults in institutional settings. In C.M. Franks (Ed.) *Behavior therapy: Appraisal and status*. New York: McGraw-Hill, 1969. Pp. 220–278.

Dollard, J. & Miller, N.E. *Personality and psychotherapy*. New York: McGraw-Hill, 1950.

Egan, G. *Encounter: Group processes for interpersonal growth*. Belmont, Calif. Brooks/Cole, 1970.

Goldstein, A.P., Heller, K. & Sechrest, L.B. *Psychotherapy and the psychology of behavior change*. New York: John Wiley & Sons, 1966.

Goldstein, J.A. Investigation of doubling as a technique for involving severely withdrawn patients in group psychotherapy. *Journal of Consulting and Clinical Psychology*, 1971, **37,** 155–162.

Goldstein, S.G. The effects of "doubling" on involvement in group psychotherapy as measured by frequency and duration of patient utterances. *Psychotherapy,* 1967, **4,** 57–60.

Gruenberg, E.M. The social breakdown syndrome: Some origins. *American Journal of Psychiatry,* 1967, **123,** 12–20.

Heap, R.F., Boblitt, W.E., Moore, C.H. & Hord, J.E. Behavior-milieu therapy with chronic neuropsychiatric patients. *Journal of Abnormal Psychology,* 1970, **76,** 349–354.

Honigfeld, G. & Gillis, R. The role of institutionalization in the natural history of schizophrenia. *Diseases of the Nervous System,* 1967, **28,** 660–663.

Isaacs, W., Thomas, J. & Goldiamond, I. Applications of operant conditioning to reinstate verbal behavior in psychotics. *Journal of Speech and Hearing Disorders,* 1960, **25,** 6–12.

Jacobs, A. & Sachs, L.B. (Eds), *The psychology of private events.* New York: Academic Press, 1971.

Jones, K. & Sidebothem, R. *Mental hospitals at work.* London: Routledge & Kegan Paul, 1962.

Jones, M. *The therapeutic community: A new treatment method in psychiatry.* New York: Basic Books, 1953.

Kelley, J.G., Blake, R.R. & Stromberg, C.E. The effect of role training on role reversal. *Group Psychotherapy,* 1957, **10,** 95–104.

King, G.F., Armitage, S.G. & Tilton, J.R. A therapeutic approach to schizophrenics of extreme pathology: An operant-interpersonal method. *Journal of Abnormal and Social Psychology,* 1960, **61,** 276–286.

Kraft, A.M. The therapeutic community. In S. Arieti (Ed.), *American handbook of psychiatry,* vol. 3. New York: Basic Books, 1966.

Krasner, L. Role taking research and psychotherapy. *VA Research Report,* November, 1959, No. 5.

Lazarus, A.A. Behavior therapy in groups. In G.M. Gazda (Ed.), *Basic approaches to group psychotherapy and group counseling.* Springfield, Ill.: Charles C Thomas, 1968. Pp. 149–175.

Lazarus, A.A., Davison, G.C. & Poleka, D.A. Classical and operant factors in the treatment of a school phobia. *Journal of Abnormal Psychology,* 1965, **70,** 225–232.

Lindsley, O.R. & Skinner, B.F. A method for the experimental analysis of the behavior of psychotic patients. *American Psychologist,* 1954, **9,** 419–420.

Maley, R.F. Changes in the behavior ratings of chronic patients on a token economy ward. Submitted manuscript.

Maley, R.F. & Feldman, G. The use of a "standard stimulus situation" to evaluate the treatment effectiveness of a token economy system with chronic schizophrenics. Submitted manuscript.

Mann, J.H. Experimental evaluations of role playing. *Psychological Bulletin,* 1956, **53,** 227–234.

Mednick, S.A. A learning theory approach to research in schizophrenia. *Psychological Bulletin,* 1958, **55,** 316–327.

Miskimins, R.W. Milieu therapy: History and interpretation. *Journal of the Fort Logan Mental Health Center,* 1965, **2,** 167–179.

Mowrer, O.H. *Learning theory and behavior.* New York: John Wiley & Sons, 1960.

Myers, A. Team competition, success, and the judgement of group members.

Osgood, C.E. *Method and theory in experimental psychology.* New York: Oxford University Press, 1953.

Patterson, G.R. & Reid, J.B. Reciprocity and coercion: Two facets of social systems. In C. Neuringer and L. Michael (Eds.), *Behavior modification in clinical psychology.* New York: Appleton-Century-Crofts, 1969.

Paul, G.L. Insight versus desensitization in psychotherapy two years after termination. *Journal of Consulting Psychology, 1967,* **31, 333–348.**

Paul, G.L. Chronic mental patient: Current status-future direction. *Psychological Bulletin,* 1969, **71,** 81–94.

Pfeiffer, J.W. & Jones, J.E. *A handbook of structured experiences for human relations training.* 3 volumes. Iowa City, Iowa: University Associates Press, 1970.

Richard H.C., Dignan, P.J. & Horner, R.F. Verbal manipulation in a psychotherapeutic relationship. *Journal of Clinical Psychology,* 1960, **16,** 364–367.

Schacter, S. Deviation, rejection and communication. *Journal of Abnormal Psychology,* 1951, **46,** 190–207.

Schaefer, H.H. & Martin, P.L. Behavioral therapy for "apathy" of hospitalized schizophrenics. *Psychological Reports,* 1966, **19,** 1147–1158.

Sherif, M. & Sherif, C.W. *Groups in harmony and tension.* New York: Harper, 1953.

Stoller, F.H. Focused feedback with videotape: extending the group's functions. In G.M. Gazda (Ed.), *Innovations to group psychotherapy.* Springfield, Ill.: Charles C Thomas, 1968.

Ullmann, L.P. & Krasner, L. (Eds.), *Case studies in behavior modification.* New York: Holt, Rinehart & Winston, 1965.

Whitaker, K.S. & Lieberman, M.A. *Psychotherapy through the group process.* New York: Atherton, 1964.

Wolpe, J. *Psychotherapy by reciprocal inhibitions.* Stanford, Calif.: Stanford University Press, 1958.

5. *Understanding and Modifying Aggression in Behavioral Groups*

Arnold A. Lazarus

Arnold Lazarus argues that the direct expression of aggression by group members toward each other is most likely to elicit counter-aggressive behaviors from the targets. Instead, he teaches participants in his groups to contain their aggressive feelings and to suspend immediate retaliations until the point of view of the other person has been considered.

Group members sometimes have an initial difficulty in reconciling this admonition of restraint with the emphasis on authenticity in behavioral groups. However, Lazarus emphasizes the importance of distinguishing between aggressive feelings and aggressive behaviors. To deny one's angry feelings will usually result in unfortunate sequelae, he suggests, but so will verbal bombardments. Behavior which is gentle, as well as honest, is the most helpful, asserts Lazarus, because such behavior is least threatening to the need of individuals to feel worthy.

An excerpt from a group treatment session is used to demonstrate how behavioral-group leaders attempt to create a climate of cohesiveness and a lack of defensiveness in order to facilitate change in group members. In addition, it is educational to observe how the group leader makes use of such principles as that of reinforcement, derived from social-learning theories, in order to modify the behavior of the participants.

The main difference between behavioral groups and other treatment and/or encounter group procedures is the *explicit* use of modeling, operant analysis, vicarious learning, extinction and other techniques derived from social-learning theory. Behavioral group leaders are not constrained to limit themselves only to precise behavioral procedures. They are free to employ useful techniques derived from any discipline (Lazarus, 1971), but their penchant to lean most heavily upon experimentally tested procedures possibly distinguishes them from most other group leaders.

One of the primary reasons for practicing behavior therapy in groups is that the increased cohesiveness and lack of defensiveness generated by supportive groups is an important facilitator of change (Lazarus, 1968). The present chapter will try to underscore these points with special reference to the modification of aggressive or hostile reactions.

THE PROBLEM OF AGGRESSION

While there is still considerable dispute as to whether human aggression is inborn it certainly is widespread. It is well-known that man almost stands supreme in the wanton destruction of his own species. Human history is in many ways a catalogue of horrors involving repulsive cruelty and brutality, and the final chapter may yet encompass the total destruction of mankind.

In his daily work, the practicing therapist comes face to face with individuals, couples, families and groups who have not come to terms with their own aggression. Whether it be in the subtly vicious form of a dyadic power struggle or the violent explosion of paranoid hostility, the net result and intent of an aggressive act is some form of injury or pain.

The behavioral literature has drawn a crucial distinction between *assertion* and aggression. Without assertive responses, human endeavor would undoubtedly be deprived of its vigor, and man's impressive attainments could hardly have been achieved. Unfortunately, anxiety, frustration and a variety of threats can readily provoke one to overstep his assertive prerogatives and resort to anger, rage, hostility and violence.

In separating an assertive response from an aggressive reaction, an arbitrary degree of subjectivity is often inevitable. An assertive response, by definition, implies that the behavior is proportionate to the antecedent stimuli. This obviously involves a judgment. "Proportionate" according to whom and by what standards? In behavioral group therapy, an assertive response is contextually considered "any active or expressive reaction which seems fair and fitting to the majority of the group members." As will be outlined below, the group can serve as a utopian microcosm and teach the transfer of ideal responses in an idealized society into adaptive responses in our real but sadly nonidealistic and thoroughly irrational world.

Many forms of group therapy are based upon notions that pent-up aggressive urges can be discharged by cathartic techniques. Members in cathartic therapy groups are taught to give vent to their aggressive drives on the assumption that psychic drainage, be it direct or vicarious, will reduce hostile energy. This view is being subjected to increasing criticism. Berkowitz (1970), for instance, points out that "the catharsis hypothesis blinds us to the important social principle that aggression is all too likely to lead to still more aggression." Behavioral groups are based upon social learning theory (Bandura, 1969), which emphasizes that the best way to reduce aggressive behavior is neither by direct expression of aggression, nor by vicarious participation, but by developing and reinforcing constructive (nonaggressive but assertive) alternative response patterns.

Before describing the format of some behavioral group strategies that have been helpful in reducing certain aggressive behaviors, a few final points of emphasis need to be underscored. Aggression is, of course, a complex biochemical, psychosocial response that is by no means fully understood, and as Storr (1968) has eloquently pointed out, "anyone who promises a solution to a problem so perennial is too arrogant to be trusted." Indeed "a solution" cannot as yet be provided, but some successful clinical interventions will be described in the hopes of offering a meaningful step in this direction.

SUBJECTIVE AND BEHAVIORAL COMPONENTS

Participants in behavioral groups learn an important distinction between aggressive feelings and aggressive behaviors. A basic assumption is that an aggressive act (except under extremely threatening circumstances or for purposes of self-defense) is rarely warranted and is almost always psychologically destructive. Tuning in to aggressive feelings, on the other hand, is quite a different matter. This differentiation can readily be appreciated by reference to some common examples.

An employer discovers that a generally efficient secretary has made a number of careless blunders. His immediate reaction is one of extreme annoyance and irritation. Although, strictly speaking, his anger is irrational (he is imposing "shoulds" upon her;—she *should* have been more careful; she *should* have known better; she *should* have doublechecked each and every item, etc.), human fallibility being what it is, we can empathize with his affective reaction and perhaps even condone it. But if his behavior toward the secretary is a direct mirror of his emotions, the final outcome is likely to be anything but constructive. Thus, if he intemperately upbraids her, insults her or otherwise abuses or assaults her, he is likely to jeopardize their relationship, or win her future cooperation at a cost. The adaptive response is not to inhibit or to deny his anger but simply to confront her assertively and constructively. "Miss Jones, I was annoyed to find three errors in the bills. I can't understand this because you have always been so careful in the past." Their mutual needs will best be served if his tone of voice is supportive rather than accusatory.

A simple but expedient principle of effective human interaction is the point at issue. It is foolhardy to deny anger, or to suppress it or displace it, but it is equally imprudent to display it by unfettered verbal harangues or physical assault. Instead, group members are taught to "contain" their aggressive feelings (i.e., to examine the content and probable irrationality of their feelings and to suspend immediate retaliatory action until they have also considered the other person's point of view), whereupon the residual feelings are shared constructively. "Tom, it bothers me when you ignore me like this because I know you are a compassionate man. I wish you'd tell me why you seem to enjoy putting me down." This type of confrontation usually facilitates close and satisfying communications, whereas the dichotomous nature of many people's reactions (they either withdraw when angry or attack) creates distance and promotes irreparable rifts. Compare the foregoing with: "Look here Tom you son of a bitch! The next time you ignore me when I am speaking, or the next time you put me down in any manner whatsoever, I'll get even with you, you bastard!"

Since considerable emphasis is also placed upon *authenticity* in behavioral groups, some members have initial difficulty in reconciling what has been outlined above with the honest and open sharing of feelings and emotions. If one feels angry or aggressive but fails to express these impulses, is this not tantamount to embracing a phony and deceptive mode of life? Indeed, many therapists advocate the overt expression of anger and aggression as a healthy antidote to anxiety and psychosomatic ills. Even if it can be documented that obnoxious people are ulcer-free, one cannot help wondering if the price is right. It must be emphasized again that to deny one's anger, to hide it, suppress it, displace it, or to vent it passively or covertly, will usually result in unfortunate sequelae. But so will hostile verbal onslaughts and bombardments. A dignified and civil confrontation, however, is quite another matter. Perhaps a personal incident will help to clarify the point.

I had noticed that one of my trainees was inclined to use my office without permission and would often leave it in disarray. On one occasion I found that coffee had been spilled on the rug. My immediate response was one of anger and aggression. I exploded to (not at) a colleague who was present, "I'd like to kick him in the balls!" and proceeded to rant for several minutes. I was allowing myself to feel my anger while fully realizing that to vent it in this manner to the recipient of my displeasure would prove anything but constructive. Since I had two objectives in mind, (1) to maintain an amicable working relationship while (2) modifying his inconsiderate behavior, it was necessary to contain (not deny, suppress or deflect) my anger and to communicate it constructively. Stating very civilly, but assertively, that I had been "mad as hell" when I found that my office had been used without my consent and that coffee had been spilled on the rug, lent him the freedom to apologize and to make amends. Aggressively cursing at him or yelling at him would most probably have elicited his own counteraggressive resources which may have resulted in veiled hostility or open antagonism. The freedom to feel murderous rage and to fantasize brutal and violent forms of retaliation, while bearing in mind that, in order to be helpful and constructive, the actual behavior needs to be gentle but honest, bridges the gap between aggressive impulses and assertive behaviors. The emphasis upon gentleness is predicated on the observation that most people are fragile, that they hunger for any affirmation of their self-worth, and become distressed when their imperfections are brought to the fore. This is not to deny the unfortunate fact that some people have been so conditioned that aggressive tactics are necessary if one is to get through to them.

SHOULDS AND SHOULDN'TS

Ellis (1962, 1970) has shown that hostility and aggression are largely a function of one's subjective and moralistic attitudes, and that the cognitive component usually consists of an arbitrary "should" or "shouldn't" imposed upon a person or situation. "He shouldn't talk to me that way." "She should have invited me to her party." "You should know better." "They shouldn't say or do those things." "It shouldn't be necessary to keep after you all the time." "People shouldn't be the way they are, and the world shouldn't be the way it is." Participants in behavioral group therapy are alerted to their own and other people's "shoulds" and are encouraged to eliminate as many "shoulds" and "shouldn'ts" from their own thinking as possible. It is pointed out that the words "should" or "shouldn't" (and all their synonyms such as "ought to," "have to," "must," etc.) betray a dictatorial and authoritarian attitude that is hardly conducive to closeness and love. Besides, they generate tension and discontent in the people who harbor then. Group members are asked to appreciate the crucial emotive differences between the following sorts of remarks: "You shouldn't throw your clothes all over the place." vs. "It would be nice if you put your clothes away neatly." "You should spend more time with your mother." vs. "It really would please mother if you spent more time with her." "People shouldn't be so unfriendly to one another." vs. "It would be nice if people were more friendly to one another."

Most group members readily become adept at recognizing their own and other people's arbitrary "shoulds" and in helping one another overcome their pernicious effects. The effects of feedback are greatly enhanced when group members add the weight of their influence to the group leader's remarks. The following excerpt may assist in clarifying the point.

GROUP MEMBER: I blew up at Charlie again. I know it's silly, but he gets me so mad and uptight that I just want to tear his hair out.

ANOTHER GROUP MEMBER: O.K., which one of your "shoulds" did he violate this time?

GROUP MEMBER: Oh, I don't know. I mean he just bugs me. The guy never does a goddamn thing around the house. He promised to sweep out the garage months ago. He sees me lugging heavy things around, but do you think he lifts a finger to help? I don't think it's unreasonable to expect a little help from him.

GROUP LEADER: It would be nice if Charlie was more helpful around the house, but by insisting or demanding that he should help, he must help, he ought to help, you are laying your trip on him, and from the sounds of it, all you succeed in doing is defeating the very ends you seek to accomplish.

ANOTHER GROUP MEMBER: Yeah, you really would find it helpful to knock off the idea that he should be helpful. Why *should* he? I mean I can see why it would be terrific but if you make it into a law——

GROUP MEMBER: Damn it! The guy lives there. He should help out instead of sitting on his ass.

GROUP LEADER: Like Tony said, why *should* he? We all agree, as I said before, that it would be nice. Once you eliminate the "should" and stop being self-righteous, you will come on to him in a way which will make it possible for him to be helpful. How do you feel when someone says, "You should take out the garbage," and when he says, "Will you be a pal and take out the garbage for me?"

GROUP MEMBER: But whenever I ask him to do anything he always says, "Later."

ANOTHER GROUP MEMBER: Do you *ask* him or *tell* him?

The personal and interpersonal freedom that follows from the reduction or elimination of these malevolent "shoulds" opens warm and loving channels of communication that are impossible between people who impose rigid standards of behavior upon one another. The basic philosophy is antiperfectionistic, and recognizes the fact that people are essentially fallible and can strive to be less fallible but not pretend to be (or hope to become) infallible.

THE CLIMATE OF INTERACTION

Many therapy groups employ so-called "friendly banter" in which group leaders and participants use verbal sparring, sarcasm and hostile humor to discourage self-pitying and self-defeating behaviors. I consider these tactics more harmful than helpful. While there is merit in teaching people not to take themselves too seriously and to appreciate the way in which they compound minor events into major tragedies, therapists' wisecracks seldom achieve these ends. It is not surprising that Strupp (1960) found that nearly a third of the therapists he studied might be considered to have antitherapeutic attitudes. More recently Bergin (1971) has commented on the widespread nature of therapist-caused deterioration.

To cite a specific example of the wisecracking tactics to which I referred above, I was present at a group meeting in which a patient described his trepidation over a new employment situation he was about to enter. "I'm really nervous about it," he explained. To my dismay, the group leader responded by sneering at the patient with words to the following effect: "Why don't you take your mommy along to hold your hand?" The other group members followed suit, and the patient found himself the butt of various snide remarks until he flew into a violent rage at which the group leader offered his first and only words of approval —"That's great! Let all the anger out:" then abruptly switched his attention to another group member who had begun to sob during the tirade. After the group I inquired about the leader's rationale and asked why he had not simply told the man that most people fear new situations and then perhaps offered some words of encouragement. The only explanation I received was that the patient needed a "good kick in the ass."

The climate of interaction in my behavioral groups is distinctly different from the above. The group leader's orienting remarks emphasize acceptance, tolerance and understanding, the absence of destructive criticism, humiliation, wisecracks and sarcasm, and underscore the fact that "everybody will be expected always to try his utmost to be of genuine help and assistance (Lazarus, 1968)." The group tries to function as "an ideal community where everyone is helpful, honest, cooperative, and sincere (Lazarus, 1971, p. 190)." Emphasis is placed upon the fact that group members are there to learn from one another. The following excerpt illustrates the manner in which aggressive outbursts are managed within this supportive context:

DICK: Paula, I wish you'd shut up already. Yak, yak, yak. Who gives a shit about your goddamn father. If you want psychoanalysis go join another group. You piss me off. Go get a board and march for Women's Lib.

JOHN: What the hell's gotten into you, Dick?

PAULA: Dick, you can go to hell! I don't interrupt when you talk——

DICK: You sure do you bitch!

LEADER: Hold it! Hold it! Let's simmer down in here. Let's try and see what's really going on.

EDITH: Dick's mad at Paula. That's what's going on.

LEADER: He's behaving aggressively but I wonder what he *feels*.

EDITH: Angry.

DICK: She just bugs the hell out of me.

LEADER: I wonder which of your "shoulds" has been infringed?

DICK: That she should never have been born.

LEADER: Come on, Dick. Your outburst sounded more like pain than anger. Let us into your feelings.

DICK: Let's forget it. I apologize for my temper.

JENNY: Dick, this is not a cocktail party. You don't have to cover up with us.

LEADER: Give us some specific behaviors in Paula that bug you.

DICK: I don't know. Let me . . . uh . . . When I think . . . uh . . . Well, whenever I talk Paula gets up and pours herself coffee. I mean it's more than coincidental, you know.

LEADER: And it makes you feel that she's not interested in what you're saying?

DICK: Have you noticed that she's never spoken more than once or twice to me directly? She's mentioned my name occasionally, spoken *about* me, but not *to* me.

PAULA: That's not true.

LEADER: Hang on. Right or wrong you have a feeling. You feel ignored by Paula. Right?

DICK: It's not just a feeling. It's a fact.

LEADER: O.K. But the fact that you blew up suggests that you value Paula and want more attention and concern from her.

PAULA: But I haven't ignored Dick. I mean I value his opinion.

DICK: Do you see what I mean about her talking *about* me, not *to* me?

LEADER: Let's pull the pieces together. It seems that Dick has gotten the feeling, right or wrong, that Paula ignores him, sometimes makes a remark about him but seldom talks to him. Furthermore, when he gets into things she ups and pours coffee for herself. This makes him feel even more convinced that Paula dislikes him.

NEIL: Hey! And his outburst came just when Paula was into that bit about ignoring her father because she dislikes him.

JENNY: Right on.

DICK: Boy, Jenny and Neil sound like frustrated headshrinkers psyching me out. What about Debbie and Pete? You two haven't said a word.

JOHN: You're getting defensive again.

LEADER: I agree. It seems that your anger meant something like this: "Paula, I value you and therefore I want you to value me. But every time I talk you get up and pour coffee, and you make me feel in other ways too that I don't add up to much in your eyes." Now instead of covering up with a smokescreen of protective anger, I wonder what would have happened if you had simply stated it like that?

DEBBIE: Maybe you could have tied it in with what she was saying about her dad?

DICK: How do you mean?

DEBBIE: Like saying that she ignores her dad because she dislikes him and then maybe pointing out that she ignores you, and asking right out if this means she also dislikes you.

PAULA: But this is absurd. Dick, I do not dislike you. But you tend to go on and on about engineering and stuff like that which I don't understand. So that's why I may get up and pour myself some coffee.

LEADER: May I suggest that we go back in time about three minutes. Paula, continue telling us about your father, and Dick, this time, instead of blowing up, will you confront Paula with your real feelings?

PETE: Excuse me. Just before we go back in time . . . um . . . I'm just not clear about something. Was the "should" behind Dick's feelings something like, "Paula should listen when I speak?"

JENNY: Can I have a go at it? Uh . . . It's like . . . uh- . . . "Paula should talk more to me and she should listen to me and she should not get up and pour coffee when I am speaking."

NEIL: Yes, but back of it all is "I like her and therefore she should like me."

DICK: Have you noticed how Jenny and Neil love to play amateur psychiatrist? I was about to blast the two of you, but instead let me say . . . uh . . . how can I put it without . . . yeah . . . I realize that you guys are trying to be helpful, but sometimes you come across to me like you are more interested in showing off your insights, like I said, playing psychiatrist.

LEADER: Great! Dick, that's a real change. Instead of blowing up at Neil and at Jenny, you have shared an honest feeling like a mature and civilized human being.

NEIL: Can I share something with Dick? You know, in here I feel that part of our function is to be therapeutic. You know, I mean I think that's what group therapy is all about. Am I wrong?

LEADER: Let's get back to your feelings in a moment, Neil. I would still like us to go back in time and have Paula telling us what she was into about her father, and then I want to see how Dick handles it with openness and nonaggression.

DICK: Do you want me to ask Paula if she ignores me because she dislikes me as she feels about her father?

LEADER: More than that. Bring out all the things about her pouring coffee and not talking to you, and you really want and value her friendship.

DICK: Well, I think it's obvious to you all that I've got a kind of thing for Paula, like I mean she really turns me on, and that's why I got upset.

LEADER: Beautiful. That took guts. Now how terrific it would be if you got into the habit of sharing your real feelings like that right from the start instead of getting aggressive to cover up your feelings. And I don't only mean in here, but also outside of the group.

DISCUSSION

The foregoing is a slightly edited transcript of what occurred during part of the fifth meeting of a behavior therapy group.

Names have been changed and certain additional remarks that may betray the confidentiality of the group have been excised. By the time my behavioral groups proceed beyond eight or ten sessions, aggressive reactions within the group are conspicuously absent. This promotes a warm, cohesive atmosphere in which people are willing to disclose their basic feelings without fear of ridicule or retaliation. These groups usually have about eight to ten members (preferably made up of an equal number of men and women) and run for approximately two and one-half hours once a week for about 20 weeks.

It was highly gratifying to receive a laudatory report from an experienced psychiatrist who sat in on the 16th meeting of a behavioral group. He expressed surprise at the fact that people could spend over two hours discussing affect-laden material without becoming angry or overdefensive. He was curious, of course, as to whether this behavior transfers or generalizes beyond the protective confines of the group. Since behavioral groups deliberately focus upon interactions outside of the group as well as between the members within the group, there is less chance that participants will merely become good at group therapy. Specific "homework" assignments also facilitate therapeutic transfer. Followup studies are presently underway in order to assess the durability of these results.

REFERENCES

Bandura, A. *Principles of behavior modification.* New York: Holt, Rinehart & Winston, 1969.

Bergin, A.E. The evaluation of therapeutic outcomes. In A.E. Bergin & S.L. Garfield (Eds.), *Handbook of psychotherapy and behavior change: An empirical analysis.* New York: John Wiley & Sons, 1971. Pp. 217–270.

Berkowitz, L. Experimental investigations of hostility catharsis. *Journal of Consulting and Clinical Psychology,* 1970, **35,** 1–7.

Ellis, A. *Reason and emotion in psychotherapy.* New York: Lyle Stuart· 1962.

Ellis, A. Personal communication, 1970.

Lazarus, A.A. Behavior therapy in groups. In G.M. Gazda (Ed.), *Basic approaches to group psychotherapy and group counseling.* Springfield, Ili.: Charles C Tomas, 1968. Pp. 149–175.

Lazarus, A.A. *Behavior therapy and beyond.* New York: McGraw-Hill, 1971.

Storr, A. *Human Aggression.* New York: Atheneum, 1968.

Strupp, H.H. *Psychotherapist in action: Explorations of the therapist's contribution to the treatment process.* New York: Grune & Stratton, 1960.

6. The Group as Agent in Facilitating Change Toward Rational Thinking and Appropriate Emoting

Albert Ellis

Many authors assert that it is man's capacity to manipulate abstract symbols which most clearly separates him from other organisms and enables him to produce the elaborate and flexible culture in which he embeds his activities. Albert Ellis, in the tradition of the General Semantics Movement, argues that it is also man's misuse of symbols that produces his neurosis and misery.

Social intervention in Ellis's Rational-Emotive Therapy (RET) is conceptualized as a reeducation process for unscrambling mislabeled events and for teaching individuals to think rationally. However, Ellis also goes beyond General Semantics in his behavioral orientation to intervention. Patients are required to learn by doing in the group and in the outside world.

Rational Emotive Therapy does not neglect the environment. Families are treated as groups. Bridges are built from the intervention system to the ecology by assigning homework to patients, and by conducting after-treatment meetings without the presence of the therapist. A private school has also been organized where children are taught didactically and experientially how to "stop upsetting themselves" as well as how they "may sometimes help . . . others stop making themselves disturbed," in the same manner and location in which they are taught academic subjects.

Ellis enumerates the advantages of intervening with groups rather than via dyadic relationships. He proposes that the greater potential for impact on group members inherent in groups, and the larger pool of resources available for intervention, are among such advantages.

When leaders in the fields of individual and group psychotherapy talk about facilitating change, they have distinct assumptions about what kind of cognitive, emotional and behavioral changes would better be facilitated. But unfortunately they rarely make these assumptions explicit or clear—even to themselves! Being, presumably, rational—which is an elegant term for *efficient in helping human beings experience less needless pain and more enjoyment in the course of their lives*—I like to make my assumptions exquisitely unambiguous. Then, at least, my colleagues and I can be reasonably agreed on what the hell we are mainly differing about and what our real differences are.

In this paper, I shall therefore first make clear what rational thinking and appropriate emoting are, in my estimation, and how they can be achieved in psychotherapy. Then I shall try to show how the group process in particular can be remarkably useful in the practice of cognitively oriented therapies, and especially in my own system, rational-emotive therapy.

Let me say at the start that I am an unabashed hedonist. I believe that there is no intrinsic, given or "real" purpose in life; that the universe doesn't seem to give a shit for the human individual, and probably never will; and that if this individual is rational or wise he will existentially *choose* to live a good number of years, to be concerned primarily with enjoying himself and secondarily with helping others enjoy themselves, and to minimize his (and others') pains and maximize his (and their) satisfactions. To this end, knowing that he is likely to live about seventy-five years, he will strive (1) to focus on and delight in the here and now and (2) also consider and plan for the pleasures of the future (Ellis, 1962, 1971; Ellis & Harper, 1970a).

When the individual importantly or mainly chooses an irrational way of life, and significantly keeps defeating his own best interests and/or keeps antisocially sabotaging the interests of others, he usually is doing so because of some kind of childish demandingness. *Demandingness,* in fact, is the essence of virtually all emotional disturbance. The nondisturbed individual strongly *desires* while the person with disturbances dogmatically demands, insists or commands that (1) he do well and receive others' approval; (2) other people treat him fairly and considerately; and (3) the world be a fairly easy and gratifying place in which to live. Significant personality change, to my way of thinking, comes about when the individual clearly sees, acknowledges and works very hard at surrendering or minimizing his puerile demandingness; and when he thereby not only is able to tone down his intense and persistent feelings of anxiety, guilt, depression and hostility (and the defenses he erects against wallowing in these feelings) but also acquires such a realistic, grownup, nonwhining philosophy of life that he automatically, for the rest of his days, rarely makes himself severely disturbed again.

Human disturbance or demandingness, in other words, may be inelegantly and temporarily alleviated by various kinds of indulgence or ingratiation, such as the therapist's or group's overtly giving love or approval to the client, providing him with pleasurable sensations, letting him joyfully scream about how horribly hurt and angry he is, or teaching him methods of succeeding in fulfilling his demands. It may also be quite inelegantly squelched or covered up by different kinds of therapeutic diversion, such as the therapist's or the group's working with a client who demands approval and teaching him to engage in diversionary activities such as work, sports, art, politics, yoga exercises, meditation, relaxation exercises, etc. It may even less elegantly be appeased by magical solutions, such as the therapist's or group's leading the troubled individual to believe that God will help him, that if he suffers enough on earth he will be gratified in heaven, or that if he really understands himself thoroughly (especially by reviewing every historical detail of how his parents abused him during his early childhood), he will suddenly and miraculously lose his emotional hangups.

Human demandingness or disturbability, in other words, may be transiently short-circuited and sidetracked by a vast number of psychotherapeutic methods, which are variously labeled psychoanalysis, encounter therapy, hypnosis, meditation, deconditioning, Christian Science, Scientology, voodoo, witch-doctoring, religious faith, etc. All these methods work to some extent but the vast majority of them seem to be largely palliative. This is because they tend to concentrate on doing something about the individual's demands, and the symptoms he is plagued with when these are not gratified to his liking; but they rarely help him effectively to minimize the demandingness itself and thereby once and for all to undercut the roots of his propensity to disturb or upset himself. Encounter-group therapy, for example, usually shares with the client his whining insistences that he direly needs love and trust from others, that he has to feel terribly hostile and overtly to express his hostility when he is balked or deprived and that he *must* gain new heights of physical sensation in order to make life bearable and to solve some of his basic problems. Although, therefore, the grandiose demander who participates in this kind of therapy will very frequently *feel* better, it is highly unlikely that he will often *get* better in the sense of training himself to become less grandiose and less demanding.

My own form of psychological treatment, which is called rational-emotive therapy (RET, for short), is specifically designed to help the childish demander accept reality, give up all magic, stick rigorously to the logicoempirical method of dealing with himself and the external world and thereby to make a systematic, persistent attack on his demandingness. It is a comprehensive form of therapy which employs a good number of evocative expressive, experiential and emotive as well as many action-centered, motorial, behavioristic, in vivo desensitization techniques. But, above all else, it is a highly cognitive, philosophic, didactic approach to basic personality change; and, what is more, almost all of the verbal and nonverbal methods that it employs are specifically designed to have pronounced cognitive effects, and to help change the individual's fundamental value system or what George Kelly (1955) calls his personal constructs. It frankly, at times, employs therapeutic palliation—such as support, reassurance, and assertion training. But it does so when these means of suaving the human psyche help the individual achieve the more elegant goal of philosophic restructuring, or when there seems to be little or no chance that a particular client is going to work toward achieving the more elegant goal of philosophic restructuring.

Rational-emotive therapy makes considerable use of group work to facilitate change in rational thinking and appropriate emoting. Its fundamental theory states that while emotion is an integral part of human living and while its absence would render people practically inhuman, not all emotions are equally appropriate to the stimuli impinging on the individual, and some emotions—such as severe anxiety, guilt, depression and hostility—are almost always inappropriate. When the individual experiences, at Point C (the emotional Consequence) a disruptive feeling, such as feelings of worthlessness, it is not because he has previously experienced, at Point A, some Activating Event (such as notable failure or rejection). Rather, it is his Belief System (at Point B) which invariably activates or causes C. And his Belief System normally consists of both sane or rational, and insane or irrational, values or philosophies.

In the case of his feeling depressed (at Point C) after he has experienced rejection (at Point A) he is first rationally convicing himself (at Point B), "How unfortunate! I wish I hadn't been rejected. Isn't that too bad!" And if he stayed solely with these rational Beliefs (rB's) he would only experience appropriate feelings of sorrow, regret, frustration and annoyance. But he foolishly and quite irrationally tends also to convince himself, "How *awful!* I *can't stand* being rejected! I *shouldn't* have acted so badly as to get her to reject me! What a *worthless individual* I am!" *Then,* as a result of these magical, empirically unvalidatable statements, he makes himself thoroughly depressed.

The elegant therapeutic solution here is to show the client how to use the logicodeductive, scientific method to challenge his demandingness and absolutism. Thus, he can be shown how to Dispute, at Point D, his irrational Beliefs (iB's) by asking, "*Why* is it awful for me to be rejected? It is obviously undesirable and inconvenient; but *awful* really means *more* than undesirable and inconvenient; and it means that *I should not, must* not be inconvenienced. But this is obviously nonsense: nothing is more than undesirable and there is *no* reason why I must not be inconvenienced."

Again, he can Dispute his irrational Beliefs by asking, "Where is the evidence that I can't stand being rejected! I'll never like it. But why can't I stand what I dislike? Why do I *need* and *have to get* what I want? Clearly I don't!"

And again, he can Dispute his dogmatic statement, "I *shouldn't* have acted so badly as to get her to reject me!" by asking himself, "Why *shouldn't* I have done so? It would have been *preferable,* if I had acted better; but why *should* I, *ought* I, *must* I do what would be preferable? Why should I not be the fallible human I shall always be and make—and *keep* making— such woeful errors?"

Finally, he can ask himself, "Why am I a *worthless individual* for acting badly with this person and encouraging him (or her) to reject me?" And he can, after much cogitation (and not by parroting by rote), answer, "Of course I am not! A crummy *act* or *deed* hardly makes me, in toto, a crummy *person!* I am a very complex, ongoing, ever-changing individual who will probably always do exceptionally stupid, self-damaging acts. So I'll never be perfect! Tough shit!"

If the individual persists, quite determinedly and vigorously, in disputing, questioning and challenging his own irrational Beliefs, after he fully acknowledges that he is emoting in an inappropriate, self-sabotaging manner as a result of absolutistically holding these Beliefs, he will not only, I hypothesize, almost immediately diminish or eliminate this dysfunctional emoting, but he will also soon begin to acquire a radically different, reality-centered philosophy of life that will nip similar emotions in the bud later, and encourage him to react appropriately to noxious stimuli.

Assuming that my hypothesis is correct, and that the aim of efficient therapy is to facilitate change toward rational thinking and appropriate emoting, how does the group process specifically abet this aim? In many ways; and through several kinds of group processes. Thus, in RET, I and my associates at the Institute for Advanced Study in Rational Psychotherapy in New York City (and at various of our branches in other parts of the country) find group work exceptionally advantageous. At the moment, we are employing four main kinds of group processes: (1) family groups, with the therapist sitting in for regular sessions with a husband and wife, a couple and its children, a single parent and one or more children or two or more children without their parents. (2) regular weekly group therapy sessions, with a therapist and an assistant or cotherapist leading, usually on a once-a-week basis for about two and a quarter hours, 10–13 group members; (3) marathon weekends of rational encounter, with a therapist (and often a cotherapist) spending 24 hours in a two-day period (usually with nine hours for sleeping in between the two days) with 10–16 participants leading them in specially devised encountering exercises and including a good many hours of showing the members of the group specifically how to solve some of their major life problems in a rational-emotive manner; and (4) workshops in rational living, with a therapist demonstrating the rational-emotive method with a volunteering individual who talks to him about his specific problem but does so before an audience of from twenty to a few hundred people. After the therapist speaks with the volunteer for about 20 or 30 minutes, the members of the audience who wish to do so are actively encouraged to speak to the therapist and to the volunteer, so that the latter encounters the feelings and hears the suggestions of as many as 20 or 25 people besides the therapist. Regular workshops for the public are given on most Friday evenings of the year at the Institute for Advanced Study in Rational Psychotherapy in New York and other workshops of this nature, for both professional and lay groups, are conducted by the Institute and its branches in varous other parts of the United States and Canada at certain times.

Lectures, seminars, films, tape recordings, and other kinds of educational presentations in the principles of rational living are given at the Institute's adult education program during the year and at the Living School, a private school for normal children which the Institute operates in New York City. Particularly at the Living School, emotional education is continually given along with academic education, so that the children are literally taught, for prophylactic and therapeutic reasons, the theory and practice rational-emotive psychology. Thus, if a child becomes upset about anything during a regular classroom session, the teacher (who is specially trained in RET procedures at the Institute) often will stop the class and deal with his emotional problem, and try to induce some of the other children to help her deal with this problem, before she returns to the academic procedures. Also, the children are given regular sessions of group counseling every week, in the course of which they bring up any problems about which they are disturbed, and the teacher acts as group leader during these counseling sessions and shows the children how to approach their problems in a rational-emotive manner, just as an RET leader of an adult group teaches them to handle their difficulties rationally.

All these methods of group therapy have proven to be highly effective, each in its different way, for individuals having minor or major emotional problems, as well as for individuals (such as those at the Living School or those who participate in the Institute's Friday night workshops) who may not be afflicted with any emotional upsets at the moment, but who can prophylactically learn what to do if and when they make themselves disturbed about anything. Through conducting and observing these various kinds of groups for the past twenty years, I find that they help the individuals who participate in them sporadically or regularly in a number of important ways:

(1) Since the essence of RET is to teach the person how to accept reality and to try to change it by concerted work instead of whining demands, several members of a group usually are more effective in bringing his dictatorialness to his attention than is a single therapist. Just because some of the members of a group process are themselves, as different circumstances arise, often rigidly enmeshed in two-year-old thinking and emoting, they can fairly easily recognize its manifestations in others and dramatically bring these manifestations to a complainer's attention.

(2) RET, perhaps more than any other of the major therapy systems, emphasizes not only showing the individual what he is thinking and how his muddled thoughts are causing his self-destructive feelings, but also demonstrating the logical parsing, the vigorously attacking, and the empirical contradicting to this disordered thinking. In a group situation, the querying, contradicting and attacking the individual's crooked cognitions can be forcefully done by several group members, who are likely to have a greater impact, all told, than a single therapist has.

(3) In RET, the therapist is an exceptionally active, probing, challenging person. In group therapy, he may well be aided in all these functions by suggestions, comments, and hypotheses from other group members, which may deflect him from neglecting some important factor, give him hypotheses which he can check on and add to, reinforce some of his main points and allow him at times to stand on the emotive and intellectual shoulders of other group members and thereby add to his therapeutic effectiveness.

(4) RET notably includes specific activity-oriented homework assignments. Thus, a client may be assigned the outside task of looking for a new job, dating a girl he is afraid to date or deliberately visiting his mother-in-law, whom he may detest.

Such homework assignments are often more effectively given and followed up when given by a group than by an individual therapist.

(5) RET includes a number of role-playing and behavior modification methods—such as assertion training, in vivo risk-taking and behavior rehearsal—which can partly be done in individual sessions but which sometimes require a group process. Thus, if an individual is afraid to talk before a group of people, he may be induced to talk regularly in the group itself.

(6) The group provides a laboratory where emotional, gestural and motorial behavior can be directly observed rather than learned through the client's secondhand reports. An individual who keeps telling his individual therapist that he no longer becomes enraged at others may get away with this report for quite a while. But the same individual engaged in a group process may unwittingly give away his enraged feelings by the way he acts in the group, and such denied feelings may then be spotted by the therapist or other group members. When this occurs, RET procedures can then be effectively employed to show him exactly what irrational Beliefs he is holding to create his rage, and what the can do about changing them and it.

(7) In RET, clients frequently fill out homework report forms and give them to the therapist at the beginning of each session to go over and correct. These forms teach them how to go through the A-B-C's of their most upsetting experiences, and when they are corrected, enable them to use the RET theory and practice more effectively next time. In group sessions, a few homework-assignment forms are often read and corrected during the session, so that all the members of the group, not merely the individual handing in the form, may be helped by seeing specifically what emotional Consequence was experienced (at Point C); what Activating Events disordered occurred to spark it (at Point A); what rational and irrational Beliefs the individual told himself (at Point B) to create his dysfunctional Consequences; and what kind of effective Disputing he could do (at Point D) to minimize or eradicate his irrational Beliefs and his subsequent disordered Consequences. By hearing about other group members' main problems and how they dealt with them on the Homework Report, most clients are helped to use these Reports properly themselves.

(8) In the group process, the individual is helped to see that he is hardly alone in being troubled, and that he has the same foolish disturbance-creating ideas as many others have. He is thereby shown that he is not unique in this respect and that he need not condemn himself for having disturbances. He gains the help of others who are in much the same boat as is he; and he learns how to try to talk these others out of their irrational Beliefs, and thereby to unconsciously and consciously attack his own similar Beliefs. In the group, he learns the RET theory and application by actually *practicing* it; or, as John Dewey (1930) stated many years ago, he learns by doing.

(9) The individual gets valuable feedback from the group. He begins to see himself more and more as *others* see him, to realize some of the poor or wrong impressions he makes on these others, and to learn how to change some of his behaviors which encourage these impressions. He frequently gains social skills, during the group process and in socializing with group members after or between sessions. Some of this gain is only palliative, since he largely learns better skills rather than to accept himself *whether or not* he is notably skillful. But he also can be philosophically jogged by other group members, especially in his social relations with them or in the course of telephone conversations, so that he acquires a distinctly new view of himself and the world.

(10) When the individual tries to deal with other people's problems in the group and questions them wrongly, makes inappropriate conclusions about them, advises them foolishly or keeps offering them only palliative solutions to their basic problems, the therapist (and other group members) are able to observe his errors, immediately bring them to his attention and get him to think through what more appropriate responses would be. He thereby receives a corrective emotional and didactic experience as the session is proceeding.

(11) The individual is able to observe the progress, and especially the philosophic and behavioral progress, of other group members, and thereby to see (a) that treatment can be effective, (b) that he can similarly change, (c) that there are specific things he can do to help himself and (d) that therapy is hardly magic but almost always consists of persistent hard work.

(12) The group member is frequently offered a wider range of

possible solutions to his problems than he would normally be offered in individual therapy. Out of ten or twelve people present at a given group session, one person may finally zero in on his central problem (after several others have failed) and another person may offer an elegant solution to it (after many ineffectual or lower-level solutions have hitherto been offered him). Where a single individual, including a single therapist, may well give up on a difficult issue (or person), a few group members may persist and may finally prove to be quite helpful.

(13) Revealing intimate problems to a group of people may be in itself quite therapeutic for the individual. In a regular RET group the client discloses many ordinarily hidden events and feelings to a dozen or so of his peers, and by being encouraged—and occasionally almost forced— to do so, he frequently sees that nothing is really so shameful as he previously thought it was. In RET workshops he may reveal himself to a hundred or more people; and, especially when he is a normally shy and inhibited individual, he often finds that this is one of the most useful risk-taking experiences of his life. Such disturbance-dispelling experiences occur in almost all kinds of therapeutic groups. But in RET groups, in particular, the therapist (or another group member) specifically tries to show the previously held-in person that he has taken a risk of others' disapproval; that he has come through it with little of the criticism and attack he falsely predicted; and that even if he were roundly excoriated and laughed at, that would not in the least be ego-downing or catastrophic; it would merely be unfortunate.

(14) RET, like most cognitively-oriented systems of therapy, is highly educational and didactic. It frequently includes explanations, information-giving, and the discussion of problem-solving techniques. It is usually more economical for the therapist to do this kind of teaching in a group rather than an individual setting, and is of course more time-saving and money-saving for the client. Besides, teaching is more meaningful in a group than in an individual setting, and encourages certain kinds of questioning of the therapist and discussion of the points he is raising that would be less effective in one-to-one teacher-pupil relationships. Education, moreover, as John Dewey (1930) and Jean Piaget (1970) have shown, is much more effective when the individual actively enters the teaching-discussing-doing process than when

he is mainly a passive recipient. And group therapy tends to provide a more stimulating and more activating kind of involvement than individual treatment often does.

Although there has recently been a kind of revolution in the field of education which includes a good deal of affective or emotional education along with the regular academic procedures, and which takes cognizance of the fact that children can learn to understand themselves and their own emoting processes, just as they can learn to understand arithmetic, history, geography and other subjects, this new direction has been too much influenced by the encounter movement and sensitivity training. It assumes that emotional knowledge can only be taught "affectively": that is, through direct experiences, through encouraging direct relationships among children, through physical sensations and through other emotive techniques.

While these methods may be both enjoyable and instructive, they hardly cover the entire range of emotional education. In our experimental work at the Living School in New York, with children from six to nine years of age, we have found that didactic means of imparting affective knowledge may also be effective. Thus, we teach our youngsters, in classroom discussions, during their play activities, through art and dramatic productions, with audiovisual materials and in a variety of other ways, that they do not *get upset* by external events but that they invariably *upset themselves*. And we show them, with rational-emotive psychology, how to stop upsetting themselves, as well as how to understand how their peers and parents disturb themselves and how they may sometimes help these others stop making themselves disturbed. Just as we employ congnitive and emotive methods to teach them academic subjects, so do we also employ both these modes to teach them emotional insights into themselves and others.

(15) The group session tends to be a highly effective interrupting device for many clients, partly because of its length. Whereas individual sessions tend to run for a half hour or three-quarters of an hour, group sessions at our Institute run for a total of two and a quarter hours and are frequently followed by the group members spending another hour or so with each other without a formal leader. This somewhat massive time intrusion during which they think and act against their strongly held

self-defeating philosophies can be therapeutically cogent and potent.

(16) Group procedures can be especially helpful for rigidly bound individuals who have a most difficult time jolting themselves out of old, dysfunctional behavior patterns into newer, healthier ones. Individual therapists, for example, frequently have considerable trouble inducing fixed homosexuals, alcoholics or food addicts to experiment for a sufficient length of time with radically different modes of living. If, however, one or two such individuals are placed in a group where most of the other members unblamefully accept him with his problems but keep showing him that he *can* change and that they intend to keep after him until he does, such severely phobiac or addicted individuals are frequently helped to try and continue new behaviors until they become accustomed to them and even learn to enjoy them.

For many reasons, of which the foregoing list is hardly exhaustive, group processes are not only exceptionally useful in attacking the troubled individual's irrational premises and illogical deductions and helping him reconsider and reconstruct his basic self-destructive philosophies; but they frequently are more effective in this respect than are the same therapies used individually. That is why many of the leading cognitive-oriented therapists—such as Berne (1964), Corsini (1966), Dreikurs (Dreikurs & Grey, 1968), Ellis (1962, 1971, 1972; Ellis & Harper, 1970a, 1970b), Lazarus (1971), Low (1952), and Phillips & Wiener (1966)—have made such extensive use of various kinds of group procedures.

This is not to say that group methods do not have intrinsic disadvantages when compared to other therapy modes; for they definitely do. In my own work, I have often found that group members can easily, out of overzealousness and ignorance, mislead other members. They give poor or low-level solutions; and they can waste so much time that there is little opportunity for the client with a problem to be shown a higher-level solution. They can bombard the individual with so many and so powerful suggestions that he is overwhelmed and partly paralyzed. They can allow a member, if the therapist does not intervene, to get away with minimal participation and hence minimal change.

They can irrationally condemn the person for his poor behavior or for his refusing to do anything about it.

In onesidedly oriented encounter-type groups the group process is much more likely to be inelegant or even antitherapeutic and to discourage rational thinking and appropriate emoting. For the basic attitude—or may I say religion?—of such groups is that the group member should mainly "get in touch with his feelings" or let his emotions unreflectively hang out; that intense emotionality of *any* kind is marvelous in itself; that if the individual stops to think about his feelings he is being overintellectual, defensive, and mechanical; and that he has several powerful and unchangeable needs, such as the need to be approved by others and the need to get terribly angry at them when they balk him, and if he does not fulfill these needs directly and immediately he can only remain in terrible anguish or can be a bottled-up zombie. Because of this highly indulgent, irrational, emotion-deifying philosophy of many encounter groups, they tend to coerce their members into conforming behavior, aggravate their dire love needs, and give them various kinds of physical diversions (such as body massage, screaming, wailing, and muscular relaxation) which enable them to feel better rather than to get better and to avoid the basic issue of ever interrupting and changing their childish demandingness (Ellis, 1969). A considerable amount of experimental and clinical evidence exists to show that emotional catharsis usually does little good and some harm (Berkowitz, 1970), but since the encounter movement is now often led by actors, dancers, architects, masseurs, housewives, gym teachers and other nonprofessionals who are not too eager to read or to heed the psychological literature, this evidence is not likely to help stop the present questionable group-therapy trends.

Let me say in conclusion that man is exceptionally prone to self-defeating thinking and inappropraite emoting and behaving; and perhaps, unless he radically changes his entire biosocial makeup, he will always be. He can significantly change his cognitions, emotions and behavior, however, in a number of ways—most of them accidental and some of them designed. Considering the enormous amount of needless emotional suffering which he now tends to experience—including long periods of intense anxiety, depression, guilt and hostility—he would be wiser if he clearly understood exactly what he was thinking and doing to create his so-called emotional upsets, and if he exerted the choice, which he uniquely has as a human being, to think and to act differently, and thereby quickly undo his upsets and arrange for their infrequent subsequent occurrence.

He can most elegantly do this if he avoids preoccupying himself with A, the Activating Events of his life, and fully acknowledges but resists endlessly reexperiencing C, the inappropriate emotional Consequences which frequently follow after and falsely seem to stem from A. He has the choice, instead, of keenly discerning, parsing, examining modifying, and uprooting B, the irrational Beliefs which he so easily tends to convince himself about some of the Activating Events at A. He can decide to persistently and vigorously work at changing his irrational Beliefs on his own, or can get help in doing so from straighter-thinking friends, books, lectures, demonstrations, tape recordings and other sources. He can also work with an individual therapist or group leader. If he chooses the group process, and picks a cognitively oriented group that also employs a comprehensive method of attacking his stubbornly held irrationalities and illogicalities, that includes selected evocative-emotive and activating-behavioristic techniques, he will thereby avail himself of a multifaceted and powerful therapeutic procedure. I stoutly hypothesize that this kind of group intervention is most likely to lead him to quicker, deeper and more elegant solutions to the ubiquitous human condition of childish demandingness and perennial disturbability than any other contemporary form of psychotherapy.

REFERENCES

Berkowitz, L. Experimental investigations of hostility catharsis. *Journal of Consulting and Clinical Psychology,* 1970, **35**, 1–7.

Berne, E. *Games people play.* New York: Grove Press, 1964.

Corsini, R. J., with Cardono, S. *Role playing in psychotherapy: a manual.* Chicago: Aldine, 1966.

Dewey, J. *Human nature and conduct.* New York: Modern Library, 1930.

Dreikurs, R. & Grey, L. *Logical consequences: A handbook of discipline.* New York: Meredith, 1968.

Ellis, A. *Reason and emotion in psychotherapy.* New York: Lyle Stuart, 1962.

Ellis, A. A weekend of rational encounter. In Burton, A. (Ed.), *Encounter.* San Francisco: Jossey-Bass 1969.

Ellis, A. *A casebook of rational-emotive therapy.* Palo Alto, Calif.: Science and Behavior Books, 1971.

Ellis, A. *Emotional education.* New York: Julian Press, 1972.

Ellis, A. & Harper, R. A. *A guide to rational living.* Englewood Cliffs, N.J.: Prentice-Hall; Hollywood, Calif.: Wilshire Books; 1970a.

Ellis, A. & Harper, R. A. *A guide to successful marriage.* (Original title: *Creative marriage).* New York: Lyle Stuart; Hollywood, Calif.: Wilshire Books; 1970b.

Kelly, G. A. *The psychology of personal constructs.* New York: Norton, 1955.

Lazarus, A. A. *Behavior therapy and beyond.* New York: McGraw-Hill, 1971.

Low, A. A. *Mental health through will-training.* Boston: Christopher, 1952.

Phillips, E. L. & Wiener, D. N. *Short-term psychotherapy and structured behavior change.* New York: McGraw-Hill, 1966.

Piaget, J. *Science of education and the psychology of the child.* New York: Orion Press, 1970.

7. *Constructive Aggression in Growth Groups*

George R. Bach

Disagreements inevitably arise between individuals and those others in their social system with whom interdependencies have been most strongly established, regarding the relative importance of the various components of their intimacy structure. Discrepancies with regard to how much closeness, power and trust is provided and how much is expected by each member of the dyad are unavoidable, and the resultant disappointment and frustration often errupts into hostile interchanges. George Bach contends that the destructive aspects of this hostility can be modified by training which substitutes constructive and growth stimulating aggressive alternatives for the growth inhibiting hostility.

The Haircut, *the* Vesuvius *and the* Museum *are among the exercises developed by George Bach which are designed with the specific objective of desensitizing partners to the expression and reception of hostility. These hostility rituals, as Bach has designated them, may, in addition, elicit useful information upon which to base future negotiations for behavior change by partners.*

The Museum exercise, for example, begins with the composition by fight-training participants of a list of all of the grievances accumulated from the outset of a pairing relationship. The list is analyzed for discardable and negotiable grievances.

Exercises in Confrontation (Impacts) represent the second element in Bach's fight-training program. The "beef for change" is the process by which partners deal with a specific issue, and a demand for change by one participant. Feedback is a crucial aspect of the Fight for Change, with careful monitoring by group and trainer to ensure that the fight participants are not distorting the information delivered by each to the other. An ingenious scoring format has also been developed which allows observers to deliver specific feedback which identifies, for the antagonists, important dimensions of their fight styles.

Exploratory research conducted by Bach leads him to conclude that the training described above has promise for enabling couples to manage conflict more effectively. The program also has applicability to other systems.

Many years of clinical practice and research with growth-stimulating groups have convinced this writer that interpersonal hostilities between member-member and leader-member can have a growth-stimulating rather than a growth-stymieing effect. Dealing with hostility in the group situation has a number of advantages over individual forms of treatment, as will be enlarged on later. Suffice it to say at this point that among such advantages are the opportunities of group members to learn to identify patterns of aggression and to receive feedback from others regarding their own styles of aggression, and the power for constructive change resulting from group witness of commitments.

Hostile interactions frequently occur in intimate groups of emotionally interdependent individuals, such as family, love-pairs, therapy groups and other face-to-face "in groups." The individual who is the object of the hostility is usually forced to interpret for himself whether the interaction is intended to create "good will" or "ill will." When the aggression is in the context of ill will it usually implies, "I hate you because you are evil and I must punish or destroy you for it—you can't improve, don't try to." Aggression in the context of good will has less punitive and more corrective impact and indicates, "I hate you, I am angry at you, I feel hurt by you—because you are mean and have committed such and such fouls. I must object and demand you to cut that out, so that I can love you again."

Aggression in the service of better growth is the hallmark of any responsible devoted parent-child, teacher-student, therapist-patient relationship. The Rogerian notion that the essence of therapeutic helpfulness lies in the absence of critical rejection and depends primarily upon "unconditional acceptance, positive regard and tender loving care" may be a truth specific to and limited by selected nondirective individual therapy contracts in which the therapist-guru commits himself for 50 minutes or so to the contrivance of suspending or suppressing of overt anger and aggression. However, in both natural and assembled intimate groups such as Families and Therapy Groups, such nonaggression pacts—if ever agreed upon—are sooner or later broken, as they are recognized as unrealistic. Seductive illusions exist which accommodate the romantic wish for peace and avoidance of conflict. Yet conflict, frustration and aggression are inherent in any face-to-face group of two or more emotionally interdependent people who wish to grow together and to improve their lot and their existential meaning in life.

A previously published series of research studies raised the question, "Can individuals be taught to selectively utilize growth stimulating types of aggression rather than growth inhibiting techniques? (Bach, 1967a, 1967b, 1967c)." In these studies, therapy-group participants were asked which of the following standard dimensions of interactions they found most growth-stimulating after 24 or more hours of Marathon Group Contact with the member chosen to be "most helpful":

(1) Identification or modeling
(2) Acceptance and warmth
(3) Problem-solving
(4) Insight mediation
(5) Aggression confrontation
(6) Other write-in dimensions of helpful interactions

Number 5, "Aggression confrontation," was checked as often as the other dimensions. Number 2, "Acceptance and warmth," was by no means the preferred choice for the most growth-stimulating interaction experience.

This research and other findings stimulated the systematic exploration of utilizing aggression therapeutically as a constructive rather than destructive form of interpersonal influence. This interest resulted in the development of an educational system for the socialization of aggression. We first focused our group therapeutic work on training the foul-fight patterns of adult intimates—especially spouses and other lovers—and developed a so-called Fair Fight System, the details of which are published in three recent books (Bach & Wyden, 1970; Bach & Deutsch, 1971; Bach & Bernhard, 1971).

The therapeutic Fair-Fight Training System is based on the assumption that interpersonal fighting is healthy and necessary, and that destructive aspects of hostility between emotionally interdependent partners can be modified by retraining the partners in more effective uses of the interpersonal communication system which they have developed, pair-specifically, during the history of their relationship. These pair-specific communication styles are assumed to be modifiable.

Our data suggest that the mismanagement of conflict and aggression through denial or evasion on the one hand or brutalization on the other may well be the crucial cause of couple and family disturbances. In view of the availability of an educational method that teaches constructive ways of dealing with aggression in face-to-face intimate confrontation, there is hope for reducing if not preventing the destructiveness of family and marital deterioration.

The purpose of the Fair Fight System is the modification of behavior through direct coaching, reinforcing techniques and group pressure. In aggressive encounters between basically committed significant others, a minimal degree of good will toward improving a relationship—in most cases—can be assumed to exist. Hostilities may have a growth-stimulating, rather than a growth-retarding, function where such good-will contracts exist. Fight-training attempts to maximize the information-yielding function of aggression and to minimize the hostile-hurt orientation. In addition to hurting and informing, aggression is also viewed as an influencing strategy for effecting changes, hopefully for the better, in a relationship.

Theoretically, this orientation can be expressed by the following heuristic formula:

$$AG(C) = \frac{I.I.}{H.H.}$$

The degree of constructiveness of aggression (AG (C)) depends on the relationship between informative impact (I.I.) and hurtful hostility (H.H.). To the extent that the experiential value of receiving relevant information and/or asserting effective impact for change is greater than the painful hurting, aggression is constructive, and such "fights" are assumed to have growth-stimulating value for each partner as well as to strengthen the bonds between partners.

Guided by this constructive-aggression model, the Fight Training System consists of a number of exercises in aggressive communication. They are divided into two different but interrelated formats. One format is designed to channel hurtful hostilities into mutually acceptable (although intrinsically painful) *rituals.* The second format, called *impacts,* trains partners to influence one another in a forceful manner in order to stimulate and discover new ways of providing enjoyment and fulfillment in their relationship. In the course of training, the partners have an opportunity to recognize and explore the operationalization of *intimacy,* in the context of their relationship.

DESENSITIZING THROUGH RITUALS

The utility of hostility rituals is to provide an outlet for the complete, yet safe, expression of accumulated resentments from the past; to allow playful, yet dramatic and authentic, expressions of hostility in a manner which makes these expressions informative, emotionally involving and also enjoyable and entertaining. Rituals also display a great deal of experiential content which has previously been hidden. From this content, partners can, upon later reflection, read the areas of vulnerability and sensitivity to hurt. In the heat of ritualized fighting, some of the burning sore points in a relationship are brought to full, dramatic awareness. This aids the partners in delineating the conflicted issues in their state of togetherness that will have to be faced later in the *impacts,* which are more rational fights for change.

External controls are placed on rituals in the form of an appointed time and place, mutual consent, respect for beltlines and "arms limitation." These limits reduce or eliminate the need for rational control over the content, thus providing a method for bringing into the open, previously unconscious, or at least undefined, feelings, hopes and concerns. The experience of acting out hostilities with structured verbal and extraverbal rituals tends to reduce fear, shame and guilt over the paradoxical existence of hate in the context of good will. Through the procedure of rituals, individuals are desensitized to the expression of hostility and become more receptive to the helpful information that will be offered during the impact encounters.

INFORMING THROUGH IMPACTS

Obviously, mastering ritualistic gamelike expressions of hostility is not enough, because rituals tend to preserve, rather than change, the very states of interdependence, which may be ripe for change, because they have outgrown their utility as far as the growth and well-being of the marriage are concerned. The second format of exercises, the impacts or "fights for change," also require a highly structured framework governed by basic rules which include, for example, a preparation for engagement, the necessity of taking turns, active listening, feedback, specificity of issues, reality oriented reasoning, change readiness, etc.

Another feature of the fight-for-change procedure is that it can be scored with the use of a formal score sheet and definitions of various fight styles that may emerge in the encounter.

Scoring the fight styles by third and fourth parties in a couples group sharpens the observational sensitivities of the scorers, while the resultant scores give the fight partners some indication of how foul or fair, how alienating or bonding their fight styles are. Over the typical training course of 13 four-hour sessions, the need for cleaning up dirty fight-styles becomes obvious to the pair involved, to the fight trainer and to the group. This knowledge motivates self-improvement and the group's awareness constitutes a reinforcing factor to try out new and less alienating fight systems.

As a fringe benefit, the scoring procedure allows the gathering of useful research data. For example, in one tabulation of 250 scored fights involving 50 couples,[1] the discovery was made that male spouses score significantly more often in the "dirty" or alienating columns in the early training sessions than women do.

[1] Data analyzed by Stephanie Bach, Research Assistant

And it will please the feminist movement that there was no evidence of "feminine wiles" in this material (Bach, 1971a).

It should be emphasized that the highly structured communication exercises in either the ritual or the fair-fight formats are meant to be transitional bridging methods, which become highly modified or even abandoned as soon as each couple has discovered their own spontaneously emerging and highly pair-specific strategies and styles of dealing with conflict and aggression.

It seems that partners learn a deeper trust and mutual respect through having gone together through these highly structured and "artificial," often trivial-appearing, exercises. However, the mastery of the Fight Training System offers the partners freedom from the fears of aggression and gives them the courage to deal henceforth with whatever serious conflicts may emerge in their groping for growth towards ever-deeper levels of intimacy.

EMPIRICAL DIMENSIONS OF INTIMACY

What does "depth" mean in interpersonal terms? What are "shallow" and what are "deeper" levels of intimacy? How are "deep" fulfillments mutually reached? Our assumption is that the satisfaction of each partner's individual needs or wants, including achieving mature autonomy and full self-actualization, depends on the pair's competence and skill in maintaining a growth-stimulating, psychologically-nurturing encounter system.

A further objective of fight training is to help partners become more fully and directly aware of the basic phenomenological parameters of these pair-specific encounter systems, called *intimacy*. In the early phase of fight training the coaches first concentrate on fight styles, regardless of what the issues are that partners have chosen to battle over. This allows the individuals involved to see through the apparently trivial nature of the manifest issues and discover some of the covert, deeply significant concerns. Untrained partners barely feel these at first, but basic issues begin to emerge as the education in aggression proceeds. Some of the themes which commonly define the problems of intimacy are as follows:

Optimal Distance

The partners of nearly every couple have been found to differ in the amount of closeness or "togetherness" that they need or can tolerate. Often one spouse feels "smothered with love" while the other feels excluded and shut out of the partner's life. The most frequent demands heard are for "more time with you and/or more intense involvement in the time we spend together" and for "privacy" or "time for myself."

Power Struggle

Who defines a situation? Does the husband or the wife decide when children need to be disciplined? When the husband socializes with business friends, is it business, as he says, or pleasure, as his wife claims?

Trust Formation

Openness in the sharing of gut-level feelings is the mark of truly intimate communication. This will be limited or expanded, relative to the quality of depth of trust that partners achieve with one another. We have clinically observed that the formation of trust in a marriage and in love-pairings depends as much on familiarization and socialization of anger and hostility as it of course depends on positive regard and "stroking." Partners trust each other more when they know—from painful experience—where, when and how they tend to hurt one another. Trust levels also depend upon the interaction occurring in situations of vulnerability as well as in heightened states of dependency (e. g., pregnancy, erotic excitement, loyalty in confrontations with outsiders, etc.). Fair-fight training includes specific "trust tests" which shortcut the pains of bitter experience by bringing out in full display: (1) beltlines, below which a partner is most vulnerable; (2) when a partner is likely not to honor the beltline, and has the tendency to hit below the belt (e. g., in company); (3) transverbal and physical (including sexual) patterns of dealing with disparities and imbalances in physical strength, emotional maturity, endurances and competencies.

In an intimate system trust grows to the extent that the "tit-for-tat" contractual orientation is overcome in favor of a high tolerance for imbalances. Differences and disparities in the qualities and resources which each individual possesses exist in any partnership. A more equitable relationship occurs when each individual learns to tolerate this inherent imbalance.

Reciprocation

To expect to get as much of that which one has given or will give is a mark of the marketplace, but not of intimacy. The deeper development of trust also thrives when the competitive, win/lose, upmanship orientation, so prevalent in nonintimate social contexts, is eliminated. The competitive tendencies in couples are cooled rather than fanned by our fight coaches by emphasizing that the quality of aggression is produced by the interaction of the two partners of a pair. The individual superiorities and inferiorities in fair-fight styles between husbands and wives are to be tolerated and clearly recognized as self-identity features of individuals. Judgmental competitive comparisons are considered as hurtful rather than helpful and growth-stimulating effects. Playful use of competitive comparisons in pairs, learning how to fight better with one another, may, however, create humor and good will. On the other hand, the superior-inferior approach—prizewinning, individual competition for better fight-styles—tends to reduce trust, alienates and encourages disengagements.

Self-Defense of Self-Identity

Intimates tend to tell each other why they are or should be according to their romantic ideals. Because intimates have good will towards these usually positive mystiques, they will severely bend their authentic identities to accommodate, even collude with, them. They will cast each other into mystique-validating but ego-alien roles, and for a while cheerfully accept roles foreign to their nature, because it does make the partner happy when the intimate interactions conform with the romantic mystique. However, individual growth is diverted, if not stunted, by too much accommodation. Such fantasy-supporting, collusive intimacies are usually short-lived phantoms which leave a bad taste and guilt over conning, even though the manipulations were in the name of a good cause; making the partner "happy." To achieve realistic intimacy, authentic individual identities of each partner must not only be preserved, but carefully nurtured along.

Concern with Centricity

How important am I to you? For example, the husband demands that his wife give up a class she is taking because she does not get home in time to prepare his dinner. He means, "Give up your activity to prove to me that I am more important to you than anything else."

Reality Testing of Cherished Illusions or Expectations

For example: "I thought you would send me flowers or at least a Valentine card, but you let the day go by without a single gesture. Did you forget, or should I not expect such things from you?"

Concern with Social Boundaries

The pair needs to define their place within the social nexus and the "sociological ecosystem." For example, "How often will we entertain or visit friends; what clubs or groups shall we join; how much will other people be involved in our recreation together? Shall we bring the children?"

Being able to fight effectively over these and related issues is one of the major objectives of the program. Our aim is not to do away with either conflict or aggression in marriage and family life. On the contrary, it is to make conflict and aggression a familiar, nonthreatening, almost daily event, as an intrinsic growth-stimulating aspect of authentic togetherness.

DESCRIPTION OF THE FIGHT TRAINING SYSTEM

As a matter of policy and conviction, the goal of fight-training is defined as arriving at the *truth about the actual state of the relationship.* The truth that emerges may be the painful fact that the two individuals, even after mastering constructive ways of dealing with conflict and aggression, find that they bring out the worst in each other. With whatever good intentions, they retard rather than promote one another's growth. In these cases, the fight-training procedure leads to a realistic exit. *Exit rituals* have been developed to maximize the learning from the defunct relationship, to reduce the guilt and shame of failure and to give hope and effective skills for engaging in new relationships. A "creative divorce" procedure is also available. For divorced persons and never-married singles, a course called "Pairing" is available both at the Institute of Group Psychotherapy and on various campuses of the University of California. In both Fight Training and Pairing classes, it is stressed that individuals are free to choose between being married and being single as alternative lifestyles of equal validity and potential for individidual growth. It would be most unethical to misuse the fair fight training system as an artificial booster shot for an intrinsically growth-restricting marriage.

The following is a partial list and description in brief of exercises in aggressive communication used in fight-training sessions. The typical group consists of from five to eight couples and meets weekly for four hours under the leadership of a fight trainer who coaches each couple as they take their turn in the "hot seat." Group members, in addition to the trainer, score and offer comments about fight style and may suggest "homework assignments." Each couple is encouraged to make a commitment for a minimum of 13 weeks of fight training in order to master the system and to apply it to everday living.

Hostility rituals usually serve as the starting point of all confrontations. They are cathartic insult-exchanges by mutual consent and appointment, with whatever equalizing rules are necessary to allow a couple to express hostility freely while remaining within the structure of one of the rituals. Rules may consist of time limitations (usually one or two minutes), restriction of content and use by one or both partners of physical aggression by means of "Batacas." These soft rubber bats provide the experience of beating and being beaten, but make it most unlikely to inflict serious physical harm.

Rituals are based on the Zero-Sum Game-Playing Model, with the extra bonus of a double win. Both partners gain, by taking turns at having an assured "listening ear" (without defensive retaliation) and an emotional "unloading." In practice, both partners deescalate feelings of rage and give information such as anger-inspiring specifics, frustrations and unabsorbable hurts. After a *rage-release ritual* the partners are more able to open avenues that increase the bonding capacity of the relationship. The emotional effect may be compared to lancing a boil or to releasing the steam from a pressure cooker. Rituals put past grievances aside, at least temporarily, and clear the decks for dealing more rationally with current issues of the relationship.

KINDS OF HOSTILITY RITUALS

The haircut is an expression of anger caused by a current specific hurt by one partner directed at the other. The partner who receives the request ("May I give you a haircut?") has the right to set the time limit, as well as the right to refuse or postpone acceptance. (Each individual must learn to gauge his tolerance for listening to rage-release rituals and set appointments and time limits accordingly.) If the "haircut" is accepted, the partner is obliged to listen to a tongue-lashing without defense, for the time contracted. The information disclosed may, at a later time, be the basis for a behavior-change request (fair fight for change).

When permission for a haircut (or any ritual) is denied, the problem arises of what to do with the accumulated rage. A specific homework assignment for each individual early in fight training is to find alternative idiosyncratic rage releases which do not require a listener, e.g., pounding a pillow, smashing crockery, working out on a punching bag, scrubbing floors, Bataca beatings, etc.

The Vesuvius is a verbal unloading of hostile steam about anything or anyone (including the partner). For example, "My boss demands too much of me and the traffic is a mess and my mother called me five times without saying anything at all and the gardener did a sloppy job on the roses and I'm sick and tired of this whole bloody stupid phony system." A respectful listenting ear is demanded and consent must be granted before a Vesuvius eruption. The time limitation set introduces the process of containment within the cathartic release.

The Virginia Woolf is a two-way, simultaneous, verbal

insult-exchange with no holds barred. By mutual agreement this ritual permits the unmentionable and intolerable insults and threats to be used. All blows are aimed "below the belt." While doing a Virginia Woolf, partners recognize the intensity and the content of their rage. The ritual provides the means for expulsion of their rage. The physical aggression of Batacas is often used in this ritual, a verbal punishment accompanied by a hit: "And this is for the time you forgot my birthday!" Whack! The airing of accumulated rage, limited by rules of physical and emotional safety, begins the process of partial evaporation. It makes the old grievances less lethal, opens them for content consideration, and gives information about pain in the relationship and danger to it. Virginia Woolfing allows the recognition and adjustment of beltlines—discovering a new insult that is intolerable, or an old one that no longer needs to be avoided.

The museum (or gunnysack) is the list of all grievances accumulated to date from the start of the pairing relationship. Confrontation of the partners with their sepatate museum lists may be an initial assignment for a couple entering fight training. (Each assignment is pair-specific, based on emotional readiness and the "state of the marital union" of the couple.) The museum is used as a base of information for change and growth tasks.

The first step is to determine which items on the "list" or "museum catalogue" are no longer important. These items are given a "burial ceremony" incorporating attitudes of forgiveness and renunciation of their use as partner-punishing weapons. In a court of law, each crime is assigned a suitable and limited punishment which ends at the expiration of the sentence. In marital unions, too frequently, the punishment for sins is endless. The burial procedure offers an escape from excessive punishment and a change in the state of the marital union.

The next step is the use of the museum list to discover negotiable items of grievance in hierarchical order. Each item may result in the establishment of a beltline or form the basis for a fight for change. The items are considered one at a time, beginning with the one most immediately practical to negotiate. Dealing with the contents of a couple's museum lists starts the process of unloading the emotional garbage that is suffocating the relationship and creating barriers to intimacy.

The *Bill of Rights* is a declaration by each partner to the other of items which the partner feels entitled to and will not allow to be infringed upon. The items are fundamental rights necessary to the feeling of self-respect, self-liking and self-worth, and without which one feels enslaved, used or degraded. Examples would be "The right to spend Saturday afternoon with my parents" or "The right to one evening a week completely alone, or doing whatever I want to do." Dealing with the Bill of Rights is a process of information-giving, self-assertion, confrontation, limitation and negotiation in the implementation of rights.

Autonomous territories are those segmented parts of intimate living in which each partner wants the right of *final decision-making.* These become defined areas of power in a relationship, e.g., a man's business management or a woman's art studio.

The clearinghouse is a daily or weekly pair-specific scheduled exercise in emptying the current gunnysack of grievances. The encounter is negotiated to designate time, place and duration. The purpose is to listen to each other's complaints, grievances and frustrations which arose since the last clearing house. This exercise gives practice in transparency and information-giving. Grievances are aired merely by stating them, with no discussion allowed. The immediate emotional need may be satisfied with the mere statement, or may form the content for further negotiation at a later designated time.

The expectations exercise is a confrontation to expose the reality of the roles one partner assigns to the other. The task is to tell what a partner assumes the other knows, e.g., "I assume that if I go to visit my family out of town, you will take care of my responsibilities for feeding the dog, watering the lawn, etc." After the telling, the information is checked out for "fit."

Mind-reading is a ritual exercise to see how far away one partner is from the being of the other. Positions are first defined, and the task of each partner is to listen to the other. The next step is an exchange of mind-reading: "I think you think . . ." The process becomes a clarification of the living space of each partner, a process of knowing instead of guessing. Mind-reading check-outs determine only the state of knowing or not knowing the other at that particular time, and have no predictive value. The term mind-raping is used for mind-reading without checkout; in other words, acting as if the unchecked assumptions about the partner's attitude are true. In extreme mind-raping, the victim is told what he feels and any protestations to the contrary are denied or ignored.

Trust-testing is a physical exercise giving indication of the trust level at any moment in a relationship. In the exercise called the "Trust Fall," one member of the couple closes his eyes and focuses on his feelings about his partner at that moment. When the partner who faces his back says, "Fall into my arms; you can trust me to catch you; I will not let you fall to the floor . . ." he relaxes his body as much as he can at that moment and falls backward as freely as he can. Then roles are switched. After this physical demonstration, each partner offers the observations he made about the other's fall: What did I notice in your fall? How did I feel falling in your arms? What did I focus on in my preparation to fall? What did I fear most in trusting you? Did you test my physical trust by making me fall a long distance before catching me? etc. The physical demonstration process provides a launching pad for getting in touch with and expressing fears of trusting.

EXERCISES IN CONFRONTATION (IMPACTS)

When partners differ and are in a state of conflict there can be no genuine resolution without aggression. The base of change is authentic communication, open encounter and confrontation. These exercises emphasize the what, when, where and how of being together. They focus on bringing about constructive change. They are interpersonal tasks to achieve an equitable balance between intimate involvement and independence. The goal is behavior modification in the direction of decreasing defensiveness and increasing transparency, explicit communication, assertiveness, and aggressive confrontation.

Fair Fights for Change

The fair fight for change (or "beef" for change in the usual terminology of fight-training groups) is the backbone of the fight-training system. It is not only the most frequently used of the rational exercises in aggressive communication, but also is the exercise which tends to yield more information, more behavior and attitude changes and more bonding capacity than any other.

The beef for change is a communication technique aimed at establishing a process for dealing with any one specific issue. It is a zeroing-in of a single gripe about a specific behavior-pattern with a demand for change by one partner of the other. Like all fight-training procedures, it begins with a request for engagement ("Will you engage in a beef for a change?"), which may be accepted, postponed or rejected. A "*yes*" answer begins the learning process of communication.

The first step is meditation on the exact thought and wording of the request for change. Often, an oral monologue giving background and feelings about the beef, as introduction, helps to clarify the issue. The fight trainer may also have a dialogue with the partner presenting the beef in order to advance the clarification. The partner receiving the beef gains information in this process but is not allowed to respond or comment until the formal presentation.

Once the beef is presented, the fight style focuses on feedback—a verbatim replay of the given message ("I hear you say . . ."). Upon confirmation ("You hear me correctly") that the message given was the message received, the next step is response, which may be agreement to make the requested change, refusal to do so, conditional acceptance, or an alternative suggestion (counteroffer). From this point the negotiation proceeds, with each communication by each partner validated in accuracy by feedback, until agreement or stalemate is reached. In case of stalemate, it is common for a couple to resume the fight with Round Two later in the session, and to try once more to reach agreement after a period of meditation and cooling-off.

Beefs for change are direct practice in eliminating the process of interpretation or "set" in the mind of the message receiver. A message may have to be restated many times before an alienated mate hears it correctly, uncontaminated by his own lacerated feelings of negative expectations and accumulated hurts.

After a beef for change has been successfully negotiated, the agreement—which has now become a *commitment to act*—is sealed by whatever physical expression the couple is able to tolerate at this moment in their relationship, e.g., a handshake, a hug or a kiss. Commitments are further strengthened because they are witnessed by the group. Every commitment to change becomes a part of the homework of the week. The following week's report to the group on assignments determines the reality of the commitment and the extent to which it was carried out. Sometimes a commitment is premature, even though given in good faith. It may then become necessary to retreat to the point of what is actually possible. A renegotiation takes place. In this way commitments are pragmatically tested and information gained.

By the rules, a beef for change must be uncontaminated by the invasion of extraneous, or past, emotional injuries irrelevant to the immediate issue, and misuses are scored for such derailment. This is to prevent the escalation of anger to the point where everything including the kitchen sink is thrown in.

A set of scoring instructions and forms (see Appendix at end of chapter) have been developed which increase the value to group participants of the fair fight for change exercise. Group members scoring a fight have an opportunity to learn to elements of fair fighting by observing the presence or absence of those components in the fight styles of others. More refined feedback can be delivered to the antagonists in the fight by means of the Fight Style Profile.

THE OUTCOME OF FIGHT TRAINING

Methods

A pilot study to get some preliminary indications as to the effects and outcome of the fight training was undertaken as follows: All private-practice couples who had taken fight training during a one-year period between June, 1969 and May, 1970, and who had actively participated together as a pair for no less than eight group training sessions, were identified. This resulted in the selection of 49 pairs who, on the average, attended 12 sessions, and who on the average paid a tuition of $240.00 total for this training.

Two copies of a specially constructed, five-page followup questionnaire "FUQC" for couples were mailed to the 49 couples, which included questions on marital history, extent of therapy, application and evaluation of F.T. after termination and 39 true-false questions relating to attitudes toward acceptance and expression of anger in self and others and descriptions of the condition of the marriage, both before and after F.T. There were a number of open-ended questions on the application of techniques and present status of marriage. About half the replies contained additional comments about the value of the experience and the changes in the individual and in the marriage relationship. Unfortunately, a severe earthquake with over 200 after-tremors occurred a few days after the reception of the questionnaires, and consequently distracted our population, who were victims of the disaster, from filling out research questionnaires. Nevertheless, we were able to determine that nine couples had moved and we were reasonably sure that they had never received the questionnaires—address was unknown. Telephone reminders to the other 40 pairs did succeed in the return of filled-in questionnaires by 15 intact couples; one was sent by a man now separated from his wife, who failed to report, and another was sent by a wife living with her husband, although the husband had refused to fill out the questionnaire on general principles of "invasion of privacy." However, not all respondents answered all the items. All respondents had their last session at least six months ago, and approximately half had terminated during 1969—about a year and a half before this writing. More than half of the respondents were within the 30-to-50 age-range, but included couples in their 20s and a couple over 60 years old.

Outcome Research Results

Qualitative-clinical impressions.—Before any statistical analysis of the results was undertaken, an independent, outside clinical consultant, a veteran professional in the marriage and family counseling field, critically perused the raw data and arrived at the following impressions (Brandzel, 1971):

> All respondents indicated awareness of changes in attitudes, before and after fight training. Changes showed a variance from a low of 4 to a high of 29 changes on 38 test items. More than half the respondents indicated highly consistent changes in terms of accepting anger in themselves and others, no longer believing that marital conflict was destructive or that intimacy was spoiled by fighting, and affirming now that children should be allowed to witness and participate in family fighting.

The various methods by which such changes could be achieved which they had learned in fight training were defined as "listen better; ask for feedback; avoid hooking in; don't walk out on a fight, verbalize anger; avoid past; don't gunnysack; be specific and avoid repetition; use negotiations instead of game playing, participation instead of fight evasion."

Violence or fear of violence was a problem for several trainees before the program, who indicated that they had been aware that "I bring out the killer instinct in my spouse" and that "I fear that my spouse is capable of murdering me." Every trainee who reported fear of violence before fight training changed in these violent attitudes during and after fight training.

The evaluation made from six months to two years after the finish of fight training, indicated that the majority of the trainees felt that the fight training had significantly affected their marriage. Four people checked "not at all," and these were all either separated or considering separation. About one fourth checked "very deeply," and the majority of these were considering separation before the program and were now managing more tolerably.

Perhaps one of the strongest evidences of the value of this program to the participants is their activity in sharing the benefits of fight training with family and friends. One woman wrote:

> Also through our sessions I have gotten our young married daughter and her husband to read your book and helped them with the "style" of fighting. Their life is better because of it.

Those participants who had been considering separation before fight training became strong proselytizers after fight training removed the acute threat of divorce. The ex-separatists listed as many as ten couples to whom they had recommended fight training.

Although the emphasis of the training was on the marital relationship, many reported with satisfaction a sense of personal growth and mastery. For example:

> Fight training has helped me overcome several serious problems which existed between my wife and myself. The

> solution of these problems have allowed me a much better opportunity to concentrate on the real problem area—myself. The time I spent in your groups showed me the direct personal advantages available to *me* when I went through the pain of changing my behavior.

This comment was from a man who had been considering separation and now says: "Fight training changed our whole marriage."

Table 7.1 shows ten attitudes on aggression in marriage on which the vast majority of our subjects changed their position from True to False or False to True, whichever indicated a greater acceptance of the reality of aggression in marriage. The responses are arranged in order of magnitude of *S*s changing in the direction of the fight-training objectives.

The content of the items in Table 7.1 clearly suggests that fight training socializes aggression and makes it an intrinsic-non-shameful part of vital marriage relationships.

Table 7.2 presents the 46 most relevant questions from the 60-item questionnaire with subtotals for husbands and wives. A number of conclusions regarding the effects of fight training can be drawn.

A significant reduction of negative value-judgments and the gaining of *freedom from shame and guilt* for anger and aggression-expressions are reflected in the after fight training unanimity of "False" answers to Items 25 and 43, items which express condemnation and shame. Before F.T. Item 25 had 11 "True" and Item 43 had 16 "True" believers, all of whom reported that F.T. changed their mind from "True" to "False."

On Item 29, "In quarreling, I tend to hurt rather than to learn," the majority answers changed from "True" to "False," showing a differentiation between the *Informant Impact* and the Hurtful *Hostility factors* in aggression.

Peace and quiet as a result of F.T. are no longer considered marks of marital success, as all but 2 of 18 pretraining doves turned into marital "hawks" on Item 32.

A *more realistic acceptance of conflict* as a frequent state in dynamic intimacy is reflected in reductions of "true" answers to Items 21, 23, 24, 33 and 36. Item 23, "I go along pleasing my spouse to avoid conflict," changed from 18 "Trues" before F.T. to 7 after F.T. and there was a concomitant reduction in "False" answers to items 40, 41, 42 and especially 51; "Children should be allowed to witness and participate in their parents' fights": 27 "False" before F.T., 8 "False" after F. T., 3 "True" before F.T., 21 "True" after F.T.

Table 7.1
The Ten Most Significant Attitude Changes Before and After Fight Training
N = 32 17 Couples—16 Males, 16 Females

(Only one respondent for two couples)

F.U.Q.C. Question Number	F.U.Q.C. ITEM
56	I can recognize and accept the aggressive tendencies in myself.
29	In quarreling, I tend to hurt rather than learn.
33	Most of our marital fights and quarrels are irrational and destructive.
37	The joys of affectionate intimacy are spoiled by fighting.
58	I accept anger in those close to me.
49	In my marriage I feel it is unnecessary to make explicit demands because my spouse will sense what is needed.
51	Children should be allowed to witness and participate in their parents' fights.
32	I believe that peace and quiet are the marks of a successful marriage.
54	Our family quarrels are destructive to my family life.
43	I feel ashamed of being hostile toward my beloved.

The *bonding* (as distinguished from the alienating) possiblities of aggressive confrontations were more clearly acknowledged (after F.T.) by significant changes in answers to Items 37 and 55, "After a fight with my spouse I feel closer;" one answered "True" before F.T., 13 "True" after F.T. However, while trainees may learn how to fight fair and learn to accept aggression as a realistic necessity, they *do not really enjoy* aggressive encounters. For example, almost half of our trainees—after F.T.—still fear,

Table 7.2
Responses to Followup Questionnaire After Fight Training

14 After discontinuing fight training at either the University or the Institute, have you practiced at home what you learned in class and/or private consultations?

Yes 23 No 7

15. How helpful have you found these at-home applications of the fight-training program?

Somewhat helpful 15 Not helpful 2 Extremely helpful 10

16. How deeply did what you learned in fight training affect your marriage?

Very deeply 8 Significantly 16 Not affected at all 5

17. How permanent or fleeting do you feel these training effects are?

Permanent 15 O.K. for a period of time 11 Very fleeting 6

18. I frequently threatened to leave my spouse:

Before F.T. Yes 10 No 22
After F.T. Yes 6 No 26

19. To the extent that fight training made any difference in your marriage, were the changes effected:

For the better 26 For the worse 2 No difference 4

20. Have you encouraged other couples to try the Fair Fight System?

Yes 24 No 7
If "Yes," how may couples? 6 (average)

Table 7.2 (Continued)

Following are a few statements about married life. Please check them as *True* or *False* as they applied to your marriage *before* and *after* you participated in fight training (F.T.)

	BEFORE F.T.					AFTER F.T.			
	Total	F-M True	F-M False	Total		Total	F-M True	F-M False	Total
21.	10	6–4	10–8	18	I try to avoid conflict and quarrels.	14	4–10	10–2	12
22.	16	10–6	6–10	16	I yell and whip abusive words at my spouse.	14	6–8	9–8	17
23.	18	9–9	6–7	13	I go along pleasing my spouse to avoid conflict.	7	4–3	11–13	24
24.	28	14–14	2–2	4	After quarreling or fighting, I feel depressed.	14	8–6	8–9	17
25.	11	3–8	13–8	21	I think that it is wrong for spouses to fight at all.	0	0–0	16–16	32
26.	12	5–7	10–9	19	I avoid criticizing my spouse directly.	8	4–4	11–12	23
27.	10	5–5	11–11	22	Our sex life is very enjoyable and mutually fulfilling.	11	6–5	10–10	20
28.	6	5–1	9–15	24	I welcome, rather than fear, a critical confrontation.	14	8–6	6–9	15
29.	28	14–14	2–2	4	In quarreling, I tend to hurt rather than learn.	8	4–4	12–11	23
30.	23	9–14	6–2	8	I avoid bringing up unpleasant, potentially hurtful subjects.	13	5–8	10–9	19

31.	14	7–7	9–10	19	I accept my anger and frustration with my spouse.	21	10–11	5–6	11
32.	18	6–12	8–4	12	I believe that peace and quiet are the marks of a successful marriage.	2	1–1	15–15	30
33.	27	14–13	2–3	5	Most of our marital fights and quarrels are irrational and destructive.	7	6–1	10–15	25
34.	20	10–10	4–5	9	Outbursts of aggression and hostility are signs of troubles and have no serious place in my marriage.	4	2–2	13–13	26
35.	11	6–5	9–11	20	I am seriously considering divorcing my spouse.	5	1–4	14–12	26
36.	20	7–13	8–2	10	I avoid argument (confrontation) for peace's sake.	9	3–6	12–9	21
37.	25	14–11	1–3	4	The joys of affectionate intimacy are spoiled by fighting.	8	3–5	12–10	22
38.	4	2–2	15–13	28	Making up after a fight is so delightful, it is worth the pain of a conflict.	6	0–6	12–9	21
39.	9	6–3	9–9	18	Fair fighting increases my capacity for enjoying intimate affections.	25	12–13	3–1	4
40.	15	9–6	4–6	10	My marriage, even though filled with conflict, is worth the commitment.	20	11–9	2–2	2

Table 7.2 (Continued)

	BEFORE F.T.					AFTER F.T.			
	Total	F-M True	F-M False	Total		Total	F-M True	F-M False	Total
41.	8	5–3	10–12	22	I do not mind my married friends fighting in my presence.	19	9–10	6–6	12
42.	4	1–3	15–11	26	I am not afraid to get involved in the marital quarrels of my friends.	14	8–6	8–9	17
43.	16	9–7	7–7	14	I feel ashamed of being hostile towards my beloved.	0	0–0	16–16	32
44.	15	7–8	9–7	16	Our marital fighting is a sign that one or both of us is neurotic.	6	3–3	13–13	26
45.	27	14–13	1–6	7	Our kind of fighting spoils good loving.	16	9–7	6–8	14
46.	29	14–15	0–0	0	The giving and taking of love must be reciprocal.	28	14–14	0–2	2
47.	23	14–9	0–5	5	Quarreling spoils good sex for me.	16	9–7	5–8	13

48.	15	9–6	7–8	15	I know intuitively how my spouse feels; I can read his/her mind.	6	4–2	12–14	26
49.	16	8–8	6–7	13	In my marriage I feel it is unnecessary to make explicit demands because my spouse will sense what I need.	0	0–0	15–16	31
50.	23	13–10	1–4	5	My areas of responsibility and competence are clearly different from my spouse's.	22	13–9	2–6	8
51.	3	2–1	13–14	27	Children should be allowed to witness and participate in their parents' fights.	21	13–8	2–7	9
52.	4	2–2	13–12	25	I bring out the killer instinct in my spouse, so we totally avoid fighting.	0	0–0	15–15	30
53.	4	3–1	11–12	23	I fear that my spouse is capable of murdering me.	4	3–1	12–13	25
54.	23	12–11	2–2	4	Our family quarrels are destructive to my family life.	8	4–4	11–11	22
55.	1	0–1	15–14	29	After a fight with my spouse we feel closer.	13	5–8	10–8	18

Table 7.2 (Continued)

	BEFORE F.T.					AFTER F.T.			
	Total	F-M True	F-M False	Total		Total	F-M True	F-M False	Total
56.	8	3–5	13–9	22	I can recognize and accept the aggressive tendencies in myself.	30	15–15	1–1	2
57.	18	12–6	4–9	13	I am very fearful when my spouse gets angry at me.	6	4–2	12–14	26
58.	8	4–4	10–11	21	I accept anger in those close to me.	26	12–14	3–2	5
59.	1	0–1	16–14	30	Our arguments are brief and to the point.	15	9–6	7–10	17

rather than welcome, a critical confrontation (see Item 28). Even after F.T. 13 spouses (mostly males) still try to avoid conflicts (Item 21). Only 20 percent of our respondents to Item 38 find the delight of making up worth the pains of conflict. Even after F.T. people feel depressed after quarreling or fighting, although the number of spouses checking "True" before F.T. (28 respondents) was reduced to 14 after F.T. on Item 24. And for nearly half of our fight-trained spouses, quarreling still tends to spoil their erotic pleasures, especially for the females (Item 47).

Turning to *differences between the sexes,* our data seem to reflect a clinically observable resistance to change and a slower learning of how to fight fair on the part of males. Males initially also tend to be more obviously fight-evasive and more conflict-phobic than the females. Does this reflect perhaps a popular male chauvinism: that only a coward would fight with a woman? In any case, the females in our fight classes seem to enjoy it more and learn somewhat faster than their male mates.

Significant sex differences were expressed in conflict *avoidance* (Items 21 and 28) where only 4 to 6 males reported any change of position. Fewer males became more tolerant about letting the children in on marital fighting (Item 51).

On the other hand, all but one of the husbands changed their *psychiatric stereotype evaluations* from "True" to "False" on Item 22; "marital fights are irrational and destructive," while 6 of their wives remained traditional on this.

Item 35, "I am seriously considering divorcing my spouse;": of the 6 wives checking "True" before F.T., 5 gave up *planning divorce,* but 4 of the 5 husbands still considered divorcing their wives even after F.T. This male ambivalence reflects perhaps on exit-fight-phobia suffered by husbands who really want to get out but "do not want to hurt the wife and the children." Such husbands may accommodate a wife's last-ditch effort to save their marriage through fight training. They may go along with their wives, not to save the marriage, but rather to find a smoother exit without provoking legal, economic and psychological penalties.

Except for the sex difference noted above, both sexes participated equally in the changes instigated by their participation in fight training.

Table 7.3 gives the depth of aftereffects, which showed a range from 0 for Couple No. 9 to 16 for Couples No. 15 and No. 4 on the

"Impact Index." A respondent earned one or two points on the impact index for appropriate responses on 7 items on F.U.Q.C., namely, Item 14 through 19 plus Item 60.

For example, the two high-scoring couples, No. 15 and No. 4, earned their high-score answers as follows: "yes" on 14; "extremely helpful" on 15; "very deeply" on 16; "permanent" on 17; change from "yes" to "no" on 18; "for the better" on 19; and "yes," they encouraged more than six couples (the average) to try the fair-fight system.

A study of Table 7.2 reveals a clear, although not perfect *correlation* between the intensity and *duration of fight training* on the one hand and the depth of its aftereffects as measured by the Impact Index on the other. The eight couples with the highest

Table 7.3
Depth of Aftereffects of Fight Training

N = 32 17 Couples—16 Males, 16 Females
(Only one responded for Couples No. 9 and 10)

Couple I.D. Number	Impact *Index* Mean Per: 8.1 pair	Male	Female	Weeks Fight Training	Supplementary Therapy
15	16	8	8	24	yes
4	16	8	8	24	yes
5	14	6	8	13	yes
13	13	7	6	13	yes
12	10	5	5	13	no
2	10	4	6	24	no
8	9	7	2	13	no
14	8	4	4	20	yes
3	8	4	4	13	no
17	8	4	4	12	no
10	7	no response	7	12	no
1	7	3	4	8	no
6	6	3	3	8	no
11	6	3	3	13	no
7	5	2	3	8	no
16	5	4	1	12	no
9	0	0	no response	10	no

Impact Index each had from 13 to 24 weeks of F.T. with an average of 16 weeks of training, while the nine couples with below-average aftereffects participated in a mean number of 10.6 weeks, which is 3 weeks short of the recommended minimum of 13 weeks.

A factor which confounds the evaluation of the depth of aftereffects of the fight-training proper is that in five out of the eight couples with above average aftereffects, at least one spouse participated in group-therapeutic programs beyond and after completing fight training. In contrast, only one of the nine couples with shallower aftereffects had therapy experience beyond the fight training. When interviewed, the four couples with the deepest aftereffects—Couples No. 15, 4, 5 and 13—reported that the fight-training course stimulated an individual growth-process for each spouse. Several of them wanted to "boost" that growth-beginning through further group therapy. All maintained that the additional group therapy was *not* focused on their marital interpersonal relationships but that, unlike the fight training, the subsequent therapy was primarily an individual development for the particular person involved in it.

Several of the low-aftereffect couples remarked that they regretted now not to have completed or expanded their fight training.

SUMMARY AND CONCLUSIONS

A therapeutic educational course for couples to re-shape and socialize their marital battles was developed by the author under the label of Fair Fight Training.

A theoretical model of the constructive communication functions of aggression is presented together with interpersonal parameters, which are assumed to be influenced by aggression.

The model differentiates between hurt-directed hostilities, including irrational violence, and useful, information-productive, impactful aggression.

The fair fight training system provides hostility rituals to discharge and control hate and anger. Differentiated from these hate rituals are procedures for "Fights for Change" or "Impacts." Impacts are aggressive, but rational confrontations to influence a partner to change his or her behavior pattern or attitudes. Both rituals and impact exercises are practiced in groups of from four to eight couples under the guidance of a "Fight Trainer" or "Coach." While one couple fights it out, the others learn how to "score" the fight for style rather than content. The scoring sheet differentiates eleven fight styles, each having a "foul" or "alienating," and a "fair" or "bonding," polarity. Thirteen four-hour weekly sessions are required by the average couple to master most of the fair fight techniques.

Followup reports by 32 spouses who had completed fight training 6 to 20 months ago reveal that 11 showed significant changes in their attitude towards and management of aggression and family conflict. The depth of learning was, however, dependent upon the length of the training and perhaps also on supplementary group therapy (Bach, 1954).

It is the author's conclusion from the above results that during fight training, couples first use the fair fight techniques rather pedantically. This proves to be a transitory learning aid which eventually is abandoned as each pair evolves their own fight styles. The simple and programmed techniques that they have learned open up the couples' spontaneous creativity concerning conflict management patterns which become very pair-specific.

Marital fight-training techniques can be applied to whole families, to dating partners (Bach & Deutsch, 1970), to interpersonal relationships in offices, classrooms and other face-to-face groups concerned with internal conflict management.

The possibility of a mass education program for the constructive usage of aggression suggests itself as a hope for the effective control and prevention of violence in families and in the community at large.

REFERENCES

The following colleagues aided in the admittedly small and incomplete but intensive followup research reported here: Yetta Bernhard, Rose Brandzel, James Elias and Herbert Goldberg.

While this chapter was drafted specifically for the inclusion in this book, some brief sections are reproduced from another current publication by permission of the copyright holder:

Bach, G. with Bernard, Y. *Aggression-lab: the fair fight training manuel.* Dubuque: Kendall-Hunt Publishers, 1971.

Bach, G.R. *Intensive group psychotherapy.* New York: Ronald Press, 1954.

Bach, G.R. Marathon group dynamics: I. Some functions of the professional group facilitator. *Psychological Reports,* 1967a, **20,** 995–999.

Bach, G.R. Marathon group dynamics: II. Dimensions of helpfulness: Therapeutic aggression. *Psychological Reports,* 1967b, **20,** 1147–1158. 1147–1158.

Bach, G.R. Marathon group dynamics: III. Disjunctive contacts. *Psychological Reports,* 1967c, **20,** 1163–1172.

Bach, G.R. & Wyden, P. *The intimate enemy.* New York: William Morrow, 1968; New York: Avon, 1970.

Bach, G.R. & Deutsch, R. *Pairing.* New York: Peter Wyden, 1970; Avon, 1971.

Bach, G.R. *Feminine wiles are masculine.* Paper presented at the meeting of the California State Psychological Association, January, 1971.

Brandzel, R. Symposium on group psychotherapies presented at the meeting of the Rush Research Foundation, Beverly Hills, California, 1971.

APPENDIX

Figure 7.1 Sample Instructions for Scoring Fair Fight For Change

How to Score a Fair Fight for Change

The fair fight style profile includes both the positive and negative elements in eight dimensions of aggressive confrontation. Although all dimensions are seldom represented in any one fight, each of these elements signifies an aspect of communication that is essential in a fair fight at some point. The purpose of "scoring" a couple's fight style is heuristic; students can learn the elements of fair fighting in the process of recording the presence or absence of these elements in their own or another pair's fight style.

Study the following definitions with examples before attempting to score a fight:

1. Realistic, authentic involvement: The fair fight issue includes the expression of a real issue of concern to the one who has the beef. This involved concern, moreover, is met with a similar realistic involvement on the part of the partner in a "good" fair fight.

versus

Irreal, phony, disengaged behavior: When either the issue or the attitudes of one or both partners suggests a shallow or "gamelike" quality, the negative aspect of this dimension is scored.

EXAMPLE: On the enclosed sample "fair fight style profile" for Jim and Nancy (J. and N.), you will see that while N's issue was real and her involvement was authentic, J's behavior was seen as disengaged by the scorer. *Please note* that this comment and all subsequent ones are made to illustrate the fight style of this couple in one particular round, and there is no intention to suggest that one partner is "better" or "fairer" as a fighter.

2. Specificity and responsibility:	The person with the beef is initially responsible for being specific, direct, and clear in the expression of both the complaint and the demand for change. The one with the beef is also responsible for eliciting full and accurate feedback and for correcting any misstatements of the complaint or demand by the partner. Both fighters are responsible for clearly admitting their feelings during the course of the fight, and for admitting the reality of something they are accurately accused of doing.

versus

Vague generalities and evasion:	Whenever a fight partner makes a statement that the scorer believes is either indirect or unclear or seems to evade the full admission of feelings or behavior, this dimension is scored negatively.

EXAMPLE: According to the sample fight style profile for J. and N. both partners made two evasive statements, although N. was scored positively for being specific in her statement of the "beef" and J. was scored positively for being clear in his rebuttal.

3. Humor: the element of joy:	Both partners are encouraged to lighten the seriousness of the fight encounter with appropriate, pair-specific humor.

versus

Derisive sarcasm or ridicule:	Neither partner is permitted to put down the other with the use of hostile humor.

EXAMPLE: Both J. and N. made some attempt at positive humor, although the scorer recorded one example of N's sarcasm in this fight.

Figure 7.2

FAIR FIGHT STYLE PROFILED

	PARTNERS
J	Jim
N	Nancy

SCORE: +5

	1	2	3	4	5	6	7	8
	Realistic Authentic Involvement	Specificity and Responsibility	Humor (joyous)	Feedback (accurate)	Time Perspective (here and now)	Partner Watching (checked)	"Crazymaking" (confront)	Change Readiness (open)
17 + (plus)	N. N.	N. (beef) N. (demand) J. (rebuttal)	J.	J. J. J. N. N. N.	J. N. N.	J. (con- fronted)		J. ↑
− (minus) 12	J. (disengaged at outset)	N. J. } evasive N. } about J. } feelings	N. ("dumb")	J. N. editing		N. N. ⟲ J.		J.
	Irreal Phony Disengaged	Vagueness Generality Evasion	Sarcasm or Ridicule	Biased Distorted Missing	List or Museum	Unchecked Private Attributions	"Crazymakers" Collusion	Resistive (closed)

8. Learning Village: Positive Control in a Group Situation

Marilyn S. Arnett
C. Richard Spates
Roger E. Ulrich

Learning Village is a corner of a Skinnerian Utopia developed as a private school. Contingency Contracting, a formula for specifying expected academic and social behaviors to students, as well as the rewards available for task completion, is the guiding educational principle of the Learning Village culture.

Education is conceptualized as a lifespan process, and the schooling of pupils begins as early as two months of age. The approach of Learning Village is truly preventative. The authors argue that children uneducated or miseducated in the first five years of life pose almost insurmountable problems to the orthodox school system. The failure of such children, who are found predominantly, although not exclusively among the poor, to further master the cultural symbol system denies these children access to the rewards of the social system.

The attempts of Learning Village to interrupt this chain of academic failure are very promising. For example, the kindergarten group at Learning Village is reported to be reading above the second-grade level in terms of national norms, in spite of the fact that half of the group are from poverty backgrounds.

Two additional features should be noted in conclusion. First, the teachers in the program include college and high school students as well as the students themselves. Elementary school children serve as teachers in an infant program and become skilled in behavioral teaching methodology. Second, the transmission of social values, and the inculcation of such appropriate social behavior as cooperation, empathy, overt affectionate behavior and honesty are imbedded in the curriculum.

THE EVOLUTION

Historically, psychologists have concerned themselves with the study of abnormal behavior and some forms of assessment, usually in settings like state hospitals, clinics and retardation centers, and occasionally in the special education division of a public school system. Sometimes one might be found in affiliation with the Guidance and Counseling department in a high school, but this generally entails only the dissemination of vocational and occupational information for students. For the most part, it is not extremely clear that these positions have been the most strategic with respect to the needs of the culture or the professional training of the psychologist involved.

If we look around us, it becomes readily apparent that a state of crisis is upon us. One does not have to look far or long to observe the many social ills with which we are faced, i.e., unemployment, racism, juvenile delinquency, mental illness, etc. To the degree that these problems threaten the very existence of the culture, it would seem of paramount importance that our attention be focused along these dimensions. Anyone who purports to concern himself with human interaction in general and the study of behavior in particular, can no longer ignore these areas of human conduct. In the words of Dr. George Albee, "If professional psychologists were truly concerned with human welfare, we could forget "psychiatric patients" for a century and turn our attention to the psychological causes of racism, sexism, and the profit motive as sources of danger to the human centered life [Albee, 1970, p. 1074]." While it is both unrealistic and impractical to think of completely turning our backs on the "psychiatric patient," it is highly feasible that we should make attempts at preventing their creation. It is along these lines that the field of early childhood education offers exceptional promise.

When broadly defined, education begins at birth and continues throughout a lifetime, with each experience adding to an individual's education and having some effect on his future actions. When a child fails to learn symbols and their sounds, he is very likely to fail at reading. Low achievement in reading results in a likelihood of failure in other subjects, which in today's society means he is inadequately prepared to achieve success in life. The occurence of this vicious chain of educational failure begins at a very early age. Once the chain has begun, it is particularly difficult to intercede in any meaningful way that allows the child to achieve success in learning and thus afford him those experiences that could make life in today's society more rewarding. It might be added that this is a situation that is not encountered by the poor alone, but that extends beyond all social, racial and economic boundaries. An educationally neglected child is unfortunate regardless of his parents' income.

The educational system is faced with the serious challenge not only of educating the nation's children once they reach school age, but at the same time of counteracting the results of the five years of training accumulated prior to beginning his official education. The results of early failure followed by perpetual failure can range from withdrawal and resignation to open hostility. The child is forced to relinquish the goals predominant in society. Unable to find achievement and self-esteem in the socially acceptable learning situation, he turns to other behaviors, many of which are clearly unacceptable to, and often actively punished by, society. Many of this country's most costly social problems could be alleviated through more satisfactory educational systems (Behavior Development Corporation, 1970).

The concept of prevention is not unusual in many fields and in fact has become routine procedure in the field of medicine, as exemplified by regular physical examinations and immunizations. Although it is fashionable within mental-health circles to talk about the concept of prevention, it must be conceded that the actual manifestation of this verbal behavior is very limited. If, by the methods to be discussed later in this paper, it is possible to structure the environments of individuals so that the result is a population with dramatically reduced behavior problems, it can legitimately be said that prevention has taken place (Ulrich, Wolfe & Cole, 1970). It is in this vein that the fields of mental health and education can no longer trod along as separate and distinct entities, but must join hands in an effort to remedy what is ostensibly a crisis situation.

Admittedly one who is possessed with ideas such as these is in trouble. The difficulties in setting up programs designed to meet the needs of the culture while concurrently involving various kinds of professional agencies, seem to be at times insurmountable. Many of the problems encountered during the establishment of the Learning Village have been outlined by Wolfe, Ulrich & Ulrich (1970). The acquisition of suitable physical space for the school was complicated by the necessity for satisfying city, county, state and federal regulations for day care centers and schools, as well as a host of other frustrations. However, the difficulties were eventually overcome, and we could turn attention to program development, our major concern.

PROGRAM INTRODUCTION

The field of elementary and nursery education had been entered, as a program under the auspices of the Behavior Development Corporation, and the Learning Village project began.

The Learning Village concept is longitudinal in nature. The purpose is to accelerate and enhance the development of children by applying scientifically sound educational practices as soon after birth as feasible and by continuing such application until the child leaves the system. The structure of this program is deliberate: designed to insure the development of children who read and write well, who think well, who can make the most of their environment and who love themselves and their fellow man.

It is the people who make the Learning Village work, both staff and students as well as parents and advisory personnel. Although the training and educational programs for all participating individuals will be treated later, a few words concerning the population is relevant at this time. One objective was to achieve a racially and economically balanced population. In this way, social and academic interaction could be shaped in relation to various types of people, regardless of the type of clothing they wear, the color of their skin, their verbal modes of expression and other variables that have usually been considered "different." As the children are about 50 percent black and 50 percent white, the teaching and administrative personnel are also mixed racially. The children range from 2 months to 11 years of age; although their academic performance determines in which learning group they are included, the general age breakdown is as follows: the 2-month to 2 1/2-year age-group comprises the Infant Program, the 2 1/2 to 4 1/2-year age-group comprises the Nursery Program and the 4 1/2 to 11-year age-group comprises the Elementary Program. As the children are mixed agewise, so are the staff. Many teachers and administrators are at various academic levels, drawn from Western Michigan University's student population, local high school population, some dropouts and parents. Those who have degrees range from high school diplomas to Ph.D. While parental involvement is talked about as a necessity for this type of program, the Learning Village boasts unusual parental involvement, with as many as 41 percent of its staff made up of parents of the students attending.

Children attend the Learning Village all day and year round. A substantial portion of the children's time in school is spent learning academic material. The amount of the time in that area, therefore, is unusual in comparison to traditional educational practices. This type of arrangement is gaining support, however, as shown in the recommendations by the Westinghouse Learning Corporation (1969) in its report, *The Impact of Head Start.* Also, as they recommend, the Learning Village is structured with a heavy emphasis on teaching necessary skills with a special preschool program that extends downward into infancy and upward into the primary grades.

The basis upon which the Learning Village was founded and upon which it operates can be summarized in the following five statements of ideals (Behavior Development Corporation, 1970):

1. Education can never begin too early.
2. When children fail in school, the fault lies with the educational system, not with the children.
3. Education, to be effective in the twentieth century, must include more than the traditional "3-R's." Our children must learn a compassion for fellow man, a respect for the environment, an understanding of human behavior, a knowledge of the need for social change, a love of learning, and a respect for one's self.
4. Education should not involve physical punishment nor the constant threats, reprimands, and general unpleasantness encountered in school and home. Learning can be, and is, fun when educational

systems are so devised that children often experience success and a joy of accomplishment.

5. The only way our present generation can *constructively* contribute to the future of mankind is through proper emphasis on the education of our youth.

The Learning Village has been in operation for only one and one-half years in what may be termed "full swing," although many of the children currently enrolled were participants in the various transient programs mentioned above (Wood, Ulrich & Fullmer, 1969). Assessment, therefore, has just begun. Since the program is longitudinal in nature, many of the results will not be available for some time—particularly in relation to the infants, as there are very few evaluative or diagnostic measures available for this age group. Anecdotal information received from teachers, parents and visitors, as well as some test data, suggests that the academic behaviors of the students at the Learning Village have indeed been accelerated. At the same time, the children appear to be happy and well-adjusted. The undesired emotional behaviors and impeded development predicted as the result of infant day care and the instruction of young children has not been observed. Parents and teachers have reported no incidents of excessive tantrum behaviors or regression to behaviors such as bedwetting or thumbsucking. Instead, they are amazed by the gaiety, spontaneity and sophistication of the students at the Village.

As mentioned earlier, many of our parents are also teachers (both certificated and noncertificated). A recent interview of the mothers yielded the following results to the question, "In general, how satisfied are you that X is in the Learning Village?" Of all the mothers, 58 percent were very satisfied, 39.8 percent satisfied and 1.5 percent not satisfied. Of the nonstaff mothers, 60 percent were very satisfied, 37.5 percent satisfied and 2.5 percent not satisfied. Of just the staff-member mothers, 52 percent were very satisfied, 48 percent satisfied and 0 percent not satisfied. According to these data, then, the majority of parents are pleased with their child's involvement. Comments also generated by this interview revealed little, if any, aversion to the methods employed for children as young as one year and as old as ten years.

A battery of tests according to a systematic evaluation program is currently being administered. These include areas of academic achievement, perceptual and motor development, intelligence and social maturity. Data collected via the Wide Range Achievement Test (WRAT) on the Elementary level indicated mean reading level for children from 7 years 8 months to 12 years 2 months at the 8.2 grade-level with the range extending from 5.1 to 11.7 grade-levels. Kindergarten children on the same test who range agewise from 4 years 11 months to 7 years 1 month achieved a mean score of 2.6 grade-level (reading). One half of these children are clearly from poverty backgrounds and have received financial assistance through our scholarship program. A recently administered (March, 1971) Gates-Macginite reading test placed these now first-grade children even higher in terms of achievement, sometimes as great as two grade levels above previous scores. Other data presently being collected should support the contention that academic behaviors are being accelerated. In fact, one child of an extremely deprived home environment (V on the Hollingshead Social Position Index) is currently at the top of her class.

It should be noted that the major emphasis of our evaluation program is not to prove or disprove that systematic usage of principles of behavior based on reinforcement theory are effective, but rather to: (1) specify special areas of remediation, (2) aid in development of structure and relevant curricula and (3) disseminate information (feedback) to those persons directly responsible for modifying behaviors. These tests do, of course, by their very nature provide a standard of comparison with other children under "normal" circumstances.

WHY POSITIVE CONTROL?

Before delving into the actual structure of the Learning Village program and the plans for its expansion, it seems appropriate to discuss the merits of positive control. This may best be introduced by discussing the various side effects produced by using aversive control techniques.

As part of our intention to maintain close contact with research, many of the staff of the Behavior Research and Development Center (of which the Learning Village is a part) are engaged in basic research in the area of aversive control techniques, especially in relation to aggression. Because of the nature of such scientific inquiry, it is often deemed necessary to rely on the infrahuman subject to tell us more about aversive stimulus properties, of both an eliciting and a consequential nature. As part of a conference on the nature of schedule-induced and scheduled-dependent phenomena, Ulrich, Dulaney, Kucera & Colasacco (1970) reviewed the recent data and presented a summary of conclusions that relate to the side effects of aversive control. They are as follows:

First, aversive stimuli produce aggression. When pain is present in the environment, the occurrence of unconditioned pain-aggression reactions must not be unemphasized. Second, environments or events frequently associated with pain can produce aggression (the familiar classical conditioning model).

This could lend an explanation as to why apparently "unprovoked" aggression accurs, due to prior association with a currently supposedly neutral stimulus. Because of the possibilities of association with an aggression producing event, behavior modifiers using aversion-therapy techniques could become conditioned aggression-producing stimuli themselves. Third, aggressive behavior can produce more aggressive behavior due to the interaction between shaped aggression which can produce enough pain, via attack, to elicit unconditioned aggression. Therefore, when methods used to control another organism's behavior are aggressive (associated with delivering aversive stimulation to another organism) the possibility of counteraggression should be expected, again probably of the more unconditioned nature. Accordingly, a fourth issue suggests that if aversive control is used to maintain operant behavior (as in escape or avoidance) the unconditioned pain-aggression reactions may interfere with the subject's performance. This, of course, is dependent on many factors including the current contingencies in operation, the subject's history, response criterion, etc. Finally when aversive control is used to suppress aggression, other behaviors can occur that make such practices inadvisable.

Based on the data, then, how advisable is it to use such measures? Under a punishment contingency for every aggressive response, Ulrich, Wolfe & Dulaney (1969) reported that at least on initial sessions, the punishment actually facilitated aggression. Controlling an organism in this situation might therefore be dependent on how big he is physically. Although later sessions of this same procedure did suppress the biting of a rubber hose in front of the subject, he exhibited other rather peculiar behaviors including self-abusive behavior (finger-biting, face-clawing, side-biting, etc.) or a general freezing of the posture. In a human situation, these types of behaviors could be more detrimental than the original behavior one was attempting to suppress. Although data regarding the effects of intermittent punishment are somewhat scarce, it appears as if it is generally ineffective at suppressing biting behavior and may in some instances facilitate it. Punishing such responses occasionally, then, may have little or no control over the behavior and should be discarded where possible. In a situation where the subject has an alternative aggressive response, when the original preferred response was punished, the alternative response increased greatly and the pattern of the aggression was disrupted. This, too, is a very serious consideration when using punishment, as perhaps subsequent aggression could be directed toward an innocent victim. Each of these considerations should be taken seriously and extreme caution concerning use of aversive control is suggested by these findings.

We have emphasized thus far how aggression is a most notable byproduct of aversive control measures. Other notable characteristics are escape or avoidance upon availability of a response opportunity, as in the example of the truant schoolchild. In any event, it seems necessary to proceed in constructing a learning environment free from such side effects. To illustrate this point further, let's take a look as some existing social situations.

The college campus is a location of many encounters across this country (as well as others). Campus protest, sometimes referred to "student unrest," was met head-on with a barrage of tear gas and clubs. This form of therapy, if you will, reached its climax during the spring of 1970 when on the campuses of Kent State University and Jackson State College (as only two examples) students lost their lives as a result of a punishment-of-aggression procedure. Following in the footsteps of the early freedom riders, many student marches were suppressed by these actions, and regrettably so. From casual observations, there seems recently to be a very sharp increase in the number of bombings or threat of bombings. A significant time-period rarely elapses without UPI or AP reporting some type of public building or private corporation building sabotaged. The solution to this problem (as usual) will continue to be very costly, requiring the aid of more expertly trained law-enforcement agencies (perhaps the military) or invention of new gadgetry for crowd control, the loss of more lives as well as the accompanying loss of property, valued so dearly by this culture. But, what are the alternative solutions, based on techniques derived from the experimental analysis of behavior?

Possible methods for reducing human aggression, then, lie in the reduction of the aversive stimuli that cause it or consequences that shape and maintain it. Although it is clearly impossible to eliminate all aversive events from our environment, there are still many such stimuli which are needlessly produced by our society. A proliferation of examples can be found in our slums whose inhabitants are more often hungry, cold and hurt than other members of society. In addition, much of their socially acceptable behavior is met by aversive consequences, as in attempting to find a job or a better home, when they are often met with social rejection from which they escape by discontinuing the search for an advanced position. Indeed, the lack of opportunity by many of our citizens to obtain the positive reinforcers common to others is perhaps aversive enough to cause aggression. It is no wonder that the rate of violent or overly aggressive criminal acts is higher in slums than elsewhere.

These illustrations, as examples, are extrapolations from the experimental analysis of behavior to the group social situation. It is the serious nature of the present societal contingencies, which have little regard for careful programming techniques, that has turned the attention of the "hopefuls," such as ourselves, toward the youth. If aversive stimuli can be reduced, so can the unwanted byproducts. If fire is not used to put out fire (punishment of aggression), displaced aggression will not result. If more cooperation and less competition occurs, then less difficulty in all social situations will result. Such is the basis of the elimination, or near elimination, of aversive control techniques at the Learning Village. To recall an earlier point, our children must learn a compassion for their fellow men, a respect for the environment, an understanding of human behavior, a knowledge of the need for social change, a love of learning and a respect for one's self. This will not be learned through coercion.

A POSITIVE CONTROL METHODOLOGY

Pyramid Instruction

The initial step toward reaching our ideal is the provision of consistent positive behavior-modifiers to serve as contingency managers or teachers. The use of high school and college students as teachers in the Village increases the usually minimal involvement of the student in the educational process and could serve as a model to revolutionize education. If effective teaching behavior can be developed by means of communication of behavioral teaching methodology, as it has been demonstrated at the Learning Village and elsewhere (Ulrich & Kent, 1970), the gap segregating the teacher and learner will close. The training program itself is pyramidal, the more experienced always coaching the less experienced from college and high school to junior high, to elementary school, etc. Even our elementary children teach in the Infant Program as part of a course in reinforcement theory. Such training is primarily "on-the-job," although occasional "refresher" inservice training courses are provided. It is the Learning Village philosophy that we are in a perpetual training situation and if the trainee is not successful, the trainer is not either. Practically, this system also reduces personnel costs and affords the student to experience a "real world" situation.

Departmentalization

As distinct from the traditional classroom, the Learning Village is departmentalized: that is to say, structured according to subject matter. This relieves one teacher from the chore of preparing (often inadequately) multisubject lesson plans which sometimes demand various different teaching strategies. Under departmentalized conditions, each teacher becomes a specialist in his area, better able to organize logical presentations. Most important, however, a student may progress at differing rates for differing subjects—a truly individualized instructional program while maintaining a high degree of teacher interaction.

Nine departments comprise the Village program: Reading, Mathematics, Language Arts, Science, Art, Music, Physical Education, Basic Skills and Social Studies. Objectives are defined for each department and prerequisites are outlined for each course. Basic skills primarily make up the curriculum of the Infant Program level and other basic skills for the Nursery Program are considered prerequisite for nearly all other departments. The department head and staff specify these objectives and prerequisites as well as examine and develop new teaching techniques and materials, and organize inservice training and teacher evaluation.

Curriculum materials used in each departmental organization will not be further treated here, but a closer inspection of the Social Studies Department's stated objectives should be related. Typically, classes in social studies have been concerned with a collection of facts, such as, our legislature is made up of two bodies, a House and a Senate; or, coffee beans are a major export of Brazil. Social Studies at the Learning Village, however, is concerned with teaching children how to have successful, happy social interactions with others. Some of the effects of inappropriate social behavior are exemplified in class by current problems such as divorce rates, crime rates, etc. A major job of the Social Studies Department is to identify both desirable and undesirable social behaviors and to arrange conditions such that the former are learned while the latter are extinguished. Traditional materials are only used when they are relevant to developing social attitudes of value to the society and/or to the individual. To date, the following categories of desirable behaviors have been established: cooperation, which includes sharing and helping others; empathy for others; overt affectionate behavior and honesty. Each of these classes of behaviors have been specified operationally and are worked with not only during a class period called "social studies" but also during free play time and other activities. This positive interaction extends between teacher and student, between teachers, between administrators, and indeed everyone who is a part of the organization.

Contingency Contracting

Contingency contracting, a phrase coined by Lloyd Homme (1969), is a convenient means for specifying to the student expected behaviors as well as specifying what type of reward will be available upon task completion. It is usually stated according to this formula: "If you accomplish 'X' then I will provide 'Y.'" It should always be stated in a positive fashion. Contracting is convenient since it allows flexibility for both the task and the reinforcer (which may be a high probability activity as in the Premack Principle, a token, an edible or social praise, to name only a few). The point in using this system is seen as long as one remains within its guidelines, which are summarized as follows: The contract should be fair, clear, honest, for accomplishment, positive, for small approximations to goal response. The reinforcers are given immediately following response, frequently and in small amounts. The entire process should be carried out in a systematic fashion. If so, the probability is extremely high that each small contract, in the form of a single task, will build the student's repertoire of desirable behaviors. Such explicit reinforcement contingencies are readily accepted by the children and have become part of the "culture" of the Learning Vilage. The eventual goal is to get the student to manage his own behavior covertly by establishing and following through with his own contracts.

Of course, not every desired response made by the children is reinforced. Such a procedure would not only exhaust the teacher, but would soon render almost any reinforcer ineffective. Continuous reinforcement is occasionally used to establish behaviors that have a low probability of occurrence. For most behaviors, however, particularly outside of a contract and for social behaviors, intermittent reinforcement produces more lasting rates of desirable behavior than does continuous reinforcement. Also, behaviors reinforced intermittently are much less conducive to extinction or diminishing from the student's repertoire. Social reinforcers are quite effective for most children and heavy use of praise, etc., does much to make the Village a happy, supportive and highly productive environment.

To be sure, problems do arise in the Learning Village. When a problem does occur, an attempt is sometimes made to restructure a specific feature of the environment to prevent its reoccurrence. Most likely, if an undesirable behavior is emitted, elimination of such behaviors occurs via a combination of extinction (ignoring) of the specified behavior and reinforcement of some other behavior which is incompatible. Occasionally a child may be removed from the environment which is maintaining the undesirable behavior as a "time-out" procedure, or tokens are withdrawn. Physical punishment is *never* used and would be rarely needed anyway.

The positive reinforcement of specific, desired behaviors forms the core of the educational program at the Learning Village. The reinforcement procedures insure acquisition by the children of a repertoire of skills, appropriate academic responses, appropriate verbal behavior, cooperation, nonaggressive play and good eating, toileting and other personal behaviors. In short, the reinforcement procedures help the children develop as independent, happy, active, effective individuals. The emphasis placed on the development of desirable behaviors in itself precludes development of many of the undesirable responses encountered in educational settings. A child who is reinforced for appropriate academic responses, for smiling and saying, "I like Johnny," when he plays cooperatively with other children and for eating his lunch, will not lag academically, cry and complain, hoard toys or throw his food. The preventive approach to problem behaviors is by far the most efficient and most pleasant and constructive from the child's point of view (Ulrich, Wolfe & Cole, 1970; Ulrich, Wolfe & Bluhm, 1970; (Ulrich, Stachnik & Mabry, 1970).

It seems evident, at least to the present authors, that we must admit our past mistakes in relation to how we have interacted with our children and friends over the years and begin to use deliberate, data-based practices to change the undesirable circumstances that appear to be causing and maintaining many of our cultural problems. Exactly how the culture could be modified is a subject for which there is no one easy answer. We are, however, presently engaged in a program which speaks directly to the issue. Results are beginning to appear which indicate that a behavioral technology based upon the experimental analysis of behavior, when used appropriately—that is to say, positively—can move our culture toward more promising goals. We look forward to the expansion of the Learning Vilage as an important model for group change.

REFERENCES

Albee, G. The uncertain future of clinical psychology. *American Psychologist,* 1970, **25** (12), 1071–1080.

Behavior Development Corporation. *The learning Village.* Distribution brochure. 1970.

Homme, L.C. *How to use contingency contracting in the classroom.* Champaign, Ill.: Research Press, 1969.

Ulrich, R.E., Dulaney, S., Kucera, T. & Colasacco, A. Side effects of aversive control. Paper presented at symposium on Schedule-Induced and Schedule-Dependent Phenomena, University of Toronto, May, 1970. 288–298.

Ulrich, R.E. & Kent, N.D. Suggested tactics for the education of psychologists. In: R.E. Ulrich, T. Stachnik & J. Mabry (Eds.), *Control of human behavior: II. From cure to prevention.* Glenview, Ill.: Scott, Foresman, 1970, 288–298.

Ulrich, R.E., Wolfe, M. & Bluhm, M. Operant conditioning in the public schools. *Behavior Modification Monographs,* 1970, **1** (1), 1–24.

Ulrich, R.E., Wolfe, M. & Cole, R. Early education: A preventative mental health program. Michigan Mental Health Research Bulletin, 1970, **4**, 1.

Ulrich, R.E., Wolfe, M. & Dulaney, S. Punishment of shock-induced aggression. *Journal of the Experimental Analysis of Behavior,* 1969, **12,** 1009–1015.

Westinghouse Learning Corporation. *The impact of Head Start: An evaluation of the effect of Head Start on children's cognitive and affective development.* Office of Economic Opportunity Publ. No. B894536. Springfield, Va.: U.S. Government Clearinghouse, June, 1969.

Wolfe, M., Ulrich, R. & Ulrich, C. Administrative hurdles blocking preventative mental health programs for children. *Michigan Mental Health Research Bulletin,* 1970, **4,** 44–48.

Wood, W.S., Ulrich, C. & Fullmer, M. Early education: An experimental nursery school. Paper presented at meeting of Michigan Academy of Arts, Letters, and Sciences, Ann Arbor, Mich., 1969.

9. *Social Network Intervention in Time and Space**

Carolyn L. Attneave
Ross V. Speck

The geographical mobility and the impersonalness of western culture creates large numbers of isolates and others whose social relationships are unrewarding. Social network intervention is the name given by Drs. Attneave and Speck to their attempts to stimulate a contemporary reorganization in the social world of such individuals.

The assembly of 50 potential helpers in the living room of someone in crisis marks the dramatic opening of the process. The authors describe, by means of a case study, what follows. This chapter, for the first time, sets down the theoretical and conceptual structure on which intervention is based.

Social network translates the doctor concept into that of the conductor and facilitator. The conductor is an active agent, and uses such techniques as warmup exercises, cluster groups and buzz groups, derived from social psychology and the training laboratory movement, to catalyze change in the system. The team of facilitators delineates specifically to the network members the behaviors to be modified, and the tactics which might be employed to accomplish change.

Ecological considerations are clearly paramount in social-network intervention. The primary objective of the intervention is the reconstitution of a responsible and functioning natural environ-

*A slightly different version appears in *Family Networks* by Ross V. Speck and Carolyn Attneave. Reprinted by permission of Pantheon Books, a Division of Random House, Inc.

mental support system for those individuals in crisis where the system has deteriorated or is no longer in existence. The authors assert that the behavior of individuals, including deviance, is only meaningful within its social context.

INTRODUCTION

As the interests of many therapists shifted from the one-to-one intensive individual therapy to the group, a considerable body of knowledge, technique and enthusiasm first simmered, and now bubbles just short of overflowing. Part of the enthusiasm arises with the awareness that groups provide a context within which an individual can look more deeply into himself and at the same time validate his observations by communicating with others. Another source of energetic pursuit is the opportunity groups provide for learning and practicing social skills which both affect one's self-concept and the way in which this is mirrored and responded to by others. These activities have provided a common challenge and have broadened the horizons of many disciplines related to the problems and practice of mental health. The "group" has been a focal arena for experimental applications of diverse techniques and an exciting, if elusive, target for research.

The bulk of literature that discusses groups pertains to artificial groups: therapy groups formed of outpatients or in milieu-therapy wards, pupils in school classrooms, adults and youth in encounter sessions or the activities of community centers. However, there is also a growing awareness of the real-life groupings of people in their churches, communities and families and to the relationships surrounding the staffs of agencies which serve various populations. In many ways some of the most fascinating puzzles being brought to our attention are those where the principles of the laboratory, the ward and the clinic are applied and tested in the context of the support systems for patients and for the delivery of mental-health services.

It is in this context that we would like to consider the social network as a natural group which, if understood, can play a very real part in bringing about the changes desired for one or more patients who are among its members.

Social-network intervention is a developing body of techniques and theory for therapeutic interventions involving a wide range of diagnostic categories and conditions which are interpreted as predictable and understandable behaviors when a person is isolated from or in unproductive relationships with his family, friends, neighbors, work associates and others who make up the social matrix of his life. The term *social network* seems to derive from the anthropologist Elizabeth Bott, (1964) who first applied it in a nontherapeutic, objective study of normal English families in 1957. She noted a distinctly different lifestyle in families where the ties to extended kin and school associates persisted into adult life in a viable way. As an anthropologist she was used to precise definitions of kinship roles and found that the network concept was more useful than the traditional classifications for describing this phenomenon.

Although similar contexts are sometimes described, the general domination of most therapeutic literature with individual and nuclear family terminology does not appear to have loosened until the 1960s, when Speck (1967) published his first descriptions of a new technique of treating schizophrenics by assembling and creating a social network that could support and sustain them in real-life situations as an alternative to hospitalization.

At about the same time, some of the more adventurous family therapists began experimenting with the idea of seeing extended family or friends in additon to the nuclear family. Auerswald (1970) in New York and Attneave (1969) in Oklahoma began including the welfare workers, public-health nurses, clergy, school personnel and others in their treatment of chronic problem families. Murray Bowen began setting a task of straightening out tangled family collusions and "knots" as part of his training of therapists, as well as in the treatment of patients. Laing (1965) and others in England began building therapeutic communities which created new networks and new roles for patients and therapists alike. Crisis-intervention teams began considering various components of the household, extended family and caretakers in their quick, decisive moves to restore equilibrum and ward off patienthood. Taber (1969) began looking into social networks among Philadelphia ghetto families. E. Mansell Pattison in Seattle, as well as C. L. Attneave began utilizing tribal structures as a means of working with American Indians.

The rapid exchange of ideas among the "network of networkers," and the phenomenon of widely scattered clinicians arriving almost simultaneously at similar conclusions about the importance of a social context in the lives of patients, makes tracing the literature in this field rather difficult. The compilation is far from complete, but suggests the variety and range of persons utilizing the social-network concept. There are others, some of whom have either been too busy to publish or who have not realized that they were pioneering in a new field.

In general what has been published up to the present has dealt mainly with descriptions of techniques and case reports. There seem to be a few shared assumptions, but this presentation represents one of the first attempts to go beyond the empirical description and organize a theory about social-network intervention which provides a rationale for selecting the techniques to be employed and for understanding the processes involved.

Before introducing the theory derived from network intervention experience, it might be well to summarize the assumptions that seem to be common to the group of therapists listed. First, there is a basic assumption that deviant behavior makes sense if one shifts attention from the individual to his social context. This transfers concern from a matter of merely labeling and classifying individual pathology to examining the context, in this case the social network of relationships that surround the individual. It also shifts concern from merely changing the individual—either by curing him or by helping him "adjust"—to concern for stimulating a contemporary reorganization in his social world. The problems attacked may be to damp out social pathology, to stimulate healthy social relationships, or even to create a climate and context in which stable real-life relationships can meaningfully occur.

This assumption also implies rather different assignments of responsibility in social-network intervention than for therapies aimed at curing an individual. If the *therapist* is to cure, he must retain responsibility. If the *group* is responsible for both healthy and pathological functioning, then the group must assume the responsibility for its members. As Jay Haley has suggested, the therapist's role is either "to heal" or "to fix." The social-network interventionist's role is to facilitate, stimulate and catalyze growth in individuals and groups in order that they may change from isolated, destructive relationships requiring many defensive maneuvers to direct, supporting, realistic interactions that provide a solid basis for living together.

This retribalization of living is certainly an undercurrent of many trends in society today, and seems to have its roots in ancient social wisdom that becomes almost too self-evident to argue a case for it. However, it is important to realize that social-network intervention does make the basic assumptions that human beings are socially interdependent. It also assumes that a good life is not measured by the maintenance of perfection. Neither society nor individuals are perfect. Along a range from comfortable to optimal functioning a social network of at least 30 to 50 people can meet one another's complementary needs and provide basic satisfactions. By pooling resources, ideas, energy and compassion, this social network can develop the means to cope with the problems of living. It is the releasing and channeling of this potential that is the target of the social-network intervention, whether the techniques involve the dramatic assembly and creation of this matrix around someone in crisis or whether it is a more leisurely repair of a social context that has gradually eroded away into a chronic problem state.

During the course of working with social-network interventions we have observed a recurring cycle of six distinct phases which typify the underlying processes. The cycle is not merely circular: in fact, circularity and the inability to progress may be the pathological process which explodes into crisis as tensions build within and between individuals who feel trapped. Instead, social-network intervention seems to be based upon a spiralling effect which enables the group to renew itself through an experience of retribalization. The termination point for the intervention team is that point of exhaustion-elation on the part of the network where this can be assumed to recur naturally, while the activities up to that point are designed both to capitalize on each phase and to push events and activities through each phase to the next until the cycle has gained its own momentum.

To follow this cycle it is necessary to be aware of events in time and space within the network in a variety of ways. Once the commitment has been made to the group itself as the agent of change, what is important is what happens to, between and among the network members, in their own lives, not just what happens in the presence of the interveners. Although the case example selected for illustration deals largely with events occurring within the network assemblies, these meetings are only a part of the process. It is part of the usefulness of this theory that at whatever point one focuses attention, whatever plane one slices through the time and spatial aspects of the network, these same cyclical phenomena seem to occur.

Although the discussion must of necessity be linear, it would be helpful to visualize the six phases of the cycle in their progressive spiral succession.

These phases are present regardless of the frequency or duration of the social-network intervention, and even tend to repeat themselves in the microcosm of the single session. This is important to remember in planning network strategy where the interveners may have to produce the network effect in only one network meeting, as well as in the extended series that are more typical. If the network intervener is aware of these regularly recurring phases he can use the prevailing atmosphere of the individual session as a road map to let him know where he is at any particular moment, and how much further he has to go in order to complete the work of that session. He has cues as to whether he has to step up the pace or let things coast because to get stuck in one of the early stages prevents the full spread of the network effect.

For example, a network session may get stuck in the retribalization phase, so that focusing and polarization does not occur effectively. This in turn operates as a type of resistance which might be manifested as an affective high. In other words, the network may enjoy the retribalization phase so much that it is reluctant to move into polarization and mobilization phases which are the precursors to breakthrough. If a network meeting is stuck on an affective high in the retribalization phase, the interveners must insist on polarization and mobilization, and then be prepared for an immediate depression. They hope to get through the resistance and depression to a point of breakthrough, so that the task of the intervention can be accomplished, and the elation that terminates each session can impart a forward momentum.

To cite another example during one of the middle sessions of a series, the intervener has to deal with the depression which is a precursor of the breakthrough phase. At the same time he must first supply in a ritualistic and accelerated fashion the opportunity for the network to go through the previous phases of

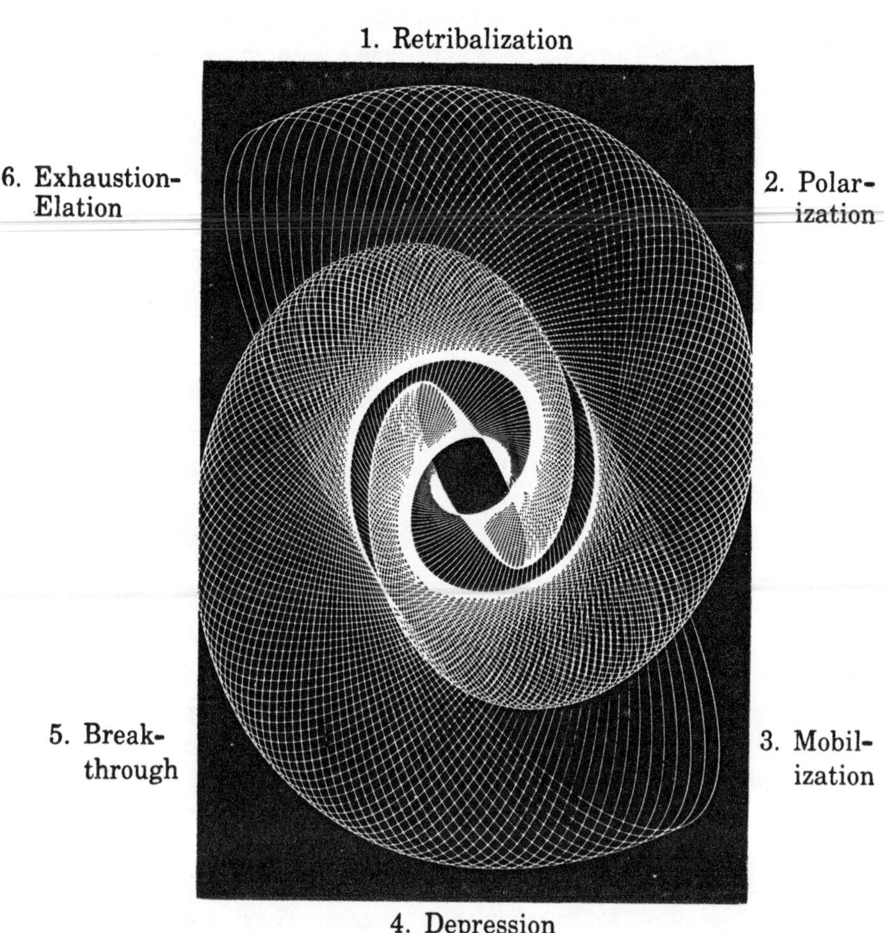

Figure 9.1 The Social Network Intervention Cycle

retribalization, polarization and mobilization in this same evening. Then the most important task of working through the depression and resistance can occur in order to be ready for the next phase of the intervention at the next meeting. Network strategy is planned between sessions by the network team. Options are always included in the strategies so that the necessary tasks can be carried out with maximum efficiency and impact in a three-hour period. Flexibility in the use of various strategies is stressed in order to deal with possible emergency situations, should they arise, or potent resistances which render certain tactics ineffective. Whenever either of these occur, a new technique or strategy is employed to prevent bogging down and to ensure that the full sequence is experienced. The techniques and the tasks vary in point of emphasis and amount of application, depending upon whether the intervener is dealing with the early, the middle or the terminal phases of the series of network meetings.

CASE HISTORY: PHASES IN A THREE SESSION ASSEMBLED NETWORK INTERVENTION

The Jones family accepted network intervention as an alternative to hospitalization for their 18-year old son whose paranoid psychosis was aggravated and embellished by shooting speed. Forty friends and relatives took part in each of three meetings, which were held in the Jones family's home at two-week intervals. This account weaves together the six sequential phases which we discovered to be characteristic of social-network intervention.

Session I

Retribalization. The meetings were all held on Thursday evenings, with assembly time announced for 7:30 P.M. When large groups assemble, however, another half hour is required for the latecomers. Therefore, we did not start our meetings formally before 8:00 P.M., but the intervention team's activities with the family and arriving members facilitated the informal knitting together of the network. By the time there were approximately 50 people in the room, noise and conversation levels were high. The retribalization process had been continuing since the first telephone call which had invited them to the network assembly. Old school friends who had not seen each other since high school days were greeting one another. Out-of-town cousins and other relatives were picking up skeins of family news. Fellow employees were meeting one another socially and in a family context.

The formal session was now due to begin, and the conductor took charge. His opening maneuver was to make use of what we generically call "nonverbals," but which really have similarities to sensitivity-encounter techniques and also have their counterparts in religious rituals, or the crowd and player rituals before the start of a football, baseball or hockey game. These are like the warmup phenomena for all performances, whether dramatic, musical, liturgical, athletic or political.

With the Jones family network the conductor first called for silence, and when he had some control of the group, asked everyone to stand up, put down everything in their hands and then join him in vigorously jumping up and down, at the same time whooping and screaming as loud as they could. The other members of the team reinforced this instruction by example. The exercise was continued for three or four minutes until most persons were overbreathing and beginning to show exhaustion. At this point they were instructed to stop, join hands with their neighbors in a long snakelike coiled chain and begin to sway with their eyes closed.

The first exercise released tension rapidly, while the second one produced an almost hypnotic type of relaxation. During the swaying the group was instructed to say in one word what they were feeling. Typical responses were "drowsy," "relaxed," "tired," "seasick," "groovy." This both reinforced the relaxation and brought about a group consciousness which is part of the retribalization process.

While this was going on the verbalization gave the conductor cues to some measure of the group resistance, as there was some reluctance to participate in the group and to follow the conductor's directions. In later sessions there was some recurrence of resistance, often more noticeable when new members joined the network during the retribalization phase of each meeting.

In the first session with the Jones family network, the conductor gave a talk for about ten minutes in which some explanation of network assembly phenomena and goals was presented. This was formulated in terms of the specific problems of the nuclear family, so that there was a careful knitting together of theory with actual suggestions about what had to be accomplished by the assembled network and how it might be done. In this network, preintervention investigation had established that Claude needed separation from the symbiotic attachments to his mother, father and sister. It was also evident that his speed-shooting habit had to be broken, and that his lack of involvement in any plans for school or work were perpetuating both the symbiosis and the drug habit.

The conductor presented possible goals for handling the family predicament, but also stimulated the assembled network to begin their own formulation of what needed to be done and possible methods to achieve this.

The introductory talk laid out a blueprint encompassing all of the phases of the network intervention. For instance, the assembly was told that they would have to focus on specific issues; that the work at times was difficult and fatiguing; that activists would have to come forward who were willing to carry out unique and innovative tasks; that complainers and laggards should consider replacing themselves in the network with other persons who had more energy and who would not give up until the tasks were completed. The group was told that they would have to assemble for three evenings at two-week intervals. (There are many exceptions where a shorter or longer series is suggested). They were also told that they would be expected to be at each session except for unusual or extenuating circumstances.

Polarization. The task of the conductor here is to use a group of techniques which will tighten vincula within the network, using the affective high which should have been generated in the retribalization phase so that the assembled network will begin to focus increasingly on the problems necessitating the intervention. One might say that this approach is as old as Hobbes, who first stated "the realization of the predicament is the pre-condition for liberty."

By allowing various subgroups to discuss the problem in the presence of the total network, the conductor is able to use the generation gap to polarize each group at times along dialectical lines, which can then be brought to a synthesis and immediately repolarized so that the entire assembled network is forced to deal with multiple levels of concepts and interpersonal relationships. This results in stimulation of the network effect in the entire assembly, comparable to the dropping of large rocks into a pool and their resounding splashes, intermingled with ripples, eddies, crosscurrents and undertows. The McLuhan tribal village is recreated in a style which encompasses the subtle depths and nuances communicated in such shows as *Laugh-In* and *The Smothers Brothers.*

The Jones family network had three subgroups composed of an inner, a middle and an outer circle, The conductor asked the dozen 16–22-year-olds to form an inner circle on the floor and to tell something about themselves as well as to discuss what they knew of Claude and his problems. They provided a good deal of peer-network support for him, but did not become particularly personal, even though several had made allusions to the experimentation with drugs by youth in general. It was not until John, a medical student in hip attire, began to tell of his own use of drugs for pure pleasure that the rest of the youthful network talked about their own drug use. (John went unrecognized by the network throughout the whole first session as a member of the intervention team. His youthful appearance suggested that he was a member of Claude's (or his sister's, peer group. Since no one asked, he and the team followed the usual policy of not telling.)

As the youthful group talked about their use of drugs, they began animatedly to discuss youth problems, the state of the world, the war, the defects of the establishment and the blind spots of their elders. During this discussion the conductor refused to allow participation from the outside circles, telling these persons that their chance would come. The more the inner group presented a polarized position, the greater the affect became in the middle and outer circle.

When it was their turn, the older parental generation, seated on the comfortable furniture about the edges of the group, was asked to criticize what the inner youth circle had talked about. They universally expressed shock at the revelation of drug use. Some became hot-tempered and chastised the young people. Most became actively involved, even surprising themselves, and again affect ran high, both within the talking subgroup and among the others. The spotlighted outer circle criticized and vehemently attacked youth values, dope, attitudes toward the war and Claude himself.

For most of the early part of the session Claude had remained aloof at the top of the stairway in his home. At this time, however, as the affect began to build up, it spilled over the neat boundaries and exchanges developed between the youth and parental circles. As Claude gained in confidence and peer support from this, he rushed downstairs and sat directly behind the conductor, who at this point was seated on the floor in direct eye-to-eye, knee-to-knee contact with Claude's father. Mr. Jones had become so involved in the polarization of the generation gap that he had come off his chair in the outer circle to encounter more closely the youths on the floor. Rapidly became embroiled in a shouting match with Frank, who was one of Claude's close friends. The father became increasingly incensed at what he called, "the lack of respect" he was getting from Frank. He finally screamed, "Get out of my house, you wise-assed young punk, and never come back!"

At this point Claude stood up. Dramatically pointing at Frank with one hand and his father with the other, he said, "That's me—that's my father! See what he always does!" This episode dramatized for the group some of the family problems, and as sympathies shifted toward Claude, a new polarization began to occur.

When the shifting polarization was sensed, the conductor asked the middle group to "take the floor" and discuss their reactions to both the older and younger groups. As anticipated, this middle group, age 25–35, attempted the synthesis of the dialectics generated by the other two groupings.

Mobilization. As the energy developed by polarization begins to become focused, it is time to mobilize and channel it constructively. At this phase of the first session, tasks are often presented to the network. In the Jones case, the meeting had been running for a couple of hours and the network effect was well into operation. Intermittently, during the earlier phases, the conductor had gently stimulated the activists in the network to be eagerly looking for tasks. Now the conductor suggested that three major areas needed the focus of attention of the network, and that suggestions would be welcome from the entire tribal assembly as to how these tasks could be implemented.

Depression. The conductor knows that the confrontation with a difficult task will meet with initial resistance, despair and even desperation. However, in a group of this size there are always a few activists who will begin to attempt practical solutions to the problem. When a number of activists begin to attempt innovative solutions to a problem and to recruit others to join or support them, the depression is replaced by determined resignation and stubborn persistence to achieve a breakthrough.

To maximize opportunities for activists to reveal themselves in the Jones network first session, the conductor formed eight subgroups, each composed of six or seven persons. They were instructed to discuss the three tasks: (1) how to get Claude away from his family and living elsewhere, (2) how to get Claude off drugs and (3) how to find employment for Claude. No primary focus was put on the Jones family because the conductor wanted a laser-beam type of confrontation centered on Claude, and an additional focus on the family would make multiple spotlights and detract from the combined network pressure to achieve a breakthrough for Claude.

Breakthrough. The network conductor must know how to transfer action from the network intervention team to the network itself. The assembled small groups in this case were assigned the task of coming up with suggestions relating to the three areas of Claude's life and then reporting back via a spokesman, at Network Session II. Once the network interveners had gotten a group process going in the subgroups, they were able to quietly leave the Jones home at about 10:30 P.M., content with the knowledge that the subgroups would run themselves for at least a couple of hours. (Breakthrough is the accomplishment of the assigned task for the intervention team, as well as for the network; this first network meeting broke up after 1:00 A.M.)

Exhaustion–Elation. Breakthrough is followed by exhaustion–elation in the team and in the network. A natural recovery period then follows between the meetings. With the Joneses, the three network interventions were held at two-week intervals.

The cycles or phases in Session I are repeated in each subsequent network meeting, as will be seen in the description of the subsequent sessions. In Session I the emphasis was placed on retribalization and polarization.

Session II

Retribalization. The intervention team arrived at the Jones home early, as usual, and suspected that the level of depression and resistance in the network had increased, as many members arrived as late as 8:00 and 8:15 P.M. In the meantime, the intervention team conversed with as many network members as possible in order to gather "network news" to be presented as part of the strategy for this meeting. The conductor began the meeting by asking for silence and used the same nonverbal techniques as in the first session.

Following this, the network news provided an information exchange about what had been happening over the previous two weeks. It occupied the position of the conductor's talk of Session I. The headline story was that Mrs. Jones reported with anger that she had discovered a spoon, some powder, a syringe and a needle in Claude's room. Claude, even when confronted with the evidence, denied that he had been using any drugs, and talked in a rambling and incoherent fashion from his perch at the top of the stairs. The retribalization phase was obviously briefer than in Session I, and the transition to polarization was almost immediate.

Polarization. The news session produced immediate polarization. Then the conductor formed an inner group composed of the seven spokesmen for the buzz groups which marked the ending of the previous formal session. Because of the high degree of affective involvement and polarization, the outer group could not refrain from interrupting the reporters and increasing irritation and chaos resulted.

This type of situation is a clear indication for a rapid shift in network intervention strategy. In fact, the conductor may scrap previously made plans and, with the team, develop new strategies on the spot designed to break through the resistance and impass.

Mobilization. There was an effort to move into mobilization by separating the two highly charged groups into separate rooms. The effect, however, was to even further strengthen the polarizations. The resulting sense of impotence, frustration and impass deepened the premature depression. Both groups became angry, at themselves and at the other group, and exhibited open hostility toward the interveners. A husband in a tense moment screamed at his wife for having her shoes off.

Depression. This phase really overlapped the preceding stages and was felt even before retribalization began. When out-of-phase sequences occur, the conductor must recycle the phase interventions in order to get the network back on the track. In this case, reassembling the whole network and a brief interlude of swaying was followed by pointing out to the group that they were depressed and stuck. This allowed a breather during which the network could again turn to the conductor for direction.

Breakthrough. The conductor rapidly suggested that a committee, called the "Claude Committee," be formed to deal with the issues which the majority of the reporters had suggested. Once mobilized, the network formed a committee and moved through the Breakthrough phase in about two minutes.

Exhaustion-Elation. The network members headed for the refreshments in the kitchen in an animated fashion, exhausted, but also in some elation at involvement in the new task. The intervention team departed forthwith in a similar state.

Session III

Retribalization. Ritualistic observance of the nonverbal activities and news reports quickly led the group through this phase.

Polarization. This time the inner group was composed of the Claude Committee. They had worked hard, and had come up with five job offers and three separate living arrangements for Claude. Two of the committee members had practically shut down their businesses in order to be with Claude constantly and prevent his use of drugs. They had also advanced him money to pay old drug debts.

By the third session the committee realized that Claude was not cooperating and that he had no intention of moving, working or getting off drugs. The committee, although feeling stuck and unable to reach their goals, had now decided to adopt a get-tough policy with Claude which they intended to apply in the next two weeks.

Mobilization—Deferred. Meanwhile, the intervention team had decided that Claude's reluctance to change was being strongly reinforced by Mr. and Mrs. Jones and by his sister. It was therefore planned to spend most of the time in this session dealing with the rest of the family. We decided that, as Claude had been the center of much of the attention in the previous two sessions, we should force him to listen while the focus was put on the others. We anticipated that Mr. and Mrs. Jones, in particular, would be very resistant to having the focus of the session put on them.

As soon as the Claude Committee reported, and before any discussion, the conductor selected Mr. and Mrs. Jones as the inner group and the rest of the network as the outer group. He then directed Mr. and Mrs. Jones to approach each other from opposite ends of the room, looking into each other's eyes, with silence, and the expectation of some kind of physical contact. This was repeated three times, with Mrs. Jones at first refusing each time, then getting panicky and attempting to run in the opposite direction, but finally sumitting to an embrace from her husband.

The conductor spent over an hour trying to get the Joneses to talk to and about each other, and about their life and relationship, independent of Claude. Mr. and Mrs. Jones protested that they had no particular problems and that their only interest was in getting help for Claude. The other network members were also unable to make much impact on the couple, who kept apologizing to the network for being a burden upon them. When the conductor suggested that a committee be formed for the parents, both stated categorically that they wanted no committee.

Depression. As the session progressed, and the network saw the extent of the resistance which included pleas to them to not interfere in the Joneses' life situation, their resistance seemed an increasing unbreakable impass. A heavy air of depression was tangible in the whole network.

Breakthrough. In order to resolve the impasse, the conductor insisted that the network form a committee for Mr. and Mrs. Jones. This was done reluctantly, with the possible exception of two spouses of members of the Claude Committee. However, the Claude Committee became mobilized realistically when they realized that Claude was trapped in a mystifying[1] relationship with his parents, who were in effect encouraging him to maintain the status quo position, while at the same time protesting against it.

The establishment of the Parent Committee, even against the wishes of the Joneses, and the renewed vitality of the Claude Committee allowed the network team to leave the third session weary but hopeful, and with a fair amount of satisfaction.

Termination

During the two weeks following the third session the two committees were able to accomplish the three tasks for which the network had been assembled. Claude found a satisfactory job. He moved to an adjoining state and lived with relatives who had attended the network meetings. Away from his peer group (who were habitual drug users) and from the frustrating symbiosis, he no longer needed to use drugs.

CYCLES AND RECYCLES

This case example illustrates that an orderly sequence of the six phases was characteristic of each network session; it provides the opportunity, also, to note that the sequential emphasis runs longitudinally between sessions. In the first meeting, the major time and energy were spent on the first two phases, retribalization and polarization. In the second session intense polarization was moved to mobilization, while in the third session the depression was first intensified, by adding new dimensions of concern, and then breakthrough and realistic retribalization followed.

This sequence of events is not atypical. Recognizing the need for recycling when the network gets stuck in a resistance-

[1]This term is used in the same sense as R. D. Laing has used it to describe certain communication patterns in schizophrenic families. Social psychiatry owes a debt to Dr. Laing, who first saw the relevance of Marx's concept of mystification to schizophrenic families.

depressed phase is one of the most useful applications of the theoretical model as a guide to intervention. The varied reactions of anger, scapegoating, non-productive efforts at solutions, and attempts to get the intervention team to take back the responsibility for solving the basic problems, are all part of a depressive reaction which is cumulative throughout the series. It should be noted that retribalization, polarization, mobilization and breakthrough are activity-oriented descriptions, while the depression phase is a mood brought on by inability to cope in expected ways when one feels one ought to be able to cope, and manifests itself in a variety of behaviors.

To some extent depression alternates with hope throughout the sequence. It occurs as the network effect is initiated and increases as soon as the network realizes, in the polarization phase, that the goals and tasks are not to be performed externally by the intervention team, but internally by the network group themselves. It reaches its peak when the volunteer activists realize that they have to mobilize in new ways, and take hitherto unrecognized factors into account. Furthermore, it is augmented when they realize that the intervention team is placing all the responsibility for further change upon them.

Thus the phase labeled resistance, or depression, is a recurrent and regularly occurring mood—a cumulative phenomenon that follows each of the first three phases. In a single-dimensional scheme this has to be represented as a fourth phase at the time of its greatest depth, when it receives the most attention from the intervention team. It is at this point that much of the subtle skills of the interveners come into play, both in resisting ploys that will get them to accept failure of the group (by taking back responsibility), and in firming up faith in the network's ability to cope realistically and effectively with the situations which have developed.

Breakthrough is the label for the relative absence of resistance and depression, and is accompanied by, or leads into, activity that accomplishes the goals of the network members. Minor or partial breakthroughs occur in each session, and the recycling of these is another task of the successful network-intervention team. For example, in the third session of the Jones family network series, the mobilization of the Claude Committee, which had decided to take a strong and tough stand with the youth, was held off by the shift in polarization to the parents in the eyeball-to-eyeball confrontation episode.

This started a completely new cycle without permitting the Claude Committee to get into action at that time. The temporarily blocked activity of the Claude Committee added further pressure to the network, who were attempting to form a second task group for the parents. The combination of this action on the part of the intervention team conductor, along with the parents' refusal and the associated visible demonstration of difficulty in getting *them* to change, led to a buildup of involvement of the total network on much more realistic grounds. Without this recycling to bring out the additional factors in the situation, the premature mobilization of effort by the first committee would have led the network back into frustration, defeat and greater depression.

CONCLUSION: RETRIBALIZATION AS A REALISTIC GOAL

When breakthrough occurs so that there is support for all parts of the system, as well as shifts in behavior and life styles that remove the original crisis, there is an aura of satisfaction and elation. This is experienced as the product of the network's activities of and for itself, rather than as a piece of professional activity. The group has knit itself together into a kind of cohesive system as a result of shared experience which makes real the retribalization symbolized by the nonverbal rituals with which the process began. Following the highpoint of breakthrough, there is a natural quiescent phase which is joined with a feeling of satisfaction at what has been accomplished. This is like normal exhaustion and rest, not tinged with depression, and seems to be accompanied by feelings of confidence that new problems, when they arise, can be shared and dealt with.

The ripples and backwashes of the network-intervention experience continue for a variable period of time after formal intervention is completed. This is not surprising since, although this discussion suggests that social-network intervention begins and ends with a series of phases of activity set off in group meetings, there is actually as much going on between sessions as in them. There is much telephoning, meeting of small clusters of concerned people, whether formally organized in committees or not, job-seeking, apartment-hunting, social affairs and discussion of the application of network-effect principles to the lives of other members of the group beyond those for whom it was originally assembled. Diffusion of the network effects almost always occurs over wide geographical distances, including renewal of contacts with friends and relatives across continents and oceans.

Once this retribalization has occurred and been reinforced by successful shared problem-solving, normal occasions for group assemblies can often keep it alive. Many of the institutions and rituals of established cultures seem to have originally evolved to perform this function: revivals, bar mitzvahs, weddings, funerals, lodge meetings, family reunions—all are familiar by their vestiges in our present culture. Older tribal societies seem to have been organized around one or two retribalizations per year, with periods of activity in the anticipatory preparations.

From this we are rather sure that the healing effect has to be renewed in order not to be lost. In the ideal case the social network would itself establish some means of perpetuating the cycle after the intervention team has taught them how to do their own interventions. The group which becomes a social network thus becomes its own agent of needed change, and the therapeutic effect becomes part of today's trend toward retribalization as an antidote to dehumanizing overcontrol by machines, electronic gadgets and computers.

BIBLIOGRAPHY

Attneave, C. L. An analysis of therapeutic roles in tribal settings and urban network intervention. *Family Process*, 1969, **8**, (2), 192–210.

Auerswald, E. H. Interdisciplinary versus ecological approach. In N. Ackerman (Ed.), *Family Process*. New York: Basic Books, 1970. Pp. 235–248.

Bott, E. *Family and social network*, London: Tavistock, 1964.

Laing, R. D. Mystification, confusion and conflict. In I. Boszormeny-Nagy & L. Framo (Eds.) *Intensive family therapy*. New York: Hoeber Medical Division, Harper & Row, 1965. Pp. 343–365.

Speck, R. V. Psychotherapy of the social network of a schizophrenic family. *Family Process*, 1967, **6**, 208–214.

Speck, R. V. Psychotherapy of family social networks. Paper presented at the Family Therapy Symposium, Medical College of Virginia, Richmond, Va. 1967.

Speck, R. V. The politics and psychotherapy of mini and micro-groups. Paper presented at Congress on Dialectics of Liberation, London 1967c.

Speck, R. V. & Morong, E. Home-centered treatment of the social network of schizophrenic families: Two approaches. Paper presented at the annual meeting of the American Psychiatric Association, 1967.

Speck, R. V. & Olans, J. The social network of the family of a schizophrenic: Implications for social and preventive psychiatry. Paper presented at the annual meeting of the American Orthopsychiatric Association, 1967.

Speck, R. V. & Ruveni, Uri. Network therapy: A developing concept. Reprinted in *Family process*, Ackerman, Nathan, (Ed.) New York: Basic Books, 1970, 92-101.

Speck, R. V. & Attneave, C. L. Social network intervention. In J. Haley (Ed.) *Changing families.* New York: Grune & Stratton, 1971.

Speck, R. V. & Attneave, C. L. The network effect. In A. Ferber & M. Mendelson (Eds.), *Training in family therapy: The complete companion.* In Press.

Speck, R. V. & Attneave, C. L. Retribalization and healing: Social network intervention techniques and applications. In Progress.

Sussman, M. & Burchinal, L. Kin family networks. *Marriage and Family Living, 1962,* **24**, 320–332.

Taber, R. H. Providing mental health services to a low socioeconomic black community without requiring that people perceive themselves as patients: An ecological system approach to a community group. Paper presented at the 46th annual meeting of the American Orthopsychiatric Association, New York, 1969.

Section III

Theory and Conceptualization

Introduction

This section contains four chapters dealing with issues of time, space, action and measurement. These are primarily "think" chapters which vary very widely in amount of documentation, with the first and third chapters being primarily concerned with developing a conceptual structure from the author's own experiences and observations of groups, and the second and fourth returning more to the existing literature. Charles Seashore addresses the first chapter to the manner in which the personal growth group facilitiates the individuals' adjustment to problems involving time and change. The author contends that participants may be better served if the intensive group experience assists them in developing a wider range of available responses, rather than attempting to acheive for all members an ideal-person stereotype characterized by openness, directness and intimacy. He argues that for some members there may be a higher payoff in learning to extract themselves from intimacy, for example. Wolfe and Proshansky, in the second chapter, examine the effects of the physical environment on the group. Size and shape of rooms, and their relationship to other space as a determinant of the activities of inhabitants of psychiatric wards in hospitals, as well as classrooms, are some of the problems considered. The chapter also reviews some of the literature on the effects of group density, visual and spatial configurations of group arrangement and the effects of the physical setting on the behavior of emotionally disturbed children. Ralph Hirschowitz, in the third chapter, describes the emotional, social, and problem-solving processes and events which occur in groups convened to make decisions about community action. The author draws from the social psychology literature, the group therapy literature and his own experience to construct a conceptual system to assist in guiding the group to its objectives. In the final chapter of this section, William Hill describes two psychological instruments he uses to measure group interactions, and attitudes of participants about such group interactions. Hill explains briefly how he uses information from these instruments to diagnose the developmental level of groups, and outlines a theory which determines the manner in which the group leader should behave based on information gathered with these instruments. In conclusion, Hill discusses such topics of general interest to group leaders as goals, selection of members, treatment settings and durations.

10. Time and Transition in the Intensive Group Experience

Charles Seashore

Charles Seashore argues that in a world of temporary structures where careers are shorter, divorces are more frequent and the membership of work teams is in continuous change, personal growth requires rapid adaptations to the changing environment. Individuals waste many years, he asserts in an unnecessary prolongation of the exploration and deliberation phases of change. Ordinarily, the natural environment of the individual contemplating change consists primarily of restraining forces exerted by those whose relationships might be threatened by such change. The intensive group may help expedite the first steps in such transitions.

The intensive group movement was initiated with a commitment to the study of change in individuals and organizations. Over the years, the social scientists who have been involved in the movement have developed a new technology for learning derived from explorations of the change process. Such innovations include the compression of learning time in the microlab (in which one 8-hour class may be substituted for the ordinary 50-minute class session spread out over 4 months), and the expansion of learning time in the cultural island concept (in which a group may meet for 2-3 weeks for as long as 16 hours per day). The laboratory of group life for social learning, and the teacher as a process consultant, are other innovations in the learning process generated by the training-laboratory movement. Inevitably, the study of social change has led back to a reevaluation of the values and the priorities of the individual.

Seashore conceptualizes the intensive group process as consisting of three phases. In the first phase, collusive relationships are developed in the service of security establishment. One's areas of greatest competence are displayed. Confrontation is the goal of a second phase, in which one, in a somewhat defensive manner, seeks a challenge to one's own views. The strategy of collaboration characterizes the third phase, which is the phase of optimal learning.

Seashore questions the belief that all members of intensive groups should attempt to achieve identical goals. He argues that some individuals may benefit more from learning to extract themselves from relationships than from learning how to be involved, intimate, and committed.

The conceptualization of intervention as an educative procedure is apparent in this chapter, as is the concern with the effect of the natural surroundings of individuals on their ability to change. Seashore also points out the interdependencies which exist among the goals of intervention. He observes that the crises which occur in the pursuit of personal enrichment may require the use of the techniques which have been developed in the context of the alleviation of symptoms and discomforts.

Sensitivity training and encounter groups were, interestingly enough, the products of the intellectual behavioral scientist looking for new methods of translating theory into action on significant social issues. Taken up by a wide range of institutions, organizations and individuals, this particular movement, in practice, has far outrun the efforts of disciples of the originators to conceptualize and build anything resembling a coherent theory of personal growth in the intensive group expereince. If one were to believe the promotion pieces, the testimonials or the accounts in the popular press, one might think that the appropriate concepts for discussing the outcomes of a typical group would be on the order of ecstacy, intimacy, despair, stripping of defenses or mind-blowing. While these kinds of feelings or states of being may exist for many participants, they are indefensible as goals or desired outcomes for the person who designs and conducts these groups. On the other hand, a far less sexy and inviting notion about concepts such as *time* and *transitions* offer both practitioner and participant a good deal more leverage in generating productive learning situations. In this paper, I would like to explore the place of these concepts in the light of my observations about the conditions which affect learning and growth in the group and the aspects of the experience which participants seem to value long after their program ended.

MAJOR AREAS OF EXPERIMENTATION IN INTENSIVE GROUP EXPERIENCES

With the aid of hindsight it is possible to point out major areas where there have been exploration in the design and conduct of learning in the intensive group. Hindsight is important since there has not been any coordinated and long term conscious program of experimentation. Rather, we have been witness to a scene of widely varying practice, marginal interest in systematic building of one innovation upon another, virtually no testing under controlled conditions, and high influence wielded by a fickle, unorganized, off-again-on-again collection of individuals and organizations who provide the marketplace for the practitioner. However, these nemeses of the compulsively organized behavioral scientist have been somewhat offset by the widespread attempts at utilization of the intensive group, the continuity of many practitioners over the 25 years since experience-based learning began to be advocated by the NTL Institute for the Applied Behavioral Sciences and the grapevine structure of the network of practitioners which seems to ooze recent techniques around the country in a manner somewhat similar to a good black-market operation.

The Schedule for Learning

The bureaucratic process seems to have become rooted in enough minds that many of us did not notice how many of our learning experiences were tied to relatively short encounters in groups which met occasionally over a semester or year. The idea of the cultural island suggested by Kurt Lewin as a way of helping people unfreeze from their traditional ways of behaving led to the development of the learning group meeting over a period of 2 to 3 weeks for as long as 12 to 16 hours a day—a drastic contrast to a class which might function for 50 minutes, 3 times a week, for 18 weeks. At the other end of the spectrum, leaders began to develop the microlab, a highly compressed design that could hopefully capitalize on the tendency of participants in a group to leave the important business to the last 5 or 10 minutes in any given meeting. The marathon falls somewhere in the middle of these two experiments, being a foray into the compression of time while at the same time fostering the notion that the group was going to go on forever or at least long enough to miss an evening's sleep. The intensity created by these experiments in schedule contrasted dramatically for most participants with the more casual, minimal-investment-of-self-model which characterizes most of what passes for education in this country. As will be seen, this intensity opens up many opportunities for learning that did not previously exist.

The Structure for Learning

The lecture stands as the traditional method for structuring learning in the social sciences, with a field trip tossed in every once in a while to keep the troops content. However, the intensive group opened up a wide variety of other modes of learning, many of which are remarkable in their similarity to laboratory work in the physical science, as well as to the myriad of informal settings of everyday life. The application of small subgroups, student-directed learning, the teacher as a process consultant rather than the content expert, the use of provisional tries in simulated settings, and the promotion of learner-controlled feedback, are but a few of the structures that have emerged in the design of intensive group experiences. While time seems to affect intensity, the structural variations have been of most importance in the search for ways for the learner to become a proactive person in his own learning and growth process rather than to be pressed by these experiments in structure.

The Blending of Cognitive and Emotional Aspects of Learning

Although any good kindergarten teacher could probably have told adult educators, college professors and high school teachers this a long, long time ago, a major contribution to the experimentation in intensive group designs is that learning which is based upon one's experience prior to generalization is a much more powerful educational technique than simple exploration at the idea level through reading or listening. The phrase *gut-level learning* perhaps describes better a process which demands the active emotional involvement of the participant as well as the use of the brain in understanding, retaining and exploring connections of the emotionally-based experience to new situations. In a broader context, it reflects the value of tying ideas to action, research to practice and knowledge to behavior. The generation of raw emotion, the use of role-playing and simulation before seminars or lectures, the stress on the process of the individual or group as well as the content, are examples of experiments in blending cognitive and emotional experiences in learning.

The Clarification of Values

The temporary nature of the intensive group experience opens up value-exploration in some very powerful ways. If a person can try out a way of behaving without longterm commitment to the style which he is exploring, he is free to explore some alternatives to usual ways of being without some of the fear of reprisal or damage. Role-playing and simulation mean that one can get evidence about the consequences of a given course of action without affecting the persons who are concerned in the real situation. The challenges to traditional concepts of authority, intimacy, organization structure, strategies of change and work become supported as an integral part of learning and growth. While far from a comfortable process, this value-clarification emphasis can be a productive force through the press it exerts on the individual to explore alternatives, to express choice, to live with consequences of choice, and to adopt this process as a part of one's own approach to problem solving in many life settings.

The Process of Change

The origins of the whole movement are based on a commitment to come to better grips with the process of change. Lewin was orginally concerned about changing patterns of intergroup relations, and the ensuing years of experimentation have all been directed at achieving change in individuals, groups, organizations or cultures. Focusing on social change or altering groups and organizations, inevitably forces the issue back to the individual level. The attempt to apply the intensive group experience to the solution of problems in the field of religion, community development, educational technique, governmental relationships, race relations and skill-training among the unemployed, has pushed the indiviuals involved to rethink their own priorities, choices, and potentials. Sometimes this process is highly confronting for the individual with accompanying stress while in other cases it produces a clarification of direction and goals which is felt to be releasing, integrating and relieving long-held ambivalent positions. In any case the individual is likely to focus a considerable degree of energy on his own transitions—in identity, family-building or dissolution, and career or work commitments.

Summary

The major areas in which there has been considerable experimentation in the design, purpose and conduct of intensive group experiences include the schedule, structure and emotional and cognitive blend of the learning situation, and a process and design which leads to value clarification and examination of the process of change. These experiments have led to the development of a technology in educational design which has significantly altered the experience of the individual learner. Specifically, it has altered the intensity of involvement, the assumption of responsibility for learning and the capacity for initiating one's own growth, and has pushed the learner past the traditional barriers such as the mind-body dichotomy to see himself as a whole person. The complexity of learning also increases as more alternatives are opened up and explored through the confrontation of values, and the necessity of coming to terms with the internal changes that will be required to achieve change in larger social units: groups, organizations or cultures. The changes in the experience of the learner as he moves from traditional learning settings to the context of the intensive group in turn influence what the individual can take away from his experience.

TIME AND TRANSITION AS KEY OUTCOME CONCEPTS

Key to the whole area of goals and outcomes of intensive group experience is the notion of individual differences. The most familiar trap we l into is thinking that there are some particular behaviors which are needed and appropriate for virtually all members of the group—such as a concept of the ideal person. That it would be good for all members to be capable of more openness, directness, closeness, trust, or intimacy is a commonly-held stereotype of what lies in the minds of group leaders, and to some degree in each of the participants. While it may be possible to take the position that none of us has reached the ultimate in these behaviors, it also completely bypasses the notion of priorities and learning which would represent the greatest gains for any given person. Experience has convinced me that a more defensible overarching goal of the intensive experience is to assist an individual in developing *a wider range of available responses* for working in the important settings of his life. Thus, for some, the highest payoff might be to learn behaviors which are quite the opposite of those listed above. Some people need to learn a functional kind of paranoia to have an alternative to their blind trust, or to learn how to extract themselves from relationships as opposed to their tendency to become overly involved, committed and intimate. Learning how to fight and enter into high-conflict situations may be more important than further honing of one's ability to express warmth and affection.

It is assumed that a person gains power over his own destiny to the degree that he has alternative ways of responding that are congruent with inner feelings of appropriateness, and that will be seen as fitting different situations depending on the context, one's own goals and the alternatives available to other persons in that situation. Widening the range of available behaviors is the key to two kinds of individual change: the better use of time and the capacity to move through transitional states.

Time

The experimentation with schedule and structure highlighted one aspect of time—ways of learning and growing at a quickened pace. The outcome for the individual after a program represents a different aspect of time—the capacity to achieve certain kinds of goals of objectives in limited periods of time. This capacity becomes increasingly important in a world of temporary structures. Careers are shorter, families do not stay together as long, moving from one location to another is done more frequently, work is organized around short-term task teams with changing membership according to need and the pace of social change forces more continual adaptation on the part of the individual while perhaps giving him a "moving target" as he tries to have an impact on the world around him. I have used the concept of "Behave Now–Pay Later" with some individuals who had acquired an infinite capacity to postpone, delay or respond in any timely way to opportunity when it arose. Obviously this admonition is appropriate only when behaving overtly has some hope of more payoff. If we look at the skill of moving quickly rather than the effect of any particular action, we are perhaps closer to what I have in mind. My grandfather stated it in pithier terms when he noted that "chance favors the prepared mind." The importance of use of time is perhaps best appreciated when looking at major changes in the family or in one's career. It is not at all unusual for people who are considering divorce or career change to indicate that they have been considering the idea for a number of years. Five or ten years is more usual than one or two. But when one looks further it becomes quite clear that not all of that five or ten years was either needed or desirable to adequately explore the change. A kind of self-imposed imprisonment results through inadaquate supports existing, externally or internally, for exploration of alternatives. The courage to change, and the supports for coping with the consequences of making the change, are quite realizable outcomes from the intensive group experience. So is that strategy for fully exploring whether or not one wants to make the transition since there is no particular reason that making a decision quickly is necessarily better than more prolonged consideration.

Transition

I have made frequent use of the concept of change in this paper. Transition is a word with many of the same connotations and is used interchangeably by lots of people. However, I would like to use it to describe a particular kind of change: namely, the process of moving from one relatively stable set of conditions to another relatively stable set of conditions. Change, on the other hand, also includes the possiblity of a relatively continuous movement without clear plateaus or breaks. Although individuals may have the feeling of creeping up on a critical event and decompressing from it afterward, I think it is usually rare for a person to experience the phenomenon of continual change with the same general degree of affect. Of greater significance is a person's capacity to initiate the transition process from a somewhat steady state of affairs. Much as the idea of inertia is used in physics, getting the ball moving in changing key aspects of one's own lifestyle requires more energy than any other part of the change process. The intensive group can help in a number of ways to point up to an individual important considerations in making that first step. For instance, in both the career change and family change situations, some of the significant restraining forces to starting the transition can be found in the individuals who are close and whose relationship would be threatened if the transition were to be made. In individual therapy one common guideline for judging progress is that the close acquaintances of the client begin to change. As he sheds those relationships which included an investment by the other person in the status quo, and reaches out to new people who share current goals and aspirations, the process of change becomes far less complex. It is also true that one can consciously start a transition by deliberately changing the reference group which one looks to for support, guidance, models and confrontation.

Summary

Time-utilization and the capacity to move through transitions are key skills for a healthy productive person. They are both dependent on a wide range of available responses to appropriately relate to one's environment. The intensive group experience can be productively used to work on all of these points, and many of the significant positive changes that people experience over time following participation in an intensive group can be easily included in these categories.

SELF-MANAGEMENT—PUTTING TOGETHER SKILLS IN DEALING WITH TIME AND TRANSITION

The term self-management for me describes a central process that requires combined skills in using time effectively and facilitating one's own transitions. The needs for self-management are great in our culture at this time. With the decline in the influence of primary groups in the form of families, neighborhoods, communities and colleagues, and the rise in the importance of temporary time-bound systems among both friends and coworkers, individuals are required to bring additional resources to cope with distress, discover joy and stretch towards their potential. The extension of the intensive group experience outside the treatment context which deals primarily with *alleviation* of suffering, and away from programs of community mental health designed to *prevent* conditions from coming about which impair individuals' functioning, has highlighted some of the contributions the group can make to effective self-management. With *enrichment* as a key objective among relatively well-functioning individuals, self-management takes on aspects of growth-seeking in addition to the kind of independence skills which are more primitive and enable basic survival needs to be met. Participants repeatedly report on several aspects of their experience as being helpful in increasing their skills of self-management.

Peak of Benchmark Experiences

During the war, training programs for spies in particular were designed to help a person get a clear view of their own capacity to function well in difficult circumstances. People who thought they would faint dead away if they looked out a three-story window found themselves successfully negotiating along a ledge on the outside of the building at the fifth-story level. In a similar fashion, some persons find a new and expanded sense of what is possible for them in dealing with other human beings. For some it is finding they can be more trusting or intimate with other people while for others it is finding new resources to deal with ambiguity, tension or attack. Others find an appreciation of the value of their contribution to others in working on a task that they had not been aware of before the program. These experiences then become new reference points that serve to raise levels of aspiration, change the value one puts on different levels of achievement and alter one's self-esteem.

Crystallizing Experiences

Every once in a while, the light bulb really turns on for an individual in the intensive group in a way which integrates and makes understandable a lot of previous experiences that were disconnected or half-forgotten because their meaning was not clear to the individual. The intensive group, as with many other settings, can be a place where this kind of crystallization can take place. The fact is that the group only serves as the final trigger to an "aha" kind of insight for which it can unfortunately take only a minor share of the credit. However, the tendency of people to attribute the entire influence to the triggering event has its rewards too, which is why I call this state of affairs ***leader's delight,*** since it blends in so nicely with his feelings of omnipotence and rescue fantasies. Nevertheless, the crystallization does provide the individual with a strong lever for dealing with problems of time-use and the transition process in new ways.

Impact Clarity

A side benefit of the unfortunate tendency of people in this culture to be somewhat less than candid with each other is the value placed on the experience of the individual in the group who gets a clear reading of the variety of reactions that individuals have to his behavior. Since effective self-management is based on good feedback systems being available to the individual, the experience of looking at the conditions and events which facilitate clear feedback on one's impact on others is a very important learning experience to many participants.

Revaluing "Negative" States

The combined intensity of the group experience with the cultural-island phenomenon which promotes sticking with difficult issues until worked through, often leads people to positively value things they have previously written off as destructive, unproductive, or just a plain waste of time. High and prolonged states of tension or conflict, ambiguous and unstructured of organization, flights from work on relevant tasks and seemingly chaotic patterns of participation, are typical of states which participants come to value for their potential contribution in working towards more easily agreed-upon goals.

Learning How to Learn

The conception of learning collaboratively with others using the here-and-now experiences of each of the group members along with the techniques of role-playing and simulation, often unfreeze the person who has been operating with a model of learning which requires outside-expert content resources. The potential classroom and daily events which may have previously seemed mundane become potential opportunites for observation, feedback and experimentation.

TRANSITIONS INTO MEMBERSHIP— ONE IMPORTANT PROCESS FOR GROWTH

The style and behavior we each exhibit as we move into more intensive membership with other members of a group may vary widely, but it seems to me that there are certain phases which we typically go through in becoming acquainted with others which are fairly constant for a large number of persons. The scheme I am proposing here is based on my observations of people in the process of moving from a collection of strangers with little in common on the surface to a group capable of providing both the abrasion and support necessary for individuals to stretch and grow in significant ways.

In Phase I the primary strategy of the individual is to set up predictable and secure patterns of interaction with the other persons. Since the other person may be in exactly the same spot, the attempt is to form collusive relationships which hopefully obscure one's underlying needs, resources and goals. What is sought is confirmation of me just the way I am, so that I may achieve my initial goal of building some security. Unfortunately, the learning outcome is nil, since the areas of greatest existing competence are being paraded to the others and the defenses against integrating contradictory information are so high that others would have to use unusually strong tactics to penetrate the closed state of mind.

If Phase I is successful, and it may take only an instant or it may never be completed, the strategy changes from seeking collusion to seeking challenge of one's own views. Confrontation is sought in the hope that the surprise will emerge—the unexpected responses, feelings or reactions which will create dissonance with what one typically experiences. The conflict aspect of the process in Phase II is likely to arouse some defensiveness, which leads to censoring and filtering of some of the inputs to the person. I call this state of learning *osmotic* to catch the notion of a membrane which allows only selected things to pass through.

Phase III is characterized by a strategy of collaboration based on a reasonable resolution of one's security needs including assurance that one can return to that state if the going gets tough, and some comfort with the confronting and conflicting behavior of others without the fear that the world is going to stop in the presence of some abrasion. What is sought is synergy, the possibility of each person contributing to another person's goals in the process of pursuing one's own growth and development. The goal becomes a mutual search, with insight and behavior change as the sought-after learning outcomes. The individuals here are in a relatively open state with minimum defensiveness and maximum capacity available for assimilating new experiences, information and perceptions.

Obviously the process of gaining membership in a group is not as orderly, coherent or pat as is suggested by the layout of Table 10.1. But this characterization does point out some interesting issues in transition. While the tendency of most of us is to spend too long in Phase I types of relationships when we are seeking deeper relationships, there are costs to not paying any attention to establishing security, testing out who is around and how safe it is in fact to become open and vulnerable with others. Similarly, moving from Phase II to Phase III is based on some resolution of competitive feelings with other members, and a level of trust which is supportive of collaboration—an inherently unstable

Table 10.1
Phases in the Development of Intensive Membership in a Group

Phase Characteristic	Phase I Low Intensity	Phase II Medium Intensity	Phase III High Intensity
Strategy	Collusion	Challenge	Collaboration
What I Want from Others	Confirmation	Confrontation	Synergy
My Objective	Security	Suprise	Search
Learning Outcome	None	Dissonance	Insight and Behavior Change
State of My Learning Capacities	Closed	Osmotic	Open

state of affairs which can be destroyed by the unilateral action of one member. In fact, the transitions seem not to go in direct order and stay at the highest level but to fluctuate back and forth, with returns to an earlier phase for rebuilding a stronger base for challenge or collaborative activity at a deeper level.

This framework does begin to provide a means for individuals to look at how they use time. In my experience with participants, a surprising number indicate that most if not all of their time is spent in Phase I types of relationships as if life were a floating set of cocktail parties with only insignificant topics of conversation serving as testing groups for never-to-be-realized deepening of the relationships. Other individuals report skills in moving fairly freely and upon their own initiative from one phase to another, including moving out of relationships that no longer seem appropriate or rewarding.

SOME CONCLUDING OBSERVATIONS

The application of intensive groups in a wide variety of settings with well-functioning individuals convinces me that significant contracts with other members of an intensive group, including the leader or therapist, may be established at a time when the individual is functioning at a peak level as well as at times when there is a greater sense of personal discomfort and need. This is especially true when there is a clear setting for application of one's learning in outside situations. In fact, it seems to me that well-functioning persons often make greater strides than those who come with a clearer sense of dissatisfaction with themselves. However, establishing a contract based on a desire for personal enrichment often leads to contact more directly related to alleviation of painful symptoms, and prevention efforts aimed at reducing the likelihood of similar difficulties in the future. I suspect this is because enrichment involves transitions which produce anxiety, tension, hostility and thus the need for more traditional supportive clinical resources.

It is also clear that frequent and regular sessions which help individuals to negotiate their roles and contracts are essential if the ongoing system such as the family or organization is to provide maximum opportunities for individual growth as well as keeping the group intact. The mountains of leftover feelings and unworked-through problems with both the family and organizations are ample evidence that these can be difficult settings in which an individual can survive, let alone grow. All too often these primary structures trap the individual so it is impossible to make transitions, and time simply becomes a measure of how long it takes to get to the inevitable.

11. The Physical Setting as a Factor in Group Function and Process

Maxine Wolfe
Harold Proshansky

An exciting new field of inquiry, psychoarchitecture, examines the manner in which man's physical environment—his buildings, rooms, vacation areas, automobiles—affects his behavior. The method of behavioral mapping *establishes, by systematic and sustained observations, what people do, where they do it, for how long and with whom.*

Drs. Wolfe and Proshansky describe the use of space by patients and staff in psychiatric wards. The spatial life-history of a psychiatric children's hospital is recorded during the first year of occupancy in order to discover the relationships between the intended and the actual use of space for social interaction versus withdrawal.

The chapter reviews some of the evidence on the relationships between population density and deviant behaviors, on the relationships between size of psychiatric hospital rooms and amount of social activity of patients and on the relationships between seating arrangements in groups and pattern of interactions.

The authors raise a number of basic issues regarding the environments of groups designed to affect social change. The durability and generalizability to settings of changes induced in individuals in special "therapeutic" or "change" environments is challenged. The effectiveness of the environment— the typical hospital ward or discussion room—in fulfilling such identity needs of the group members as those for familiarity and importance is questioned.

The authors assert that the freedom of choice of an individual to experience (or to not experience) group life is an essential ingredient of change. Physical space must, therefore, not only optimize the conditions for social interactions in groups, but also provide the individual opportunity for privacy.

We begin this discussion at a disadvantage. During the last few years some psychologists and other social scientists have become increasingly involved in a new field of inquiry generally referred to as *environmental psychology,* sometimes also referred to as *architectural psychology,* and at other times as *psychoarchitecture.* We are at a disadvantage because the term *enviornmental psychology* evokes either complete familiarity in the form of "Isn't every psychologist an environmental psychologist?" to which the answer is a resounding No; or, if not complete unfamiliarity, then a very vague familiarity which usually involves considerable distortion of the nature of this new field. A brief introduction can accomplish a great deal in correcting these distortions.

Environmental psychology is concerned with people, places and the behavior of people in places. Stated more formally, it raises theoretical questions about and undertakes empirical reseach into the relationships between the physical environment and human behavior. By the physical environment is not meant the physical stimuli of traditional psychology, e.g., light, sound, etc., nor even the integration of these basic physical stimuli with others into specific, physical objects, but rather the complexity that constitutes the physical setting in which men live and interact over extended periods of time. Great concern is given to man's built environment: its design, content, organization and meaning. More specifically, environmental psychology asks questions about rooms, buildings, hospital wards, school classrooms, houses, apartments, automobiles, airplanes, theaters, beds, chairs, urban settings, vacation areas, natural forests and other settings of varying scope.

Some examples can be cited in terms of research carried out in conjunction with the Ph.D. program in Environmental Psychology at the City University of New York. A major study recently completed concerns the influence of ward design on patient and staff behavior in psychiatric settings. We have asked and investigated such questions as how patients and staff use the space in psychiatric wards, and whether there is *regularity* over extended periods of time in their use of this space (Ittelson, Proshansky & Rivlin, 1970a). The method employed is *behavioral mapping:* it establishes by means of systematic and sustained observations what people in the ward are doing, where they are doing it, for how long, and with whom, if anybody. We have also compared wards varying in organization and design, and in fact changed the nature and organization of one room in a ward to determine its consequences for a previously established spatial utilization pattern of this ward (Rivlin, Proshansky & Ittelson, 1969). Did the difference make a difference? It did. Refurnishing and reorganizing a poorly furnished and underused solarium not only increased activity in the solarium, but changed the extent and nature of activities in other parts of the ward. We observed what we now refer to as the conservation of behavior. Whereas the change in the solarium caused a corner of the main corridor used for isolated standing by various patients at different times to be less available for this purpose because of increased traffic, the "standing area" reappeared in another part of the ward following the change.

Make no mistake, at this stage in the development of a program of research in environmental psychology, the studies being done are not based upon complex and sophisticated research designs. When we speak of activity we mean the commonplace categories of behavior, i.e., eating, talking, reading, sleeping, playing cards, arguing, watching TV, being alone, being with one other person or two other people, laughing and others. Unlike the plethora of small-group studies during the 1950s and 1960s, we are more interested at this point in the nature of the phenomenon being studied, in observing and exploring how, when and where humans use space and the objects in it either alone or in interaction, than in abstracting and quantifying selected variables. We are more likely to ask at this stage, what is happening rather than why. Highest priority is given to reasearch strategies that leave the events and settings intact, rather than to those that evolve highly sophisticated and indeed complex methodologies in search of "the right problems." Of course, we continually take into account reliability, validity and other aspects of research design and measurement, but only as a consequence of selected phenomena and the problems they generate, rather than as means for establishing what the problems are.

We by no means reject the laboratory approach if it permits us to view physical enviornmental "happenings" close up, without distorting them to any degree, as a means of evolving hypotheses or developing ideas about what is important in these events for human behavior. For example, we have designed a "novel-environment" room: a dark room with a series of mirrors with electronically-controlled surface contours, strobe lights and pulsating sounds associated with each mirror. The mirrors, lights and sounds can be sequenced and coordinated in a variety of patterns by the experimenter. To some degree the room permits us to duplicate the continuing "novelty" of sights and sounds experienced by the inner-city resident or shopper. Given this room, we have investigated how people behave in and describe novel environments, and the relationships between these behaviors and descriptions and the social interaction conditions under which they experience the room, i.e., alone or in a group (Nahemow, 1970).

The findings, thus far, indicate that when subjects are asked how they would describe the room, their descriptions can be characterized as either "experiential" or "structural." Subjects giving structural descriptions respond to the physical aspects of the room as though it consisted of a series of objects. They will describe the contents of the room, e.g., it had mirrors, lights, etc., rather than their experience in or personal response to the room. Experiential descriptions, on the other hand, emphasize these personal responses to the environment, or impressions and feelings, e.g., "it was like a trip," "images of a heartbeat." On the basis of these experiential descriptions, it would be difficult to determine what the room actually contained in terms of objects. Each of these approaches could be further categorized along a dimension of *complexity,* from quite simple description to attempts to analyze interrelationships between the component objects and/or between the objects and the feelings or experiences of the subject. Other, more tentative, findings suggest that people entering the room in a group were more likely to stay in the room for a longer period of time and were more likely to say they enjoyed the room than people entering alone. In one study, a simple predetermined pattern of the triggering of mirrors was used rather than a random sequence, and we attempted to find out if subjects were aware or interested in "figuring out" or learning the pattern. Our findings indicate that those who entered with others were less likely to learn the sequence than those entering alone.

We will cite a few other ongoing studies at the City University to give you a more diversified look at the emerging field of environmental psychology. Due to fortuitous timing, we had a unique opportunity to study the evolution of space-utilization patterns in a new children's psychiatric hospital, particularly in terms of the *intended* versus *actual* use of the new facility. Beginning with a set of predictions about the ultimate use of the space based on the architect's intentions in designing it, and the director's conception of how it could be used therepeutically, we observed the children from the first day of occupancy through the next two weeks, all through the day for the fourteen days. We then returned for a full week's observation, first, two months after the opening of the facility, and then after a six-month period. Thus, we were able to trace the "spatial life history" of the hospital during its first year of occupancy. Did specific space utilization patterns evolve? Quite clearly they did. In this particular instance, within two months the house (or living area) changed from its active use as an area for social interaction to one for withdrawal, with a decline in its social function, even though it was clearly designed for a variety of both private and small group activities. At the root of such changes are the reciprocal interrelationships involving the design of the building or its particular areas, its intended therapeutic program, and the therapeutic program which actually evolves (Rivlin & Wolfe, 1972). Other studies of this psychiatric facility are in progress with attention being given to such questions as the effects of age differences on the use of space and the relationships among such factors as pathology, group size and space utilization.

Urban transportation has become a major human problem in the 1970s, not just in terms of how quickly and efficiently we move people around a city, but from the viewpoint of their other needs, e.g., safety, privacy, comfort, in getting from one place to another in the city. With new subway lines being built in New

York City, for example, our research staff of faculty and students is investigating how individuals use subway stations, and what they expect and are satisfied or dissatisfied with in their experiences with this means of travel. Still another, very different, investigation is being undertaken by the staff with respect to the open school or open classroom, that is, the school without fixed classrooms, During the last decade such schools have sprung up in many places in the United States on the assumption that the "learning situation" under these conditions will facilitate the educational process, because it will be more responsive to the individual needs, talents and proclivities of each pupil. There is, however, much that remains to be done in optimizing the effective use of the open classroom. The value of open-space classrooms will depend on appropriate educational programs which, in turn, will require both teachers and students who themselves are willing and able to vary their role-behaviors by both giving up some of their autonomy in certain ways and increasing it in still others.

From our brief discussion and the few examples we have given of research in environmental psychology, it is possible to deduce some of its major properties as a new field of inquiry—at least as it has evolved into a research and training program at the City University of New York in the last eleven years. First, it is problem-oriented, in the sense that it formulates questions about existing physical settings, and seeks to answer these questions within the context of these settings. In what Lewin originally meant by his term *action research,* it seeks to evolve concepts, findings and schemes that can be socially useful as well as theoretically meaningful.

Second, it is as much concerned with the description and conceptualization of environments as it is with the description and conceptualization of the individual or the group. Stimuli are not environments: they are components of the environment which also include *the person* as one of its components. Theoretically there is no such reality as the person and/or versus the environment, since there is only the environment of which the person is one part. We can extract any component of the environment for purposes of analysis including the person, but it is important to stress that the person has environmental properties as well as *individual psychological* ones. And in the same way we can only speak of the "physical," "social," "psychological," "political" or any other kind of environment, for purposes of analysis. There is only *the environment*. There is no physical environment that is not embedded in and inextricably related to a social system, nor a social system that is not supported by and indeed even evolved as part of the stable and changing character of physical settings.

Finally, let us point out without too much explanation that environmental psychology—and we think a better designation would be environmental behavioral science—is interdisciplinary in character. The significant and compelling problems of man have and will continue to defy the boundaries of the social science disciplines—indeed all disciplines. Physical environments influence and in turn are influenced not just by the behavior and experience of individuals, but by groups, social organizations and even larger human systems. And by interdisciplinary we do not mean the "social science cafeteria" approach—that is, one of each. Our program at the City University of New York is closely allied with a school of architecture. We have design and architectural students and faculty, city planners, etc., on equal status with the usual psychologists and other social scientists. A study now in progress, for example, combines graduate students and faculty in architecture and environmental psychology into a problem-oriented research group that is observing behavior patterns in a psychiatric ward in order to subsequently redesign and rebuild aspects of the ward and, in turn, to evaluate the changes in behavior that occur as a result of these changes.

We are interdisciplinary in the sense that whether at the level of doctoral education or environmental research, problems of the physical environment in relation to behavior require an analytical or conceptual interface: an *interface* evolved from formulations, descriptions and interpretations reflecting the varying conceptions and methodological orientations of the social sciences and design disciplines.

We turn now to the immediate focus of the present volume: the group as an agent of change. In this chapter we are concerned with how physical settings have consequences for group function and process. If the group, in effect, is to serve as an agent of change, then those factors that maximize or minimize group function and process—of which we postulate the physical setting is not an unimportant one—will determine the extent to which the goal of individual change is achieved. In what respects, then, is the physical setting significant in group function and process, and therefore in the effectiveness of the group as an agent of change?

The response to this question can only be general. Clearly, to answer it in specific terms would require that we be asked about a particular kind of group, attempting to produce certain kind of changes in certain types of individuals to achieve certain kinds of ends. In the present discussion we only consider those general factors with respect to *any* physical setting that have implications for the effectiveness of group function and process. And even at this level our "principles" are tentative since there are little data, if any, upon which we can draw. We wish we could point to a body of literature for the reader to examine in terms of this problem, but we can't. It doesn't exist as yet.

Let us start with the obvious, and perhaps even with what is trite. No small face-to-face group can function adequately, and therefore achieve its goals, if the physical setting interferes with and precludes normal social interaction between or among its members. Can the physical setting and its dimensions accommodate the members of the groups in relation to the number of individuals, what they will be doing, for how long, and toward what end? Given a specific amount of space, increasing group density has been shown to have adverse effects on the types and frequency of social behavior. Calhoun (1962) has described the development of a "behavioral sink" in the living pens of Norway rats, reared in the laboratory under high-density conditions. Four interconnecting cages were designed so that two of the four pens would have a higher probability of use. As members of the group began spending a large amount of time in these pens, and specifically in one of the two, other neighboring groups were attracted to that place. The resulting large number of rats in that space was accompanied by a variety of sexually and socially deviant behaviors, including the dissolution of maternal behavior and marked social withdrawal.

Increasing group density in a constant amount of space has been shown to affect human behavior, as well. Hutt & Vaizey (1966) observed, recorded on film and rated the behavior of normal, brain-damaged and autistic children in a 27.5 × 17.5 foot playroom. Children were observed in three different sized play groups: small (N< 6), medium (N = 7 to 11) and large (N >12). The normal children became significantly more aggressive in the large group and showed progressively and significantly less social interaction with increasing group size, although they did not withdraw to the boundary of the room. There were different effects of increasing group size for the autistic and brain-damaged children. Brain-damaged children showed increasing aggression and destructiveness as group size increased, engaged in more social interaction and spent least time on the periphery when playing in the medium sized group. The significant findings for the autistic children were that they spent most of their time in social interaction in medium-sized groups, confining their interactions in large groups to the adults who were present. As density increased, these children spent signficantly more time at the boundary of the room.

One aspect of social interaction in relation to the physical setting deserves special emphasis. Social interaction depends on nonverbal communication as well as verbal communication, that is, on facial expressions and body gestures and positions. The work of Birdwhistell (1970), Ekman (1968), Goffman (1959) and others make it quite evident that we communicate and receive the "meaning of the other" by what we see as well as what we hear. Visual and spatial configurations—where the other sits, how far, in what position, in what contexts, over what periods of time, carrying out (or not carrying out) what movements, gestures and expressions—depend to some degree on the properties of physical setting in which the interaction occurs. Of critical importance in understanding child-adult interactions whether at home, in school or in any other context, are just such configurations. The difference in physical size, in the ability to articulate verbally, and in the skill necessary to manipulate physical objects in the setting, all suggest that visual and spatial configurations must play a vital role in their communication with each other.

The implications of the research and conceptions we described above are clear. The fact is that in the 1970s questions of whether there is enough room or whether group members can hear each other or indeed be accommodated for long periods of time, are by no means unimportant. Whether at the university, the public school, the general hospital, the industrial setting or the psychiatric facility, the problem of adequate space and its facilities and the effects of such problems on human behavior looms as a significant issue, and the need for additional research is clearly indicated.

To state as some of the existing small-group literature does, that twelve or ten is the optimum number for a face-to-face discussion group—as compared, let us say, to six or eight or sixteen—fails to specify under what kind of physical conditions. Steinzor (1950) found that seating arrangement was one of the factors determining the individuals with whom one was likely to interact in a small face-to-face group. In circular seating arrangements of groups with approximately ten members, when one person stopped speaking, someone opposite rather than alongside the first speaker was next to speak. Steinzor attributed this effect to the greater physical and expressive value a person has for those sitting directly opposite him in a circle. Subsequent research has indicated that the "Steinzor effect" is influenced by leadership style in the group (Hearn, 1957) and may be a function of the amount of eye contact which is desirable in such settings (Argyle & Dean, 1965). In a paper on small-group ecology, Sommer (1967) has summarized and reviewed the literature relating spatial arrangement to group processes. We will not elaborate further here except to state that clearly, while there are physical limits to the number of people that can function in a face-to-face group, below this limit, effectiveness will depend on —among other things of course—the nature and quality of the physical setting as we suggested above.

Now we turn to some significant issues that raise questions about particular aspects of physical settings in which groups function as agents of change. These issues will constitute the remainder of our discussion in this article.

The self-identity of every individual has elements of place in it—or as we have said elsewhere, all individuals have a "place-identity." They remember, are familiar with, like, and indeed achieve recognition, status or occupational statisfactions from certain places. Whether we are talking about "the family home," "the old hangout," "my town" or some other place, it should be obvious that physical settings are also internalized elements of human self-identity. Let us go even further. We are socialized to eat, drink, sleep, work, make love, relax, not just in certain ways, but in certain places in which certain conditions are accepted as necessary if not sufficient.

While little attention is usually paid to this spatial or physical environment aspect of self-identity, it is implicit in many problem areas that constitute the field of psychology. Nearly every major approach to child development speaks about the child differentiating himself from his environment. From Piaget's point of view, specifically, development of cognitive functioning stems from the infant's interaction on a sensorimotor level with his physical environment and gradually, through this process, developing a stable concept of himself in relation to this environment.

In the case of the emotionally disturbed child, a central aspect of symptomology is the relationship of the child to his environment. It is generally agreed that schizophrenic children display an inability to come to terms with external reality, confusing it with their own private world; these children are unable to differentiate themselves from the social and physical environment; they show a desire for sameness of objects and environment (Goldfarb, 1961). It is not unusual for the schizophrenic child to have an unpredictable response to visual stimuli, for instance, a peculiar preoccupation with a light or surface texture, an intense fear—or an equally strong liking—for a commonplace object (Stroh and Buick, 1964). While the basic factor in the therapy of such children is usually a specific type of social relationship, many psychologists have stressed the importance of the physical environment in aiding the therapeutic process. Thus, Alt (1960) has described the basic principles in the planning of facilities at a residential treatment center for disturbed children.

Berenson (in Bayes, 1967) is one of the few investigators who has dealt experimentally with the effects of the physical setting on the behavior of the emotionally disturbed child, and specifically with the role of this setting in establishing the child's self-identity. He found, for example, that there was a significant change in the appearance and behavior of a group of emotionally disturbed and near-delinquent girls when each was provided with a mirror near her bed, whereas previously there had been only one mirror in the washroom used by all the girls. The mirror, according to Berenson, served to define the "personal space" of each girl and thereby helped to provide them with a sense of who they were individually.

In general, conceptions of the qualities of the physical environment that will provide the proper therapeutic milieu for the disturbed child are of a speculative nature, most often based on the experiences of persons dealing with these children (Alt, 1960; Bettelheim, 1955). As a result there are conflicting views about the nature of the environment that will be therapeutically effective. For instance, while there is some general agreement on the necessity to avoid ambiguity in building for emotionally disturbed children (i.e., spaces and rooms should be clearly defined), a minority view held is that a deeper familiarity results when it takes the child time to learn about or understand a space or building (Bayes, 1967). Bettelheim (1955) favors planning of residential facilities in which dorms, classrooms and recreational facilities are close to each other, thus helping to establish a sense of security and reduce anxieties about separation. In contrast, other investigators (Penningroth, 1963, for example) believe that school and home areas should be separated from each other so that conditions are nearer to those experienced by the normal child. Even in relation to the desired number of children in a bedroom, it is difficult to find agreement. Bayes (1967) cites a variety of viewpoints, giving recommendations from 4 to 12 in a room. As we expect, each viewpoint is supported by convincing arguments, but without the benefit of empirical research to support these arguments.

Some other dimensions of space in relation to building for the disturbed child that have been discussed are: proper room size and shape (Bettelheim, 1955); the types and arrangements of furniture which should be utilized in a children's psychiatric setting (Docker & Drysdale, 1967; Kahn, 1967; Sorosky, Rieger & Tanguay, 1969); and the extent to which the disturbed child will adjust to a change in his environment (Bayes, 1967; Goldfarb & Mintz, 1961).

While most of these views are speculative, in that there is relatively little research to support them, it is clear that all of them express two basic assumptions either implicitly or explicitly: (1) the physical environment is a significant factor in the development and maintenance of the self-identity in the child, and (2) the physical environment, therefore, can be used as a therapeutic tool or as part of the therapeutic process in aiding disturbed individuals, particularly the disturbed child. Given these assumptions and the views which emerge from them, a host of questions arise about groups as agents of change. However, all these questions can be reduced to two major issues.

First to what degree do physical settings in which change groups operate meet the particular needs and expectancies of the individuals involved? We are not talking about meeting simple biological needs, but about meeting the individual's identity needs. Can a hospital ward or a discussion room provide the same sense of familiarity, importance and satisfaction that the individual received in the natural settings of his day-to-day existence? Of course, the natural settings of his day-to-day existence may have negative as well as positive meaning for the individual, but clearly they can't be all negative. Furthermore, what sense of satisfaction or security can the individual derive from a group setting that is so unfamiliar or alien to his previous experience that he has little to identify with?

In some of our work with psychiatric wards in general hospitals in New York City, we have raised the question whether the shift from a crowded ghetto apartment in a slum area to a sleek, pastel-colored, charmingly furnished modern ward or semi-private room is beneficial, as those of us who take the latter for granted therefore assume that such a change must have positive consequences. But does it? We are not so sure, because we have found that when ghetto children are assigned to a two-bedded room with just enough space, they sometimes move in a third child and thereby reduce their free physical space to almost nothing. We have seen this occur even when a much larger bedroom (accommodates four) is next door and could easily be used by these children (Rivlin & Wolfe, 1972).

Let us direct a more fundamental but related question to those who work in and with groups as agents of social change. To what extent can we expect lasting changes in behavior, attitudes, feelings and values induced in special "therapeutic" or "change" settings? Is the "retreat," or the therapeutic summer camp or the special group therapy room, the place to induce change in individuals who will return to their old day-to-day physical settings? Proshansky (1966), in a chapter on the development of intergroup attitudes, has noted that while intergroup contacts may be quite effective in modifying ethnic attitudes, it is also true that such changes tend to be confined to the particular contexts in which they occur, rather than being generalized to a variety of settings. Successful school integration may lead to more positive attitudes toward black schoolmates, yet not toward blacks in general, or even toward these schoolmates in nonschool contexts. Of course the question we have raised necessarily goes beyond the issue of the nature of the physical setting. Individuals return not only to familiar places, but to old relationships, conflicts and activities. Yet we cannot ignore the possibility that the mere removal of the group or the individual to a *special setting* for "self-examination" may induce situation-bound effects just because a special setting is involved. Intervention programs designed to bring about social and individual change in on-going, familiar settings, such as community-located halfway houses for drug addicts and psychiatric patients, reflect an attempt to overcome this problem in affecting meaningful change.

It is important to note that even in special settings, e.g., the reformatory, camp, hospital and others, where individuals spend considerable periods of time, group activities are carried out in still other especially designated settings. In other words, the person is asked to leave his now familiar room, bed, ward, bunkhouse or even classroom, to interact with others in another, new, special group setting.

We would like at this point to move in somewhat closer to the events that characterize *life* in a group. The groups we have in mind are those in which individuals in a hospital psychiatric ward, a prison cell, an army compound, a classroom, a summer camp, spend considerable periods of time with each other. To a greater or lesser degree they live together in the sense of the members of a family living together. Within these contexts more specific groups emerge either through design in order to accomplish certain tasks or on a spontaneous and informal basis. In many instances the goals involved are attempts at inducing change in the individual.

A simple principle can be stated: other things being equal, the effectiveness of group function and group process in affecting change will depend on the extent to which the individual not only has the freedom of choice to experience group life or not experience it as he sees fit, but also on the ability of the individual to exercise this choice when he has it.

We would all agree that to induce change by coercion, group pressure, punishment, or surveillance—indeed if this is ever possible by these means—is not likely to produce lasting change. We also know that change is more likely to occur when the individual's group membership is something he desires because it satisfies certain specific needs, including the satisfaction he derives from playing certain roles and having particular experiences in this group.

But the effectiveness of any group in terms of the satisfaction it brings to the person, depends upon the satisfaction of other needs that are invested in his sense of being (perfectly or imperfectly) a separate and autonomous individual. If a person has a need to affiliate, love and be loved, and a need to seek a host of satisfactions from others, including the sheer joy of being with others, he also has a cluster of needs that involve the freedom to be alone, to remain anonymous and indeed to escape the setting of the group. Physical space then must not only facilitate group function and process through maximizing and optimizing the conditions of social interaction; it must also allow the person the possibility of human *privacy*.

Privacy is a human need with many dimensions, yet it has received almost no attention from behavioral scientists. The need to be alone, to think out problems, to create, to engage in fantasy, to reconsider, "to lick one's wounds," to plan the next steps, to "recharge one's psychic batteries" or to enjoy just being alone, express some of the aspects of the person's need for privacy. If individuals have to learn how to function in groups, to be aware of the importance of group goals, the needs of others, and to separate these from their own nongroup-relevant or egocentric interests, then groups must in turn learn to recognize the need for autonomy and more specifically for privacy in each of its members. To function as an effective group member, the individual must first be able to function as a person in his own right. This means that the group setting must provide the conditions that facilitate the latter in order to guarantee the former.

Space limitations do not permit us to analyze the various forms which the desires for human privacy may take. Being alone may extend from literally being alone or away from human contact as, for example, the individual who takes a long walk into the country to escape the sight or even the conscious presence of others, through being alone in one's room at home or in the office, to simply withdrawing in the presence of others by not listening or responding to these others. Even in the case of the dyad involving passing acquaintances, friends or members of the immediate family, somehow or another A gets the message that B may be sitting, standing or working right next to him, but he would prefer "to be alone" by not having to listen or say things to A.

Human privacy, however, is not only an individual need, but if we may also use the same term, a "group need," or perhaps said more accurately, a condition to be met by groups at various times if group function and process are to be effective. Clearly, the presence of other nearby groups, intrusions by others in the physical setting of the group, the failure of a group to have "its place" to meet—particularly when a group is first being formed, emotionally charged over a given issue or involved in intragroup conflict—all raise questions concerning physical space and the group's need for privacy.

But as environmental psychologists we must stress the fact that not only must individuals and groups have freedom of choice with respect to their privacy, but the physical setting must afford them the opportunity to exercise this freedom. In effect, space must be designed and administered with this objective in mind.

Thus, in our psychiatric ward studies the distribution of activities in one-, two- and three-bed rooms and larger rooms were compared (Ittelson, Proshansky & Rivlin, 1970b). In the small rooms it was found that the activities are more evenly distributed over the entire range of possible activities, although social activity is relatively more frequent and isolated passivity is relatively less frequent. It would seem that the patient in this room perceives the whole range of possible behaviors as open to him. He feels free to choose from this range, and in fact to choose more or less equally from among all these possibilities.

On the other hand, the patient in the larger rooms tends to perceive the range of options from which he can choose as severely limited, as evidenced by the fact that he was more likely to engage in isolated passive behavior than in anything else. He spent from two thirds to three fourths of the time in his room lying on his bed either asleep or awake. It would appear then that the small rooms provide the patient with a considerable freedom of choice in what he does in his room, whereas the large, multiple-occupancy room limits freedom of choice and almost forces him into isolated passive behavior.

It is clear that "privacy" has its negative aspects also. In many therapeutic settings, one aspect of therapeutic philosophy is to encourage patients to interact with others. Thus design or administrative policies which allow private places to become a refuge or an escape—including a multiple-occupancy room as we noted above—may be reinforcing exactly the behavior which one would hope to change. We stress both *design and administration,* because spaces may be used in a variety of ways and the decisions as to use are generally administrative. In the children's hospital we have described, for example, the house area which was clearly designed for a variety of private, small-group and larger-group activities, began to serve as a refuge because hospital policy and programming became so structured that the child's choice was to join a group in some other place or be alone in the house. In a short time, the house became a refuge, a place for withdrawal and a place to contain children who were acting-out, and since it was physically remote from other areas of the hospital, there was practically no opportunity for a child to be on the periphery of a group while withdrawing. Thus, the "environmental message," both physically and administratively, so to speak, was, "if you won't join us, then withdraw to the house." There were no other options.

We haven't developed the concept of "freedom of choice" in relation to physical space very much in this discussion, although a more detailed discussion is available (Proshansky, Ittelson & Rivlin, 1970). Here we would only like to emphasize its importance in terms of understanding human behavior—both in terms of overt action and inner process—in relation to a physical setting. Freedom of choice is not only a function of social systems and their normative features, what groups permit and don't permit, but also of the nature of the physical setting. Patently, a setting must have the facilities and be designed to permit certain activities to go on thereby allowing the individual not only to make his choice but realize it. The fact that a room is available for an individual to be alone if he so desires is of no help if other individuals are allowed to move in and out of this room. And in contrast, a room designed for social use, as we described above, will not be used that way if hospital policy fosters its use as a place of withdrawal or containment. As Kira (1966) points out, only the bathroom has a lock on it in most American homes, thereby allowing children and parents to guarantee that at least there they can actually maintain visual and, to a degree, auditory privacy. It is also important to remember that a crowded dayroom, ward or apartment also reduces each individual's freedom of choice not only with respect to privacy, but with respect to where he can sit, engage in particular activites or even just watch TV.

Freedom of choice implies that the individual can exert some control over his physical setting, and in this regard we are confronted with the growing concern over human territoriality. Individuals not only lay claim to "privacy" for themselves as corporeal objects, but for the things they own, the spaces they occupy and their so-called personal effects. The personal pronoun "my" in the sense of "my room," "my desk," "my chair at the table," "my neighborhood," "my sheet," "my file," "my papers," etc., implies more than legal or normative ownership. These objects, spaces and places are extensions of the individual's self—or as we noted earlier, they may be elements of his self-identity—and in this sense he and only he can determine who besides himself—if anyone at all—will use them, change them or even view them.

Group function and process is facilitated—indeed can only be effective over time—if group members can satisfy their desires for "a place" both *for the group* and for themselves as individuals. To the extent that a group expects, wants, and needs a particular physical setting for their own, to this degree will the effectiveness of group function and process depend on the satisfaction of its territorial aspirations. The street corner of the delinquent gang, the clubhouse of a teenage girls' club and the corner of the dayroom of the somewhat healthier psychiatric patients, reflect the desire for territoriality in human groups. But within such groups, and those that endure over a longer period of time, e.g., family, the individual's own need for controlling his "piece" of the environment is no less important. Group functions and process depend on it in the sense that given group members must reign over certain physical areas if group tasks and functions are to be realized. Leadership is indeed expressed by putting the leader at the head of the table, and putting the secretary at his side subtly expresses the meaning and nature of this role. That mothers and wives have final authority over the kitchen—at least in some homes—expresses this same principle.

However, territoriality is critical for each group member—aside from his assigned roles. He must almost literally find his "place" in the group if meaningful face-to-face interaction is to occur. More importantly, having "his place" not only helps to establish the validity of his membership in the group, but permits him to exercise control over at least his part of the physical environment. Again, it is important to point out the significance for human individuality and autonomy of the person's sense of and claims to "my room" and "my chair," "my house" and "my neighborhood." To the extent that the individual's self-esteem is threatened in other ways, to this degree will he lay claim to what is his territory and the objects in it.

We have said enough about the physical setting and group function and process as a means of change. We will conclude with a number of generally integrative statements about our analysis in relation to the field of environmental psychology. First, what we presented are ideas and hypotheses rather than data, for as yet no real data exist. However, let us put these hypotheses in their proper perspective. In no sense are we suggesting that physical settings are responsible for a great deal of the variance that accounts for how groups function and whether or not they are effective change agents. No, we do not believe that if you design the right kind of homes for young married couples that none of them will ever get divorced. How much of the variance is attributable to physical space, and its design is an empirical question that only systematic research can answer. But whether it is a little or a great deal is beside the point. A full understanding of human behavior, whether in groups or otherwise, requires the study of man's physical environment. This is the task of the social sciences regardless of whether or not we are facing an "environmental crisis." It is time to reverse figure and ground. We can no longer afford to view the physical setting as a *backdrop* against which social, psychological and biological factors influence behavior and its development.

If there is an urgency in the study of man's physical environment and its consequences for behavior, then it is important to recognize that there is not one environmental crisis, but two. There is the crisis of human life and the consequences of air, water, food, soil and still other kinds of pollution and contamination. But there is also a crisis in human dignity. This is the failure to consider the effects that the designs of our cities, buildings, rooms, furniture, cars, recreation, have on the structure and functioning of the individual, or perhaps better said, the quality of his existence.

In our judgment, the crisis in human dignity is no less real than the crisis in human life. However, its reality in many instances is far more subtle, and it has as yet to evoke any real concern. What camouflages the crisis is the fact that to some degree modern technology views man in mechanistic, objectlike terms. Of greater importance are two assumptions which are made to rationalize the lack of concern about what physical space, its properties, organization and uses, do to people. The first is that individuals are highly adaptable, which is indicated if they neither complain consistently or manifest other overt signs of difficulty. Somehow or another people adapt to the crowded subways, inadequate office space, improperly designed furniture, congested streets, incredibly high noise levels and even more serious conditions of the physical environment. The second assumption rests on the first. If people adapt—as evidenced by no obvious or manifest difficulties including verbal complaints—then the designed environment has had no *real* negative effects on the growth and continued existence of the person.

It is these assumptions which make it a simple matter to regard the influence of the urban setting on man's behavior and growth as a low-priority consideration in planning living sites, designing equipment, and organizing his day-to-day physical existence. The importance of the physical environment in these respects is overlooked not just in a shortterm but also a long-range sense. The question becomes, which price is being paid or will eventually be paid for this adaptability? Our responsibility is to look for not just its patent, manifest effects, but its subtle consequences. As in the case of modern medicine we will have to ask what are the long-range as well as shortterm side effects on man of the various attempts to reorganize, "improve," speed-up, and "streamline" his physical existence.

The crisis in human life engendered by the modern urban environment has to some degree brought the self-deceiving assumptions about man's adaptability into question. Until they are completely rejected, the crisis in human dignity is likely to grow and provide its own set of catastrophes in the years to come.

REFERENCES

Alt, H. *Residential treatment for the disturbed child.* New York: International Universities Press, 1960.

Argyle M. & Dean, J. Eye contact, distance and affiliation. *Sociometry,* 1965, 28, 289–304.

Bayes, K. *The therapeutic effect of the environment on emotionally disturbed and mentally subnormal children.* London: Gresham Press, 1967.

Bettelheim, B. *Truants from life.* Glencoe, Ill.: Free Press, 1955.

Birdwhistell, R.L. *Kinesics and context.* Philadelphia: University of Pennsylvania Press, 1970.

Calhoun, J.B. Population density and social pathology. *Scientific American,* 1962, **206,** 139–148.

Docker-Drysdale, M. Cited in Bayes, K. *The therapeutic effects of environment on emotionally disturbed and mentally subnormal children.* London: Gresham Press, 1967.

Ekman, P. Communication through nonverbal behavior: A source of information about the interpersonal relationship. In S.S. Tomkins and C.E. Izard (eds.), *Affect, Cognition and Personality.* New York: Springer Press, 1968, Pp. 390–442.

Goffman, E. *The presentation of self in everyday life.* Garden City, N.Y.: Doubleday, 1959.

Goldfarb, W. *Childhood schizophrenia.* Cambridge, Mass.: Harvard University Press, 1961.

Goldfarb, W. & Mintz, I. The schizophrenic child's reaction to time and space. *Archives of General Psychiatry,* 1961, *5,* 535–543.

Hearn, G. Leadership and the spatial factor in small groups. *Journal of Abnormal Social Psychology,* 1957, **54,** 269–272.

Hutt, C. & Vaizey, M.J. Differential effects of group density on social behavior. *Nature,* 1966, **209,** 1371–1372.

Ittelson, W.H., Proshansky, H.M. & Rivlin, L.G. The environmental psychology of the psychiatric ward. In H.M. Proshansky, W.H. Ittelson & L.G. Rivlin (Eds.), *Environmental psychology: Man and his physical setting.* New York: Holt, Rinehart & Winston, 1970a.

Ittelson, W.H., Proshansky, H.M. & Rivlin, L.G. Bedroom size and social interaction of the psychiatric ward. *Environment and Behavior,* 1970b, **2,** 255-270.

Kahn, J.H. Cited in Bayes, K. *The therapeutic effects of environment on emotionally disturbed and mentally subnormal children.* London: Gresham Press, 1967.

Kira, A. *The bathroom: Criteria for design.* Ithaca, N.Y.: Center for Housing and Environmental Studies, Cornell University Press, 1966.

Nahemow, Lucille. Research in a novel environment. Paper presented at the meeting of the American Psychological Association, Miami Beach, September, 1970.

Penningroth, P.W. *Programs for emotionally disturbed children.* Bethesda, Md.: U.S. National Institute of Mental Health, 1963.

Proshansky, H.M. The development of intergroup attitudes. In L.W. Hoffman & M.L. Hoffman (Eds.), *Review of child development research.* New York: Russell Sage Foundation, 1966.

Proshansky, H.M., Ittelson, W.H. & Rivlin, L.G. Freedom of choice and behavior in a physical setting. In H.M. Proshansky, W.H. Ittelson & L.G. Rivlin (Eds.), *Environmental psychology: Man and his physical setting.* New York: Holt, Rinehart & Winston, 1970.

Rivlin, L.G., Proshansky, H.M. & Ittelson, W.H. Change in psychiatric ward design and patient behavior: An experimental study. Mimeographed paper. City University of New York Environmental Psychology Program, 1969.

Rivlin, L. G. & Wolfe, M. Early history of a psychiatric hospital for children. *Environment and Behavior,* 1972, *4,* 33–72.

Sommer, R. Small group ecology. *Psychological Bulletin,* 1967, **67,** 145–152.

Sorosky, A.D., Rieger, N.I. & Tanguay, P.F. Furnishing a psychiatric unit for children. *Hospital Community Psychiatry,* 1969, **20,** 234–236.

Steinzor, B. The spatial factor in face to face discussion groups. *Journal of Abnormal Social Psychology,* 1950, **45,** 552–555.

Stroh, G. & Buick, D. Perceptual development and childhood psychosis. *British Journal of Medical Psychology,* 1964, **37,** 291–299.

12. Small Group Methods in the Promotion of Change within Interagency Networks: Leadership Models

Ralph G. Hirschowitz

Some of the same issues and tactics of concern to the group psychotherapist and the trainer in a personal growth laboratory become relevant when an administrator convenes a group of community representatives with the goal of developing a collaborative program in the human services area. Dr. Hirschowitz points out that the same need exists to establish a climate of security and trust before the group can do its business as exists in remedial or growth groups.

In addition, the subsequent phases of defining the problem and deciding on the solution do not ordinarily occur in a detached and objective manner. The inevitable disagreements about what is to be done, how it is to be done and who is to do it arouse tension and turbulence in group members. Unless the group leader understands the process and has the skills to deal effectively with such points of emotional crisis, the group may not arrive at its objectives. The habitual personal styles of the participants and their methods for dealing with the tension which is aroused may lead the group to premature and therefore inferior decisions, or to procrastinate beyond the natural decision point. The leader himself must be prepared to play the role of a transient scapegoat, in order to defuse group hostility which may result from his interventions during periods of unstable development. The use of group commitment and involvement to insure that members follow through on decisions arrived at in the group is common, again, to growth and remedial groups. In the community action group such commitment is a consequence of members feeling that they have played a role in the group decision.

The variables which Dr. Hirschowitz employs in his conceptualization and the techniques he suggests, as will also be observed in some other chapters, represent a meeting ground of disciplines—in this case of social psychology and psychotherapy. For example, from traditional clinical treatment wisdom is derived the suggestion that the task of the group leader to monitor the group dynamics may be facilitated by his careful attention at periods of group crisis to nonverbal cues of dependency or flight emitted by participants. But Dr. Hirschowitz also finds social psychology's Balesian interactional chronograph a useful tool for diagnosing group dysfunction on the basis of differential densities of categories of task-oriented or socioemotional acts.

Dr. Hirschowitz closes with a plea for cooperation among human services agencies in order to improve the delivery of human services.

In order for a human-services leader to comprehend the complex interorganizational field within a community, he must be able to move with conceptual, and pragmatic, sophistication across the boundaries of community groups and community agencies. He needs to become aware of the community's tradition, its values, its sources of power and influence, the prevailing human service ideologies and its motivational matrix (Hirschowitz, 1971). As the professional maps his community, he builds relationships and develops his constituency. Until the community is adequately mapped and until the professional human-services leader has established a substantial constituency, he moves with deliberate circumspection.

Without this preliminary reconnaissance, the human-services administrator destined to be a small-group leader will flounder in his attempts to promote collaborative problem-solving. When expected to convene a small group around substantive issues, the leader prepares himself by acquiring a keen sense of the functions of the agencies, and the aspirations of agency representatives who comprise the problem-solving group. He also seeks specific information about the positions habitually occupied by these individuals in their respective agencies.

In his preliminary intelligence operations, the group leader bears in mind that the roles individuals will enact derive not only from positions occupied in their sponsoring organizations, but also from affiliations and reference groups outside the formal organization. Some expressed attitudes, beliefs, opinions or preferences may stem from actual and aspired-to positions within these other groups. A heterogeneous group is often a microcosm of the larger community—and the leader ignores the cherished differences in such a microcosm at considerable peril.

In order to facilitate the presentation and discussion of conceptual and practitioner models, the small-group stage is here conceived of as a "task force" of duly mandated and sanctioned community representatives, convened to establish interagency agreement about collaborative programs in the human-services arena. The leader has been given convening power and is the duly-designated "chairman." The programmatic purposes for which such a group might convene could range in scope and intensity from the immediacy of establishing a drug-education program to long-range planning for a child day-care program.

Establishment of the conditions necessary for the success of such a group problem-solving enterprise should involve the task-force leader in the process by which agency representatives are selected. The group task-force members should be selected so that they can work together as a "balanced aquarium." It becomes a further function of the leader to establish that members are sufficiently empowered to represent their agencies both in making decisions and in committing resources for their implementation.

A necessary assumption of the "task force" paradigm here offered, is that the group begins with an appointed or ascribed leader. As the group develops, leadership acts are shared with the group members.

THE GROUP CONVENES: BUILDING A WORKING CLIMATE

Small group problem-solving between agencies whose representatives are inexperienced in collaboration proceeds slowly; immediate movement may in fact be barely discernible. Formation of a collaborative working climate precedes significant group problem-solving attempts and expectations of early substantial task progress should be minimal. The leader who attempts to accelerate the pace of problem-solving runs the danger of alienating members and causing group tensions or disintegration.

As the leader proceeds, his tolerance for transient stress, strain and turbulence should be fortified by some sense of direction toward an eventual productive outcome. He is most likely to be able to maintain strategic mastery of self and situation if he has at his command adequate guidance models to convert uncertainty into negotiable and manageable risk. His models should provide for postdictive error-correction as well as predictive tactical planning. Examples of maps and models that can serve this purpose are now presented. While no compilation of models can chart all the complex dynamics operative within small-group systems, the models are offered in the hope that they may at times prove useful in illuminating some aspects of a group's ever-shifting field of forces.

GROUP PROBLEM-SOLVING PHASES

Once a group convenes, a sequence of necessary, predictable phases unfolds. In its early forming-yet-aborning stage, the group strives to establish functional norms; members attempt to "norm" their working environment. As they interact, they assert their own preferred definitions of structure, process and content. As generally acceptable norms are sought, some inevitable "forming-storming" will precede the group's eventual "norming" (Stogdill, 1967). Because this phase can be volatile, the leader's primary efforts must focus on building a group matrix of support, safety and security within which the group's basic norms can be established.

As the group establishes its working norms, the leader's navigating maps indicate the sequential phases which must be traversed if the group is to prove optimally effective and productive. These phases can be conceived of as four telescoping but delineable phases, each with its own end-goal, necessary functions and phase-appropriate processes. The phases are schematically indicated in Figure 12.1.

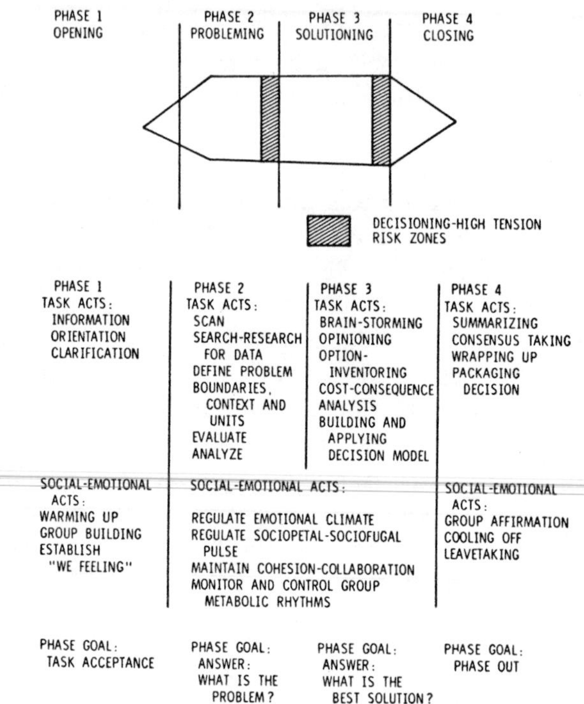

Figure 12.1. A Group Problem-Solving Paradigm

Figure 12.1 proposes a group paradigm in which group problem-solving proceeds through four phases. Each of these phases interdigitates with the next one in diamond-shaped processes which connect like trelliswork. Within each phase there are stages of opening and peak openness (and intensity) and then of eventual closure. A miniphase begins and ends "tight" and is maximally "loose" and open in its midphase. The phases are now discussed in some detail.

PHASE I: THE OPENING PHASE

This phase begins when members are seated within the structural boundary of the meeting place. At a first meeting, the leader should initiate a round of introductions and identity statements. Members need to know who the other members are, what interests they represent and what roles they enact on their respective organizational stages. The leader may take an early opportunity to declare his own identity and perception of his own facilitating role. As he foreshadows productive outcomes, he signals his own intentions and demonstrates his style and modus operandi.

In addition to encouraging some clarification of person and position by everyone present, the leader asks questions which create opportunities for mutual clarification and refinement of the group's goal and purpose. Any uncertainty or ambiguity about the group's objectives, sanctions or legitimacy should be resolved. Not only must the group's problem-solving task be absolutely clarified in this phase, but *consensual* acceptance of the group's primary problem-solving tasks must be achieved in order for Phase I to be satisfactorily concluded. If by the end of the first meeting there is no such consensus, it may be necessary for group members to return to their respective agencies and secure further clarification of their personal mandates. If preliminary briefing has not been specific enough, the leader should, between meetings, affirm or modify the shared task that has been set for the group, in concert with the superordinating agency, as well as the agencies whose representatives have been convoked.

In moving towards the realization of the first-phase goal of task acceptance, both socioemotional acts and task (or instrumental) acts will be necessary (Bales, 1950). Socioemotional acts serve to warm and build the group and are supportive, initiating, empathetic and harmonizing in nature. The leader attempts to help the group generate an *esprit de corps* which communicates to its members a vibrant expectancy of accomplishment.

Task acts in Phase I usually function to resolve problems of communication so that a "public language" of shared referents can emerge. Messages therefore give or seek essential information, clarification, orientation and confirmation, and often need to be restated in many ways. (Since language usage is highly idiosyncratic, and sometimes culturebound, verbal communication, unlike written communication, should accept the necessity for redundancy to insure that all members "get the message.") When communication is confused, it is wise for the leader to back it up, erring in the direction of reclarification, careful checking out and repetitive summarizing. When the task is clearly understood and accepted, group tension will fall and the problem-solving phase can begin.

Group problem-solving is a two-phase process, passing sequentially through Phase II, the phase of probleming, and Phase III, the phase of solutioning. Each of these phases is accompanied by necessary phase-appropriate task and expressive acts.

PHASE II: THE PROBLEMING PHASE

The end-goal of this phase is problem-definition. The questions asked in this phase are: What are the problems? In what units or subsystems of the larger community system are they found? The answer should define the boundaries and units of the problem while relating these components integrally to the time-space arena in which the problem is embedded. The task acts in this phase are therefore characterized by questioning and searching, scanning and hypothesis-generating, information-gathering and researching, analytic and synthetic processes. Contributions in this phase will be made by members who have the knowledge, skills and research temperaments appropriate to the probleming task. (While it is the researcher-analyst who is the major facilitator in Phase II, it is, by contrast, the generator of new ideas—the innovator, the brainstormer—who moves to the fore in Phase III.)

Figure 12.1 depicts a "decisioning high-tension risk zone" at the culmination of both Phases II and III. These zones signaling terminations of the phases are highlighted because they are fraught with problems of tension-management. In the concluding stage of Phase II, as information becomes adequate and a satisfactory probleming model processes the information, the group experiences the anticipatory awareness of imminent arrival at its phase goal—the definition of the problem. This awareness is accompanied by signs of excitement and tension within the group; oscillating interaction patterns occur in which information-seeking-giving-and-sharing acts alternate with search for agreement about a workable definition of the manifold realities of the problem. The search for agreement will be accompanied by the acts Bales defines as negative socioemotional acts (such as disagreement or antagonism). As proposals and counterproposals for problem formulation are made, tension rises. While some such tension is inevitable, the leader must vigilantly monitor the number and intensity of negative socioemotional acts. His interventions are timed to reduce tension to an appropriate working level. If the decisioning tension is maintained within tolerable boundaries, the group can persevere without resorting to task-avoidance, impulsive suggestion-acceptance or haphazard problem-formulation.

Task acts in the "decisioning high-tension risk zone" should include summarizing, provisional formulations, trial-ballooning and careful consensus-testing. Decisioning is usually best achieved by slow, careful superimposition of one proposal upon another, by heuristic problem-solving or "successive approximations."

PHASE III: SOLUTIONING

Phase II will, ideally, have ended when the group arrives at a satisfactory definition of the problem, its contexts, the system or systems in which the problem is embedded and the systems which impinge upon the systems in which the problem is embedded. Adequate information will have been gathered about the historical antecedents of the problem and its primary containing system, and trends will have been projected for the probable future direction and movements of that system. This provides the foundation upon which the group builds in Phase III, the answer phase, which attempts to answer the question: What is the best solution to the problem?

Since both tasks and functions in Phase III differ from the previous phases, there will be some "regrouping" while yet another cycle of "forming-storming-norming" readies the group for performance of the Phase III task. Members who have been valued contributors as formulators and researchers in early phases may have to take back seats as "brainstormers" and pragmatic action-planners now move into front seats. Required Phase III task acts include brainstorming; opinioning; the seeking of options and alternatives; the weighting and listing of these; the analysis of probable costs and consequences attached to each; and the construction of a decision scale by which to weigh alternatives. The group may for part of this phase resemble a research and development laboratory. Its style will be loose and exploratory. However, when an adequate supply of ideas and options has been generated, the group tightens up and should move in a more specific, decision-focused direction. Alternatives are then carefully screened and processed: a decision model is constructed which can select rationally these alternatives which combine the virtues of both salience—fulfilling a need—and practical feasibility—the ability to actualize that need.

The group thus moves in this phase from early reliance upon its idea men to later reliance upon its practical men. In filtering alternative solutions, the practical consequences of choosing one route over another are inventoried. A decision tree may then emerge in which alternatives may have near-equal weights attached to them. Disagreement about recommended routes are therefore inevitable—as is the strain and turbulence that will occur as the group moves through its second "decisioning high-tension risk zone." Members, quite simply, will differ in their choice of preferred solutions, the more particularly since individual or group commitment to a preferred solution will have consequences both for the individual and the group. Some measure of compromise and accommodation is eventually accepted as necessary before a solution can receive the acceptance and support of most, if not all, members (Hall & Watson, 1970).[1]

When there is very significant disagreement in this phase, without clear weighting of valued alternatives, then an extended period of creative solution-incubation may be required. When the leader is aware of hazy uncertainty within the group during the solutioning phase, he should act to postpone closure so that ongoing homework, negotiation and creative incubation can occur between the problem-solving sessions.

Phase III is concluded when the group has successfully navigated the troubled waters of decisioning to recommend a clear, unambiguous, preferred solution.

The paradigm of group problem-solving here proposed assumes that members have the requisite skills and legitimation to accomplish the group's instrumental task. If an adequate membership repertoire of task skills exists, it is unnecessary for the leader to contribute many instrumental acts in Phase II and

[1] It should be emphasized that problem-solving defines a present reality. The more certain such definition is the more the group should approach consensus. Solutioning attempts to predict the future; uncertainty must be accepted as a must; therefore, majority decision-making in this phase.

III. His preferred role is that of chairman, integrator, group-builder, maintenance man and tension-regulator. Since members are usually intensely involved in instrumental problem-solving, the leader's focus should be upon the group *qua* group; he functions as an emotional thermostat, contributing or catalyzing positive socioemotional acts to counteract negative tension. He also monitors fatigue and regulates the group's metabolic rhythms (a discussion of which follows).

PHASE IV: CLOSING OR CLOSURE

When a group has satisfactorily concluded Phase III, it usually experiences a period of residual excitement and exhilaration. A mechanism is required to help the group decrescendo and prepare for its final phase. Phase IV, therefore, has the process subgoal of winding down or cooling off, and the substantive endgoal of formal wrapup and closure.

In this final phase, the leader supports acts which attempt to summarize and package the group's problem-solving product. (In the absence of such acts, he initiates them.) He attempts to ensure that all members participate in forming and designing the group's solution proposal so that involvement and commitment are maintained. The group's decisions should be committed to paper, and shared understandings maintained; the language and style of a written report should be determined by a continuing group-participative process. The group's final task acts therefore include both verbal and written distillation and integration. Group members continue to interact until consensus about the group's proposal has been established. When this point is reached, the group's mission is concluded. As the group begins to reach this point, it becomes aware of its imminent dissolution as a temporary system. Socioemotional acts appropriate to termination should then be catalyzed. The stage should be set for final "leave-taking" and free expression of positive sentiments encouraged. Where possible, ceremonial phasing-out should be arranged. Subject to context and situation, an appropriate ceremonial might include the invitation of "notables" who are likely to influence the fate of the group's proposal.

SOME HAZARDS: ANTICIPATION AND CORRECTION

While the models here produced are not faultless navigatory maps, they do permit the signaling of "off-course" error. The leader-navigator should be able to apprehend error signals when they first occur; he can then facilitate the group's self-correction and return to course. Steering and guidance is shared as the group system becomes increasingly sophisticated in the diagnosis, monitoring and correction of its errors of omission or commission. Illustrative errors that occur with some predictable frequency include the following:

Problems of Prematurity

When the group becomes particularly turbulent, members are likely to exercise pressures upon the leader to expedite task resolution. The leader's response to such pressures can be guided by the findings of such illuminative studies as those of Hall & Watson (1970). Their study suggests that it is necessary for "strains toward convergence" to be curbed (if group synergy is to take hold and be effective). In the initial pains, anxieties and "storming" of group formation there are frequently strains toward premature closure, with demands that the leader take action and curb anxiety by "getting on with it." The leader responds best when he resists pressures towards closure, and maintains a careful problem-solving focus. Specific phase-specific examples of premature decisioning are:

(1) *Premature convening.* This occurs when a group is convened before problems have high public visibility or when inadequate sanction or legitimation to explore the problems exist. Both the group and its members may lack the power, support or commitment to carry out its task. The group then either quietly disintegrates or builds models which will never fly.

(2) In Phase I, a group hazard to be avoided is *premature probleming.* In Phase I, the questions, What is the group for? Who is it for? and Why is it meeting? must be addressed and clarified. The group should not be guided toward problem-solving before there is task agreement and some commitment to the collaborative task. Expecting too much, too fast, too soon, will produce

group noise, heat and tension, reflecting the dissonance of members' pursuit of differing definitions of their raison d'etre. A "Babel syndrome" can occur and excessive group strain may presage the group's dissolution.

(3) When the group moves into Phase II, *premature problem closure* becomes an endemic problem. The process of bounding the limits of a problem and defining its constituent elements, interrelationships and contexts is painstaking. Impatient, action-oriented members may be poorly disposed by temperament or experience to endure the rigorous search-research stages of this probleming phase. As such members become impatient, they may fail to value or comprehend the vital contributions of participating members in this phase, and may act to impose a premature "strain towards convergence." The strain is manifested as impulsive, solution-minded decision-making, which is characterized by solution-seeking before the problem is adequately defined. Global statements are then made about what the problem "really" is, in the absence of adequate substantiating evidence. Attempts, in effect, will be made to define the problem so that it fits, in somewhat autistic fashion, the solution of a proposer. Instead of seeking solutions to fit defined problems, the process is reversed, and problems are sought to fit preset solutions. Immaculate solutions are then proposed—for the wrong problems.

When such pressure toward premature closure occurs, the leader should mobilize efforts to keep discussion open by employing all the stratagems in his repertoire. He may "back it up" or acknowledge the potential of premature contributions by foreshadowing an active role for capable solutioners as soon as the problem is defined. He emphasizes that probleming proceeds by the gathering and processing of evidence and maintains an empirical, scientific evaluative posture through this phase.

(4) When the group moves into the solutioning of Phase III, the danger is *premature solution selection.* The solutioning phase is generative and requires adequate time for the gestation of ideas. Brainstorming is a loose, prolonged phase which precedes decisional closure. It is usually premature to begin to weigh options until enough have been generated. It is also premature to ask for decisions until a cost-consequence analysis of each remotely viable solution-option has been made and a decision

model constructed. When such a model has been built, the solutioning phase moves into its decisioning risk-zone. In that zone a press towards premature convergence will once again emerge. The leader may have to slow the process down so that all members have equal opportunities to weigh and deliberate; the more silent members should have the opportunity to contribute and exercise countervailing pressures upon dominating members who have a need to control the discussion.

(5) Once Phase III is satisfactorily completed, the final hazard of *premature exit* remains. Once the job appears to be done, members may "want to get the hell out" or "call it a day." Procedural structure should therefore insure that the group remains convened until consensual agreement about the presentation of the arrived-at solution is reached.

The Problem of Postmature Nonclosure

While most businesslike groups are prone to action-oriented pressures toward premature decision-making, there is an opposite error to monitor and correct; this nonclosure tendency is common with mental-health professionals who are particularly prone to the hazard of dithering past the point of closure readiness. The hazard is occupational in origin. Many professionals have acquired a trained incapacity to focus on planning, decisioning or *pro*spective acts such as *pro*gramming, *pro*posing, and *pro*ducing. They are, rather, *re*active and *re*sponsive.

The mental-health professional must therefore not only struggle to modify his habitual reactive stance but must also guard against an equally common tendency to obsessive intellectualization: an excessive preoccupation with minutiae which may impair his vision of larger Gestalts. In a group in which critics, reactors and obsessors are overrepresented, a pattern of decision-avoidance or postmature nonclosure may emerge. There is a point of ripeness when a group has gathered all the information that it realistically can hope to process. At such a point, the group is ready to make a decision and should be pushed to do so. Requests for "more information" or delay should then be countered with restatements of the relative adequacy of existing data while proactive members are supported in movement toward a decision.

Postmature nonclosure can exist in all four phases of the

group's activity, and is readily identifiable by the alert leader. While prematurity is the Scylla that a group craft will most often impale itself upon, the Charybdis of postmaturity, although revealing itself less often, will also require careful steerage if it is to be avoided by the group's helmsmen.

Acts of Individual Dominance or Control

Sometimes the group is confronted with a member whose needs for dominance and control may prove counterproductive for the group. Particularly when decision pressures escalate, the habitual tension-reducing styles of individual members may present navigational hazards. A member may attempt to counter his own anxiety by exercising excessive control or dominance upon his immediate environment. Such a member may monopolize, control or dominate the group; group members may then move away from the issue or problem as they engage in acts of counter-control. Ad hominem disputes may ensue which may have disintegrative or rupturing consequences for the group. If members do not intervene to prevent such consequences (by positive socioemotional acts), then the leader should do so. He acts best if he rapidly identifies movement toward offensive-defensive communication; as he senses imminent dyscontrol, he should reduce tension and focus the group's attention upon the problem issues. He should not delay action until the group is overwhelmed by the contagion of emergency emotions. At all times, the leader ensures that issues and problems, not members, are attacked.

PROBLEMS OF STEERAGE AND COUNTERSTEERAGE: A MODEL FOR MONITORING GROUP DYSFUNCTION

In order to decide whether a group is where it ought to be, moving neither too fast nor too slowly (i.e., stuck for an unnecessarily long time in a particular phase), a model is now proposed which superimposes the Balesian interactional chronograph upon the group problem-solving paradigm of Figure 12.1.

This superimposition is schematically illustrated in Figure 12.2.

1. The reader is reminded that the scoring pattern of Bales (1950) defines acts, verbal and nonverbal, as follows:

FIGURE 12.2
TYPICAL INTERACTION DENSITY PATTERN
IN GROUP PROBLEM SOLVING

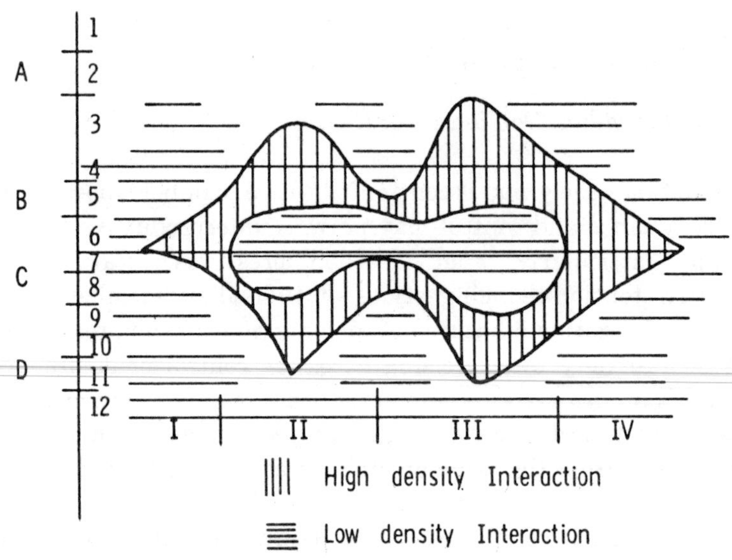

A POSITIVE SOCIAL-EMOTIONAL AREA (BALES)

B & C NEUTRAL TASK AREA (BALES)

D NEGATIVE SOCIAL-EMOTIONAL AREA (BALES)

I, II, III, & IV PHASES CORRESPONDING TO FIGURE 1.

Area A: Positive Socioemotional Acts
(1) Shows solidarity, raises other's status, gives help, rewards
(2) Shows tension release, jokes, laughs, shows satisfaction
(3) Agrees, shows passive acceptance, understands, concurs, complies
Area B: The Neutral Task Area:
(4) Gives suggestion, direction implying autonomy for other
(5) Gives opinion, evaluation, analysis, expresses feeling, wish
(6) Gives orientation, information, repeats, clarifies, confirms
Area C: Also a Neutral Task Area:
(7) Asks for orientation, information, repetition, confirmation
(8) Asks for opinion, evaluation, analysis, expression of feeling
(9) Asks for suggestion, direction, possible ways of action
Area D: Negative Socioemotional Acts:
(10) Disagrees, shows passive rejection, formality, withholds help
(11) Shows tension, asks for help, withdraws out of field
(12) Shows antagonism, deflates other's status, defends or asserts self.

Applications of the Bales scheme and Figure 12.2 are now discussed.

The density of particular acts varies with some predictability from phase to phase and during each phase. Typical density patterns are illustrated in Figure 12.2. When interactional density does not appear appropriate to stage or phase, group dysfunction is usually signified. For example, the group may be litanously and repetitively concerned with acts of giving and receiving orientation and information, covering ground which has been adequately covered. This may indicate reluctance to move from areas of relatively comfortable concrete specificity (acts in the Bales spectrum 5—8) to more abstract acts of suggestion, direction, and potential disagreement (Bales 9, 10, 3 or 2). Such clinging to safe territory may be associated with obsessive dithering in Phase II or reluctance to conclude solutioning in Phase III.

In any phase, rapid escalation of negative socioemotional acts (Bales 10–12) may signal controlling "take-over" bids. Actions which cluster densely in this zone signal danger, and corrective intervention should be immediate. Negative socioemotional acts are disintegrative; in any intensity, they generate "freezes" and disruptive emotional contagion within the group. When such acts are not balanced by positive socioemotional acts (Bales 1–3) the group risks attrition or disintegration; even if disintegration is prevented, the consequences for group morale will be disastrous.

A decision thus must rapidly be made about the significance of a sudden unpredicted shift of high intensity interaction. For example, density of interaction in the negative socioemotional area may signal little more than a high level of problem-solving frustration. When the leader is satisfied that he is registering emotional indicators of group *task* frustration, then his intervention should focus upon remedying the source or roadblock. However, when negative socioemotional acts emerge persistently from one member and not from many, the more likely explanation is that there is a significant disjunction between the personal need-disposition of one individual and his tolerance or acceptance of a group-member role. This problem of personality-role misfit is discussed by Benne and Sheats (1948) in their description of idiosyncratic "individual" roles, and has been addressed in the earlier discussion of group hazards.

FIGURE 12.3
A TOPOLOGICAL "WHERE IS EVERYBODY?" MODEL
FOR THE CROSS-SECTIONAL MONITORING OF GROUP DYNAMICS
(After Bion)

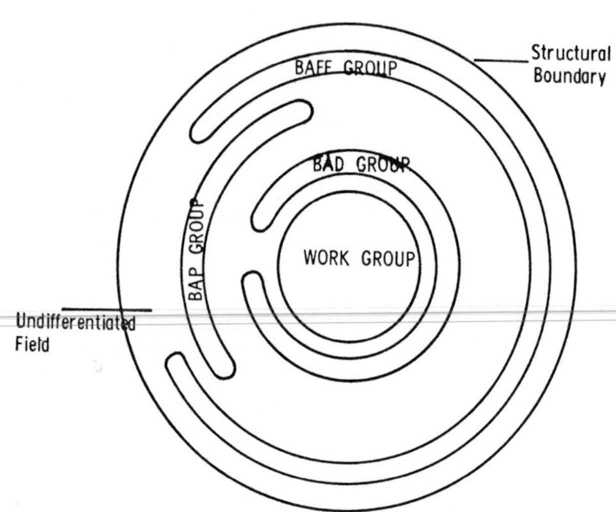

All Boundaries are permeable.

BAD -- Basic Assumption is Dependence
BAP -- Basic Assumption is Pairing
BAFF -- Basic Assumption is Fight-Flight

WHERE IS EVERYBODY?

Another model employed by the author to orient himself in particularly fluid and turbulent fields is derived from Bion (1961). Figure 12.3 is offered as a topological "Where is Everybody?" model for the monitoring of group dynamics in the chronological unfolding of group process.

The group is conceived as having a concrete structural boundary (the room in which the group is convened) within which are loosely bounded spaces with flexible, permeable sub-boundaries. The loosely bounded subterritories of the group's life space offer positions in either the central work group; a peripheral intermediate "BAD" group (the *b*asic *a*ssumption of which, following Bion, is *d*ependence); or, closer to the periphery, a "BAFF" space inhabited by members who share the *b*asic *a*ssumption of "*f*ight-*f*light." There is also a "BAP" space in which the *b*asic *a*ssumption is *p*airing. Finally, there is an undifferentiated group field through which individuals migrate, or which may be occupied by members who are in retreat, alienated or isolated.

At any point in time, the question "Where is everybody?" can be answered within the frame of this topological model. When most of the members are actively or vicariously invested in the work group, most acts will be in Bales's neutral task area with some occasional acts of disagreement or agreement (Bales, 10 or 3). The "centrality" of the work group will also be reflected by the "sociopetal-sociofugal" pulse. When sociopetality is dominant, members will be in a roundtable posture, they will be close to one another, their minds will be focused upon the central issue and their eyes upon one another; physically, they will be moving inward and toward one another. The group will be alive and energetic. Working tension will be evident in the posture, hands, faces and voices of members. The group will act and feel like a "we group" (Bales, 1971).[2] When the majority of members are in the "basic assumption of dependence" (BAD) group, the general posture and overall impression conveyed by the group will be one of passivity. Bodies will be slumped, eyes will be focused upon the leader and minds upon some external source or wisdom, power or authority. Dependent members will be literally "looking up" to the leader. Members' presentation of self and defensive demeanors will be subordinate and childlike (by contrast, the posture in the work group will be coordinate and symmetrical). As members migrate towards the BAFF (flight) group, their stance will be hypervigilant and their posture "uptight." "Fight" will be shown by a heightening of volume and acerbity of voice as well as an obvious increase in body tonus. Hands will form fists and index fingers will punctuate remarks with pistol-like thrusts. Associated signs of flight, often interweaving with those of fight, will include flightiness of language, and of eyes, hands, feet or limbs. Sociofugal patterns will be evidenced by the visible movement of chairs and bodies to the room's periphery. When "flight" is intense, members will seek to protect their rears and bodies will move toward, or out of, the group gateway. In the group dialogue,

[2]Cohesion can often be measured by the preferred use of the first-person plural pronoun.

an early sign of flight will be "throwing the ball out of field"—verbal acts lacking relevance to the manifest content of group discussion (Bales 11–12).

APPLICATION OF THIS MODEL

This model can be applied whenever the group is in crisis. It is helpful for scanning and correction for strain when, for example, in "storming-norming," the group struggles for goal-adaptive patterns and functional viability.

In the stage of "forming," the group *is* leader-dependent and his behavior is crucial in setting the stage for the formation of a work group. When a group is convened for the first time, members do have a basic assumption of dependence (at this stage, "BAD"-ness is not necessarily pejorative). Until the group is bonded (formed, stormed and normed), members are dependent upon an integrative central authority who will ensure task clarification and guide the content, structure and processes of the group. As the task is clarified and both task and group "take hold," members can abandon their occupancy of the temporary "BAD" group in favor of membership in the central work group. The leader's early initiatory thrust can thus diminish. If he has successfully catalyzed information exchange, the initial apprehension, tension and stranger-uneasiness of members will also have been transcended—and energy freed for group work (in the central work group).

While the core work group now offers rewarding and preferred positions for most members, intrarole, inter-role, or interactor strain will still occur. Such strain will be indicated by outmigration to the "BAFF" group. When this occurs, the leader goes on "emergency alert" and insures that sociofugality is curbed.

While pairing and alliances do form in temporary system task forces around shifting needs and interests, they are not of as much critical significance as they are in therapy groups. Pairing does tend to exclude other members, but in a robust task force where the group is task- and issue-focused, the pursuit of individual need-satisfactions via pairing is not usually a problem which requires critical intervention.

THE LEADER: HIS GUT AND HIS COOL

In the field, there is little time for ratiocination. The leader tends to operate atheoretically, usually "sensing" when a group is "uptight" or "fighty-flighty." In such scanning-sensory activity, a vital source of information is the leader's own gut. When emergency rather than welfare emotions are dominant in a group, the leader's gut is likely to pick these emotions up in the "vibes" or spreading emotional climate of the group. His gut can then function as a sensitive barometer of group tension. His gut calibration and additional knowledge of his own emotional reactions can then guide planned action. Without such informed action, the leader may be nonspecifically, and often irrationally, propelled by the emotions aroused within him by the group. Whether aroused by the climate within the group, or by a direct antagonistic assault upon him, it is imperative that the leader understand and master his own "fight-flight" emergency responses; only then can his intervention reduce both the group's tension and his own.

In addition to knowledge, sensibility and sensitivity regarding group process, the group leader requires patience, a keen political sense, a considerable measure of "cool" and a repertoire of tension-reducing interventions, including a culture-appropriate sense of humor. The leader whose investment is too highly personalized, i.e., who needs to have followers who revere, worship, admire or love him, is likely to be both a poor group leader and a poor change-agent. Qualities more disposed to success are tolerance for anxiety, ambiguity and those emergency emotions, such as rage, hostility, resentment and envy, which can contage or destroy group circuits. The leader should be able to tolerate these emotions in others and in himself, while maintaining enough distance to avoid seduction into the defensive alliances, cliques and cabals that may temporarily form.

OPTIMAL WORKING TENSION?

Most practiced group members and agency representatives usually have a shared definition of language, optimal working tension and reciprocal expectations in a task-force situation. Critical problems do, however, emerge in groups whose members are not uniformly skilled or practiced in conventional, middle-class, "rules of order" group situations. This is particularly true in some " community participation" situations where professional and lay participants may manifest conspicuous differences in styles and assumptions. Such heterogeneous groups demand highly structured leadership as well as a large investment of time in the construction and maintenance of a supportive, safe security system. Frequent task-focused interventions will be needed to permit acceptable group norms and procedural mechanisms to emerge. While the group is in developmental flux, the leader may have to keep a tight restraining hold upon the group and his interventions may have to be active, frequent, highly structured, controlled and sometimes controlling.[3] In their early development, these groups are intrinsically sociofugal. As the leader makes integrative (sociopetalizing) attempts, resistant and frustrated group members are likely to focus their rage and frustration upon him. At such a point, the leader who is not prepared to be a transient scapegoat to defuse the group's hostility, is likely to contribute to the scapegoating of more vulnerable members and will not be discharging a useful or defensible function.

A particular predicament for such groups derives from culturally different levels of preferred working tension. Some individuals prefer to work in an atmosphere of "pseudohostile noise." The somewhat more sober, antiseptic working climate of professionals often proves anathema to individuals who have learned to survive against a background of noise, invective and "kidding" which facilitates their work but impedes that of some professionals.

[3]As the group grows and stabilizes, much less control is needed—and more disagreement is tolerated by the group.

VALUE-ORIENTATIONS AND THE GROUP MICROCOSM

Many differences of group behavior-style stem from differing value orientations. As anthropologists have shown, orientations toward peers and authority figures are socially acquired and vary on three dimensions: the individualist, linear and collateral (Kluckhohm & Strodtbeck, 1961). These differing value orientations are expressed in groups in some of the following ways:

Hyperindividualist members will not succumb readily to the pressures of group members or figures in authority as they tend to be "inner-directed," holding out for their perceptions of what is right and best. Members who have linear orientations are more deferential toward authority figures; they are unlikely to move toward coordinate group membership without sanction and perceived support from authority. Members whose dominant orientations are "collateral" are maximally responsive to group pressure; they may readily minimize or modify their own preferred individual contributions in order to achieve group acceptance and approval.

The orchestration of human diversity with its complex heterogeneity of personal styles, needs, values and interests is crucial to the regulation of interpersonal, intergroup and intersocial relations. American society's history of confederate pluralism and its wide tolerance for diversity has evolved culture-unique patterns for the regulation of such differences. While individuals and organized groups of individuals protect and promote their perceived needs and interests, they do so in the awareness that accommodations must inevitably be struck. A small-group task-force, like a community, is therefore often a microcosm for the regulation of intergroup and interindividual differences. Issues of pluralism are brought into bold relief in such a microcosm, as small group process presses towards the pursuit of outcomes satisfactory to all members.

There is an inherent dialectical dilemma in attempting to reconcile the pursuit of commonality with simultaneous attempts to preserve individual differences, freedoms, and rights. Individual differences create an inherent sociofugal strain. Leadership must perforce exercise countervailing sociopetal pressure to combat the inherent strain toward divergence, separatism, isolation and/or competition that may permeate any social microcosm.

CONCLUSION

Human services are neither integrated nor coordinated. Agencies operate in isolation from one another or parallel to one another. Some segments of the population receive a superfluity of services while other segments receive little or none. Services are fragmented, incomprehensible to the consumer and noncomprehensive to the objective observer. Delivery is wasteful and program criteria often more agency-centered than population-centered. In attempts to promote change, federal agencies have mandated the need for public involvement and interagency agreement in new program areas such as health or mental health. In consequence, a more active public, acquiring consumer-participatory power, is multiplying demands for change.

As efforts are being made by human-services professionals, and their agencies, to effect comprehensive, coordinated program planning, the needs for skills in group problem-solving and attendant group leadership have become increasingly apparent. In recognition of these needs, this paper has proposed relevant conceptual and practitioner models. As human-services leaders become more skilled in the application of models such as these, it is hoped that pleas for human-services agencies to share domain, responsibility and accountability, will begin to move from rhetoric to reality.

BIBLIOGRAPHY

Bales, R.F. *Interaction process analysis: A method for the study of small groups*. Reading, Mass.: Addison-Wesley, 1950.

Benne, K.D. & Sheats, P. Functional roles of group members. *The Journal of Social Issues*, 1948, 4(2), 41–49.

Bion, W. R. *Experiences in groups and other papers*. London: Tavistock, 1961.

Hall, J. & Watson, W. H. The effects of a normative intervention on group decision-making performance. *Human Relations*, 1970, **23**(4), 299–317.

Hirschowitz, R. G. Dilemmas of leadership in community mental health. *Psychiatric Quarterly,* 1971, **45**(1), 102–116.
Kluckhohm, F. R. & Strodtbeck, F. L. *Variations in value orientation.* Evanston, Ill.: Row-Peterson, 1961.
Stogdill, R. M. Basic concepts for a theory of organizations. *Management Science,* 1967, **13**,B666–B676.

13. *Systematic Group Development—SGD Therapy*

William Fawcett Hill

William Hill argues in this chapter that the interventions of a group leader should be related to what he and group members are doing—an idea which seems obvious, but is resisted by many group leaders. An instrument, the HIM-G, is described, which enables the group leader to obtain such information. The HIM-G consists of a set of categories which describe theoretically relevant group interactions. A content-style dimension describes what groups talk about, and a work-style dimension describes the types of interactions which may occur. An analysis of a large number of therapy-group sessions by means of the HIM-G enables the author to conclude, for example, that one third of the time of the typical group-therapy session is spent in chitchat.

A second instrument developed by Hill, the HIM-B, can be administered to group members or leaders, and indicates the degree of acceptance of the various types of group activities scored in the HIM-G. The HIM-B is therefore a useful instrument for the selection of group members, or for examining the relationships between group composition or leadership style and group activity.

Systematic group development therapy *is the name given by Hill to the approach to group therapy which he describes in this chapter. He argues that most of the differences between therapy groups can be accounted for on the basis of group composition, leadership style and group development. The HIM scales developed by Hill can provide immediate quantitative data on all three factors.*

DESCRIPTION OF GROUP PROCEDURE

As with a famous brand of food, there seems to be at least 57 varieties of group therapy. Many group therapists hope to gain uniqueness by giving their therapy an unique name. In some cases this is the only distinguishing characteristic, and in other cases the innovative aspect may be somewhat insignificant in its contribution to the total therapeutic impact. Maximizing differences and minimizing similarities has greatly hindered the understanding of the group therapeutic process. Even in the case of the true innovators, e.g., George Bach, Rudolph Dreikurs and Frederick Perls, their approach is dependent on their firm mastery of the core functions of group therapy.

The group-therapy approach we advocate is essentially eclectic. Before elaborating on it, let us first take a look at the commonalities of therapy groups. In our attempt to shed some light on this, we collected recordings of a large and representative sample of therapy groups. We accumulated fifty groups for which typescripts or tape recordings were available. A key session of each of these fifty groups was rated on our categorization system, the Hill Interaction Matrix (Hill, 1966), which will be described in some detail later.

Analysis of these data showed the typical therapist accounting for 15 to 20 percent of the interaction, with the group spending almost half of its time on individual members—discussing where they are from, their likes and dislikes and their problems. About one fourth of the interaction was concerned with the here-and-now—exploring reactions and relationships among members. In this "statistically typical" therapy group only about one fifth of the time was spent on discussing topics external to the group itself and how it functions. As for the "task" functions of the group, we found almost a third of the time spent in chitchat and exchanging social amenities. However, approximately half of the time was spent in talking about and exploring problems of group members. As little as 5 percent of the time in the "typical" group was spent in constructive confrontation. Another 15 percent was accounted for by ventilations directed toward the establishment, the leader, other members and the group. Thus, about one fifth of the time was spent in our "typical" group in behaviors consistent with so-called attack therapy.

SGD and the Eclectic View

As eclectic group psychotherapists we are concerned with both the here-and-now and there-and-then. We strive to build a climate of acceptance and to practice accurate empathy, unconditional warmth and genuineness. Our goals are to encourage reality-testing, mutual confrontation and the development of transference, as well as providing corrective emotional experiences. However, we do emphasize two aspects of the therapeutic enterprise; systematically derived feedback and concern for group development. These constitute a variation of the eclectic or normative theme. For the purposes of this article we have named our brand of eclectic group psychotherapy *systematic group development* (SGD) therapy.

The Systematic Approach

The systematic element in SGD is best explained through understanding the Hill Interaction Matrix (HIM). The HIM is essentially a set of categories allowing the therapist to conceptualize and describe, in a systematic way, the theoretically relevant group interactions. This matrix of categories has been arranged into an ordinal scale, and rating instruments (HIM-B and HIM-G) have been developed which allow for quantitatively describing Leadership Style, Group Composition and Group Development—all within the same frame of reference. Figure 13.1 and the following paragraphs provide a brief description of the HIM category system. More comprehensive accounts are to be found in Hill (1963, 1966, 1970).

Categories were empirically derived by intensively studying a number of therapy groups. Two basic dimensions seemed paramount in distinguishing among groups. Both dimensions refer to "style" of operation. The content/style dimension, describing *what* groups talk about, has four categories: topic, group, personal and relationship. A group's style can be characterized by talking about here-and-now relationships and reactions of members to each other (Relationship, IV), problems of members in a historical manner (Personal, III), the group itself (Group, II), or all of the topics external to the group, e.g., current events (Topic, I). These can be placed in a nominal scale, but in

Figure 13.1 Hill Interaction Matrix

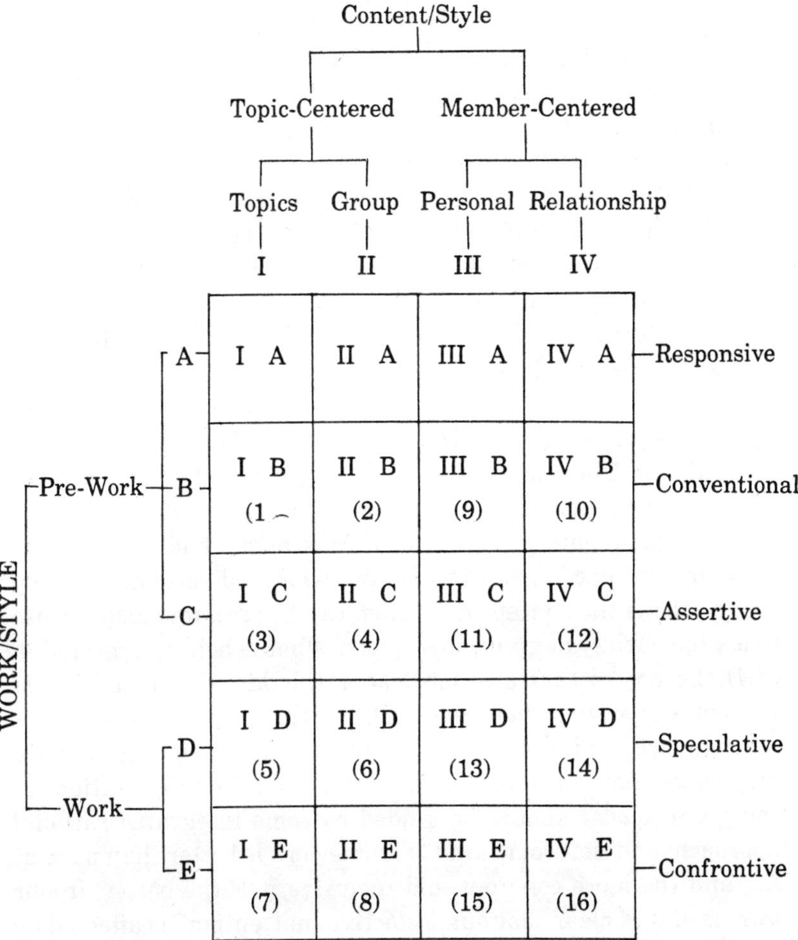

the HIM they appear ordinally in order of assumed increasing therapeutic significance from I to IV.

The other dimension, also empirically derived, describes the level of Work occurring in a group. Within the Work/Style dimensions there are two subdivisions, Work and Pre/Work. In Pre/Work, no one is attempting to gain self-understanding. The lowest level is Responsive (A), characterized by little or nothing taking place except in response to the leader's attempts to stimulate interaction.

Conventional (B) equates treatment groups with other "everyday" groups relying on social amenities, stylized transactions and chitchat; Assertive (C) is the highest rank of Pre/Work categories and represents social protest behavior, usually an assertion of independence from group pressure and a rejection of help from group members. Superficially it may look like Work—a member presenting his problem—but he is "acting-out," not "acting-on," his problem. The Work/Style dimension has the following five categories listed in order of increasing significance: Responsive (A), Conventional (B), Assertive (C), Speculative (D) and Confrontive (E). Work, a term borrowed from Bion (1964), is characterized by interaction of two group members, one playing a helping role and another a patient role engaged in an attempt to gain self-understanding.

The dimensions are arranged in matrix form in the HIM with Content/Style on the horizontal axis and Work/Style on the vertical axis. The matrix (F'gure 13.1) has 20 cells, each of which characterizes typical behavior found in therapy groups.

It is worth noting that the HIM schema had little or no difficulty in encompassing the 50 widely divergent therapy groups. Thus the conceptual system can be recommended for use to a wide variety of group therapists. What is being suggested in SGD therapy is that a group leader should have some kind of explicit and systematic framework by which he assesses what is taking place in his group and it is further suggested that the HIM may serve that purpose. Our position is that the interventions of the group leader should be guided by some integrated rational approach, and that some kind of framework is better than none at all, and the more coherent and inclusive it is the better. In our own case it is clear that our "selective inattention" is affected by the categories of the HIM, but they nonetheless seem to encompass enough of the group phenomena to be useful in understanding most situations that arise in the group. The fact that there have been over 50 studies (Hill, 1971) completed using the HIM, lends some validity to the system and some sense of confidence to the users.

Ideally, SGD goes beyond the simple notion that a good group therapist should have a sytematic conceptual grasp of interaction processes. What is being advocated is that the group leader should base both his therapeutic tactics and strategies on feedback data from his group. The HIM not only makes this

Figure 13.2
Hill Interaction Matrix Scores
HIM-G

Computer Printout

Cell Sequence
TS TM MP MF

	Topic I	Group II	Personal III	Relation-ship IV		Raw Score	Percent	Interpersonal Relationship	TH/M	MP/MF
Conventional-B	1122	2122	2132	0011		23	.209	0	.533	1.143
	= 6	= 7	= 8	= 2		23	.209	0	.533	1.143
Assertive-C	2123	2112	2012	2011						
	= 8	= 6	= 5	= 4		23	.209	+	.769	.625
Speculative-D	3223	2121	2213	3022						
	= 10	= 6	= 8	= 7		31	.282	−	.938	.778
Confrontive-E	2213	2210	3234	2312						
	= 8	= 5	= 12	= 8		33	.300	+	1.200	.667
Raw Score	32	24	33	21						
Percent	.291	.218	.300	.191						
Interpretation	0	+	−	0						
TH/M	.778	1.182	.737	.909						
MP/MF	.636	1.200	.727	.833						
Responsive-A	1	3	2	2	= 8	.40				

Total Score = 110
Total TH Ratio =
Identification Number 64265129
Risk Ratio = 5.185
Intragroup Ratio = 1.731
TH Part 20-40%

Figure 13.3
Hill Interaction Matrix Scores
HIM-A or B
Computer Printout

	Topic I	Group II	Personal III	Relationship IV
Conventional-B	6	7	6	10
Assertive-C	6	3	6	10
Speculative-D	3	4	1	4
Confrontive-E	6	4	4	6
Raw Score	21	18	17	30
Percent	.244	.209	.198	.349
Norm (Score)	0	0	0	7
Norm (Percent)	.00	.00	.05	07
Interpretation				

Raw Score	Percent	Norm (Score)	Norm (Percent) Interpretation
29	.337	1	.00
25	.291	7	.07
12	.140	0	.07
20	.233	0	.00

Total Acceptance Score = 86
Total Norm = 0
Identification Number 5759
Administration Number 1

possible, but also feasible because a number of rating scales have been derived from the conceptual schema. In particular, the HIM-G and HIM-B could be used for this purpose as they only take about 20 minutes to fill out and can be computer-scored to allow for rapid feedback to the therapist.

The HIM-G is a 72-item rating-scale to be filled out by a rater, possibly the therapist, after he has attended a session of a group, listened to it on audio, viewed it on videotape or read a typescript of the session. The test items are descriptive of typical group behaviors and activities, and the rater is not required thereby to be particularly sophisticated in group work or versed in the HIM. These items are keyed to the cells of the HIM, however, and the rater is merely required to discern to what extent, if at all, these behaviors occurred during the group session. As previously indicated, a group can be rated on the HIM-G in about 20–25 minutes, and as it can be computer-scored a printout can be made available to a group leader within a half hour following a group session. Administration, scoring and interpretation of the HIM-G as well as the HIM-B is dealt with in depth in another publication (Hill, 1970), but for the purposes of demonstrating the feedback principle in this article, a sample HIM-G computer printout is offered in Figure 13.2. With brief instruction a group leader could determine, by perusing Figure 13.2, that this group session was characterized by high confrontation and assertive behavior (risk-taking categories) and was highly relative to therapy groups in general in terms of time spent in talking about the group itself (Group or II). The Th/M ratio column tells us that the therapist accounted for much of the high volume in the confrontation and group categories. The foregoing is merely illustrative. Much more can be gleaned from the HIM-G, and it is most revealing where a series of meetings have been rated and changes from session to session can be detected in the ratios, categories and cells.

The HIM-B is essentially similar in construction to the HIM-G. It is a 64-item scale describing typical events that occur in groups and is administered to group members or group leaders who are required to indicate the degree of acceptance they feel toward each of the 64 group situations. These test items are keyed to the HIM categories (4 for each HIM cell). A prospective member can complete the test in 20–25 minutes, and as it is computer-scored the printout can be made available to the group leader almost immediately. A sample printout is made available in Figure 13.3. With brief instruction a group leader could determine by perusing Figure 13.3 that this individual should be able to participate well in a group, as he has a Total Acceptance Score of 86 and the norm average is 70. Also, he is high in Assertive and Relationship as far as the categories are concerned, and in terms of the cells he prefers quite markedly IVB and IVC, which means that he prefers to relate to others in a group and to share reactions with them. The foregoing is merely illustrative; much more can be gleaned from the HIM-B, and it is most revealing where the individual's pattern on the HIM-B can be compared with the composite of the members of his group or prospective group.

It is our contention that most of the variance between groups can be accounted for by three factors: Group Composition, Leadership Style and Group Development (plus a situational factor). If all the members take the HIM-B, the composition of the group can be ascertained. Similarly, if the group leader takes it, leadership-style preferences can also be determined. Where a series of HIM-G readings have been taken, the development, or lack of it, in a group can be traced. Thus utilization of the HIM scales can provide immediate quantitative data on these three factors, and all within the same frame of reference. It is presumed that this feedback can be very useful as a guide to the leader's assessment of where the group is and where it might go. One further word: it has been demonstrated innumerable times that the impressions of group leaders as to what is taking place in their groups are badly distorted when compared to carefully gathered quantitative data.

Our efforts in SGD, therefore, are directed toward making group therapy a little more of a science and a little less of an art, which it is now almost exclusively. We have encountered much resistance to our program. The dissenters seem to be saying, as we interpret it, that a therapist will lose his sensitivity and spontaneity if he knows what he is doing, and furthermore that a scientific approach to human relations tends to be dehumanizing. The following quotation expresses our position on the matter:

> There can be no doubt . . .
> all learning is scientific which
> is systematically laid out and . . .
> that a genuine humanism is scientific
> [Matthew Arnold].

The Group Development Approach

The "group development" aspect of our group-therapy approach is based on the assumption that groups do have a somewhat regular growth pattern, and the therapist's main endeavor is to help in the group's development (Whitaker & Lieberman, 1964). He should be guided in his performance by considerations of the

Figure 13.4
Adaptation of Martin & Hill Theory of Group Development

Level	Description of Behavior	Group Cognitive Style	Therapist's Behavior	Therapeutic Valve	HIM Characteristic
Phase I	Egocentric, Unshared Individualistic-oriented Productions	Free Association	Joins In and Upgrades	Socialization	B
	Transition from Phase I to II	Ennui, Anxiety, Dissatisfaction	Interprets, Models Phase II	Awareness of Source of Dissatisfaction	A & C
Phase II	Reaction to Group Pressure	Asserting Individuality and Protest	Joins In and Upgrades	Presentation of self	C
	Transition from Phase II to III	Ennui, Anxiety, Dissatisfaction	Interprets, Models Phase III	Awareness of Source of Dissatisfaction	A, B, & C
Phase III	Exploration of Individual Potential	Oriented to Individual Psychology	Joins In and Upgrades	Insight into Self	III D III E
	Transition from Phase III to IV	Ennui, Anxiety, Dissatisfaction	Interprets, Models Phase IV	Awareness of Source of Dissatisfaction	
Phase IV	Exploration of Potential	Oriented to Interpersonal Psychology	Joins In and Upgrades	Insight into Relationships	IV D & IV E
	Transition from Phase IV to V	Ennui, Anxiety, Dissatisfaction	Interprets, Models Phase V	Awareness of Source of Dissatisfaction	A, B, & C
Phase V	Exploration of Group Dynamics	Oriented to Group Psychology	Joins In and Upgrades	Insight into Group Process	II D II E

development level and developmental need of the group. The primary task of the therapist is to develop the group. The various innovative techniques, stratagems and devices have little significance where good development is neglected.

In keeping with this procedure we are not oblivious to the needs and strivings of individual members. Nonetheless, our behavior as leader is strongly influenced by its effects on the development of the group. For example, we might ignore or attempt to curb a chronic monopolist. Or, in the case of a persistent nonparticipant, we might attempt to draw that member out. The fact that it was in our judgment "good" for the patient at that time would be sufficient cause, but a necessary cause would be the fact that such behaviors might be impeding group development. Thus, in a group I spend considerable time attempting to understand what is going on with the group: the common group tension, the group process and the underlying group dynamic or hidden agenda. Systematic feedback from the HIM-G helps in diagnosing the developmental level and developmental needs of the group.

What I do in a group at any given moment is therefore in part a consequence of the developmental level of the group. Figure 13.4 presents a brief outline and adaptation of the Martin & Hill (1957) theory under which I try to operate as a group leader. As can be seen from Figure 13.4, my role in the transition phases, where I *lead* the group, is different from my role in the phase plateaus, where the group is locked into a mode of operation. I rest my case for group development on the following quotation with which I strongly concur: "We will not get healthy individuals until we have healthy groups" [Kurt Levin].

The Ideal SGD Group

The ultimate development of SGD therapy would be to instruct group members as well as the group therapists in a theory of group development and in a conceptual system of group behavior. Actually a booklet has been written (McCarty, 1969) which in programmed instruction format teaches the HIM category system. Thus it is envisaged that the group member in the SGD of the future would not have to spend much of his time trying to figure out what is and what should be going on in the group (and what the therapist expects), but by recieving printouts on the structure and function of the group get a glimpse of what is going on in his group and possibly, from time to time, discuss with the other informed members the significance of the feedback data.

Clinical Experience with SGD

So much for the guiding concepts to our group procedure; what about SGD itself? Actually my procedure has only been formally studied on two occasions, and these will be reported here.

In order to do an adequate investigation of group development, a group must be sufficiently stable and meet often enough for systematic phenomena to emerge. A decade ago, when I was working at Utah State Hospital, I conducted over a thousand sessions with the same group. Ten sessions of this group were rated on the HIM at a time when research was being conducted on the group. At that time the group had a very stable membership. In figure 13.5, average HIM ratings are plotted for the ten sessions.

These results were viewed as being very representative of what was going on in the group at that time. In figure 13.5 results of the HIM ratings are graphed. Average percentages in each category are converted to percentile ranks. These percentile ranks are obtained from our group norms (Hill, 1966). As can be seen from Figure 13.5, this group was relatively high in the Group, Relationship and Confrontive categories. This is consistent with my goals for the group, and the daily feedback from the research staff resulted in producing an almost perfect "goodness of fit" with the desired outcome.

In 1969 at Olive View Hospital I conducted a series of 16 weekend sessions with the same clients in what is aptly called *saturation group therapy* (Vernallis, 1969). This provided an ideal situation for demonstrating group development principles. But since there were no process ratings immediately available to the therapist, no systematic leader feedback was provided. HIM ratings for this group are reported in Figure 13.6.

This group does not have a "good" profile in terms of what most modern theorists would demand. In particular, it seems to be quite high in B (Conventional) and low in D (Speculative), which suggests a low level of operation, and only the relatively high E (Confrontation) makes it acceptable as a "good" group. I was

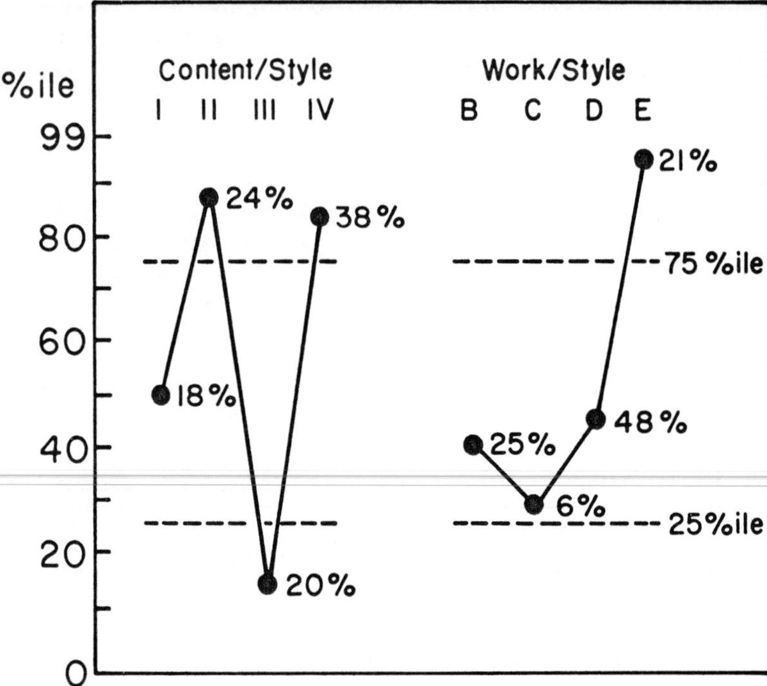

Figure 13.5. Modal measures of percentage of participation in each HIM dimension plotted in terms of percentile norms for Utah State Hospital group.

surprised that this group was not higher in Group (II) and Relationship (IV), and was shocked to find it so high in Conventional (B). If I had HIM-G ratings made available to me on an ongoing basis as was the case in the Utah State Hospital group, this state of affairs would not have continued. This demonstrates how a therapist cannot always accurately gauge what is going on in his group. Even the author of the HIM was "found out" by his own rating instrument!

When prepost scores of my group were compared to those of other group therapists in the project, my group did not improve as much as several of the others on outcome measures. Nonetheless, they did better than the controls. Even more significantly, they continued to improve when measured six months after these 16 weekend sessions. A preliminary report on SGD is now in print (Vernallis, 1969), and a complete analysis of the data will be forthcoming.

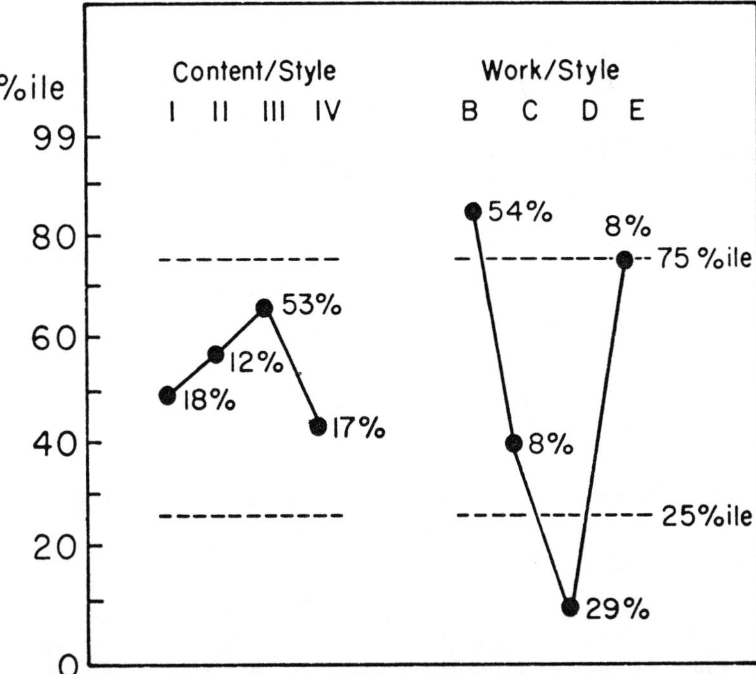

Figure 13.6. Modal measures of percentage of participation in each HIM dimension plotted in terms of percentile norms for Olive View Hospital group.

On the basis of this and other experiences it would seem that the group development approach is likely to have more Conventional ratings than those whose style is deliberately to zoom in on individual members. Also, there is the hint that the effects of the group development approach are slower in taking effect but are perhaps longer-lasting. It conjurs up a spansule theory of recovery.

THEORETICAL RATIONALE

In defining the procedure of SGD in the first section, I could not refrain from indicating something of the underlying rationale for the approach. In this section I will try to be a bit more explicit, a little more personal and hopefully somewhat scholarly.

The underlying assumptions of the SGD are consistent with

what we understood to be those of the National Training Laboratory (in-group development, as it was originally known) and where I served as a researcher under Herbert Thelen in 1951 (Thelen, Ben-Zeev, Hill, Gradolph, Rogers, & Stock, 1954) and as a Training Associate with Jack Gibb in 1952. It was my interpretation that NTL believed that an understanding of group development, like knowing the truth, would free a man and that group leadership should be as much a science as an art. In fact, I recall staying up very late every night to analyze the proceedings in a T-Group and sharing the analysis with the T-Group leaders prior to the next T-Group session.

The idea seems obvious to me that some sort of systematic feedback, whether it comes from the HIM or not, should have utility and lead to better therapy for the group. However, resistance to the idea is considerable among many group leaders. They act as if sensitivity and spontaneity are not compatible with knowledge that is not intuitively derived. That art must make some room for science in clinical practice seems to this writer indisputable. Nonetheless, one is hesitant to go all the way with this approach and suggest that systematic data should also be fed back to the group members. However, studies by Roffers (1969), Hellervik (1968) and Lee (1968) all indicate that clients can be modified behaviorally to operate at higher HIM levels. Yalom et al.'s (1967) study indicates that group members do operate at higher HIM levels when they are given some orientation prior to participating in a therapy group. In any case, a more complete statement of the scientific position in the practice of group therapy is given elsewhere (Hill 1967).

In any event, the group-development approach is important because some of the determinants of a member's behavior are a result of group pressures, group climate, and other group level influences. A member has to see that he has both a cause and an effect relationship with group process. Therefore complete understanding of his behavior cannot be obtained by exclusive concern with psychodynamics, but must include group dynamics. To be more specific, we see stages or levels of mental health development paralleling the stages of group development. Thus in Phase III, (Figure 13.4) the psychology is individual, i.e., it concerns itself with individual psychodynamics whereby the client obtains insight into himself (Foulkes, 1960). This is a step forward and is a necessary but not entirely sufficient condition. In

Phase IV the psychology is interpersonal. This adds the dimension of knowledge about dyads and understanding the transactions between persons rather than just understanding the other person or the self. This adds another developmental layer for coping in the world. Finally, in Phase V, the psychology is group. And to understand this phase is to protect oneself from being the unwitting victim of group processes in therapy, work and social situations. To be able, in addition, to influence the processes is to be well on the road to becoming that mythical self-actualizing man. Again we conclude with a quotation, this time from George Bach (1954), which summarizes all I have said:

> . . . a group therapist cannot be satisfied to be a therapist to the individual in isolation; he must also be a therapist of the group. He must facilitate the growth of the group from its initial states of immature assembly to the more mature states of therapeutically significant communication. . . . it is impossible for the individual to grow psychologically without a concomitant change in the group atmosphere to which he belongs. (p. 268.)

GOALS FOR GROUP

The goal of all group therapy should be the treatment and improvement of the individual and not just the enhancement of the group experience. The outcome data mentioned earlier indicate that, on the average, this goal was to some extent accomplished in the saturation group therapy project. The goal was to maintain an eclectic approach. To my way of thinking, group interaction should embrace all cells of the HIM. Incidentally, the SGD variation did in fact have the best HIM cell coverage in the project. Obviously, it was the goal of this therapist not only to tap the full potential of the group as manifested in the HIM categories but also to get the group through all the phases of our genetic theory. The therapeutic benefits to be derived for each developmental level are explicit in the theory. In brief, the goal was to have members experience both a strong impact from the group and from the therapist's presence. I believe both were accomplished. There is some evidence that the impact will continue to be felt for a number of years to come.

SELECTION OF MEMBERS

Most practitioners do not have the luxury of applying rigorous selection criteria to their groups. Consequently they reject only those condidates who are grossly inappropriate for the purposes of their groups. This often results in having groups with built-in problems that can only be diagnosed and treated by assessing the composition of the group. We have found that data obtained on the group members from the Bion Q Sort, FIRO-B, or HIM-A (simpler-language version of the HIM-B), can be helpful in this regard. Certainly, as additional members are added to a group, some selectivity can be exercised. One must be concerned with what is missing rather than only what is present, and this requires experience or test data to make such determinations. In any event, two factors are involved: maximizing the ránge while at the same time maintaining compatibility of the membership. One should also avoid putting an individual into a group where he might become a psychological isolate. This is covered under the so-called Noah's Ark principle.

There seems to be no limit to the types of classes of people that might benefit from group psychotherapy. If a person is not an appropriate candidate for existing groups because of his pathology, background, I.Q. or whatever, one should find other persons with similar qualities and form a group with them. Thus no one is rejected from group therapy, but he may be rejected from a *particular* group because the group could not function adequately with that person as a member. People are selected or rejected in terms of the conditions under which the group is conducted, compatibility with members and goals of the group.

OPEN AND CLOSED GROUPS

Most traditional therapy groups are open groups, but some have more stable memberships than others. As our theory of group development indicates, it is difficult to develop a therapeutic group if the membership is constantly changing. One of the attractions of marathon group therapy for group therapists may well be that it is a closed group having a relatively long continuous run in terms of number of therapy hours.

It is important to bear in mind Furst's dictum about shortterm and longterm benefits, in which homogeneity favors the shortterm and heterogeneity favors the longterm. In other words, if the turnover of membership is expected, one should maximize homogeneity of grouping for best results. In stable groups that meet for considerable periods of time, greater heterogeneity in membership is desired—within the bounds of compatibility, of course.

TREATMENT SETTING

Not all the variance between therapy groups is accounted for by therapist style, group composition and group development. Some must be attributed to treatment setting. Obviously the physical setting itself is important, and where it is difficult to form a circle or seat people adequately, the therapy suffers. Institutional settings do have their effects, and this is often because of imposed administrative limitations. More often the limitations come from the informal norms operating among the inmates of an institution. Again these are limiting rather than preemptive factors, and group therapy, like a weed, seems to exist, if not prosper, under all kinds of unpropitious conditions.

DURATION OF TREATMENT

What we have been saying in previous sections applies here: namely, that group therapy takes all kinds of forms. There is every conceivable kind of member, a wide variation in settings, and we now observe that the duration of treatment is also highly variable. We now have minilabs and marathon groups as well as brief and extended groups that are open or closed or contractual.

Stoller (1970) observed that for this dimension, as we have indicated for the others, it is not a case of one time-series being better than another but of different therapeutic potentials being emphasized under different conditons. Thus, for the practioner, it is a matter of matching goals to techniques, or in this case, the packaging of group time. Again one can only state that further research is needed on this dimension in order to tease out differences and similarities between contract and open-ended groups and between accelerated and traditionally distributed time groups—including the gains and losses for each condition.

TRENDS AND INNOVATIONS

We read with great empathy the observation by Yalom (1970) that in England he felt like he was avant-garde and when he returned to California he felt almost obsolescent as a group therapist. Again, if there is a variation that can be conceived by a therapist, there is a group somewhere in California putting it to practice. While we rearguard types, who a few short years ago were avant-garde, look on with fascination, envy and doubt—doubt about the ethics, rationale or durability of the professed results—the nonverbal, feeling, gestalt, encounter and nude groups proliferate.

It is my considered opinion that the rationales for most of these innovations are perfectly sound—as rationales go. However, I hold with Yalom (1970) that the "core' must be studied or evaluated with the "front" aspects of these groups. In my terms, this means that we must know the theme as well as the variations.

SUMMARY

SGD therapy is not a wildly innovative approach to group therapy but is orthodox-eclectic with an emphasis on:

(1) utilization by the group leader of an explicit theory of group development
(2) utilization of systematic feedback, e.g., HIM, by the group leader
(3) sharing the theories, concepts and feedback data with the group members.

REFERENCES

Bach, G. R. *Intensive group psychotherapy.* New York: Ronald Press, 1954.

Bion, W. R. *Experience in groups.* New York: Basic Books, 1964.

Foulkes, S. W. *Therapeutic group analysis.* New York: International Universities Press, 1960.

Hellervik, L. W. An operant conditioning approach to changing counselor interview behavior. Unpublished doctoral dissertation, University of Minnesota, 1968.

Hill, W. F. Hill Interaction Matrix (HIM) Scoring Manual. Los Angeles, California: Youth Studies Center, University of Southern California, 1963.

Hill, W. F. Hill Interaction Matrix (HIM) Monograph. Los Angeles, California: Youth Studies Center, University of Southern California, 1966.

Hill, W. F. (Ed.). Group therapy for social impact. *American Behavioral Scientist.* 1967, **11,** (1), 1–49.

Hill, W. F. Supplement to Hill Interaction Matrix (HIM). Los Angeles: Youth Studies Center, University of Southern California, 1970.

Hill, W. F. Annotated Bibliography of HIM Studies and Reports. Los Angeles: PSRI, University of Southern California, 1971.

Lee, G. R. Operant conditioning of within-interview verbal behavior of counselors-in-training. Paper presented at meeting of the American Psychological Association, San Francisco, September, 1968.

Martin, E. A. & Hill, W. F. Toward a theory of group development. *International Journal of Group Psychotherapy,* 1957, **7,** 20–30.

McCarty, T. M. *It all has to do with identity.* Salt Lake City: Institute for the Study of Interaction Systems, 1969.

Roffers, T. Conditioning a style of interaction in group therapy and its effects on behavior and attitude change. Unpublished doctoral dissertation, University of Minnesota, 1969.

Stoller F. H. Psychotherapy and the time grain: Pace in process. *Comparative Group Studies,* 1970, 410–418.

Thelen, H. A., Ben-Zeev, S., Hill, W. F., Gradolph, W., Rodgers, R. & Stock, D. Methods of studying work and emotionality in group operation. Human Dynamics Laboratory, University of Chicago, 1954, No. 1.

Vernallis, F. F. Saturation group therapy, Olive View, California. Olive View Hospital Report No. 1, 1969.

Whitaker, K. S. & Lieberman, J.A., *Psychotherapy through the group process.* New York: Atherton Press, 1964.

Yalom, I. D., Houts, P. S., Newell, G. & Rand, K. H. Preparation of patients for group therapy. *Archives of General Psychiatry,* 1967, **17,** 416–427.

Yalom, I. D. *The theory and practice of group psychotherapy.* New York: Basic Books, 1970.

Section IV

Data and Research

Introduction

Section IV consists of four chapters which have more of the quality of review chapters than the chapters preceding. John Cone and E. Wayne Sloop, in the first chapter of the section, present a historical review of the use of parents as treatment agents for their children, and a somewhat discouraging evaluation of the success of traditional methods of child therapy. The main thrust of the chapter, however, resides in a description of the principles which are taught to parents trained in the methods of experimental analysis of the behavior of their children, and a review of some of the current literature referring to training parents of a single family, and to training groups of parents as behavior modifiers. The second chapter, Affect in Groups, begins with a discussion of the concept of emotion and how it is related to social illness and health on the one hand and to intervention by group methods on the other. The chapter proceeds to review current research on the role of emotion in group interventions, including studies on the emotions which arise during group interventions, on the affective consequences of group intervention. The chapter also presents information regarding the relationships between the emotional characteristics of participants or groups of participants, and behavior during and at the conclusion of the group intervention.

The third chapter, Learning-Oriented and Training-Oriented Approaches to the Modification of Emotional Behavior in Groups, reviews some current literature on intervention in groups and systems produced by adherents of three different learning orientations. The training of group leaders, clients and "significant others" in interpersonal skills such as empathy by those who espouse systematic experiential learning is covered first. A second section reviews recent literature referring to the work of those using behavior rehearsal methods, such as systematic desensitization, in groups to diminish undesirable emotions such as anxiety. The third section describes the principles and some of the very recent literature which refers to the use of social-learning principles and operant techniques as devices for group intervention.

The final chapter, The Use of Feedback in Groups, considers some of the issues and knowledge surrounding the use of feedback in groups. This chapter reviews some of the current literature on verbal feedback and the use of audio and videotape reproductions of behavior to deliver feedback in groups. Recent experiments by the author and colleagues on the reception of verbal feedback in groups are also described.

14. Parents as Agents of Change

John D. Cone
E. Wayne Sloop

Training parents to be behavior modifiers is a logical extension of the operant approach to treatment, assert John Cone and Wayne Sloop, because parents and other caretakers have the most control over environmental stimuli which powerfully influence the behavior of children. Experimental analysis, in this approach to treatment, identifies the behavior of the parent as the focus of the intervention, rather than that of the child who has heretofore been designated as the patient. Also, the potential preventative value is apparent of teaching to parents general techniques which can be utilized with other children than those in need of treatment, and can be applied to most behavior difficulties which may arise in their families.

The inclusion of parents in the treatment plan for children with behavior disorders is not a new invention, as the authors point out. However, traditional child-treatment methods have emphasized intrapsychic concepts and much inference regarding the internal reactions of the patient, and therefore it would be difficult to train the average parent in the use of such techniques with their children. In addition, Cone and Sloop review evidence which raises questions regarding both the efficacy and efficiency of traditional child treatment methods.

The users of the operant approach, on the other hand, have reported substantial success in the treatment of a variety of child-behavior disorders by training parents. Ingenious attempts have been employed to model and to reinforce change in parental behavior, and more sophisticated conceptualization is occurring regarding the nature of parent-child interaction. However, most of these studies have described the treatment of only one or two children, and other studies were characterized by various methodological shortcomings such as the omission by the research of descriptions of exactly what was taught to parents and how much the parents learned.

Very few studies exist at present which have evaluated the training of parents in groups as behavior modifiers. Cone and Sloop are skeptical that it has been convincingly demonstrated that parents can be effectively trained in groups, or that the critical ingredients of the training program have been identified.

INTRODUCTION

The use of parents as therapeutic agents of change has a relatively long history. Until the past few years, however, parent participation has generally been limited to passive enhancement of the therapeutic atmosphere in their child's treatment or concurrent inclusion in a therapy of their own. Training parents as active modifiers of children's behavior is an enterprise of relatively recent origin. The present paper surveys the history of the use of parents as change agents and then focuses on the efforts of behaviorally oriented investigators to train parents in the principles of behavior modification. Our intent is to present a moderately extensive coverage of the literature in this area. However, in keeping with the general emphasis of the book we have focused more on group strategies of parent training than on studies attempting to train one or more parents of a single family.

It is difficult to appreciate the full significance of a major new development in any field without viewing it in historical perspective and in the context of other major developments and problems within that field. Thus, the first four sections of the chapter present an historical perspective, an evaluation of traditional modes of child therapy, some comments on mental health manpower needs and a brief overview of the growing development and application of behavior-modification techniques. Rather than assume a "bag of tricks" view of behavior modification, an effort has been made to emphasize the coherence of the set of principles underlying the training of parents as behavior modifiers. These principles are best summarized under the rubric "experimental analysis of behavior" (Skinner, 1964). Consequently, the section on the growing development and application of experimental-analysis principles is followed by a brief section detailing the rationale for including parents in efforts to modify their child's behavior.

The essence of the chapter is then presented in the section titled "Strategies of Training." Here we have endeavored to divide the literature into those studies training one or both parents of a single family (single-family approach) and those training groups of parents (multiple-family approach) as behavior modifiers. Rather than cover the single-family approach extensively a few examples are presented in some detail. These provide a flavor for work in this area while at the same time conserving space for the more thorough presentation of the multiple family (group) approach which follows.

HISTORICAL PERSPECTIVE

The deliberate inclusion of one or both parents as agents in the therapy of their child has a history almost as old as that of contemporary psychological treatment itself. As Guerney (1969) has noted, Freud (1950) was the pioneer in this regard with his treatment of the phobias of a five-year-old boy. That now classic therapy was conducted almost entirely with the father acting as therapist, and Freud emphasized the therapeutic contribution afforded by the unique father-son relationship. The historical significance of "Little Hans" stems more from its contributions to the psychoanalytic understanding of childhood neurosis, however, than from its demonstration of the value of incorporating parents into the treatment process as active therapeutic agents.

Following Freud, psychoanalytically oriented therapists have reported a variety of case studies in which one or both parents have been included in the child's treatment. It is interesting that many of the current attempts to use parents as modifiers of their child's behavior have, at least, superficial similarities to early psychanalytic efforts.

One of the prevalent assumptions underlying psychoanalytic treatment of the child is that many of his difficulties may be traced to unconscious conflicts, thoughts and feelings of the parents themselves (e.g., Hampton, 1962). Hence, the collaborative treatment of mother and child by social worker and psychiatrist was the prevailing mode in the child guidance movement (Noyes & Kolb, 1963, p. 497). Many therapists have gone further, including both mother and child in the same therapy session, and have offered anecdotal evidence for a variety of advantages in doing so. For example, Schwarz (1950) and Kolansky (1960) pointed out that including the mother reduces the likelihood of the child's developing a loyalty conflict between parent and analyst and moderates the guilt a child might experience about disclosing family secrets in the therapy hour. Other advantages are said to include helping the mother recognize her own unconscious feelings (Furman, 1950; Ruben & Thomas, 1947), helping the parents toward more realistic expectations of their child (Schwarz, 1950), permitting direct treatment of the parent-child relationship itself rather than the separate personalities of its constituents (Elkirsch, 1953), effecting economies of patient and therapist time (Bonnard, 1950), and establishing the basis for a possible spread of therapeutic effect to other children in the family who are not treated directly (Bonnard, 1950; Schwarz, 1950).

As with Freud's case of "Little Hans," most of the psychoanalytic case reports of parents being included in their child's treatment have had little to say about the therapeutic process per se, tending to focus instead upon understanding the psychodynamics of the particular child (Guerney, 1969). The therapeutic emphasis appears to be focused more upon analyzing and interpreting unconscious conflicts of child or parent than upon teaching the parent specific techniques for handling the child's problems on his own. A few psychoanalytic case reports mention the value of the parent's learning the analyst's ways of relating to the child, but these appear to rely mainly upon unsystematic modeling opportunities provided during the therapy hour and vague exhortations to "draw out and show acceptance" of all the child's feelings.

The scarcity of psychoanalytic reports detailing the training of parents as therapists is not difficult to understand when one considers the nature of psychoanalytic theory and its application to child therapy. The data of psychoanalysis, i.e., intrapsychic phenomena, are extremely difficult, if not impossible, to infer reliably, making adequate training a highly demanding and complex affair. If, for example, the analyst's goal is the "redirecting of instinctual energy" from inappropriate objects to appropriate ones (Rangell, 1950), how does he train parents to facilitate this process? How does he train them even to recognize which objects the child has already cathected? Moreover, how does he sell the parents his own interpretation of their child's dynamics? These are obviously extremely difficult undertakings, ones which analysts themselves take years to perfect. It is questionable whether the average parent could easily learn such an abstract, indirect mode of understanding and handling the very concrete problems she is confronting in her child. Furthermore, the efficacy of intrapsychic strategies in even the deftest of hands has been called into question repeatedly, as a subsequent section of this paper will show.

Therapists of a client-centered persuasion have also been involved in attempts to incorporate parents into the therapy of their children (e.g., Carkhuff & Bierman, 1970; Fuchs, 1960; Guerney, 1964). The most extensive and well-developed efforts in this direction are those of Guerney (Guerney, 1964; Guerney, 1966; Stover & Guerney, 1967; Guerney, 1969) and his colleagues at Rutgers. Under the label *filial therapy*, these investigators have developed a method of training parents to act essentially as client-centered therapists during play-therapy sessions conducted at home with their child several times each week.

Filial therapy has been described by Guerney (1964) as involving three general stages. During the first stage, groups of nonspouse parents averaging about six to eight in number meet for a series of sessions designed to train them in the specific techniques they will use in later play-therapy sessions with their child. The benefits of play therapy are presented to the parents in terms of "release from tension-producing inner conflict, freer communication processes from child to parent, and giving the child a greater sense of self-direction, self-respect, and self-confidence" (Guerney, 1964).

These advantages are said to accrue through the parent's use of specific Rogerian therapy techniques such as reflection, clarification of feeling and structuring. Demonstrations of these techniques are conducted by the trainers using normal children or children of group members. Role-playing is also used and opportunity is provided for the exploration of feelings and attitudes of the parents in a client-centered, nondirective way. During the final phase of the first stage each parent is observed conducting a play session with his own or another group member's child, and the session is discussed later by the entire group.

The second stage is entered somewhere around the seventh or eighth session with the parents' beginning to conduct play therapy with their child at home. Standard play-therapy equipment purchased by the parents is used, and they are encouraged to take notes of the session or tape-record it for later evaluation by the group. While technique remains a common subject of group discussion during this stage, more emphasis is given to the parents' and children's emotional reactions to the therapy. The third and final stage involves termination.

Unlike psychoanalytic reports which included parents in their child's therapy but emphasized understanding of the child's psychodynamics, Guerney has attempted to specify carefully the actual techniques taught to the parents. A prominent assumption in filial therapy is that the parent will be the most active agent in his child's recovery. Such an emphasis upon the specifics of technique is commendable. However, filial therapy shares a common difficulty with the psychoanalytic approach, i.e., a theoretical basis in intrapsychic phenomena. Parents are told to observe carefully, with "the child's needs uppermost in mind," to encourage the child's increased freedom to express himself in order that the parent gain "greater understanding of the child from which the parent can in turn gain more realistic expectations and attitudes" (Guerney, 1964). The advantages of the parent's providing a 24-hour therapist are recognized but explained in such abstractions as enabling the child to "lift repression and work through conflicts more quickly" (Guerney, 1964).

As with psychoanalytic approaches, the use of abstract, global concepts may not carry much face validity for parents confronted with very concrete problem behaviors in their child. Furthermore, one might expect such obfuscation to result in relatively long and expensive parent-training programs. Indeed, Guerney's (1964) report of two filial-therapy groups still in progress after eight and ten months should be compared with the results of explicit cost analyses provided by Patterson, Ray & Shaw (1968), which show much greater economies of therapist time using behaviorally oriented techniques.

Such comments are not intended to overshadow the important contributions filial therapy has made, however, The systematic attempt to train parents in the use of specific techniques in task-oriented group sessions is certainly to be applauded. Providing parents with clearly defined roles and corrective feedback from the therapist and other group participants is a vast improvement over the passive participation provided in most early psychoanalytic parent-child treatment schemes. Ultimately, the usefulness of filial therapy will have to be evaluated with controlled outcome studies, and an encouraging start in this direction has been provided by Stover & Guerney (1967).

It should be pointed out that the goals of psychoanalytic and client-centered approaches are different from those of more behaviorally oriented strategies. Whereas the latter focus upon changing specific behavior in an identified child and his parents, the former are more concerned with personality restructuring and reorganization. It is eminently reasonable that a more modest focus on specific behavior may take less time and fewer resources. Which set of goals is more useful in terms of longrange mental health requirements is an empirical question, of course, the answer to which is only recently beginning to unfold.

EFFECTIVENESS OF TRADITIONAL CHILD PSYCHOTHERAPIES

With the exception of recent efforts to evaluate the effectiveness of filial therapy, there have been no systematic assessments of either the psychoanalytic or client-centered approaches to training parents as therapists for their own children. However, there have been studies assessing the effectiveness of these modes of therapy applied directly to the child. Indeed, it is the rather bleak results of such studies which have influenced the rapid development of behaviorally oriented parent-training strategies. For this reason, a brief summary evaluation of traditional modes of child psychotherapy will be presented here.

The best-known attempts to assess the effectiveness of

traditional child psychotherapy are those of Levitt (1957, 1963, 1971). Using Eysenck's (1952) article on adult psychotherapy as a model to assess the effectiveness of psychotherapy with children, Levitt (1957) chose as his baseline unit of measurement evaluations of the degree of improvement of the patient by concerned clinicians. Under the general heading of "improved" Levitt included individuals listed as "much improved, improved, partially improved, successful, partially successful," etc., while individuals listed as "slightly improved, unimproved, unadjusted, failure, worse," etc., were included as "unimproved" cases. As "control" subjects Levitt chose "defectors," i.e., children who had been accepted for treatment by a clinic but who never reported for treatment (Witmer & Keller, 1942; Lehrman, Sirluck, Black & Glick, 1949). In the Witmer and Keller study subjects were appraised 8 to 13 years after clinic treatment, and 78 per cent were rated as improved. The Lehrman et al. study employed a one-year follow-up interval and found 70 per cent improved. The overall rate of improvement in both reports was 72.5 per cent, and this figure was used as the baseline for evaluating the results of child psychotherapy. A total of 37 reports were included by Levitt, who attempted to use only cases which would crudely be termed "neuroses." Of the 37 reports, 13 gave evaluations at the close of treatment, 12 at followup; 5 furnished both close and followup data (yielding a total of 18 at close, 17 at followup); and an additional 2 studies yielded data based upon a combined close-followup rating.

The 18 studies providing evaluations at close indicated 67 per cent of the children were rated improved, while the 17 studies providing followup evaluations indicated that 78 per cent were rated improved at followup intervals ranging from 6 months to 27 years. The two studies using a combined close-followup evaluation found 74 per cent of the patients rated as improved. When the results of the 37 outcome reports were compared with the 72.5 per cent rate of improvement found in the baseline groups, Levitt (1957, p. 195) concluded "the results of the present study fail to support the view that psychotherapy with 'neurotic' children is effective."

The use of defector groups to yield base rates of spontaneous remission has been criticized by a number of writers (Eisenberg & Gruenberg, 1961; Heinicke & Goldman, 1960; Hood-Williams,

1960; Kessler, 1966). Replying to Hood-Williams, Levitt (1960) cited a number of studies which tended to show that defectors are not, in fact, a biased control group and can therefore be used to provide evidence of improvement in the absence of psychotherapy. Of the studies cited, one of the most impressive, Levitt, Beiser & Robertson (1959), involved the comparison of 192 patients and 93 defectors on 26 variables derived from psychological tests, objective facts of adjustment, parents' ratings, self-ratings and clinical judgments of the interviewers. No significant difference between the two groups was found on *any* of the 26 outcome variables.

Another critique of Levitt (1957) pointed out that he failed to distinguish between diagnostic categories (Eisenberg & Gruenberg, 1961; Eisenberg, Gilbert, Cytryn & Molling, 1961). Acknowledging the merit of this criticism, Levitt (1963) reviewed 22 publications involving clients separable into the following diagnostic groupings: neurosis, acting-out, special symptoms, psychosis and mixed. The overall improvement rate for the 1741 cases involved was 65 per cent. Evaluations at close and followup were not separated and the earlier pooled defector rate of improvement of 72.5 per cent (Levitt, 1957) was used as the baseline. The defector rate was greater than the 65 per cent rate yielded by the 22 studies reviewed. Removal of the psychotic and acting-out diagnostic categories from the 1963 review yielded an adjusted rate of improvement of 68 per cent, still less that the defector rate of 72.5 per cent. Levitt concluded:

> The results of this second review of evaluations of outcome of therapy with children are similar to those of the earlier review, and like those earlier findings, do not differ markedly from results obtained with defector cases. And again, the inescapable conclusion is that available evaluation studies do not furnish a reasonable basis for the hypothesis that psychotherapy facilitates recovery from emotional illness in children [1963, p. 49].

Two additional studies which yielded essentially the same percentage improvement for treated cases as those found by Levitt (1957, 1963) can be cited. Lucas & Ochrock, in a study cited by Kessler (1966, p. 393), grouped the published studies chronologically by year of publication. In the decade from 1930 to 1940, nine studies reported that 68 per cent of the patients improved; from 1940 to 1950, eight studies reported 78 per cent improved, and from 1950 to 1962, three studies reported 56 per cent improved. Shepherd, Oppenheim & Mitchell (1966) report the results of a comparison between a group of 50 children attending child-guidance clinics and a similar group of children matched by age, sex and behavior disorder. After a two-year follow-up 63 per cent of the clinic cases had improved and 61 per cent of the matched children who received no formal therapy were also judged improved. The Shepherd et al. results show slightly less improvement overall than seen in the Levitt (1957, 1963) reports, but the conclusion to be drawn obviously must agree with those of Levitt.

In summary, little evidence exists to support the belief that "traditional" child-psychotherapy techniques are more successful than no formal treatment in ameliorating childhood behavioral disturbances. Certainly the burden of demonstrating the efficacy of "traditional" intervention procedures must lie with adherents of these approaches.

MENTAL HEALTH MANPOWER: QUESTS FOR NEW MENTAL HEALTH CARE DELIVERY TECHNIQUES

The rather bleak outcome figures of the "effectiveness" studies cited in the preceding section must be added to an equally grim mental-health manpower picture. The present and projected shortage of manpower in the core mental health professions of psychiatry, psychology, social work and psychiatric nursing are well-known and have been amply documented (e.g., Albee, 1959, 1968; Arnhoff, 1968; Arnhoff, Rubinstein, Shriver & Jones, 1969; *Report of the Joint Commission on Mental Health of Children*, 1969). For example, the *Report of the Joint Commission on Mental Health of Children* (1969) spends a considerable amount of time discussing the manpower deficit and mentions the necessity for developing programs to produce associate-professionals such as psychiatric technicians, child-care workers, case aides in social work, etc., as a partial answer to the manpower shortage.

Each of the four professions has convened various high-level committees, study groups and national manpower conferences over the past 10 to 15 years. "And the conclusion reached (current need for services outdistances available or projected manpower supply) has been monotonously repetitious, with only the name of the profession changed in the .al reports and conclusions of each of the four professions [Matarazzo, 1971, p. 363]." From the vantage point of mid-1971, it is quite obvious that the four core professions, and their members, have done a considerable amount of talking and writing about the manpower shortage. However, very few innovative programs utilizing nontraditional mental-health manpower have been initiated by these professions. While the writing, talking, and meeting continues, "other segments of society appear to have tired of waiting and have recruited, trained, and already put to work thousands upon thousands of nonprofessional persons . . . [Matarazzo, 1971, p. 363]." Matarazzo (1971) has documented the tremendous recent surge in such programs.

Within the "core" professions, recent attention has been given to streamlining the whole process of child treatment so that more children can be seen more efficiently by existing personnel (e.g., Chess & Lyman, 1970; Livingstone, Portnoi, Sherry, Rosenheim & Onesti, 1970; Mackay, 1967). These changes represent significant, long-needed innovations. However, even if widely adopted they will not do the entire job. Other alternatives, along the lines suggested by Guerney (1969), Hobbs (1964), Matarazzo (1971) and the *Report of the Joint Commission on Mental Health of Children* (1969), need to be pursued. What is needed is not "more of the same" but a quantum leap in delivery potential, something akin to the dramatic increases in capacity provided by the third generation in electronic computers.

From the standpoint of remediation and prevention, one of the most dramatic and potentially fruitful developments heralding a third generation in mental-health-care delivery is the increasing use of "symbionts" (Guerney, 1969, p. 246), such as parents, teachers and peers. Mental-health manpower needs and the empirical accomplishments of behavior therapy noted in the next section have combined to lay the foundation for the effective use of parents as modifiers of their child's behavior.

THE GROWING DEVELOPMENT AND APPLICATION OF THE PRINCIPLES OF THE EXPERIMENTAL ANALYSIS OF BEHAVIOR

The fact that behavior is largely controlled by its consequences was not invented by social scientists but has long been studied by them (Thorndike, 1898). The implications of this fact for the behavior of man have only recently begun to be realized, however. Slightly more than a decade ago Skinner (1958) correctly noted that the experimental analysis of behavior is "only slowly reaching into the field of human behavior." This slow reaching has positively accelerated at such a rate over the past ten years that there is now scarcely a corner of human behavior that has not been influenced to some degree.

Early work with lower animals demonstrated unequivocally that much behavior is shaped and maintained by environmental events following the response. Experimental work with cats (Thorndike, 1898), rats (Skinner, 1938), pigeons (Ferster & Skinner, 1957) and other animals demonstrated that the frequency of certain behaviors, e.g., opening a door, pressing a lever or pecking a disk, could be brought under the control of consequent stimuli such as food and water. Similar studies have led to the development of a consistent body of principles often set forth under the general rubric "experimental analysis of behavior" (Skinner, 1964).

A wide range of children's behavior has been shown to be understandable in terms of experimental-analysis principles. Retarded behavior (Birnbrauer, Bijou, Wolf & Kidder, 1965; Birnbrauer, Wolf, Kidder & Tague, 1965; Peterson & Peterson, 1968), autistic behavior (Ferster & DeMyer, 1961; Lovaas, Berberich, Perloff & Schaeffer, 1966; Wetzel, Baker, Roney & Martin, 1966); delinquent behavior (Burchard & Tyler, 1965; Meichenbaum, Bowers & Ross, 1968; Tyler & Brown, 1967), elective mutism Blake & Moss, 1965), encopresis (Barrett, 1969; Gelber & Meyer, 1965; Neale, 1963), speech deficiencies (Cook & Adams, 1966; Reynolds & Risley, 1968), behavior related to brain injuries (Hall & Broden, 1967) and echolalia (Risley & Wolf, 1967) are some of the behavior problems to which these principles have been applied.

Moreover, the techniques of experimental analysis have been used in a wide variety of settings. These have included psychological laboratories (e.g., Wahler, Winkel, Peterson & Morrison, 1965), nursery-school playgrounds (e.g., Buell, Stoddard, Harris & Baer, 1968), nursery-school classrooms (Brown & Elliott, 1965), elementary-school classrooms (e.g., O'Leary, Becker, Evans & Saudargas, 1969), institutions (e.g., Barton, Guess, Garcia & Baer, 1970), Appalachian community mental-health centers (Wahler & Erickson, 1969), and the home (e.g., Patterson, Ray & Shaw, 1968; Zeilberger, Sampen & Sloane, 1968; O'Leary, O'Leary & Becker, 1967).

Though operant techniques appear to provide us with very powerful ways of modifying behavior, it is a bit too early to evaluate their full range of application and effectiveness. General reviews of behavior modification (Gelfand & Hartmann, 1968; Grossberg, 1964; Pawlicki, 1970) have implied that the greater effectiveness of behavioral over traditional modes of change is more a promise than a fact at this point in their history. Indeed, Gelfand & Hartmann (1968) suggested that many of the child behavior therapy studies they reviewed represented "no improvement over the traditional case study method in terms of experimental rigor [p. 212]." Pawlicki (1970), reviewing 54 behavior-therapy studies with children published during the period 1965–1969, concluded that "most of the research reviewed did not meet basic requirements of scientific research [p. 169]." Some of the methodological problems which need to be overcome will be discussed in a later paper. Methodological difficulties notwithstanding, however, experimental analysis principles and supporting empirical evidence have provided the necessary foundation upon which to base extensive efforts to train parents as behavior modifiers.

RATIONALE FOR TRAINING PARENTS AS BEHAVIOR MODIFIERS

The increasing frequency of this type of parent training may be seen as the logical outgrowth of a number of influences. The repeated failure to demonstrate the effectiveness of traditional modes of child therapy has led to disenchantment with them and a search for useful alternatives. This search has been accelerated by the realization that the supply of mental-health manpower is being more than outpaced by rapidly increasing demands for its services. Alternative modes of meeting current and future mental-health requirements are needed, for, as Hobbs (1964) has stated, "it will be of no moment simply to train ourselves to do better what we are already doing." Underscoring Hobb's statement, Bandura (1969) has added:

> Even if the traditional forms of psychotherapy had proved highly effective, they would still have limited social value. A method that requires extended and highly expensive training, that can be performed only by professional personnel, that must be continuously applied on a one-to-one basis over a prolonged period of time, and is most beneficial to self-selected highly suggestible persons cannot possibly have much impact on the countless social problems that demand psychological attention. Major progress will be made in resolving these problems by concentrating on the development of highly efficacious principles of behavioral change and by utilizing the large pool of nonprofessional persons who can be trained to implement programs under competent guidance and direction. This approach would provide more prople with more help than they receive under current professional practices [pp. 60–61]."

As already mentioned, the mental-health manpower pool is being expanded by increasing the use of potential influential agents within the social milieu of the client (Matarazzo, 1971). Parents, teachers and peers are three categories of significant others, or symbionts, that have been shown to possess such influence. A number of conceptually different approaches have been suggested for the incorporation of these agents into the therapy of a specific client. However, the approach most frequently used has been based upon principles derived from the experimental analysis of behavior.

The reason for this preference are fairly easy to understand. A growing number of case studies applying operant techniques with children have used relatively well-controlled designs and demonstrated effective control over the behavior in question (e.g.,

Harris, Johnston, Kelley & Wolf, 1964; Wiltz, 1970). Furthermore, the principles of operant techniques are straightforward and easily understood, and they direct attention in an objective, commonsense manner to the concrete problem-behaviors parents are concerned with in their children. In addition, a variety of commercially prepared books and pamphlets are available which present operant concepts to parents and others in an easily understandable, often programmed manner (e.g., Becker, 1971; McIntire, 1970; Patterson & Gullion, 1968; Valett, 1969).

However, the most important reason for training parents to use operant techniques is that logically consistent adherence to experimental analysis principles requires it. Parents and other caretaking agents invariably have control over environmental stimuli which powerfully influence their child's behavior. Moreover, control of these stimuli is vested in the parents significantly more often than 50 minutes a week. Even if professional therapists were to gain effective control over certain behaviors during the usual 50-minute session, there is little reason to suppose this would generalize to the nontherapy environment. On the contrary, the deviant behavior was probably shaped and maintained by the social environment of the child in the first place (Patterson, McNeal, Hawkins & Phelps, 1967). Returning him to an unchanged set of reinforcement contingencies is simply to invite retention of the problem.

Such a view suggests that the logical approach to changing behavior is to "reprogram the social environment" in which it occurs (Patterson et al., 1967). As parents are usually the most significant "mediators" of reinforcement (Tharp & Wetzel, 1969) in the child's social environment, it follows that they should be taught new, more effective ways of mediating. It should be apparent that this position changes the focus of the professional's effort from the "identified patient," the child, to the parents. Indeed, some studies (e.g., Peine & Munro, 1970) have included only parent behaviors as the dependent variables of interest. Most have attempted to include both parent and child behaviors, and the more sophisticated (e.g., Patterson & Reid, 1970; Mash & Terdal, 1970) have studied the interaction between them. The following two sections provide an overview of the work that has been accomplished thus far.

STRATEGIES OF TRAINING

This section discusses a number of strategies that have been used in training parents as behavior modifiers. In a sense, all of the studies we shall mention have involved a group approach, if one is willing to define groups as consisting of as few as three persons and not require their concomitant interaction. However, for ease of exposition the studies are divided into those using single-family versus multiple-family strategies. The latter conform most closely to traditional definitions of groups and, in keeping with the general theme of this book, they will receive more emphasis. First, however, single-family studies will be summarized and evaluated briefly.

Single-Family Approaches

This section will focus upon reports which have described the training of parents as behavior modifiers within a single-family constellation. The principle requirement for inclusion in this section is that the report describe a behaviorally oriented intervention program which places one or both parents of a single family in the role of primary therapeutic agent. Conditioning treatment of nocturnal enuresis, using a buzzer or bell device, is one area wherein parents have almost always served as therapists for their own children. However, the nature of parent participation in this kind of program differs significantly from the parent involvement demanded in studies included here. In conditioning treatment for enuresis, the parent serves basically as an "apparatus supervisor" (except in the recent articles by Kimmel & Kimmel, 1970, and Nordquist, 1970) in the sense that they are generally given the responsibility for carrying out routinized procedures involving the child and the conditioning apparatus. Studies in this area have been reviewed elsewhere (e.g., Lovibond, 1964; Yates, 1970) and will not be covered in this chapter. Neither will any attention be given the intriguing efforts of a few researchers who have recently begun applying an operant strategy in family and marital therapy (cf. Liberman, 1970; Patterson & Hops, 1970). Continued work in this area may develop avenues for training whole families in the systematic application of behavioral principles.

A moderately exhaustive search of the literature yielded 49 studies involving single-family interventions in which one or both parents acted as the agent of change. A total of 135 children were included in these studies, and the problem behaviors ranged from encopresis to psychogenic seizures. The vast majority of the 49 reports dealt with only one (N=31) or two (N=9) children. Among the studies which dealt with more than two children, some have dealt with a number of children all of whom display essentially the same kind of problem behavior, and the investigators have applied basically the same procedures to each child (Kennedy, 1965; Kimmel & Kimmel, 1970; Ryback & Staats, 1970; Wagner & Ora, 1970; Wahler, 1968). For example, Kennedy (1965) developed a routinized procedure which he applied in working with 50 children who showed what he called Type 1 school phobia. Other studies involving work with more than two children (e.g., Patterson et al., 1968; Wahler, 1969b; and Wahler *et al.*, 1965) have dealt with at least two differing major problem-behaviors.

Most of the studies reviewed for this section used observational data as the basis for judging the success or failure of the intervention attempts. The experimenter served as the data collector in 17 of the 49 reports, while both experimenter and parents collected data in 11 of the studies. From the standpoint of data reliability and validity, studies in which the experimenter collected some of the observational data (e.g., Allen & Harris, 1966; Bernal, Duryee, Pruett & Burns, 1968) are preferable to those in which the data were collected entirely by the parents (e.g., Johnson, 1969; Russo, 1964). However, this varies somewhat with the behavior in question, being more of a problem with some, e.g., compliance, than with others, e.g., chronic constipation (Lal & Lindsley, 1968; Peterson & London, 1965; Tomlinson, 1970), school phobia (Kennedy, 1965) and similar "unitary" problems.

In addition to considering who collects the data, the locus of collection is important. Some researchers have been aware of possible incomparability of data collected in the clinic and in the natural environment. A total of 13 of the 49 studies reviewed involved data collection by the experimenter in the actual setting where the deviant behavior occurred rather than relying solely upon parental reports or clinic observation. Although at times it is difficult, if not impossible, to observe the target behavior *in situ*, this procedure is advisable whenever possible.

The reports by White (1959) and Williams (1959) represent the beginning of the behaviorally-oriented single-family approach to the direct training of parents as therapeutic agents. Williams (1959) successfully trained the parents of a 21-month-old boy, via a brief series of interviews, to deal with the tantrum behaviors he emitted when put to bed in the evening. The procedure used was essentially one of extinction. The parents were advised to leave the bedroom and not reenter after putting the child to bed. After 17 nights the child's bedtime tantrum-behaviors had ceased. However, inadvertent reinforcement by an unwary aunt necessitated a second extinction procedure which again succeeded in eliminating the tantrum behaviors after seven nights.

White (1959) described a treatment program aimed at overcoming a five-and-a-half-year-old girl's refusal to eat for her mother after her father had died. The treatment program "involved both stimulus-substitution and the generalization continuum [p. 228]." As conceptualized by White, the father was a "conditioned stimulus upon which the conditioned response of eating had come to depend, reinforcement being supplied both by satisfaction of hunger, as well as by anxiety-reduction through sitting on the father's knee and being fed by him [p. 228]." The first week of the treatment program occurred while the child was a psychiatry inpatient and involved daily sessions in which White and the child took care of the food needs of a doll family. During this time the child began to drink tea from a doll-sized cup and to eat miniature biscuits. After the initial week the child was seen as an outpatient, at least four times per week, and the play sessions with the author continued with larger cups and biscuits being substituted for their doll-sized counterparts. During the middle of the second week the child's mother reported that the child had accepted food from two of her neighbors. Progress continued until, after about three months of treatment, the child would eat a regular breakfast and at times even said she was hungry. Six months after the initial referral, the child's eating behavior was no longer of concern to her family. "By this time the psychologist had managed to transfer a large part of the father's mantle onto two uncles . . . [pp. 228–229]." From normal eating behavior for her uncles, the child gradually acquired a normal pattern of eating with her mother which was maintained three years after the treatment program was discontinued.

To summarize the flood of studies which have followed those of Williams (1959) and White (1959), we have attempted to present subsequent reports in this section according to the strategy of intervention followed. By "strategy of intervention" we mean the procedures used in gathering data about the problem behaviors, and the method used to evaluate the impact of the intervention technique.

By far the most commonly used approach has been one which might be called "treatment only." This approach, which essentially involves a description of the problem behaviors by the parents and a recommendation by the therapist, was used in 16 of the 49 studies reviewed. For example, Boardman (1962) based his treatment recommendations on a lengthy, detailed, anecdotal account from a mother of a six-year-old boy who manifested a number of problem behaviors including nocturnal enuresis, running away, school truancy, defiance and destruction of property. After the history had been obtained from the parents, the child was seen once for a few moments and the family was sent home to follow a set of instructions provided by the therapist. In essence, Boardman instructed the parents "to carry out procedures in which Rusty would always be given a choice between unacceptable behavior and clearly defined acceptable behavior and would be punished severely and continuously while he persisted in undesirable acts and rewarded promptly and adequately when he shifted to appropriate behavior [p. 295]." According to Boardman, Rusty's behavior had been brought under his parents control six days after their consultation with him.

Some criticism (cf. Bandura, 1962) notwithstanding, the report by Boardman is generally representative of most "treatment only" studies in which parents are "taught" behavioral change principles, apply them at home, and report to the therapist-researcher on the effectiveness of the principles employed. Such a strategy has been followed in treating selfscratching (Allen & Harris, 1966); bath phobia (Bentler, 1962); temper tantrums (Coe, 1970; Wetzel, Baker, Roney & Martin, 1966); extreme disobedience (Engeln, Knutson, Laughy & Garlington, 1968); fire-setting (Holland, 1969); encopresis (Keehn, 1965); school phobia (Kennedy, 1965); delayed speech (Ora & Burgess, 1971; Risley & Wolf, 1967); bowel retention (Peterson & London, 1965); violent outbursts, rudeness, hyperactivity, impulsiveness (Russo, 1964); diurnal enuresis, disobedience, defiance (Shah, 1969); refusal to eat (White, 1959); and to desensitize a child's anxiety to its mother (Straughan, 1964). Although apparently successful in enabling parents to effect desired changes in a child's problem-behaviors, many of these reports have an inherent limitation for both the clinician and the researcher in that they lack specific information regarding precisely what principles were taught and how.

A second major intervention-strategy, obtaining a baseline measure of the behavior before applying the actual treatment, was incorporated in 13 of the 49 studies reviewed. Mathis (1971) followed this procedure in working with a parent whose child manifested deficiencies in verbal communication skills. In particular, the mother described his speech as being intelligible, but largely irrelevant and nonsensical, with some phrases being repeated over and over again. Before treatment began the mother agreed that the child would not be seen by the therapist but that "she would act as a participant-observer and attempt to carry out the instructions of the staff to the best of her ability based upon weekly conferences and outside readings [p. 234]." Before the treatment procedures were initiated, the mother was taught to use data sheets for recording appropriate and inappropriate speech, and she was instructed to tape-record five minutes of daily interaction with her son. During the treatment phase the mother attended weekly sessions to which she brought the behavioral records and audiotape recordings and during which she received instructions to be followed the coming week. In his short descriptions of 20 sessions, Mathis details the content of each session, including specific instructions given to the parent. Baseline observations revealed that the child engaged in appropriate speech approximately 35 per cent of the time. Beginning with Week Seven (six weeks after treatment began), the child began to exhibit 100 per cent appropriate speech and continued at this level until treatment was terminated.

The baseline-treatment, or A-B strategy, has also been followed by investigators concerned with encopresis (Barrett, 1969); chronic constipation (Lal & Lindsley, 1968); the "brat syndrome" (Bernal, 1969; Bernal, Duryee, Pruett & Burns, 1968); compliance (Browning & Stover, 1971); overactivity and overdemandingness (Johnson & Brown, 1969); nocturnal enuresis (Kimmel & Kimmel, 1970); disruptive behavior at dinner (Johnson, 1969); underachievement and disruptive behavior in the classroom (Patterson, 1969); fire setting and stealing (Patterson & Reid, 1970); unresponsiveness to parents and "bizarre" behavior (Patterson, McNeal, Hawkins & Phelps, 1967); noncompliance (Patterson, Shaw & Ebner, 1969); teens on probation (Thorne, Tharp & Wetzel, 1967), and oppositional children (Wahler, 1968).

The third most commonly used intervention strategy, the "reversal" or A-B-A-B design, involves establishing a baseline, introducing a treatment routine, withdrawing or reversing the treatment procedures and, finally, reintroducing them. The technical aspects of this strategy have been adequately presented elsewhere (Bijou, Peterson, Harris, Allen & Johnston, 1969; Dinsmoor, 1966; Sidman, 1960) and will not be repeated here.

Ten of the 49 studies used an A-B-A or A-B-A-B design in assessing the results of parent-training programs. O'Leary, O'Leary & Becker (1967) followed this strategy in modifying the interactions of a six-year-old boy and his three-year-old brother who frequently engaged in assaultive and destructive behavior. During the baseline period the experimenter and an observer conducted 5 30-minute observations in which they recorded the frequency of three general classes of behavior: deviant (kicking, hitting, pushing, name-calling and throwing objects at one another); cooperative (asking for a toy, requesting the other's help, conversation, playing within three feet of one another); and isolate (the absence of verbal, physical or visual interaction). The observations were carried out in a basement playroom of the family's home without the mother present. The mother was allowed to come down and discipline the children as she saw fit, but these times were excluded from the observation data.

During the first experimental period the experimenter continuously reinforced each instance of cooperative behavior by either child by placing an M&M candy in the child's mouth and simultaneously saying "good." On the third and fourth days of this experimental period alternate cooperative responses were reinforced. A token reinforcement system was introduced and explained to the boys on the fifth day. The token reinforcement system consisted of the experimenter putting checks on a blackboard for cooperative behavior and removing them for deviant behavior. Checks were added up at the end of each session and exchanged for backup reinforcers (e.g., candy bars, bubble gum, kites, comic books, etc.). The first experimental period remained in effect for 16 days, during which the mean percentage of cooperative play rose to 85 percent from a 46 percent baseline level. A reversal period was then instituted with an observer present but without token reinforcement for cooperative play. During the reversal period cooperative play dropped to 50 percent. Experimental procedures were then reinstated, with the experimenter again managing the token reinforcement system, and cooperative play increased markedly. Two days after the second experimental period began, the boys' mother was given instructions on running the token system. In addition, she was instructed in the use of a "time out" procedure (Ferster & Appel, 1961), in which the boys were isolated in the bathroom contingent upon kicking, hitting, pushing, name-calling and throwing objects at one another. Also, a "stretchout" of the token system was begun by the mother, requiring checks to be earned over several days for payoff. To assist the mother in learning the procedures, the experimenter used hand signals to indicate when token reinforcement or time-out should be administered. The hand signals were gradually withdrawn as the parent became proficient in executing the procedures. The combination of the token reinforcement system and time-out by the mother during the second experimental period produced a high rate of cooperative behavior (mean frequency = 90 percent).

Other reports describing the use of reversal designs in single-family approaches to parent training have dealt with finger sucking (Friedman & McIntire, 1970); a difficult-to-manage child (Hawkins, Peterson, Schweid & Bijou, 1966); oppositional behavior and nocturnal enuresis (Nordquist, 1970); bowel retention (Tomlinson, 1970); "oppositional" children (Wagner & Ora, 1970; Wahler, 1969a, 1969b); three children described successively as "manipulative," "very dependent" and extremely "stubborn" (Wahler, Winkel, Peterson & Morrison, 1965); and a child described as aggressive and disobedient (Zeilberger, Sampen & Sloane, 1968).

Several reports could not be classified under any of the three major intervention strategies thus far considered. These studies employed a miscellany of strategies dealing with the modification of psychogenic seizures (Gardner, 1967); childhood schizophrenia and extreme hyperactivity in a brain-damaged child (Krapfl, Bry & Nawas, 1968); temper tantrums, negativistic and immature behaviors (Patterson & Brodsky, 1966); climbing behavior in an autistic child (Risley, 1968); tantrums, sleeping and eating problems, refusal to wear glasses and bedtime problems in an autistic child (Wolf, Risley & Mees, 1964).

A number of different training techniques varying widely in content and the clarity of their exposition have been used in these miscellaneous studies. One method has been to have the parent observe the therapist while some of the techniques are explained to the parent by a colleague (e.g., Engeln et al., 1968; Wetzel et al., 1966). Another technique often used has been to explain the principles of behavior modification to the parents during a few sessions in the office and then send them home to practice what they have been "taught." For example, Barrett (1969), working with the parents of a five-and-a-half-year-old boy in an attempt at bowel training, states:

> Our goal was to enable the parents to eliminate what they considered to be the most distressing behavior in their child. Observation and treatment were carried out by the parents at home. The choice of treatment and assessment procedures was theirs. *Our contribution to their efforts was to explain to them the rudiments of behavior modification* and to encourage them to maximize the contingencies existing in their home [italics added] [p. 173].

The first consultation involved getting the parents to record instances of their child's disturbing behavior for one week. During the second consultation the parents were advised not to dispense daily snacks of chocolate cookies unless the toilet was used for bowel movements and to take away the child's favorite pillow for inappropriate bowel movements rather than yelling at him or slapping him, as had been the usual practice. Further consultations (three office visits and one brief home visit) dealt with attempts at having the parents apply the recommended procedures after every misplaced bowel movement. The program was judged successful by the parents after a total of 75 days.

Reports such as that of Barrett (1969), Boardman (1962), and numerous others which do not provide specific detail regarding precisely *what* principles were taught and *how*, do not furnish clinicians with information sufficient to enable them to repeat the training process in their own work. Nor do they provide enough detail to allow researchers to assess different aspects of the training process in any systematic manner.

Examples of the kind of specification of training routine which are more valuable for such purposes are to be found in recent reports by Bernal (1969), Johnson & Brown (1969), and Patterson *et al.* (1968). Bernal (1969) described a format for training parents in child management which involved two essential features: (1) operant learning principles and (2) behavior feedback via videotape. Bernal explicitly indicated the content of each therapy session (called an "intervention") in describing work with two children classified as exhibiting behaviors characteristic of the "brat syndrome." To summarize, the following quote indicates the essence of Bernal's treatment program: " Once the treatment begins, each intervention consists of playing excerpts from previous video tapes to the parent to demonstrate various points and giving the parent a set of instructions to follow during video taped interaction with the child which takes place immediately after tape viewing and instruction [p. 375]." In addition to the investigation of the use of videotape feedback, Bernal's article is an exemplary one in that she clearly specifies the content of the treatment sessions.

Johnson and Brown (1969) report the use of a variety of behavioral techniques in working with the parents of two children. The first case involved a two-year-nine-month-old girl who required constant supervision because of her intense overactivity. In working with her mother and grandmother, Johnson and Brown employed direct instruction (explication of techniques of reinforcement, shaping and schedules of reinforcement), group discussion with another family whose child presented similar behavior problems, behavioral direction in which a red light was used to signal the parent to reinforce the child appropriately, parent reinforcement which involved use of a light signal to indicate when the parents had rewarded the child appropriately and modeling sessions in which the therapist played with the child and attempted to demonstrate the procedures explained in "direct instruction." The second case relied primarily upon a modeling procedure to effect change in parental control of an overdemanding child.

Patterson et al. (1968) followed a four-step intervention program in which parents were first trained in the language and concepts of social learning via a programmed text. "The parents were then trained to observe and count child behavior. Following this, the entire family participated in a series of 'sample' intervention programs which were first modeled by the experimenters and then imitated by the family members [p.6]." The last step involved the family members' practicing specific programs on their own.

A description of the Patterson et al. (1968) four-step intervention program can best be given by presenting a specific case. The R family had as its problem child Russ, a six-year-old boy who was described as being extremely aggressive toward his three-year-old brother, noncompliant, very nervous and suspicious of adults and unable to get along with peers. The intervention program began with Russ's parents reading selected sections of *Living with children* (Patterson & Gullion, 1968), a programmed textbook. After both parents had read the appropriate sections of the text, an office interview was held to pinpoint the child's problem behaviors. Each parent agreed to observe Russ for one hour each day and to record each incidence of the following: hitting, pushing or shoving his brother, noncompliance with parental requests and commands, refusal to wipe himself after going to the toilet and failure to dress himself. The parents were also to record the consequences provided for each of these behaviors, and, because all these behaviors were low-rate responses, they were to record the number of positive social reinforcers they used in interacting with Russ.

After four days of recording by the parents, the investigators entered the home to conduct the first training session. During this session the experimenter initiated a series of practice trials in which both boys earned points (later traded for M&M candies) and social reinforcers. The parents also carried out several practice trials while being supervised by the investigator. At the end of the first training session the parents were instructed to carry out regular practice sessions for compliance and to continue collecting observation data on a full array of designated problem behaviors. In the second home-training session, procedures were introduced to train Russ for compliance with parental commands. For example, the parents were shown how to reinforce him as he learned to button his shirt and tie his shoes. At the final family-training session, the parents were given instruction in the use of time out as a consequence for hitting behaviors or for refusing to dress himself. A number of followup telephone calls indicated that the intervention programs were proving successful.

The Patterson et al. (1968) procedures can be summarized in the following four steps: (1) parents respond to a programmed text aimed at teaching the language and concepts of social-learning theory; (2) parents are trained to observe and count child behaviors; (3) the investigators conduct a series of "sample" intervention programs which they first model and then supervise the parents in implementing; (4) the family members practice the specific programs when the experimenters are not present.

The Patterson *et al.* (1968) study, as well as those of Bernal (1969), Johnson & Brown (1969) and Mathis (1971) reviewed earlier, may be taken as representative of the kinds of reports which are probably most useful at this stage of the development of single-family approaches to parent training. The specification of the treatment strategy, including an outline of the content of individual therapy sessions, provides enough detail to allow for adoption of the procedures by a clinician and should make it possible for the researchers to vary systematically different aspects of the training routines in order to compare their relative effectiveness.

The brief overview of single-family studies presented in this section has shown that a wide variety of childhood behavior problems have been treated by training parents in behavior modification techniques. It was noted that observational data, recorded by parents, researcher or a combination of parents and researcher, have constituted the basic dependent measures used to assess the effectiveness of the intervention attempts. It was also shown that observations have been made in the home, school or clinic setting with a number of researchers braving the hazards of making *in situ* observations themselves. Three major intervention strategies for single-family parent training were identified and a study representing each strategy was reviewed in detail. The lack of specificity regarding the techniques taught to parents and the methods used to teach them was noted as a general deficiency of many of the studies reviewed. Future investigators should provide as much detail as possible regarding parent-training procedures in order that the procedures may be more effectively utilized by others interested in this area. The single-family approach to training parents in behavior modification techniques seems to have had a successful beginning and currently enjoys a considerable degree of popularity. The limits of its utility and the magnitude of its benefits can only be determined by future research.

Multiple Family Approaches

Thus section focuses primary emphasis upon empirical efforts to evaluate the usefulness of multiple-family strategies in training parents as behavior modifiers. Therefore, some anecdotal reports (e.g., Rose, 1969; Gorelick, 1970) are not included. Multiple-family strategies involve any attempt to train simultaneously the parents of more than one family. This approach thus includes efforts to train two or more mothers in behavior modification techniques at the same time. The principal requirement of our definition is that more than one family be represented. The training of several different members of a single family is included under "single-family strategies."

The composition of the parent group trained with multiple-family strategies varies greatly as will be seen. Frequently, only mothers are included. Sometimes both mothers and fathers compose the group, and these may or may not be spouses. Systematic evaluations of the effects of varying these and other training group characteristics have not been carried out. In fact, empirical investigations of the effectiveness of group training of parents as behavior modifiers is merely a fledgling enterprise at the present time. The author's search of the literature in this area yielded very few reports dealing with the subject, and most of these are unpublished doctoral dissertations or papers presented at professional meetings.

As recently as 1969, Hirsch & Walder (1969) were able to find only one reported study in which parents in groups were trained in behavior modification techniques. Wiltz (1970) found only one such study (Ray, 1965) which used observational measures rather than parent reports to assess outcome. As is characteristic of most scientific forays into uncharted wilds, these early studies are more notable for their temerity than for the reliability of their scientific yield.

The earliest group attempt to train parents as behavior modifiers and to assess the effectiveness of training is to be found in an unpublished paper by Pumroy (1965) (unless one is willing to include the "nondepth, commonsense" approach of Phillips, 1960). Pumroy assigned parents to one of three lecture-discussion groups or a "control" group and reported anecdotal comparisons on a number of dependent measures after ten one-hour treatment sessions. The emphasis in all three lecture-discussion groups was on the application of operant principles to child behavior. The "control" group was actually a comparison group treated by another therapist in an unspecified manner. Pumroy reported no differences in "attitude change" between experimental and control groups, but got a favorable response from the former when he asked what they had gotten out of the sessions. A test over the material showed parents had learned the principles of behavior modification, and 10 of the 11 families who said they would try the techniques reported "favorable behavior change two months after the sessions had concluded."

Other studies (Walder, Cohen, Breiter, Daston, Hirsch & Leibowitz, 1969; Hirsch & Walder, 1969) have continued the training of parents in didactic groups, and have incorporated a variety of additional features. Walder et al. (1969) used a three-stage strategy involving "educational group meetings, consulting with individual pairs of parents, and structuring a more controlled laboratory-like environment within the home." Their research is remarkable for the obvious attempt to apply operant principles consistantly at each stage of the training. Even the behavior of the trainer was observed, recorded and appropriately consequated.

The unique and most extensively developed of the three stages of Walder et al.'s approach was the educational group meeting. Groups of three pairs of parents met one evening a week for 16 weeks with two professionals in one-hour sessions. During these sessions one professional acted as observer of the other's group-leader behaviors in order that a functional relationship between these and parent behaviors could eventually be formulated. The 16 educational group meetings represented what might be termed a cram course in the principles of operant conditioning. Parents were taught how to observe and record behavior accurately while viewing brief two-person interactions through a one-way mirror. They were required to complete homework assignments, which involved reading behavioral vignettes describing specific behavior problems and writing answers to questions about each one. Written answers were required for admission to the next group meeting. Training also involved home observation by parents of their child's behavior for a brief period daily. Reports of these observations were turned in at the subsequent session. Parents were also exposed to staged interactions involving "contrived contingencies" which they had to learn to identify. Verbal conditioning tasks, shaping certain behaviors of another group member, a film on "Reinforcement Therapy," shaping two behaviors in food-deprived rats and case presentations of behavior change projects at home rounded out the group training.

Though Walder et al. (1969) presented no data evaluating their effectiveness, a companion study (Hirsch & Walder, 1969) has provided a useful start in this direction. These authors assigned 30 white mothers from mostly upper-middle-class professional families to two conditions: No wait (N=15), and Wait (N=15). Nine one-and-one-half-hour group sessions were conducted over a period of five weeks, all groups receiving the same treatment. Meetings consisted of "highly organized lectures" on the principles of behavior modification, discussion of each mother's individual child and advice on implementing a behavior change program in the home. Each mother was required to deposit $50 with the investigators, which was returned contingent upon perfect attendance at the group sessions.

It is important to note that, in keeping with the general theoretical rationale for teaching parents to mediate reinforcement for their own children, mothers and not children were the subjects of Hirsch & Walder's study. Hence, as in Pumroy's earlier investigation, most of the dependent measures used to evaluate the success of this approach were taken on the mother.

Pre-post comparisons revealed the greatest change for the behavioral vignettes, essentially a test of how well the mothers learned the principles of operant conditioning. Mothers' records of child behavior in the home indicated significant pre-post changes in the improvement direction. In addition, Hirsch & Walder found that scores on present versus ideal ratings, behavior ratings and achievement ratings all showed improvement. Interestingly, such improvement occurred whether "subjects had been treated, were in the process of waiting, or were being followed up after treatment." The authors suggest that mothers, wanting to see improvement, are likely to indicate it even when there is no reason to be any. These data, reminiscent of similar findings by Clement & Milne (1966) and Radke-Yarrow (1963), highlight one of the more difficult methodological problems in this area. Clearly objective recording of mother-and-child behavior by an unbiased observer is necessary to demonstrate whether the mother has indeed changed her mediating behavior and whether this change has produced a concomitant alteration in the behavior of her child.

Hirsch and Walder also reported that mothers' Henmon-Nelson I.Q.'s and group size had no effect on the outcome. It is interesting that group size had no effect, and more attention needs to be given this variable, especially in view of Mira's (1970) finding of greater economy of professional time when parents are trained individually.

Finally, Hirsch & Walder (1969) report 100 percent attendance at all meetings, a fact they attribute to the required $50 deposit. The use of incentives in parent training is also an important factor which needs further investigation (cf. Patterson, 1971). Indeed, stimuli sufficient to maintain mediator behavior are critical to the maintenance of changed behavior in the child.

Howard (1970) has reported the results of a six-week parent-training program that was part of the larger Project Re-Ed described by Hobbs (1964). In his study, 20 parents of emotionally disturbed children were assigned to a training group (N = 10) which attended six two-hour class sessions, or a control group (N = 10) which attended none. Howard reported that the parents were heterogeneous regarding education, intelligence, race, sex and socioeconomic standing. Class sessions, conducted by two professionals, were a mixture of lecture and discussion. A variety of learning adjuncts were used, including assignments in programmed texts by Patterson & Gullion (1968) and Smith & Smith (1966). Movies, videotape and role-playing by the instructors were also incorporated into the training. The effectiveness of the program was assessed by pre-post comparisons of the treatment and control groups on the following measures: (1) seven dichotomously scored items relating to confidence in handling child behavior, (2) a semantic differential measure of "present child–ideal child" discrepancy and (3) frequency counts of annoying behaviors. Significantly more parents indicated confidence in handling child behavior after the six-week program than before it if they had been enrolled in the classes. The parents in the no-treatment control group showed no such change. On the semantic differential measure, treated parents showed a significant reduction in the discrepancy of their "present child-ideal child" ratings, whereas the controls showed no change. The frequency count of annoying behaviors, potentially the most interesting of the dependent measures, also showed significant reductions for the treated group but no change for the controls.

An intriguing attempt at exploring the effectiveness of a number of behavioral techniques to shape and maintain parent participation in a group training program has been reported by Peine & Munro (1970). Twenty-eight parents of children labeled autistic, brain-damaged, emotionally disturbed, psychotic or slow-learner were assigned to one or two groups "according to their availability for meetings." Group I, composed of six couples and two single parents, attended ten two-hour sessions over a five-week period. Training for Group I was comprised almost entirely of lecture and demonstration. Group II, composed of four couples and six single parents, met for the same number of sessions over the same time-period and received most of its material in the form of lectures. However, from the beginning of training Group II was placed on a token economy. A wide variety of classroom behaviors, e.g., attendance, punctuality, completing assignments and hand-raising, were reinforced with poker chips worth one cent each. Tardiness and failure to complete various assignments resulted in token loss. Members of Group II also signed contracts specifying the reinforcement contingencies. Two instructors managed the classes for each of the groups.

Presumably the same two instructors conducted both groups, though the authors did not make this clear. Group II, in addition to receiving tokens and signing contracts, also engaged in more role-playing and more general class discussion.

The other systematically introduced differences between the groups occurred in sessions seven and eight. For Group I a token economy was instituted in Session Seven with tokens provided for hand-raising and, intermittently, for attending behavior and asking questions. During Session Eight, tokens were replaced with pennies and nickels, nickels for hand-raising and pennies for attending and asking questions. The token economy was discontinued during Sessions Nine and Ten. Group II was placed on extinction for hand-raising during Session Seven and, in Session Eight, hand-raising was subjected to a response cost contingency. Previously operative contingencies were reinstated in sessions nine and ten. Inter-rater reliability for hand-raising, computed for two experienced observers, yielded a correlation of .94.

Results of the study were reported in terms of comparisons between the two groups across the ten training sessions on four dependent measures: (1) attendance, (2) punctuality, (3) turning in assignments and (4) hand-raising. Attendance was consistently higher for the contingency managed group: $\overline{X}$=79.6 percent versus 59.7 percent. The members of this group also tended to be more punctual ($\overline{X}$=86.7 percent versus 44.9 percent on time), and they handed in more assignments ($\overline{X}$=9.7 vs. 3.7).

Hand-raising was reinforced by tokens during Sessions Three to Six for Group II, resulting in consistently higher rates of that behavior. When placed on extinction for handraising in Session Seven, Group II actually showed an increase in that response. However, when subjected to the response cost contingency in session eight, hand-raising in Group II decreased markedly.

In Session Seven, Group I was also reinforced with tokens for hand-raising, but showed no increase. However, when tokens were replaced by nickels in Session Eight, hand-raising increased considerably. Reinstating the original contingencies for both groups in the remaining two sessions resulted in the return of hand-raising to its levels prior to the seventh session.

The tokens earned by members of Group II were exchanged for money at the rate of one cent per token. Earnings were computed three times during the five-week program, and checks were sent to the participants. It should be noted that attendance was reinforced at the accelerating rate of 75 tokens for the first seven meetings followed by 150, 300 and 600, respectively, for Sessions Eight, Nine and Ten. The total cost of the token economy of Group II was $229.68.

Considering the nature of the dependent measures used in this study one might question its inclusion in a review of literature dealing with parent-training groups. Might not such data just as well have been gathered on lecture-discussion groups constituted for any of a variety of other purposes? Perhaps so, but Peine & Munro were concerned with imparting operant principles to parents of deviant children, and effective classroom procedures may be an important ingredient of any such training approach. Though it was not specifically demonstrated in his study, it is reasonable to assume a functional relationship exists between attendance and active participation in an educational program and the benefits to be derived therefrom.

The multiple family strategies considered thus far have been concerned with their effectiveness in bringing about changes in certain parent behaviors. The primary thrust has been in demonstrating the efficacy of a group approach via pre-post changes in measures taken on the mother. Even studies seeking information on changes in child behavior have relied upon ratings or observations taken by the mother. Strictly speaking, such dependent measures are really based only indirectly on child behavior and should probably be viewed as data on the mother in the absence of independent evidence of a high degree of correspondence between them and what the child actually does.

A growing number of studies (e.g., Mash, Lazere, Terdal & Garner, 1970; Mash & Terdal, 1970; Patterson, Cobb & Ray, in press; Wiltz, 1970) have attempted to extend the range of direct measurement beyond the mother to the child and to the interaction between them. These authors have argued that the appropriate subject in parent-training programs is neither the parent nor the child alone, but a behavioral unit consisting of the antecedent-consequent relationship existing between them. Such an emphasis is seen as especially desirable as research moves from the "single behavior, single manipulation" paradigm to those in which "complex, multiple contingency behaviors are observed (Mash & Terdal, 1970)". Mash, Terdal & Anderson (1970) have developed a three-term contingency method for recording interactive behavior of mother and child simultaneously. Similar views have led Patterson and his colleagues (e.g., Patterson & Reid, 1970) to develop ANOVA methods for examining reinforcement reciprocity in single family studies.

Mash, Lazere, Terdal & Garner (1970), unlike the multiple-family strategists already mentioned, attempted to get corroborative evidence of *in situ* child behavior changes by comparing pre-post differences on records taken by the investigators in the home. Mothers of mildly retarded children were assigned (nonrandomly) to an experimental (N = 4) or control group (N = 5) and their interaction with their child was observed in a 15-minute laboratory free-play situation. Data were taken on mother's commands, child's response to the commands and mother's consequation of the child's response. In addition, observations of the some behavior were made in the home for the experimental subjects, though not for the controls.

Mothers in the experimental group then participated in ten one-and-one-half-hour sessions conducted by two psychologists. The general focus of the group sessions was on training the mothers in effective "command behavior, social reinforcement for compliance, and withholding approval for noncompliance." The major techniques used in the training were demonstration and group discussion. One of the experimental mothers who had been through previous behavior modification training served as a "demonstrator mother." Each session began with group discussion centered around a review of previous material. This was followed by a 15 to 20-minute observation period in which the demonstrator mother interacted with her child behind a oneway mirror. During the demonstration the group leaders pointed out effective and ineffective techniques used by the demonstrator. Following this, the demonstrator mother rejoined the group for discussion of the tactics she had employed and ways in which the observer mothers might employ some of the more effective methods in their own situations.

At the end of the ten sessions all mother-child pairs were again observed in 15-minute laboratory free-play sessions, and a second home observation session was made for members of the experimental group. The effectiveness of the training was evaluated, using a variety of measures comparing experimental versus control mothers and observers versus demonstrator within the experimental group. Only a summary of the results will be presented here.

In general, the compliance behavior of children of trained mothers increased markedly in a laboratory free-play situation. That of the controls showed only a slight increase. Mean percentages of compliance pre- and post-training were 40.2 and 91.2, versus 32.5 and 40.5 for experimental and control groups, respectively. The demonstrator mother, not included in the experimental group mean, produced a change in her child's compliance from 26.9 percent to 50.0 percent, substantially less than that recorded for the rest of the experimental subjects.

In terms of consequent behavior for compliance, experimental-observer mothers showed a slight increase in praise and interaction $\bar{X}$=47.6 percent to 55.2 percent). The demonstrator increased from 72.7 percent to 89.2 percent, wheras the controls decreased ($\bar{X}$=24.7 percent to 15.6 percent). All experimental mothers completely eliminated any negative consequating behavior for compliance ($\bar{X}$=10.3 percent to 0.0 percent), while control mothers showed a very small increase ($\bar{X}$= 1.3 percent to 4.6 percent). Increased compliance appeared to generalize to the home situation, with pre-post means being 12.4 percent and 25.7 percent, respectively, for the children of observer mothers. The demonstrator's child increased from 2.2 percent to 8.0 percent. Commands and command-questions, termed "mother directiveness" by Mash et al., were reduced ($\bar{X}$=50.2 percent to 32.6 percent) by experimental-observer mothers, whereas the demonstrator increased slightly (36.5 percent to 41.9 percent), and controls remained unchanged ($\bar{X}$=56.5 percent versus 56.4 percent).

Discussing these results, the authors suggested that modeling procedures may be beneficial in training parents as behavior modifiers. They pointed out that mothers appeared to learn effective behavior-management skills primarily from observation and discussion, since no opportunity was provided for them to practice new skills under supervision and no formal feedback was available. Furthermore, the demonstrator mother, who had no opportunity to observe others, displayed changes on the dependent measures which seemed unrelated to those of the experimental observer mothers. In general, the demonstrator did not experience the improvement characteristic of the observers, a fact interpreted by the authors to support the value of using modeling procedures. Mash et al. caution against overgeneralizing the results of this exploratory study but suggest that they lend support to the view that "mothers can learn techniques of child management by observing and discussing critical interactions occurring in another mother-child pair."

A more elaborate investigation by Mash & Terdal (1970) attempted group training of mothers in the use of effective modes of interacting with their child in play situations. Arguing the preventative mental-health advantage of focusing on nondeviant behavior, these authors trained five groups of eight to ten mothers in more effective ways of playing with their retarded children. Training was carried out in a series of ten one-hour group sessions. Prior to training each mother-child pair was observed in laboratory free-play for 15 minutes. Interactions were again recorded using the three-term contingency system developed by Mash, Terdal & Anderson (1970), with two recorders simultaneously recording antecedent-consequent behaviors of both mother and child.

Teaching "effective" play behavior was the focus of the first two training sessions. The authors did not explicitly define what they meant by effective play behavior, but it appeared to involve increasingly greater stimulus-control by the mother over her child's activities. This control was to be achieved through training in the use of operant principles which would "assist the parents in providing an atmosphere for the child to express himself without threat or coercion" (Mash & Terdal, 1970). The remaining eight sessions were spend discussing behavior modification principles operative in noncompliant behavior, self-help skills and communication.

The focus of the Mash & Terdal paper was upon the procedures employed during the first two sessions. Whereas Mash et al. (1970) used a demonstrator mother to provide a model for parent-child interactions which could then be discussed by the group, Mash & Terdal (1970) used videotaped examples of appropriate and inappropriate parental behaviors. Apparently, training was restricted to observation of the tapes and subsequent discussion of their contents. Two psychologists again served as group leaders. Following the tenth session, mother-child pairs were observed and their behavior recorded during 15-minute laboratory free-play periods.

As in the Mash et al. (1970) study, data were presented for a variety of dependent measures on the mother, the child, and their interaction. A summary of their important findings is presented here.

Results on a variety of dependent measures indicated that mothers could be taught more effective ways of playing with and encouraging independent play in their children. Mothers in all five experimental groups showed a decrease in their rate of commands during free play. They also showed a drop in their rate of question-asking and an increase in appropriate consequation of various child behaviors. All groups showed increased amounts of interaction with their children and less control over and greater encouragement of the children's initiative during independent play.

Apparently eminently in response to these changes in their mothers (though not a demonstrated functional relationship), children showed a slight increase in compliance, and a concomitant decrease in behaviors incompatible with compliance. Children also showed an increase in appropriate responses to questions from their mothers.

Mash and Terdal note that training mothers to modify and encourage nondeviant play behavior may be an important form of preventative mental-health practice, a point which should be underscored. It is imminently reasonable to assume that training parents in behavior-modification techniques will result in more effective parents and fewer behavior-problem children in the long run. Even studies attempting to deal with relatively specific behaviors are, when successful, providing parents with skills which should generalize to other behaviors and other children. To the extent that they do, such training procedures offer one of the greatest preventative strategies available to mental health professionals today. There is some evidence (e.g., Patterson, Ray & Shaw, 1968) that generalization of the techniques is not automatically forthcoming, however, and generalization-inducing procedures need to be built into the overall training program.

The final two studies to be mentioned were carried out by Patterson's group at the University of Oregon. In a doctoral dissertation, Wiltz (1970) assigned parents of behavior problem boys to a treatment and "wait" control group chronologically as they applied for help at a mental-health agency. The first six families applying during a several-month period were assigned to the training group. Six subsequent families, the "wait" controls, were matched with the training group on age of child, socioeconomic standing and proportion of deviant child behavior. Ages of the boys ranged from 6 to 14 years. Baseline data were recorded for ten weekdays in the home of each of the 12 families, whereupon training was begun for parents in the experimental group. Two-day observation probes were made for both groups after five weeks, and again after nine weeks for the experimental families. Training included responding to Patterson & Gullion (1968), pinpointing and recording a child behavior, and attending eight to ten group meetings. Training sessions consisted of group discussions regarding the parents' behavior recording projects.

Data were analyzed in terms of baseline to fifth-week changes in deviant behavior. During this period experimentals showed a 50 percent decrease, whereas controls increased about 30 percent. The ANOVA F representing this interaction was significant at $p < .07$. Deviant behavior continued to decrease for the experimentals as shown by a baseline-to-ninth-week drop of 60 percent.

No effort was made to assess those aspects of the training program which may have been responsible for the improvement in the experimental families, and details were presented too sketchily for us to speculate about the relative effectiveness of various program components. The most notable feature of the study was its sophisticated attempt to deal with a number of methodological shortcomings present in earlier investigations. Thus, although parents were not randomly assigned to treatment and controls groups, these groups were carefully matched on proportion of deviant behavior based upon observational baseline data taken in the home. Moreover, six different observers were trained to satisfactory levels of reliability based on a strict criterion before baseline data were collected. Periodic retraining was continued throughout the study to guard against reliability slippage. Finally, as a check on both observer bias and reliability by false consensus, a "calibrating observer" was included. This rater was required to make observations with other observers on a random basis but was kept naive regarding the group membership of each of the families. Agreement between calibrator and regular observers ranged from 46 percent to 88 percent with a mean of 70.7 percent for 28 checks made throughout the study.

Patterson, Cobb & Ray (in press), using some of the same families studied by Wiltz (1970), provide our final example of parent-training using a multiple-family strategy. A total of 13 families having behavior-problem boys ranging in age from 6 to 13 years was studied. All 13 families were enrolled in a linearly sequenced training program similar to that of Wiltz. Following 6 to 10 hours of baseline recording, parents responded to Patterson & Gullion (1968). Successful completion of a test over this material gained entrance to a pinpointing-and-recording phase during which parents were trained to focus upon and record the frequency of a single problem-behavior. Daily phone calls monitored progress during this period. Admission to group training sessions was contingent upon adequate data collection during the pinpoint-and-record phase.

The training groups consisted of three to four sets of parents who met once a week for approximately eight weeks. Group meetings centered around discussions of each family's project. Thirty minutes (regulated by a kitchen timer) were allowed for each family, with scheduling determined by order of arrival at the meeting: i.e., first arrivals presented first. Parents' graphs were passed around for comment, and specific details of programs and estimates of their probably success were the principal focus of discussion. Noncompliance was usually the first behavior dealt with by the parents, with two basic sets of procedures emphasized: token programs for adaptive, compliant behavior, and time-out for deviant or noncompliant behavior. Initially, progress was monitored via daily phone calls, but these were gradually faded as training continued.

Results were evaluated for four major dependent variables: changes in frequency of targeted behaviors, generalization to other behaviors of the child, generalization to sibling behavior and changes in parent perceptions of the child on 47 bipolar adjectives described in Patterson & Fagot (1967). Measures were taken in the home using procedures similar to Wiltz (1970). Data were collected at six points: two baseline periods, following parents' reading of Patterson & Gullion (1968), following four and eight weeks of group sessions, and at termination. Specific details may be found in the original paper (Patterson, Cobb & Ray, in press). In general, targeted deviant behavior was reduced 46 percent for the 13 families from baseline to termination $F = 4.31$ $p < .01$). Nontargeted problem behavior decreased 19% by termination, indicating only slight generalization of the effects of training to other behaviors of the problem child. In terms of generalization to other children, data showed a 47% decrease in the occurrence of deviant behaviors in siblings at termination ($F = 2.367$ $p < .10$).

Pre-post changes on the 47-item rating-scale revealed that parents had acquired a "highly generalized disposition to view the deviant child in a more favorable light." Greatest changes were manifested in areas related to out-of-control behaviors, i.e., the boys were described as less aggressive. Changes in the mothers' descriptions, analyzed by the Wilcoxon test, were significant at $p < .05$.

Complete followup data, available for 5 of the 13 treated cases, showed continued maintenance of reduced rates of targeted behavior twelve months after "termination." Nontargeted deviant behaviors of the child also maintained or showed slight improvements in their levels over termination. Followup data on siblings' deviant behavior revealed great variability and a slight tendency for rates to return to baseline levels. Overall efficiency of the program was analyzed in terms of the cost in hours of professional time spent with each family. Training in the home cost "25.67 hours (median = 18.15) with a range from 5.7 to 133.15 hours up to the point of 'termination' [p. 77]." About one third of the cases required concomitant programs designed to alter deviant behavior in the school. These programs cost about as much professional time as the home training, or a combined outlay of approximately "sixty hours of professional time for an average family [p. 78]." Finally, assessing their effectiveness in terms of the number of successfully treated families, Patterson et al. report an overall success rate of 50 percent when the improvement criterion requires at least a 46 percent drop in rate of deviant behavior from baseline to followup and premature terminators are counted as failures.

CONCLUSION

We have attempted in the preceding sections to present a comprehensive coverage of the literature describing efforts to train parents as behavior modifiers. The history of early psychoanalytic attempts to include parents (usually mothers) in their child's therapy or in their own, concurrently running therapy, was followed by discussion of client-centered approaches, primarily those of Guerney (1969). The reliance of both psychoanalytic and client-centered strategies upon intrapsychic independent variables and their consequent minimizing of overt, concrete problem-behaviors was discussed. The evidence for the efficacy of these strategies in traditional child psychotherapy was cited and the conclusion was reached that more effective and more economical modes might now be available. The empirical accomplishments of investigators using behavioral techniques were presented to support the rationale for attempting to train parents to use these methods with their own children.

The literature describing the training of parents as behavior-modifiers was divided under two main headings: (1) those studies attempting to train the parent(s) of only one family at a time, and (2) those studies training the parent(s) of several different families together in groups. While a few representative studies of the first type were described in detail, greater emphasis was placed on the latter. It was noted that general trends and statements of the most effective tactics are impossible at the present early state of the art. It must be concluded that single-family studies have generally involved a higher level of methodological sophistication than have multiple-family-group designs.

Nonetheless, it is heartening to note the progression in methodological sophistication which accompanies the order of presentation of the papers in the preceding section. Indeed, the last mentioned study (Patterson, Cobb & Ray, in press) is most notable for its attention to a number of methodological intricacies inherent in parent-training research. The stability and representativeness of baseline data, observer bias, observer reliability, the effects of programmed materials, and generalization to other behavior and other children, were all examined. Future investigations could profit immeasurably from the incorporation of Patterson's technological and methodological advances.

From the present perspectives it would appear that behavior modification remains the Zeitgeist and there is every reason to expect the extension of behavioral technology to work with parents will continue. Some preliminary theorizing has begun in the area (see the reciprocity-coercion hypothesis of Patterson & Reid, 1970, and the triadic model of Tharp & Wetzel, 1969), and a healthy use of material from other disciplines is emerging (cf. Patterson & Hops, 1970).

It appears that, as with behavior modification generally, the first blush of enthusiasm surrounding parent training is beginning to wane and serious investigators are starting to address themselves to some of the difficult issues. Basic to their concern need to be such questions as whether the methodology employed in studies to date has been sufficient to demonstrate convincingly that parents can indeed be trained. A critical evaluation of methodological issues, undertaken in another paper (Cone & Sloop, in preparation), has suggested that well-controlled demonstrations of program effectiveness are in short supply in this area.

Once there have been reliable demonstrations that parents can be trained, then a variety of questions concerning critical ingredients in training programs need to be raised. Is group training more efficient than a single family approach? Does this depend upon the skills and training of the group leader, the homogeneity of the group, the size of the group, etc.? What variables are effective in maintaining changed parental reinforcement mediation? How should training programs be sequenced? Are programmed materials useful? These questions and more will doubtless be raised by investigators in the near future. One can only await their answers with intrigue and a bit of excited impatience.

REFERENCES

Albee, G. W. *Mental health manpower trends.* New York: Basic Books, 1959.

Albee, G. W. Models, myths, and manpower. *Mental Hygiene,* 1968, **52,** 168–180.

Allen, K. E. & Harris, F. R. Elimination of a child's excessive scratching by training the mother in reinforcement procedures. *Behaviour Research and Therapy,* 1966, **4,** 79–84.

Arnhoff, F. N. Realities and mental health manpower. *Mental Hygiene,* 1968, **52,** 181–189.

Arnhoff, F. N., Rubinstein, E. A., Shriver, B. M. & Jones, D. R. The mental health fields: An overview of manpower growth and development. In F. N. Arnhoff, E. A. Rubinstein & J. C. Speisman (Eds.), *Manpower for mental health.* Chicago: Aldine, 1969.

Ayllon, T. E. & Azrin, N. H. Reinforcement and instruction with mental patients. *Journal of the Experimental Analysis of Behavior,* 1964, **7,** 327–331.

Bandura, A. Punishment revisited. *Journal of Consulting Psychology,* 1962, **26,** 298–301.

Bandura, A. *Principles of behavior modification.* New York: Holt, Rinehart & Winston, 1969.

Barrett, B. H. Behavior modification in the home: Parents adopt laboratory-developed tactics to bowel-train a five-and-one-half-year-old. *Psychotherapy: Theory, Research and Practice,* 1969, **6,** 172–176.

Barton, E. S., Guess, D., Garcia, E. & Baer, D. M. Improvement of retardates mealtime behaviors by timeout procedures using multiple baseline techniques. *Journal of Applied Behavior Analysis,* 1970, **3,** 77–84.

Becker, W. C. *Parents are teachers.* Champaign, Ill.: Research Press Company, 1971.

Bentler, P. M. An infant's phobia treated with reciprocal inhibition therapy. *Journal of Child Psychology and Psychiatry,* 1962, **3,** 185–189.

Bernal, M. E. Behavioral feedback in the modification of brat behaviors. *Journal of Nervous and Mental Disease,* 1969, **148,** 375–385.

Bernal, M. E., Duryee, J. S., Pruett, H. L. & Burns, B. J. Behavior modification and the "brat syndrome." *Journal of Consulting and Clinical Psychology,* 1968, **32,** 447–455.

Bijou, S. W., Peterson, R. F., Harris, F. R., Allen, K. E. & Johnston, M. S. Methodology for experimental studies of young children in natural settings. *The Psychological Record,* 1969, **19,** 177–210.

Birnbrauer, J.S., Bijou, S.W., Wolf, M.M. & Kidder, J.D. Programmed instruction in the classroom. In L.P. Ullmann & L. Krasner (Eds.), *Case studies in behavior modification.* New York: Holt, Rinehart & Winston, 1965. Pp. 358–363.

Birnbrauer, J.S., Wolf, M.M., Kidder, J.D. & Tague, C.E. Classroom behavior of retarded pupils with token reinforcement. *Journal of Experimental Child Psychology,* 1965, **2,** 219–235.

Blake, P. & Moss, T. The development of socialization skills in an electively mute child. *Behaviour Research and Therapy,* 1965, **2,** 227–232.

Boardman, W.K. Rusty: A brief behavior disorder. *Journal of Consulting Psychology,* 1962, **26,** 293–297.

Bonnard, A. The mother as therapist in a case of obsessional neurosis. In *The psychoanalytic study of the child,* Vol. V. New York: International Universities Press, 1950.

Brown, P. & Elliott, R. Control of aggression in nursery school class. *Journal of Experimental Child Psychology,* 1965, **3,** 102–107.

Browning, R.M. & Stover, D.O. *Behavior modification in child treatment.* Chicago: Aldine-Atherton, 1971.

Buell, J., Stoddard, P., Harris, F.R. & Baer, D.M. Applying "group" contingencies to the classroom study behavior of preschool children. *Journal of Applied Behavior Analysis,* 1968, **1,** 55–61.

Burchard, J.D. & Tyler, V.O., Jr. The modification of delinquent behaviour through operant conditioning. *Behaviour Research and Therapy,* 1965, **2,** 245–250.

Carkhuff, R.R. & Bierman, R. Training as a preferred mode of treatment of parents of emotionally disturbed children. *Journal of Counseling Psychology,* 1970, **17,** 157–161.

Chess, S. & Lyman, M.S. A psychiatric unit in a general hospital pediatric clinic. In S. Chess & A. Thomas (Eds.), *Annual progress in child psychiatry and child development.* New York: Brunner-Mazel, 1970. Pp. 540–550.

Clement, P.W. & Milne, D.C. Group play therapy and tangible reinforcers used to modify the behavior of eight-year-old boys. Unpublished manuscript, Harbor General Hospital, Torrance, California, 1966.

Coe, W.C. Dick and his parents: A case study. Presented at the conference "The Troubled Adolescent and His Family," Mendocino, California, March, 1970.

Cook, C. & Adams, H.E. Modification of verbal behaviour in speech deficient children. *Behaviour Research and Therapy,* 1966, **4,** 265–271.

Dinsmoor, J.A. Comments on Wetzel's treatment of a case of compulsive stealing. *Journal of Consulting Psychology,* 1966, **30,** 378–380.

Eisenberg, L., Gilbert, A., Cytryn, L. & Molling, P.A. The effectiveness of psychotherapy alone and in conjunction with perphenazine or placebo in the treatment of neurotic and hyperkinetic children. *American Journal of Psychiatry,* 1961, **117,** 1088–1093.

Eisenberg, L. & Gruenberg, E.M. The current status of secondary prevention in child psychiatry. *American Journal of Orthopsychiatry,* 1961, **31,** 355–367.

Elkirsch, P. Simultaneous treatment of a child and his mother. *American Journal of Psychotherapy,* 1953, **7,** 105–130.

Engeln, R., Knutson, J., Laughy, L. & Garlington, W. Behavior modification techniques applied to a family unit: A case study. *Journal of Child Psychology and Psychiatry,* 1968, **9,** 245–252.

Eysenck, H.J. The effects of psychotherapy: An evaluation. *Journal of Consulting Psychology,* 1952, **16,** 319–324.

Ferster, C.B. & Appel, J.B. Punishment of Ss responding in matching to sample by time out from positive reinforcement. *Journal of the Experimental Analysis of Behavior,* 1961, **4,** 45–56.

Ferster, C.B. & DeMyer, M.K. The development of performances in autistic children in an automatically controlled environment. *Journal of Chronic Diseases,* 1961, **13,** 312–345.

Ferster, C.B. & Skinner, B.F. *Schedules of reinforcement.* New York: Appleton-Century-Crofts, 1957.

Freud, S. *Collected papers,* Vol. 3, London: Hogarth Press, 1950.

Friedman, H.L. & McIntire, R.W. Modification of a child's finger-sucking behavior in the home with the mother as therapist. *Proceedings of the 78th Annual Convention of the American Psychological Association,* 1970, **5,** 769–770.

Fuchs, N.R. Play therapy at home. *The Merrill-Palmer Quarterly,* 1960, **3,** 89–95.

Furman, E. Treatment of under-fives by way of their parents. In *The psychoanalytic study of the child,* Vol. XII. New York: International Universities Press, 1950.

Gardner, J.E. Behavior therapy treatment approach to a psychogenic seizure case. *Journal of Consulting Psychology,* 1967, **31,** 209–212.

Gelber, H. & Meyer, V. Behaviour therapy and encopresis: The complexities involved in treatment. *Behaviour Research and Therapy,* 1965, **2,** 227–232.

Gelfand, D.M. & Hartmann, D.P. Behavior therapy with children: A review and evaluation of research methodology. *Psychological Bulletin,* 1968, **69,** 204–215.

Gorelick, M.C. Teaching parents to shape behavior of autistic children. Paper presented at the meeting of the Western Psychological Association, Los Angeles, April, 1970.

Grossberg, J.M. Behavior therapy: A review. *Psychological Bulletin,* 1964, **62,** 73–88.

Guerney, B.G., Jr. Filial therapy: Description and rationale. *Journal of Consulting Psychology,* 1964, **28,** 304–310.

Guerney, B.G., Jr. The use of parents as therapeutic agents. Paper presented at the meeting of the American Psychological Association, New York, September, 1966.

Guerney, B.G., Jr. *Psychotherapeutic agents: New roles for nonprofessionals, parents and teachers.* New York: Holt, Rinehart & Winston, 1969.

Hall, R.V. & Broden, M. Behavior changes in brain injured children through social reinforcement. *Journal of Experimental Child Psychology,* 1967, **5,** 463–479.

Hampton, P.J. Group psychotherapy with parents. *American Journal of Orthopsychiatry,* 1962, **32,** 918–926.

Harris, F.R., Johnston, M.K., Kelley, C.S. & Wolf, M.M. Effects of positive social reinforcement on regressed crawling of a nursery school child. *Journal of Educational Psychology,* 1964, **55,** 35–41.

Hawkins, R.P., Peterson, R.F., Schweid, E. & Bijou, S.W. Behavior therapy in the home: Amelioration of problem parent-child relations with the parent in a therapeutic role. *Journal of Experimental Child Psychology,* 1966, **4,** 99–107.

Heinicke, C.M. & Goldman, A. Research on psychotherapy with children: A review and suggestions for further study. *American Journal of Orthopsychiatry,* 1960, **30,** 483–493.

Hirsh, I. & Walder, L. Training mothers in groups as reinforcement therapists for their own children. *Proceedings of the 77th Annual Convention of the American Psychological Association,* 1969, **4,** 561–562.

Hobbs, N. Mental health's third revolution. *American Journal of Orthopsychiatry,* 1964, **24,** 822–833.

Holland, C.J. Elimination by the parents of fire-setting behaviour in a 7-year-old boy. *Behaviour Research and Therapy,* 1969, **7,** 135–137.

Hood-Williams, J. The results of psychotherapy with children: A reevaluation. *Journal of Consulting Psychology,* 1960, **24,** 84–88.

Howard, O. Teaching a class of parents as reinforcement therapists to treat their own children. Paper presented at the meeting of the Southeastern Psychological Association, Louisville, Ky., April, 1970.

Johnson, J.M. Using parents as contingency managers. Paper presented at the meeting of the Southeastern Psychological Association, New Orleans, February, 1969.

Johnson, S.M. & Brown, R.A. Producing behavior change in parents of disturbed children. *Journal of Child Psychology and Psychiatry,* 1969, **10,** 107–121.

Keehn, J.D. Brief case report: Reinforcement therapy of incontinence. *Behaviour Research and Therapy,* 1965, **2,** 239.

Kennedy, W.A. School phobia: Rapid treatment of fifty cases. *Journal of Abnormal Psychology,* 1965, **70,** 285–289.

Kessler, J.W. *Psychopathology of childhood.* Englewood Cliffs, N.J.: Prentice-Hall, 1966.

Kimmel, H.D. & Kimmel, E. An instrumental conditioning method for the treatment of enuresis. *Journal of Behavior Therapy and Experimental Psychiatry,* 1970, **1,** 121–123.

Kolansky, H. Treatment of a three-year-old girl's severe infantile neurosis: Stammering and insect phobia. In *The Psychoanalytic Study of the Child,* Vol. XV. New York: International Universities Press, Inc. 1960.

Krapfl, J.E., Bry, P. & Nawas, M.M. Uses of the Bug-in-the-Ear in the modification of parents' behavior. In R.D. Rubin & C.M. Franks (Eds.), *Advances in behavior therapy.* New York: Academic Press, 1968. Pp. 31–35.

Lal, H. & Lindsley, O. R. Therapy of chronic constipation in a young child by rearranging social contingencies. *Behaviour Research and Therapy,* 1968, **6,** 484–485.

Lehrman, L. J., Sirluck, H., Black, B. J. & Glick, S. J. Success and failure of treatment of children in the child guidance clinics of the Jewish Board of Guardians, New York City. *Jewish Board of Guardians Research Monograph,* 1949, No. 1.

Levitt, E. E. Results of psychotherapy with children: An evaluation. *Journal of Consulting Psychology,* 1957, **21,** 189–196.

Levitt, E. E. Reply to Hood-Williams. *Journal of Consulting Psychology,* 1960, **24,** 89–91.

Levitt, E. E. Psychotherapy with children: A further evaluation. *Behaviour Research and Therapy,* 1963, **1,** 45–51.

Levitt, E. E. Research on psychotherapy with children. In A. E. Bergin & S. Garfield (Eds.), *Handbook of psychotherapy and behavior change.* New York: John Wiley & Sons, 1971. Pp.474–494.

Levitt, E. E., Beiser, H. R. & Robertson, R. E. A follow-up evaluation of cases treated at a community child guidance clinic. *American Journal of Orthopyschiatry,* 1959, **29,** 337–347.

Liberman, R. Behavioral approaches to family and couple therapy. *American Journal of Orthopsychiatry,* 1970, **40,** 106–118.

Livingstone, J. B., Portnoi, T., Sherry, N., Rosenheim, E. & Onesti, S., Jr. Comprehensive child psychiatry through a team approach. In S. Chess & A. Thomas (Eds.), *Annual progress in child psychiatry and child development.* New York: Brunner-Mazel, 1970. Pp. 551–561.

Lovaas, O. I., Berberich, J. P., Perloff, B. F. & Schaeffer, B. Acquisition of imitative speech by schizophrenic children. *Science,* 1966, 151, 705–706.

Lovibond, S. H. *Conditioning and enuresis.* Oxford: Pergamon, 1964.

Mackay, J. The use of brief psychotherapy with children. *Canadian Psychiatric Association Journal,* 1967, **12,** 269–279.

Matarazzo, J. D. Some national developments in the utilization of non-traditional mental health power. *American Psychologist,* 1971, **26,** 363–372.

Mathis, H. I. Training a "disturbed" boy using the mother as therapist: A case study. *Behavior Therapy,* 1971, **2,** 233–239.

Mash, E.J., Lazere, R., Terdal, L. & Garner, A. Modification of mother-child interactions: A modeling approach for groups. Unpublished manuscript, University of Oregon Medical School, 1970.

Mash, E. J., Terdal, L. & Anderson, K. The response class matrix: A procedure for recording parent-child interactions. Unpublished manuscript, University of Oregon Medical School, 1970.

Mash, E. J. & Terdal, L. Modification of mother-child interactions: Playing with children. Unpublished manuscript, University of Oregon Medical School, 1970.

McIntire, R. W. *For love of children: Behavioral psychology for parents.* Del Mar, Calif.: CRM Books, 1970.

Meichenbaum, D., Bowers, K. & Ross, R. Modification of classroom behaviour of institutionalized female adolescent offenders. *Behaviour Research and Therapy,* 1968, **6,** 343–353.

Mira, M. Results of a behaviour modification training program for parents and teachers. *Behaviour Research and Therapy,* 1970, **8,** 309–311.

Neale, D. H. Behaviour therapy and encopresis in children. *Behaviour Research and Therapy,* 1963, **1,** 139–150.

Noyes, A. P. & Kolb, L. C. *Modern clinical psychiatry.* Philadelphia: W.B. Saunders, 1963.

Nordquist, V. M. The modification of childhood enuresis: Some response-response relationships. Paper presented at the meeting of the Southeastern Psychological Association, Louisville, Ky., April, 1970.

O'Leary, K. D., Becker, W. C., Evans, M.B. & Saudargas, R. A. A token reinforcement program in a public school: A replication and systematic analysis. *Journal of Applied Behavior Analysis,* 1969, **2,** 3–13.

O'Leary, K.D. & Drabman, R. Token reinforcement programs in the classroom: A review. *Psychological Bulletin,* 1971, **75,** 379–398.

O'Leary, K. D., O'Leary, S. & Becker, W. C. Modification of a deviant sibling interaction pattern in the home. *Behaviour Research and Therapy,* 1967, **5,** 113–120.

Ora, J. P. & Burgess, M. M. Operant conditioning of a deviant child by a psychiatric patient-mother. *Psychotherapy: Theory, Research and Practice,* 1971, **8,** 106–108.

Patterson, G. R. The mother as a social engineer in the classroom. In J. Krumboltz & C. Thoreson (Eds.), *Behavioral counseling: Cases and techniques.* New York: Holt, Rinehart & Winston, 1969. Pp. 155–161.

Patterson G. R. Behavioral intervention procedures in the classroom and in the home. In A. E. Bergin & S. L. Garfield (Eds.), *Handbook of psychotherapy and behavior change.* New York: John Wiley & Sons, 1971. Pp. 751–775.

Patterson, G. R. & Brodsky, G. A behaviour modification programme for a child with multiple problem behaviors. *Journal of Child Psychology and Psychiatry,* 1966, **7,** 277–295.

Patterson, G. R., Cobb, J. A. & Ray, R. S. A social engineering technology for retraining the families of agressive boys. In H. Adams & L. Unikel (Eds.), *Georgia symposium in experimental clinical psychology,* Vol. II. Springfield, Ill.: Charles C Thomas, in press.

Patterson, G. R. & Fagot, B. I. Selective responsiveness to social reinforcers and deviant behavior in children. *The Psychological Record,* 1967, **17,** 369–378.

Patterson, G. R. & Gullion, M. E. *Living with children: New methods for parents and teachers.* Champaign, Ill. : Research Press, 1968.

Patterson, G. R. & Hops, H. Coercion, a game for two: Intervention techniques for marital conflict. Unpublished manuscript, University of Oregon, 1970.

Patterson, G. R., McNeal, S., Hawkins, N. & Phelps, R. Re-programming the social environment. *Journal of Child Psychology and Psychiatry,* 1967, **8,** 181–195.

Patterson, G. R., Ray, R. S. & Shaw, D. A. Direct intervention in families of deviant children. *ORI Research Bulletin,* 1968, **8** (9).

Patterson, G. R. & Reid, J. B. Reciprocity and coercion: Two facets of social systems. In C. Neuringer & J. Michael (Eds.), *Behavior modification in clinical psychology.* New York: Appleton-Century-Crofts, 1970. Pp. 133–177.

Patterson, G. R., Shaw, D. A. & Ebner, M. J. Teachers, peers and parents as agents of change in the classroom. In F.A.M. Benson (Ed.), *Modifying deviant social behaviors in various classroom settings.* Eugene, Ore.: Department of Special Education, College of Education, 1969. Monograph No. 1.

Pawlicki, R. Behavior-therapy research with children: A critical review. *Canadian Journal of Behavioral Science,* 1970, **2,** 163–173.

Peine, H.A. & Munro, B. C. Training parents using lecture demonstration procedures and a contingency managed program. Unpublished manuscript, Bureau of Educational Research, University of Utah, 1970.

Peterson, R. F. & London, P. A role for cognition in the behavioral treatment of a child's eliminative disturbance. In L. P. Ullman & L. Krasner (Eds), *Case studies in behavior modification.* New York: Holt, Rinehart & Winston, 1965.

Peterson, R. F. & Peterson, L. The use of positive reinforcement in the control of self-destructive behavior in a retarded boy. *Journal of Experimental Child Psychology*, 1968, **6**, 351–360.

Phillips, E. L. Parent-child psychotherapy: A followup study comparing two techniques. *Journal of Psychology*, 1960, **49**, 195–202.

Pumroy, D. A new approach to treating parent-child problems. Paper presented at the meeting of the American Psychological Association, New York, September, 1965.

Radke-Yarrow, M. Problems of methods in parent-child research. *Child Development*, 1963, **34**, 215–226.

Rangell, L. A treatment of nightmares in a seven-year-old boy. In *The psychoanalytic study of the child*, Vol. V. New York: International Universities Press, 1950.

Ray, R. S. The training of mothers of atypical typical children in the use of behavior modification techniques. Unpublished master's thesis, University of Oregon, 1965.

Report of the Joint Commission on Mental Health of Children. *Crisis in child mental health: Challenge for the 1970's*. New York: Harper and Row, 1969.

Reynolds, N. J. & Risley, T. R. The role of material reinforcers in increasing talking of a disadvantaged preschool child. *Journal of Applied Behavior Analysis*, 1968, **1**, 253–262.

Risley, T. The effects and side effects of punishing the autistic behaviors of a deviant child. *Journal of Applied Behavior Analysis*, 1968, **1**, 21–34.

Risley, T. & Wolf, M. Experimental manipulation of autistic behavior and generalization into the home. In R. Ulrich, T. Stachnik & J. Mabry (Eds), *Control of human behavior*. New York: Scott, Foresman, 1966. Pp. 193–198.

Risley, T. & Wolf, M. M. Establishing functional speech in echolalic children. *Behaviour Research and Therapy*, 1967, **5**, 73–88.

Rose, S. D. A behavioral approach to the group treatment of parents. *Social Work*, 1969, **14**, 21–29.

Ruben, M. & Thomas, R. Home training of instincts and emotions. *Health Education Journal*, 1947, **5**, 119–124.

Russo, S. Adaptations in behavioural therapy with children. *Behaviour Research and Therapy*, 1964, **2**, 43–47.

Ryback, D. & Staats, A. W. Parents as behavior therapy technicians in treating deficits (dyslexia). *Journal of Behavior Therapy and Experimental Psychiatry*, 1970, **1**, 109–119.

Schwarz, H. The mother in the consulting room: Notes on the psychoanalytic treatment of two young children. In *The Psychoanalyt-*

ic study of the child, Vol, V. New York: International Universities Press, 1950.

Shah, S. A. Training and utilizing a mother as the therapist for her child. In B. G. Guerney, Jr. (Ed.), *Psychotherapeutic agents: New roles for nonprofessionals, parents, and teachers.* New York: Holt, Rinehart & Winston, 1969. Pp. 401–407.

Shepherd, M., Oppenheim, A. N. & Mitchell, S. Childhood behavior disorders and the child-guidance clinic: An epidemiological study. *Journal of Child Psychology and Psychiatry,* 1966, **7,** 39–52.

Sidman, M. *Tactics of scientific research.* New York: Basic Books, 1960.

Skinner, B. F. *The behavior of organisms.* New York: Appleton-Century-Crofts, 1938.

Skinner, B. F. The flight from the laboratory, In J. T. Wilson et al., (Eds.), *Current trends in psychological theory.* Pittsburgh: University of Pittsburgh Press, 1958.

Skinner, B. F. What is the experimental analysis of behavior? Paper presented at the meeting of the American Psychological Association, Los Angeles, September, 1964.

Smith, J. & Smith, D. E. D. *Child management: A program for parents and teachers.* Ann Arbor, Mich.: Ann Arbor Publishers, 1966.

Stover, L. & Guerney, B. G., Jr. The efficacy of training procedures for mothers in filial therapy. *Psychotherapy: Theory, Research and Practice,* 1967, **4,** 110–115.

Straughan, J. H. Treatment with child and mother in the playroom. *Behaviour Research and Therapy,* 1964, **2,** 37–41.

Tharp, R. G. & Wetzel, R. J. *Behavior modification in the natural environment.* New York: Academic Press, 1969.

Thorndike, E. L. Animal intelligence: An experimental study of the associative processes in animals. *Psychological Review Monograph, Monograph Supplement,* 1898, 2 (Whole No. 8).

Thorne, G. L., Tharp, R. G. & Wetzel, R. Behavior modification techniques: New tools for probation officers. *Federal Probation,* 1967, **31 (2), 21–27.**

Tomlinson, J. R. The treatment of bowel retention by operant procedures: A case study. *Journal of Behavior Therapy and Experimental Psychiatry,* 1970, **1,** 83–85.

Tyler, V. O., Jr. & Brown, G. D. The use of swift, brief isolation as a group control device for institutionalized delinquents. *Behaviour Research and Therapy,* 1967, **5,** 1–9.

Valett, R. E. *Modifying children's behavior: A guide for parents and professionals.* Palo Alto, Calif.: Fearon, 1969.

Wagner, L. I. & Ora, J. P. Parental control of the very young severely oppositional child. Paper presented at the meeting of the Southeastern Psychological Association, Louisville, April, 1970.

Wahler, R. G. Behavior therapy for oppositional children: Love is not enough. Paper presented at the meeting of the Eastern Psychological Association, Washington, D. C., April, 1968.

Wahler, R. G. Oppositional children: A quest for parental reinforcement control. *Journal of Applied Behavior Analysis,* 1969a, **2,** 159–170.

Wahler, R. G. Setting generality: Some specific and general effects of child behavior therapy. *Journal of Applied Behavior Analysis,* 1969b, 2, 239–246.

Wahler, R. G. & Erickson, M. Child behaviour therapy: A community program in Appalachia. *Behaviour Research and Therapy,* 1969, **7,** 71–78.

Wahler, R. G., Winkel, G. H., Peterson, R. F. & Morrison, D. C. Mothers as behaviour therapists for their own children. *Behaviour Research and Therapy,* 1965, **3,** 111–124.

Walder, L. O., Cohen, S. I., Breiter, D. E., Daston, P. G., Hirsch, I. S. & Leibowitz, J. M. Teaching behavioral principles to parents of disturbed children. In B. G. Guerney, Jr. (Ed.), *Psychotherapeutic agents: New roles for nonprofessionals, parents, and teachers.* New York: Holt, Rinehart & Winston, 1969. Pp. 443–449.

Wetzel, R. J., Baker, J., Roney, M. & Martin, M. Outpatient treatment of autistic behaviour. *Behaviour Research and Therapy,* 1966, **4,** 169–177.

White, J. G. The use of learning theory in the psychological treatment of children. *Journal of Clinical Psychology,* 1959, **15,** 227–229.

Williams, C. D. The elimination of tantrum behavior by extinction procedures. *Journal of Abnormal and Social Psychology,* 1959, **59,** 269.

Wiltz, N. A. Modification of behaviors of deviant boys through parent participation in a group technique. *Dissertation Abstracts International,* 1970 (May), Vol. 30 (11-A), 4786–4787.

Witmer, H. L. & Keller, J. Outgrowing childhood problems: A study in the value of child guidance treatment. *Smith College Studies in Social Work,* 1942, **13,** 74–90.

Wolf, M., Risely, T. & Mees, H. Application of operant conditioning procedures to the behaviour problems of an autistic child. *Behaviour Research and Therapy,* 1964, **1,** 305–312.

Yates, A. J. *Behavior therapy.* New York: John Wiley & Sons, 1970.

Zeilberger, J., Sampen, S. E. & Sloane, H. N., Jr. Modification of a child's problem behaviors in the home with the mother as therapist. *Journal of Applied Behavior Analysis,* 1968, **1,** 47–53.

15. *Affect in Groups*

Alfred Jacobs

The research on personal-growth groups suggests that homogeneous groups composed of friendly, expressive and person-oriented members are consistently more effective than homogeneous groups which lack members with such attributes. Neuropsychiatric patients are less likely to be sociable and expressive than normals, and therefore treatment groups composed exclusively of patients are most similar to those groups which research has shown to be the poorest. Studies are urgently needed to examine this issue, as well as its implication that mixed groups of normals and patients may deliver more effective treatment. Mental hospitals and prisons, to take the logic a step further, should also be poor treatment environments.

The search for generalities in the literature pertaining to emotions and group interventions is otherwise disappointing. Much speculation and endorsement of the importance of emotions by authors exists, and has stimulated studies. However, a shortage of standard instruments for measuring the important components of the intervention processes has hampered research, and the use of idiosyncratic measuring devices makes it difficult to compare studies which seem to be addressed to the same issues. A striking absence is observed, of empirical studies of the intervention process itself, of studies of the manipulation of the variables of intervention and of studies of interventions designed to produce specific outcomes. Most of the early research is observational and descriptive, as might be expected in a new research area. However, evidence is accumulating that discomfort can be reduced, that affective responses can be modified and also become more valued and that empathy and warmth may be two important ingredients in the process.

INTRODUCTION

I propose in this paper and the next two to discuss the role of affect or emotion, and of feedback in groups designed to change human behavior. As the general context for the material to follow, let me state at this point that I identify feedback as one of the primary vehicles for the input of new information to group participants. Emotions are associated with the motivational, incentive and reinforcement characteristics of events which transpire in the group. Such events may interfere with or may facilitate and stabilize the absorption of information and the production of attitudinal and behavioral change.

I believe that the power latent in a group resides primarily in the advantages of a number of people acting in concert in order to deliver a greater quantity of more credible information to each other, to serve as role models to each other and to exert more influence on each other in accordance with the principles of social learning. Therefore, the therapist or group leader must mobilize and train group members to motivate, reinforce, model and give accurate information to each other. In recent years, many of the distinctions between psychotherapy groups, growth groups, discussion groups, community groups, etc., have blurred for me, as it becomes more apparent that many of the principles for effective group functioning are identical in all situations.

The material to follow will refer to a variety of conceptualizations that therapists have developed to attempt to explain the importance of these two variables, emotion and feedback, to the functioning of groups, as well as some of the research literature relevant to these issues.

Let me begin by explaining the choice of these two variables for my papers. To begin with, I have had a longstanding interest in emotions, and in their relationship to the learning process. However, I was pleasantly reassured to discover considerable support for the position that emotions and feedback were two of the most important dimensions in group process. For example, Campbell & Dunnette (1968), in their review of the effectiveness of T-group experiences in managerial training and development, state, "Thus the participants must be able to inform each other how their behavior is being seen and interpreted and to describe the kinds of feelings generated [p. 76]." Egan's (1970) book on personal-growth groups identifies emotional issues as one of the focuses of the personal-growth group and feedback as an important dimension of group treatment.

Group therapy patients who benefited most from treatment seem to agree with Egan, and with Campbell and Dunnette. Patients report that catharsis (emotion) and personal input (feedback) are the most helpful occurrences in group psychotherapy (Yalom, 1970).

Certainly, the ubiquitousness of concepts referring to emotional states in the writings of more or less traditional and contemporary individual and group therapists from Freud to Ellis is so obvious that it needs no documentation.

The order of presentation of topics of this chapter will be as follows:

Emotions and Groups—Theories and Fancies begins with a general discussion of the concept of emotion, which is defined as a class of private events. It is asserted that confusion has resulted from the naive assumption of researchers that verbal reports, complex social behavior and physiological manifestations are all equivalent measures of emotions.

A second section categorizes the common conceptualizations of the relationship of emotion to social illness and health, and the manner in which these various conceptualizations have been related to intervention by group methods. Two such major sets of categories exist. Emotional disorder theories contend that psychopathology or bad mental health is a consequence of the excessive or deficits which arise in certain classes of emotional responses of individuals. Psychopathology of the normal theories emphasize the inadequacy of our ordinary practices of social education which lead to socioemotional incompetencies in the typical individual. It is rare that the theories or hypothesis in any of the above categories elaborate the specific advantages of group methods of intervention.

The last section describes two major positions with regard to the role of emotions in the group intervention process. One group of theorists contends that the arousal of negative emotions and states of discomfort in participants is essential to the effectiveness of group interventions. A second group of theorists emphasizes the importance of the creation of a positive emotional climate of trust or group cohesiveness in order to produce beneficent outcomes in group intervention. The proponents of each of these conditions bases its position on one or two of the several motivating and inhibiting properties which characterize such states of subjective distress as anxiety. However, the general agreement of the theorists that emotional events are important, and should be studied, stimulated the descriptive research summarized in this the next major section of the chapter.

Research on the role of emotions in group interventions is the topic of the next major chapter section. I have found it difficult to draw many generalizations from this material because of the lack of comparability of intervention techniques and instruments from study to study, and the general unsystematic nature of the research which exists at present.

The section covers six major topics. The research of the first section suggests that negative emotions characterized the first half of the intervention period, and positive emotions the second half. From studies of the affective consequences of group interventions, the second section, it may be concluded that patient discomfort may be reduced by psychotherapy, and that a number of other emotional changes are achieved by sensitivity training. The third section examines the literature on the personal characteristics of those who benefit most and least from groups. Anxious patients seem to improve more after psychotherapy than other patients; anxious normals seem to benefit least from laboratory training. Section Four examines the group behavior of emotionally different types of participants and finds that anxious patients seem to talk more in groups. The T-group literature is addressed to different issues, and suggests that friendly, expressive participants are friendly and expressive during laboratory sessions. In Section Five, studies of groups composed of different types of individuals are reviewed and a conclusion similar to that of the previous section is drawn. Groups composed exclusively of friendly, expressive members seem to do better than homogeneous groups which lack such participants. The final section studies the emotional characteristics of the leader, and shows that empathy, genuineness and warmth seem to be related to patient improvement.

Time and space is the next major chapter topic. Research on the marathon group, in which the duration of sessions is lengthened, is reviewed. Research suggests that the longer sessions are more effective than the more traditional one-or-two-hour session. Manipulation of variables has also characterized investigations of such spatial dimensions as the proximity of group members. Initial studies suggest that the relationships to emotion are probably complex.

In the Summary and conclusions, reasons for the primitiveness of the research are explored, such as the shortage of measuring instruments. The failure of the early studies to study the intervention process itself is also noted.

EMOTIONS AND GROUPS—THEORIES AND FANCIES

The Concept of Emotion

Let us begin our examination of the relevance of emotional concepts to group processes by defining emotion. I have chosen to conceptualize affective states as private events which are represented centrally. Emotions are probably generated historically by the experiences of individuals with gratifying or aversive events. Differences in the frequencies with which such events have occurred in the past, the proportions of negative to positive events, the magnitudes of each and the social contexts within which each is encountered, produce momentary or more durable anticipations and evaluations in individuals (Jacobs, 1971). The large number of classes of verbalizations associated with such sequences of events are commonly classified as affective, and include such terms as liking or disliking, happiness, fear, depression, anger, etc.

The importance of maintaining the criterion of verifiability of concepts in empirical science, in order to preclude demonological or other pseudo explanations, has led many experimentally oriented psychologists to avoid the study of issues relating to such private events. However, public operations such as the verbal report under specified conditions, gross molar behavior such as withdrawal and a variety of physiological indices have often been utilized to define emotional states (Jacobs & Sachs, 1971). Although the actual degree of concomitance among verbal, gross behavioral and physiological "measures of emotion" is demonstrably low (Jacobs, Edelman & Wolpin, 1971; Lang, 1969; Jacobs & Wolpin, 1971; Leitenberg, Agras, Butz & Wineze, 1971), researchers, having reified emotions, have generally been unwilling to face this fact and its consequence, that the three response classes above are independently modifiable. It is, therefore, not plausible that an intervention whose design makes it most appropriate for the modification of one class of emotional behavior should use a different class of behavior as the criteria of change. Much of the inconsistency in the research literature is attributable to such illogical research designs. The issues have been further clouded by the injection into the confusion of the reductionism question, and the question whether some definitions are more valid than others, instead of whether some are more fruitful.

Defined in any of the three response modalities, as well as in terms of certain common stimulus constellations, emotions have been demonstrated to be associated with motivational—that is, energizing or deenergizing—processes in organisms (Miller, 1948; Brown & Jacobs, 1949; Konrad & Jacobs, 1965). In groups, such processes can facilitate change or cause change to be resisted.

The material to follow has been drawn from studies which have defined emotion by verbal reports, including such instruments as rating scales, check lists, self-report inventories and questionnaires, and from studies of typical social behaviors associated with affective states. Studies of emotions such as depression, fear and anger, and emotional behaviors such as flight and tantrums, which are universally accepted as members of the class of emotional events, have been given preference.

Emotions, Social Illness, Health and Groups

There appear to be two major categories of conceptualizations which relate emotions, and mental health, to group intervention. In emotional disorder theories, certain emotional states are purported to cause, either directly or indirectly, the symptomatology of concern to the individual or social group. One of the most explicit examples is that of Mowrer's integrity therapy (Mowrer, 1968). Mowrer asserts that emotional disturbance begins with some type of mismanagement of one's contractual systems. Those who attempt to conceal their contract failures from themselves and others experience guilt and fear of discovery, which leads to persistent affective discomfort and somatic symptom systems. More elaborate and cognitive symptoms may develop as attempts to avoid the discomfort. Mowrer's remedy includes confession, which reduces the fear of discovery, and restitution to decrease the guilt. The group is important in Mowrer's formulation because it represents (or is) the community which receives the confession, and whose monitoring provides the motivation to complete the restitution and to avoid further contractual failures.

Probably most variants of traditional psychotherapies based on the paradigm that fear or discomfort lead to avoidance, repression or distortion also fall into this class; however, such theories are not always explicit with regard to the advantages of group treatment.

Compatible with the emotional-disease model is also the point of view that certain emotions, i.e., anxiety and depression, may cause excessive discomfort when they are habitual and intense in individuals, and it is, therefore, ordinarily desirable to attempt to diminish the intensity or the frequency of such emotional reactions. Because of its emphasis on psychopathology, the emotional disease model does not seem as often or as strongly to assert a second corollary: that individuals may also suffer from deficiencies in the occurrence of positive emotional states such as belongingness or feelings of affection. It is conceivable that a case could be made for the greater efficiency or effectiveness of group processes over individual for dealing with both the above conditions.

A second group conceptualization, probably more relevant to encounter and personal growth groups, may be subsumed under the heading of the *psychopathology of the normal,* for lack of a better term. Such conceptualizations refer to the presumed culturally produced deficits in expressions and recognition of emotional responses in self and others (Egan, 1970). For example, some critics of our culture have remarked on the absence of formal training in our educational systems of emotional responses. Other observers assert that there are informal pressures, particularly on males, to suppress expression, demonstration or recognition of strong emotional states. Social scientists identify socialization processes designed to discourage assertive, aggressive or hostile behavior in females.

Proponents of the use of groups as vehicles for personal growth contend that groups have advantages over dyadic relationships for the acquisition of such positive social-emotional skills as the development of intimacy or the establishment of trus which are ordinarily neglected in the social training of most people. In the areas of negative emotions, such theorists as Bach and Lazarus, as may be seen in earlier chapters, use groups as settings in which to train more effective aggressive or more assertive behavior. Some of the disadvantages of the dyad for such purposes are obvious. Clearly, that the group is superior in demonstrating the universality of emotional responses available, as well as in providing a range of models, cannot be disputed.

However, rather than curing people of feelings of alienation, or training them to better cope with such problems in the social environment, one might argue that it is a sufficient purpose for the group to satisfy such needs during its contracted period of existence. Or, to escape further from a treatment or training model, the fact that certain kinds of group experiences make people feel good is as legitimate a basis for the existence of groups as it is for the existence of roller coasters or movie shows (assuming that the purpose of such groups is not misrepresented). The more fervent healers and social engineers among us might not choose to lend our time organizing or participating in such groups.

The Emotional Characteristics of the Intervention Process

A number of authors have speculated that predictable sequences of emotional events occur in group treatments or laboratory experiences. Little agreement appears to exist regarding which sequences are more likely to characterize effective group interventions. However, the issue regarding the desirability of arousing negative emotional states in participants separates the theorists into two camps. Samples of typical assertions regarding the flow of emotional events follows, first for those who contend that the arousal of discomfort facilitates treatment.

Schein & Bennis (1965) posit a three-phase system, consisting of what they call unfreezing, changing and refreezing. The cycle is initiated by a dilemma or some disconfirming information information, which creates *social anxiety* to "produce powerful emotional responses" and guilt. If the person comes to feel safe, he will then seek further information about himself, which will allow him cognitively to redefine some beliefs about himself or his relationship to others.

Stoller (1968) comments that negatively loaded responses come predominantly in the early phases of a marathon session. More positive reactions tend to come later when there is a general air of increased honesty within the group, and also in the context of having been earned through behavior. Corsini (1968), in discussing Immediate Therapy in groups, describes the beginning of the process as one which the patient experiences the feeling of acceptance, belonging and identification with the group. The patient is then manipulated into a situation of intense anxiety, which the author describes as a state of panic. The patient is then rejected from the group, and is allowed to be alone with his anxiety. Ordinarily, reports Corsini, within a two-day period, the patient suddenly "understands" and becomes tranquil and calm.

Contrasted to these theorists who have in common their agreement that the early presence of intense negative experiences are necessary for change are theorists like Gibb & Gibb (1968), Rogers (1951) and Yalom (1970). The approaches of all three emphasize the creation of a positive climate as a condition of change. In his TORI conceptualization, Gibb (1971) asserts that growth is facilitated by nondefensive inner conditions and high trust in interpersonal relationships. Therefore, relationships that are trusting, open and contain the potential for realization and for interdependence are more likely to produce personal growth than those characterized by defensive relationships, where there is a need to ward off perceived or anticipated threats. Rogers (1951) emphasized the importance of unconditional regard from the therapist, as one of the ingredients that enable the patient to explore himself undefensively. Rogers has recently suggested that group-member acceptance and understanding may carry with it a greater power and meaning than acceptance by the therapist.

Yalom (1970), in his review of the relationship of cohesiveness to treatment, concludes that group cohesiveness (liking for a group) is a necessary precondition for effective therapy. He summarizes evidence that suggests that the cohesiveness of the group, and individual attraction to the group, may be related to therapeutic outcome. He presents some persuasive arguments with regard to the various relationships between cohesiveness and such variables which might relate to therapeutic outcome, as amount of acceptance, amount of support, level of self-esteem, frequency of attendance, etc.

A differential emphasis on some of the properties of anxiety, and an exclusion of consideration of the other properties is the basis for this division between those theorists who advocate the arousal of anxiety in groups, and those who contend that anxiety arousal is detrimental. Schein & Bennis, in the first group of theorists, capitalize on the principle that the escape from or avoidance of distress, as has been well established, provides powerful motivation and reinforcement for response change. The inhibiting power of aversive stimulation is used by proponents of anxiety arousal to prevent the occurrence of those habitual responses of participants which interfere with the self-exploration which may be necessary for growth.

Those theorists who contend that anxiety arousal has detrimental effects on group interventions point to the habit-evoking characteristics of aversive stimuli, and the high probability that defensive habits such as flight, denial and distortion will be elicited from individuals in periods of discomfort. The maintenance of high anxiety levels in participants during interventions, these theorists imply further, may increase the difficulty of elicitation of desirable responses, such as those of self-disclosure, which tend to be inhibited for fear of social disapproval even in more favorable circumstances.

It has been demonstrated elsewhere that other, more complex, reactions to distress exist in humans which probably affect the evaluation of and the participation in group interventions. Among these are the dissonance-reducing processes of humans, which sometimes motivate the assignment of positive evaluations to painful experiences in preference to the alternative of accepting the conclusion that one may have volunteered for a worthless as well as an uncomfortable experience. More sophisticated theories of group intervention may incorporate all the properties of anxiety which have been described so far, as well as additional characteristics, as our knowledge of the mechanics of group processes increases.

Such theories as have been described in this section of the chapter have also contribued contributed conceptualizations and stimulated research into the role of emotion in group interventions. The theories have also generated the general belief that the emotional events which occur in groups are important, and should be studied.

Among these classes of conceptualizations and research are the following types:

(1) changes in the emotional responses of group participants during and after interventions
(2) relationships deriving from the habitual emotional attributes of participants, or various combinations of participants
(3) emotional reactions of participants to components of the intervention process

In the main, the conceptualizations are directed at the facilitation of inhibitory quality of emotional events as they affect the shortterm and longterm objectives of intervention. The next two major sections of the chapter consist primarily of a summary of some of the descriptive research on group intervention which is addressed to the above issues. I mean to underscore by the selection of the term *descriptive research* to describe these studies, that the research of this era ignored the study of the intervention process itself as if it were a given, and concentrated for the most part on its consequences, and on its participants.

The reader may experience some difficulty adding up and integrating all the studies, as I have had myself, because of the unsystematic character of most of this research. The apparent inconsistencies and information gaps are perhaps not too unexpected in a new research area. The confusion is compounded by two major trends which the reader may note. One is the lack of standard instruments or techniques for the measurement of group interactions, which has led researchers to invent scales or to use instruments developed for the assessment of individuals. The comparability of results from study to study sometimes becomes difficult to determine when different instruments purporting to measure the same or similar attributes have been used.

Second, the concepts of group psychotherapy research have been psychiatrically generated, and seem to be primarily concerned with the modification of habitual negative or deficit affects and behavior, whereas the T-group literature has been more addressed to the study of socially and educationally derived conceptualizations and the improvement of affective skills. For these reasons, I have ordinarily attempted to present the psychotherapy studies and T-group studies separately in the material to follow.

RESEARCH ON EMOTIONS IN GROUPS

Emotional Phases in Group Intervention

Conceptualizations such as those in the previous section have generated some research regarding the sequence of affective events in group situations. One of the earliest phase theories having to do with emotion is that of Bales and Strodtbeck. The theory and its evaluation are summarized in Goldstein, Heller & Sechrest (1966). Bales and Strodtbeck hypothesized that the early phases of problem solving in groups would be characterized by interactions involving evaluation, and subsequently by interactions emphasizing control. The progression would be characterized by increases in the relative frequencies of positive and negative interactions. An equilibrium process was also hypothesized by which the initial acts in groups would lead to a balanced proportion of positive, negative and other reactions. An attempt by Talland to verify the presence of the same processes in psychotherapy groups was a failure; a better designed study by Psathas with psychotherapy patients reported the existence of both processes.

Stock (1964) summarizes other early studies, including one in which Back reported that two T-groups expressed relatively more negative feelings during the second half. He also reported that the trainers consistently expressed more positive than negative feelings. On the basis of the Stock review of a number of other studies in which measures of emotional responses were recorded, I would conclude that very little consistency of results is obtained in these phase studies.

Bass (1962) reported that depression reliably increases over a ten day Training laboratory although it declines at the end, and activation and skepticism decrease. Surprisingly in the light of other evidence, little anxiety was expressed by participants in the Bass study.

Two studies by Lubin and colleagues (Lubin, Dupre & Lubin, 1967; Lubin & Zuckerman, 1967), using an adjective checklist of emotions (a self-report measure consisting of adjectives describing emotions which are endorsed by Ss to indicate their feelings at the moment), report that depression in both studies, and anxiety and hostility in the second, are highest in the middle week of sensitivity training. An attempt to calibrate the extent of the emotional disruption which occurs in T-groups in a third study (Lubin and Zuckerman, 1970) reveals that the level of emotion aroused at the peak of T-group experience, is significantly less than that aroused by six hours of perceptual deprivation experiment experience, and about at the top of the normal range of scores on his check list. A similar type of adjective checklist evidence (Jacobs & Jacobs, 1971) showed that the level of apprehensiveness at the very beginning of a simulated laboratory experience for graduate students in psychology (a dry run intended to prepare the students to serve as trainers in a future personal growth laboratory) was twice as high as the average apprehension reported by a somewhat simiar population of graduate and upper-division students in a month-long study of typical mood-levels.

Dunphy (1968) more recently used a computer system of content analysis, to analyze journalized weekly reports written by undergraduate Harvard students in a year-long T-group-like course. He concludes, with respect to emotional changes over this course of time, that early attempts to achieve interpersonal closeness and emotional involvement in the group are resisted and avoided. Emotional arousal, affection, depression and anxiety increase about the middle of the sequence. The last two phases show high emphasis on emotional concerns, particularly affection, as the group ends.

Moderate to high discomfort seems to characterize the middle and perhaps the beginning of the training groups. The expression of positive feelings by participants appears more likely to occur during the second half of a T-group. The same may be true of psychotherapy groups. Whether this sequence of emotion is unavoidable, and whether it contributes to the success of the intervention, as some have theorized, has not been established. The antecedents to these emotional events have not been identified. Egan (1970) speculates that the ambiguity and/or lack of structure which often characterizes the beginning of laboratory training and psychotherapy groups may be responsible for this early arousal of discomfort. The "hot seat" technique, in which members of groups take turns at becoming the target for group evaluation and criticism, might also be expected to arouse mounting discomfort as members await their turn.

The Affective Consequences of Group Intervention

A large number of studies have concerned themselves primarily with the nature of affective outcomes in various types of group interventions.

Bednar & Lawlis (1971), in their review of outcome-group literature, report that two studies showed decreases in the Minnesota Multiphasic Personality Inventory (a self-report inventory of psychiatric symptoms) neurotic-triad scores after treatment, especially the depression scale, which is frequently considered to be a measure of general subjective discomfort.

Kelman & Parloff (1957) report corroborating results. The authors show significant changes in staff members' ratings of patient discomfort after treatment, as well as in several other outcome criteria measures, but little evidence for the existence of relationships between changes in patient comfort and changes in patient effectiveness or patient self-awareness.

Gibb (1971) concludes that there are several studies that clearly indicate that feelings are the most salient stimuli in group situations and the primary locus of changes in sensitivity. He bases his conclusion on such evidence as the fact that trained subjects, when placed as unknowns in new test groups, are rated as having higher "general emotional adjustment" in one study, and as receiving higher ratings on the tendency to "own one's feelings" in another. There is further evidence, asserts Gibb, to indicate that feelings are valued more than thoughts after training, that training decreases wanted affection and that, after treatment, the largest reduction in disparity between own behavioral tendencies and those desired in others occurs in group members who originally show strong control and weak affection tendencies and who desire low control and high affection, as measured by the FIRO Scales. (The FIRO is a self-report inventory developed to measure attitudes of participants in groups.) The scores, as suggested above, describe such affective attributes of the endorser as affection, and also the amount of affection which he would desire from others.)

However, Holbert, Cormier & Friedman (1971), in a recent study, find no differences between experimental and control leaderless classroom sensitivity groups on the FIRO affection scales.

It is of interest to me in reading the literature how much research seems to be devoted to the problem of whether group psychotherapy and laboratories are effective and so little to the relationship between the nature of interventions and their objectives. In any case, a substantial amount of evidence seems to exist to suggest that a variety of interventions may modify the affective processes of the participants, and that self-reports of discomfort are decreased after intervention. The T-group literature particularly, as reported here and later in the chapter, provides support for the proposition that sensitivity training *does* achieve one of its goals, in that participants become more aware of feelings and assign more importance to them.

The Emotional Characteristics of Participants Who Benefit Most from Group Intervention

The most recent study of initial status and psychotherapeutic change is Truax (1971). Truax evaluates previous research (as much based on studies of individual rather than group therapy) and concludes that clients with greatest pretherapy "felt disturbance" and least overt behavioral disturbance benefit most. The Bednar & Lawlis review of the literature, referred to earlier, also concludes that groups are effective for participants with mood disturbances. Truax evaluates his own study on inpatients, outpatients and delinquents receiving group treatment as tentatively supporting the previous hypothesis.

However, the Truax study used therapist's ratings of improvement, freedom from hospitalization and changes in patients' self-reports of symptomatology after treatment as criteria of improvement, and only the last measure of improvement is consistently related to amount of initial mood disturbance. Even this last relationship may be partly artifactual. As in studies reported earlier, different criteria of improvement are not related to each other. As a matter of fact, some of the anxiety indices derived from this initial testing with the MMPI are significantly related to *more* days of hospitalization after treatment in Truax's inpatient mental-hospital population.

The issue of which type of patient benefits most from which type of intervention is clearly an important practical question. However, the evidence is obviously sparse and, in any case, has had little effect on practice. It seems clear from Truax's study that the problem of the relationships between initial status and extent of improvement after treatment are complex and that the solution may differ according to population, type of treatment and instruments used to evaluate results.

Stock (1964), in reviewing the T-group literature on learning, concludes that there is evidence that individuals demonstrating such emotional behavior as too-high anxiety, threat orientation and tendencies towards dependency and flight, gain little from laboratory experiences. These conclusions seem somewhat contradictory to those derived from the group psychotherapy literature with regard to the role of anxiety level. However, differences in populations and nature of interventions may resolve such apparent contradictions. Patients whose symptoms consist primarily primarily of anxiety may simply represent the least "sick" or most accessible to treatment, when compared to the remainder of the psychiatric population, where additional layers of behavioral or other more complex secondary symptoms may have developed to reduce the discomfort of persistent and intense anxiety. On the other hand, the anxious participant may be handicapped, when compared to the less-anxious intact normals with whom the anxious T-group volunteer interacts in a laboratory training experience.

Emotional Characteristics of the Member and Group Process

The personality variables of interest to the psychotherapy research, as the reader has observed by this point, have been psychiatric conceptualizations, such as neurosis and psychosis.

Negative affect such as habitual anxiety and associated deficit behaviors such as withdrawal characterize this area of group research.

Stern & Grosz (1966a, 1966b), in two studies of the relationship of extroversion and neuroticism (habitual anxiety?) to group process, report that extroversion is related to patient-to-patient interactions and neuroticism to patient-to-therapist interactions in psychiatric groups. In the second study the authors report that extroverts interact with extroverts, and those high on the neuroticism dimension react with other high scorers on neuroticism, whereas the low scorers on each dimension interact with each other. Eisenman (1966) reported that anxious patients talk more than nonanxious patients in group therapy.

Holmes (1967) found that adjective-checklist mood-measures of depression taken at the end of sessions did not relate to interaction measures. Geidt (1961) reported that ratings of affect were the least effective of four sets of ratings of work behavior for predicting quality of participation in group therapy.

Anxious patients seem to talk more than nonanxious, and particularly with the therapist and other anxious patients, seems to be the major conclusion that one might draw from this literature. Ratings of affect by others, which may be less reliable than ratings of overt behavior which are less inferential, or may not be as highly related to overt behavior as to other measures of affect, do not seem to be a promising predictor of group interaction.

The T-group literature on personality, process and outcome has shown more interest in such personality variables as friendliness and liking for people, and willingness to express positive and negative emotions. The group process and outcome variables which have been used include productivity, expression of emotions, sensitivity and the value placed on the importance of personal feelings.

Stock (1966) reviews a number of studies in the T-group literature which examine the emotions of the participants and group processes. Among the studies reviewed by Stock is that of Ben Zeev, who reports that members of a T-group who participate with those they like show tendencies on projective tests to express warmth and friendship and inhibit expressions of hostility and anger. Those who did not participate with those they liked showed the reverse pattern. Stock also reviews a study by Roseberg, who reports that the least productive T-group members were less friendly, and more competitive and energetic, than the most productive.

Harrison & Lubin (1965) conclude that whereas person-oriented members are more expressive, warm and comfortable in T-labs, task-oriented participants learn more. The results seem somewhat contradictory to those of Roseberg who reports that the least productive T-group members were less friendly and more competitive and energetic than the most productive. Harrison & Lubin (1965) conclude that whereas person-oriented members are more expressive, warm, and comfortable in T-labs, task oriented participants learn more: the results seem somewhat contradictory to Roseberg. Campbell & Dunnette (1968) review a study by Mathis, who concludes that those scoring highest on a scale of intrapersonal conflict, and also on tendencies towards the open communication of aggression and affection, are rated higher on sensitivity, sophistication and productivity at the end of a laboratory than the low scorers. The results again seem somewhat inconsistent with the findings of Ben Zeev above, that those who participate with those they like tend to inhibit aggression.

Steele (1968) reports in a more recent study that a preference for intuitive perception is related to endorsement of such laboratory values as trust and the importance of personal feelings both before and after training in volunteers for human relations laboratory training, but there is no increase in the relationship after training. No relationship exists before training for middle managers, but the correlation becomes significant after training. Intuitive perception preference is also related significantly to a number of process and outcome ratings by peers and trainers, although I am somewhat skeptical regarding the independence of the rating dimensions.

The evidence is unclear regarding the value of emotional characteristics of the Ss in the prediction of group productivity. Some of the contradictions are clearly related to whether productivity is defined in terms of the performance on objective tasks or in terms of more affective and interpersonal criteria. Those who like people, and those who participate with members they like, seem to like the laboratory group more than participants with opposite characteristics—a finding that may not surprise the layman.

Let me add here the Olch and Snow study (1970), which shows that the personality characteristics of sensitivity group volunteers as measured by the CPI are significantly lower than those of nonvolunteers, including performance on self-report scales measuring emotional characteristics such as liking for social activities and self-control. The authors suggest that students may be motivated to seek sensitivity groups because of self-perceived problems, in a manner similar to that of students who seek counseling. An alternative explanation is that part of differences may be attributable to less concern on the part of the volunteers about making a good impression via conforming responses.

Group Composition and Process and Outcome Variables

A number of authors have tried to manipulate group composition, and evaluate process and outcome. Although such studies are not strictly descriptive, some are included here for convenience. Stock (1964) summarizes several such studies. Gradolph, for example, composed groups of either work-pairing (friendship work-oriented) or flight members, and two groups of mixed members. Assessors reported that the flight-group members were uninvolved, work-pairing members expressed much affect and the mixed groups were frustrated and angry.

Harrison (1965) reports that homogeneous groups composed of person-oriented types are seen as behaving more expressively and warmly, and are more comfortable and feel stronger interpersonal ties than work-oriented groups.

Lieberman, Stock (1964) reports, ran one laboratory group containing equal numbers of members with primary tendencies to express one of each of five kinds of affect, and a second omitting pairing members. He observed that the affective comments regarding pairing were initially lower in the second group than the first, but gradually increased to an equal level. Stock and Luft found, Stock (1964) reports, that a group composed completely of members with a preference for the exploration of feelings and interpersonal issues was highly verbal, process-oriented and very self-analytic. The members were initially very excited, but the group seemed to stagnate. A second group, lacking such members, but composed of members with a preference for high structure was very efficient, but the discussion remained shallow. A group composed of half of each type seemed to have little tolerance for conflict. Stock concludes that such evidence as above suggests that dichotomous groups are less efficient and are likely to become more frustrated; homogenous groups seem to permit and reinforce expressions of the characteristic tendencies of their members.

Schutz (1961) reported that groups homogeneously composed on the basis of scores on the FIRO B test indicating tendencies to express emotions such as affection performed better than groups made up on the basis of the tendency of members to not express affect (such as tendency to avoid the expression of affection). Schutz suggests, because of the tendency of homogeneous groups formed in this manner to go into depth on one topic to the exclusion of others, homogenity of members might be better for treatment groups and heterogeneity for training groups.

Edwards (1969), on the other hand, using the same type of criteria of compatibility, found little relationship between within-group compatibility and several outcome measures. However, patient-therapist compatibility was related to improvement. The author also reports that the FIRO B affection scale was positively correlated with outcome.

Silver & Mood, in a recent study (1971), found few differences after T-group training between homogeneous and heterogeneous groups composed on the basis of scores on Leary's Dominance and Love dimension (scores derived from endorsement of adjectival self-descriptions). The authors report that Ss with high scores in these dimensions before treatment have lower scores after treatment, and that those with low scores before treatment achieve higher scores afterwards. Since these kinds of results are frequently reported when Ss are readministered tests with no intervening treatment, it is not an impressive finding. The authors also report some differences between efficiency rankings of each other made by members of the two sets of groups suggesting a high consistency of peer rankings after the first session with those of the last session for the homogeneous groups, and a high peer-self consistency for the heterogeneous groups after training. The authors conclude that the heterogeneous groups change more, and are therefore superior.

The most recent study is that of Pollack (1971). Again using the

FIRO B, four homogeneous groups were composed on the basis of high and low expressed and wanted control, and compared to twelve heterogeneous groups. Changes in the differences between expressed and wanted dimensions after treatment were defined as positive changes. Pollack finds greater numbers of positive changes in the control dimension in the heterogeneous groups, using the 10 percent level of significance, but not for inclusion or affection. More significant changes in ratings of satisfaction of participants occurred in the heterogeneous groups than in the homogeneous, leading Pollack to conclude that the heterogeneous groups are superior. Pollack's evidence is not strong.

Two recent studies by Yalom and coworkers have explored the relationships between cohesiveness and outcome. In the first (Yalom & Rand, 1966), Yalom reports that compatible groups whose members are matched on the basis of FIRO B scores are significantly more cohesive than incompatible groups. Incompatible group members are not only less satisfied with the group, but are more likely to terminate prematurely.

Yalom, Houts, Zimerberg & Rand (1967) find that a cohesiveness questionnaire reflecting overall satisfaction with the group correlates significantly with patient but not interviewer ratings of change. The cohesion variable seems a promising one to investigate, because a considerable social psychology literature exists (Yalom, 1970) which demonstrates that members of cohesive groups influence and attempt to influence each other more, are more productive and maintain group memberships longer.

Bednar & Lawlis (1971), reviewing primarily the psychotherapy literature, conclude that the relationships between three major sets of affective dimensions and outcomes have been investigated. Expression of feeling, meaningful participation, and empathy, warmth and genuineness emanating from the therapist and the group have been related to a number of measures of constructive changes. Stated as above, the statement seems to me somewhat more impressive than the amount of evidence on which it is based, which consists of seven studies. Four were studies of psychiatric populations, the remaining three each using different populations, and with each of the seven studies using different criteria of effectiveness and different independent variables.

The general evidence suggests to me that groups composed of

person-oriented, friendship-oriented, emotionally expressive members do express more positive affect than groups composed of work-or flight-oriented members, for example. The question may be raised whether the positive orientations described above indeed represent different dimensions, or rather, different ways of defining something like sociability. Cohesiveness, which is partly liking for other group members, and which seems to have some relationship to outcome, may be another sociability index. We may have discovered that groups artifically composed of friendly and expressive members express more positive affect, are happier with the group and feel that they get the most out of it. A similar conclusion is drawn in the previous section.

The homogeneity-heterogeneity issue is not clear. Two studies present meager evidence but conclude that heterogeneous groups are superior. Three studies report that homogenous groups are better when formed along certain dimensions. Homogeneous groups composed of avoiders, those who do not express feelings or those who are not person-oriented, do not appear to achieve much success. Two studies suggest that groups composed on the basis of dichotomized measures are disruptive. The resolution of this issue may very well depend on the goal of the intervention, the type of intervention, and the instruments and dimensions used to select group members, as determinants of whether specially composed groups are more successful or not.

Group Leader Emotional Variables

Although a great deal of speculation, and some research, suggests that the emotional characteristics of those who do individual therapy is related to effectiveness, (Luborsky, Chandler, Auerbach, Cohen, & Bachrach, 1971), little work has been done on such characteristics of group leaders. The exception is the work of Truax & Carkhuff, who have systematically investigated the therapist dimensions of empathy, genuineness and non-possessive warmth in a number of studies which suggest that such qualities are related to various criteria of improvement in a variety of patient populations (1967).

The authors, in a series of later studies, present evidence that low levels of these therapist qualities may be related to deterioration in patients; that high levels are related to extent of self and intrapersonal exploration by patients and that the qualities are trainable in group leaders and others. The most recent review of the work of this group of colleagues (Truax & Mitchell, 1971) provides impressive evidence for the efficacy of the therapist variables under study, including some interesting data suggesting substantial longrange effects on decreasing amount of hospitalization over an 18-year period in an inpatient population. The possession of these personality variables in roommates of college students, and in teachers of grade-school children, the evidence also suggests, may also be related to amount of academic achievement. The most recent study I have seen (Truax, Wargo & Volksdorf, 1970) suggests that with a juvenile delinquent population, self-report outcome measures of mood, emotional stability and anxiety are not related to therapist characteristics. Other plausible measures of successful outcome are not highly related to self exploration in clients. Only one of three anxiety measures, in participants in group therapy and neither mood nor stability is related to ratings of Depth of Intra-personal Exploration. The high intercorrelations between ratings of therapist characteristics with a heterogeneous group of therapists (.97, .93, .80) make one somewhat suspicious whether three dimensions really exist, even though Truax & Carkhuff (1967) have reported some negative correlations between the dimensions in earlier work.

Summary and Conclusions

Substantial evidence exists that during the first half of laboratory types of intervention more negative emotions are expressed by participants and that more positive emotion is expressed during the second half. Some authors contend that the early negative reactions are beneficial because they provide motivation for participants to seek new information and to change behavior. There seems to be no evidence to support this contention. If it is true, as Egan argues, that the initial anxiety may be obstructive to the achievement of group goals, then the use of techniques similar to those he suggests to reduce the ambiguity and lack of structure which may contribute to the early anxiety, may lead to better outcomes. The viewing of videotape reproductions of typical group behavior by participants about to enter groups, as well as the presentation to such volunteers of formal and explicit descriptions and instructions (contracts), are among the potential anxiety reducers listed by Egan. A number of meaningful problems exist there for the researcher.

That group interventions can reduce feelings of discomfort in participants, that warm and empathic leaders have more success and that training laboratory experiences have an effect on the emotional responses of participants, also seems to be established.

One of the most important conclusions, or perhaps speculations, one may arrive at from the data of this section is that psychotherapy groups may be the worst modality for the treatment of patients. I base this on a number of assumptions which seem plausible. The first is that psychotherapy groups and personal growth groups do not involve basically dissimilar processes. That group cohesion and the exploration of feelings, for example, are common to both types of intervention, would probably be agreed upon by a number of the researchers whose work is reviewed in this chapter such as I. D. Yalom and R. Carkhuff. The research literature suggests that homogeneous personal-growth groups composed of friendly, expressive and person-oriented members are consistently more effective than groups composed of members of opposite attributes. Since patients are ordinarily less sociable and expressive than nonpatients, groups composed completely of patients would ordinarily be more similar to the less effective groups. If the results of the research on personal-growth groups is applicable to psychotherapy groups, then the patients in psychotherapy groups should have a poor prognosis.

If modeling and reinforcing are important elements of interventions, as is suggested in the following chapter, then the unlikeliness that patients will serve as good reinforcers (see Chapter Four), the fact that fearful and incompetent models have less avoidance-reducing effect on phobic viewers (Zupnick, 1971) than fearless or competent models, represent plausible explanations for the inferiority of intervention systems composed primarily of patients. If, as the research of Truax, Carkhuff and colleagues which we have reported suggests, therapists can harm as well as help patients, it is plausible that patients can have similar effects on other patients. The excellent results of treatment reported in Chapter Three may be partly attributable to the fact that the treatment groups are often composed of as many students as patients.

To carry the speculation further, one might question the wisdom of treating people in mental hospitals or correctional institutions, since the social environment here also probably consists of more individuals of low social competence than high. Mental hospitals and prisons have certainly been notable for their ineffectiveness at treatment and rehabilitation. The approach of treating individuals within their communities is more logical in view of the above considerations.

Much valuable research could be conducted on such problems of group composition. For example, what are the optimal proportions of well-functioning to poorly functioning group members of various kinds?

TIME AND SPACE

In concluding this chapter, I would like to discuss briefly the role of such grossly manipulable variables as time and space, which have been asserted to be related to group process and affect. Time and space are dealt with in a broader context in Chapters Ten and Eleven.

Time

I conceive of time as a convenient way to measure the probability that certain numbers and types of events have transpired, processes have occurred or expectations have been created, rather than as a basic parameter in its own right. At the present time, we are largely ignorant of which are the important events and interactions, and our statements about the causal relationships are largely speculative.

A number of recent studies have attempted to explore the affective consequences of extending the length of the meeting period of treatment groups from the traditional one- or two-hour sessions to larger time-units—a technique pioneered by George Bach (1967a, 1967b, 1967c,) and Frederick Stoller and referred to as the marathon or accelerated interaction group. Therapists who have had experience with such groups report a high intensity of emotionality.

One of the earliest of these studies (Myerhoff, Jacobs & Stoller, 1970) attempted to compare the response of mental-hospital patients meeting for three consecutive six-hour periods to a similar population meeting in three two-hour sessions each week for three weeks. An adjective checklist was used to measure emotional responses after each two hour period in each group. The major differences was that marathon members sustained a high level of negative emotional responses, which peaked during each session, in contrast to the regular smooth decrease in expression of negative emotion observed in the traditional group. Cohesiveness was also higher in the marathon group at the completion of training than in the traditional group. The authors speculate the fewer warmup periods needed in the marathon format, the fatigue which might develop more intensely in the marathon group because of the necessity to maintain defenses for a longer period or some other complex condition, may account for the differences.

Three studies relating to time and affect appear in a recent issue of *The Journal of Comparative Group Studies*, a memorial issue dedicated to the memory of Fred Stoller. Foulds, Girona & Guinan (1970) compared a personal-growth group which met for 24 hours to a no-treatment control group, using an adjective affect scale designed to measure positive and negative affect. Members of the marathon group rated themselves and others positively after the experience whereas the control group members did not. The finding is perhaps not too surprising.

A second study by Sklar, Yalom, Zim & Newell (1970) studied six treatment groups in a psychiatric outpatient department during their first 16 sessions. Three of the groups held a six-hour first session, while the other three held a six-hour eleventh session. Two questionnaires were administered. One measured such items as comfort in talking about intimate details and expressing feelings of liking for the group, and the other measured member involvement. The effects on group involvement of the use of a six-hour session at the beginning of treatment appeared to be negligible, whereas the use of a six-hour session later in treatment appeared to produce substantially more involvement in the following session. However, the groups are not appreciably different four sessions later. Similar results appear to obtain for the variable of involvement with other members of the group, except that the superiority of the late six-hour interval persisted longer. However, this latter result appears to be partly an artifact, and related to a substantial decline in the scores on the member-member involvement questionnaire criterion by the group with the early six-hour session. Yalom also pointed out that the therapists were inexperienced, and therefore may have reacted differently in the two experimental conditions.

A final study by Dies & Hess (1970) compared male patients accepted for treatment into three marathon and three short-term groups. The marathon groups convened once for 12 consecutive hours while the short term groups met an hour each day for 12 successive weekdays. The ratings of samples of the interactions on degree of self-disclosure and the frequency of self-disclosure (self-disclosure being defined as including sharing emotional experiences and disclosing intimate feelings), showed the superiority of the marathon condition. However, ratings by patients at the conclusion of treatment did not differentiate between the treatments on a good-bad rating scale, although a number of other significant results were found.

It seems clear that much research needs yet to be done regarding the time dimension and groups but that it is a promising variable for maximizing interaction and intensity. The exact mechanisms which may contribute to the effectiveness of marathon groups have not yet been identified.

Space

Space, like time, is another variable which may engage a number of processes. I would include in this category such speculations as those of Schein and Bennis (1965) having to do with the "cultural island" notion. The authors maintain that having the group set in a residential laboratory,where the participant suspends his membership in other social systems, provides a safety for experimentation with new responses as well as arousing anxiety by removing the individual from his customary source of support and feedback.

Other spatial concepts include the pattern of seating arrangements which the social psychologists have shown to clearly relate to the communication patterns which evolve, and to the satisfaction of individuals with the group experience. As summarized by Goldstein, Heller & Sechrest (1966), more centralized networks, for example, where all communications between group members must pass through one member, were efficient yet had lower morale than the less centralized groups. The circle tends to be unorganized and erratic, and yet is enjoyed by its members. The wheel, a circle with a member at the center through which communication must pass, at the other extreme is less active, and has a distinct leader. It is stably organized as well as less erratic, and yet is unsatisfying to most of its members.

The type of leadership, amount of eye contact and status and dominance of members in groups, have also been recently discussed in the context of a review article by Sommer (1967), who concludes that most of the studies were post hoc analyses, and conducted in laboratory rather than more naturalistic settings. A typical study is that of Hare & Bales (1963), who, using five-man laboratory groups and a paper-and-pencil measure of dominance, found that in "task" sessions the centrally seated members received more vocalizations, while in social sessions talk was directed more to adjacent rather than central members. Dominant individuals chose more central seating positions and talked more.

A recent article by Griffitt & Veitch (1970) studied the influence of population density and temperature on affective responses, using an emotional checklist as a measure. *Ss* were seated side by side in a standard chamber in small groups of 3 to 5 or in groups of 12 to 16, so that the available space per person in the low-density group averaged almost 13 square feet per person, whereas available space was only 4 square feet per person in the high-density group. For half the subjects the temperature was maintained at 74 degrees, for the other half at 94 degrees. *Ss* in the high-density condition rated themselves as vigorous, affectionate and happy; the room was less attractive, pleasant and comfortable; and the experiment generally more negative. The effects of high temperature also caused greater amounts of negative emotional reactions. Attraction to a hypothetical stranger who agreed with the subject on a high proportion of issues was also lower when Ss were exposed to uncomfortable temperatures and high population densities.

Much speculation but little careful research exists in the area of personal space. Hall (1966) marshals a great deal of anthropological evidence to support the contention that the phenomenon of personal space is a universal one.

However, Snyder (1968) found that varying Hall's personal and social distances and seating arrangements did not yield significant differences in the number of verbal interactions, or in ratings of group attractiveness. And Van Meter & Jacobs (in preparation) also failed to find clearcut differences attributable to simple variations in personal distance in a study which points out the probable complexities of the personal space issues.

Spatial proximity, sociability and topic intimacy were studied in groups of female undergraduates. Ss participated in five-person discussion groups in chairs 9 inches apart (intimate space) and 23 inches apart (personal space). Number of verbalizations, sociograms constructed by participants, ratings of liking for the discussion and group members and the Jacobs Survey of Mood and Affect II were the dependent measures. No differences could be attributed to the personal space dimension. Analyses of covariance to remove initial differences of mood revealed that high-sociable participants rated themselves as happier and more sociable and their group as more enjoyable after treatment; low-sociable Ss ratings showed more uneasiness and disinterest. The more intimate topic, sex, also caused more anxiety and cautiousness than the casual one. Clearly same-sexed group-members from the same reference group may not respond to the intimate distance variable in the same manner as heterosexual group Ss, or as strangers in a park.

Summary and Conclusions

Manipulations of time and space have been shown in this section to affect the emotional responses of participants in group situations. The few studies on time manipulation which have been reported compare interventions of longer duration to short interventions and find that the longer sessions seem to be more effective. The Sklar et al. study is an interesting exception which attempts to determine whether it is more effective to extend the length of sessions at the beginning of treatment, or at a later date. No studies as yet are addressed to the identification of the time-associated events which are responsible for the differences which have been obse d between the effects of long and short sessions of treatment.

There is much laboratory-type research as well as speculation to make one suspect that the seating arrangements and physical proximity of group members may influence emotional responses. Little research on these questions has been conducted thus far in more naturalistic settings. The research reviewed in this chapter suggests that the relationships between spatial variables and emotional reactions may be quite complex.

CONCLUSIONS

The legitimacy of the descriptive studies, which compose most of those to which I have referred so far is unarguable. I am uneasy about them however, for a number of reasons. We are all well aware of the existence of such phenomenon as experimenter and therapist bias (Rosenthal, 1966) which can make it possible for the therapist, by means of his own behavior and influence on other group members, to unwittingly produce the phases or consequences that he has predicted. Such confounding, and the small number of Ss and groups used for the research reported, is so common that I have not bothered to comment on it.

I also found myself wondering frequently exactly what was going on in the psychotherapy and laboratory groups being studied, particularly when therapists or trainers were identified as adherents of different theoretical positions. Intervention, the primary variable under study, is almost always mysterious and undescribed, as if what happens in all laboratories or treatments is the same, or as if the differences which may exist are irrelevant or unimportant. The objectives of the intervention are often unspecified in the studies reported, and the selection of outcome criteria related more to what test instruments are available, or in style, rather than to the objectives of the intervention. I also am often suspicious that no clear objectives actually exist, and that the intervention is supposed to do whatever interventions are supposed to do.

I am also somewhat taken aback that so little of the research seems to go anywhere, and so much seems to be devoted to proving that intervention works. Outcomes, and how they may be differentially achieved, are clearly the most important class of criteria. But the research on the relationship of personal characteristics to outcome and process has not, as far as I can see, led to differential selections of participants either in practice or in subsequent research. Process studies have led to relatively little research into the generation of beneficent group climates. Truax & Carkhuff are a laudible exception to my first generalization in their translation of therapist qualities into leader-training programs.

The research seems to support the contention of the theorists that emotions are somehow important in group interventions. Discomfort can be allayed by group experiences and other emotional responses of participants modified. Empathy and warmth appear to be important characteristics of the group leader, and probably of group members. Such characteristics are trainable. Sociability factors, such as interest in people and liking for groups, may also be important attributes of those who benefit most from groups.

Research on the effects of manipulation of the duration of group sessions, such as the marathon group, shows a promising beginning. Research on the emotional consequence of manipulating the proximity of members and other spatial variables in the group situation, suggests that the relationships involved are probably quite complex. The research in neither of those two areas has yet come to grips with the identification of the events associated with time or space which are responsible for the emotional effects.

I believe the recentness of the interest and research into group process is somewhat responsible for the primitive level of conceptualization that the descriptive studies represent. The lack of standard instruments is also a handicap, which is not surprising at this point of development of the group research area. However, other conceptual alternatives are beginning to emerge, and more appropriate tools (see Chapter Thirteen). Group leaders are becoming less vague about what they would like to accomplish, and what intervention alternatives are available to them. I believe it is becoming more general for group leaders to be more specific with regard to what group behaviors should be encouraged (group solidarity, for example), and what the effect of modeling behavior by the leader (self-disclosure, for example) may have on group members.

I expect that research in the field of applied behavior change will be greatly facilitated in the near future by the data that already exists in the field of social psychology with regard to how individuals influence each other, by the developments in the area of social learning, and by the increasing sophistication of adherents of the Skinnerian approach. In the following chapter on emotion, I will review some of the research on affect in groups, which is derived primarily from the latter two of these sources.

REFERENCES

Bach, G.R. Marathon Group Dynamics: I. Some functions of the professional group facilitator. *Psychological Reports,* 1967a, **20,** 995–999.

Bach, G.R. Marathon Group Dynamics: II. Dimensions of helpfulness: therapeutic aggression. *Psychological Reports,* 1966, **20,** 1147–1158.

Bach, G.R. Marathon Groups Dynamics: III. Disjunctive contacts. *Psychological Reports,* 1967a, **20,** 1163–1172.

Bass, B.M. Mood changes during a management training laboratory. *Journal of Applied Psychology,* 1962, **46,** 361–364.

Bednar, R.L. & Lawlis, G.F. Empirical research in group psychotherapy. In A.E. Bergin & S.L. Garfield (Eds.), *Handbook of psychotherapy and behavior change: An empirical analysis.* New York, London, Sidney, Toronto: John Wiley & Sons, 1967. Pp. 812–838.

Brown, J.S. & Jacobs, A. The role of fear in the motivation and acquisition of responses. *Journal of Experimental Psychology,* 1949, **39,** 747–759.

Campbell, J.P. & Dunnette, M.D. Effectiveness of T-group experiences in managerial training and development. *Psychological Bulletin,* 1968, **70,** 73–104.

Corsini, R.J. Immediate therapy in groups. In B.M. Gazda (Ed.), *Innovations to group psychotherapy.* Springfield, Ill. Charles C Thomas, 1968. Pp. 15–41.

Dies, R.R. & Hess, A.K. Self-disclosure, time perspective, and semantic differential changes. *Journal of Comparative Group Studies,* 1970, **1** (4), 387–395.

Edwards, W.P. Interpersonal relations orientation compatibility as related to outcome variables in group psychotherapy. *Dissertation Abstracts*, 1969, 29, 10-B, 3909–3910, Order #69-5091.

Egan, G. Encounter: Group processes for interpersonal growth. Belmont, Calif.: Brooks/Cole, 1970.

Eisenman, R. Birth order, anxiety, and verbalization in group psychotherapy. *Journal of Consulting Psychology*, 1966, **30**, 521–526.

Foulds, M.L., Girona, R. & Guinan, J.F. Changes in ratings of self and others as a result of a marathon group. *Journal of Comparative Group Studies*, 1970, **1**, (4), 349–355.

Geidt, F.H. Predicting suitability for group psychotherapy. *American Journal of Psychotherapy*, 1961, **18**, (4), 582–591.

Gibb, J.R. The effects of human relations training. In A.E. Bergin, & S.L. Garfield (Eds.), *Handbook of psychotherapy and behavior change: An empirical analysis*. New York, London, Sidney, Toronto: John Wiley & Sons, 1971. Pp. 839–857.

Gibb, J.R. & Gibb, L.M. Emergence therapy: The TORI process in an emergent group. B.M. Gazda (Ed.), In *Innovations to group psychotherapy*. Springfield, Ill.: Charles C Thomas, 1968. Pp. 96–129.

Goldstein, A. P., Heller, K. & Sechrest, L.B. *Psychotherapy and the psychology of behavior change*. New York: John Wiley & Sons, 1966.

Griffitt, W. & Veitch, R. Hot and crowded: Influences of population density and temperature on interpersonal affective behavior. *Journal of Personality and Social Psychology*, 1970, **17** (1), 92–98.

Hall, E.T. *The hidden dimension*. Garden City, N.Y.: Doubleday, 1966.

Hare, A.P. & Bales, B.F. Seating position and small group interaction. *Sociometry*, 1963, **26**, 480–486.

Harrison, R. Group composition models for laboratory design. *Journal of Applied Behavioral Science*, 1965, **1**, 409–432.

Harrison, R. & Lubin, B. Personal style, group composition, and learning. *Journal of Applied Behavioral Science*, 1965, **1**, 286–301.

Holbert, W., Cormier, W. & Friedman, M. The semantic differential in sensitivity training. *Journal of Comparative Group Studies*, 1971, **2**, 36–42.

Holmes, J.S. Relation of depression and verbal interaction in group therapy. *Psychological Reports*, 1967, **20**, 1039–1042.

Jacobs, A. Mood, emotion, affect. In A. Jacobs & L. Sachs (Eds.), *The psychology of private events*. New York: Academic Press, 1971. Pp. 131–163.

Jacobs, A., Edelman, M. & Wolpin, M. The effects of differential anxiety level and the repression-sensitization dimension in systematic desensitization therapy. Paper presented at the meeting of the American Psychological Association, Washington, D.C., September, 1971.

Jacobs, A. & Jacobs, M. Emotional responses to positive and negative feedback. In preparation.

Jacobs, M., Jacobs, A., Gatz, M. & Schaible, T. The credibility and desirability of positive and negative structured feedback in groups. Submitted for publication.

Jacobs, A. & Sachs, L.B. (Eds.) *Psychology of private events.* New York and London: Academic Press, 1971.

Jacobs, A. & Wolpin, M. A second look at systematic desensitization. In A. Jacobs & L.B. Sachs (Eds.), *Psychology of private events,* New York and London: Academic Press, 1971.

Kelman, H. C., & Parloff, M. B. Interrelations among three criteria of improvement in group therapy: Comfort, effectiveness and self-awareness. *Journal of Abnormal and Social Psychology,* 1957, **54** (3).

Konrad, W. & Jacobs, A. A. social therapy program with schizophrenics to change mood and social responsiveness. Paper presented at the California State Psychological Convention, April, 1968.

Lang, P.J. The mechanics of desensitization and the laboratory study of human fear. In C.M. Franks (Ed.) *Behavior therapy appraisal and status.* New York: McGraw-Hill, 1969. Pp. 160–191.

Leitenberg, H., Agras, S., Butz, R. & Wineze, J. Relationship between heart rate and behavioral change during treatment of phobias. *Journal of Abnormal Psychology,* 1971, **78** (1) 59.

Lubin, B., Dupre, V. & Lubin, A. Comparability and sensitivity of set 2 (lists E, F, and G) of the depression adjectives checklists. *Psychological Reports,* 1967, **20,** 756–758.

Lubin, B. & Zuckerman, M. Affective and cognitive patterns in sensitivity training groups. *Psychological Reports,* 1967, **21,** 365–376.

Lubin, B. & Zuckerman, M. Level of emotional arousal in laboratory training. *Journal of Applied Behavioral Science,* 1969, **5,** 483–490.

Luborsky, L., Chandler, M., Auerbach, A., Cohen, J. & Bachrach, H. Factors influencing the outcome of psychotherapy: a review of quantitative research. *Psychological Bulletin,* 1971, 75 (3), 145–185.

Miller, N.E. Studies of fear as an acquirable drive I: Fear as motivation and fear-reduction as reinforcement in the learning of new responses. *Journal of Experimental Psychology,* 1948, **38,** 89–101.

Mowrer, O.H. Loss and Recovery of Community. In G.M. Gazda (Ed.), *Innovations to group psychotherapy,* Springfield, Ill.: Charles C Thomas, 1968. Pp. 130–189.

Myerhoff, H. L., Jacobs, A., & Stoller, F.H. Emotionality in marathon and traditional therapy. *Psychotherapy: Theory, Research, Practice,* 1970, **7** (1), 33–36.

Olch, D. & Snow, D.L. Personality characteristics of sensitivity group volunteers. *Journal of Personnel and Guidance,* 1970, **48,** 848–850.

Pollack, H. Changes in homogeneous and heterogeneous sensitivity training groups. *Consulting and Clinical Psychology*, 1971, **37**, 60–66.

Rogers, C. *Client centered therapy*. Boston: Houghton Mifflin, 1951.

Rosenthal, R. *Experimentor effects in behavioral research*. New York: Appleton-Century-Crofts, 1966.

Schein, E.H. & Bennis, W.G. *Personal and organizational change through group methods: The laboratory approach*. New York, London, Sidney: John Wiley & Sons, 1967.

Schutz, W.C. On group composition. *Journal of Abnormal Social Psychology*, 1961, **62**, 275–281.

Silver, A. & Mood, D. Group homogeneity, conformity and flexibility of interpersonal perception. *Comparative Group Studies*, 1971, **2**, 25–35.

Sklar, A.D., Yalom, I. D., Zim, A. & Newell, G.L. Time-extended group therapy: a controlled study. *Journal of Comparative Group Studies*, 1970, **1** (4), 373–386.

Stoller, F.A. Marathon group therapy. In G.M. Gazda (Ed.), *Innovations to group psychotherapy*, Springfield, Ill.: Charles C Thomas, 1968. Pp. 42–95.

Snyder, O. Arrangement and distance as factors in small group interaction. Unpublished master's thesis, West Virginia University, 1968.

Sommer, R. Small group ecology. *Psychological Bulletin*, 1967, **67**(2), 145–152.

Steele, F. Personality and the "laboratory style." *Journal of Applied Behavioral Analysis*, 1968, **4**, 25–46.

Stern, H. & Grosz, H.J. Personality correlates of patient interactions in group psychotherapy. *Psychological Reports*, 1966a, **18**, 411–414.

Stern, H. & Grosz, H.J. Verbal interactions in group psychotherapy between patients with similar and with dissimilar personalities. *Psychological Reports*, 1966b, 19, 1111–1114.

Stock, D. A. Survey of Research on T Groups. In L.P. Bradford, J.R. Gibb & K.D. Benne (Eds.), *T-Group theory and laboratory method innovation in re-education*. NewYork, London, Sidney: John Wiley & Sons, 1964. Pp. 395–441.

Truax, C.B. The initial status of the client and the predictability of psychotherapeutic change. *Journal of Comparative Group Studies*, 1971, **2** (1), 3–16.

Truax, C. & Carkhuff, R. *Toward effective counselling and psychotherapy: Training and practice*. Chicago: Aldine, 1967.

Truax, C. & Mitchell, K. Research on certain therapist interpersonal skills in relation to process and outcome. In A. E. Bergin & S. L. Garfield (Eds.), *Handbook of psychotherapy and behavior change: An empirical analysis*. New York, London, Sidney, Toronto: John Wiley &

Sons, 1971. Pp. 299–343.

Truax, C., Wargo, D. & Volksdorf, N. Antecedents to outcome in group counseling with institutionalized juvenile delinquents: Effects of therapeutic conditions, patient self-exploration, alternate sessions, and vicarious therapy pretraining. *Journal of Abnormal Psychology*, 1970, **76**, 235–242.

Van Meter, W.I. & Jacobs, A. Spatial proximity, sociability and topic intimacy. In preparation.

Yalom, I.D., Houts, S., Zimerberg, S.M. & Rand, K.H. Prediction of improvement in group therapy. *Archives of General Psychiatry*, 1967, **17**, 159–168.

Yalom, I.D. & Rand, K.H. Compatibility and cohesiveness in therapy groups. *Archives of General Psychiatry*, 1966, **15**, 267–274.

Zupnick, S. Effects of varying degrees of a peer model's performance on extinction of a phobic response in an individual or group setting. Proceedings of the 79th Annual Convention of the American Psychological Association, 1971, 433–434.

16. Learning-Oriented and Training-Oriented Approaches to the Modification of Emotional Behavior in Groups

Alfred Jacobs

Contemporary psychologists are taking seriously the plaintive social commentary of the Beatles that the world needs love. Those who deal in Systematic Experiential learning are teaching counselors, patients, school children, etc., to have accurate empathy, warmth and positive regard towards their fellow man. The style of the Skinnerians is less ebullient, and they translate the message of the Beatles into redirecting and increasing the amount of positive reinforcement and social approval in the home and school. The behavior rehearsal movement theme is still predominantly to eliminate the negative.

All three movements are characterized by a refreshing emphasis on the specification and measurement of the objectives of interventions. A substantial literature has begun to develop in each area in the short time since the beginning of the interest of these practioner-scientists in groups and systems. I suspect that it is the greater psychological accessibility of behavioral conceptualizations, and techniques of behavioral assessment and investigation which has accelerated the generation of information by these three groups of psychologists.

The most important contribution of each group, so far, can be summarized as follows:

(1) Systematic experiential learning has identified empathy, warmth and other attributes of the psychotherapist as related to improvement by the patient. A technology has also been developed

to increased the amount of these effective helping behaviors in therapists, patients and others by training.

(2) Behavior rehearsal scientists have invented simple, brief and easily trainable procedures for the reduction of discomfort and avoidance.

(3) Skinnerians have demonstrated that a wide variety of the behaviors associated with fear, anger and other emotions can be modified in relatively short time-periods by rapidly trained interveners who have been taught to manipulate the environmental consequences of behavior.

Exciting potentialities are raised by the new interest of the Skinnerians and the systematic experiential learning group in areas of socioemotional education.

INTRODUCTION

Three main movements are included in this chapter. The systematic experiential learning movement of Truax, Carkhuff and colleagues has emphasized such variables and techniques as role-playing, exercises, feedback and the creation of empathy, warmth and genuineness in a variety of populations of treaters and treatees. The cognitive-rehearsal movement of Wolpe and Lazarus has concentrated on the reduction of fear and avoidance responses but also on the training of assertiveness (see Chapter Five) and reducing depression. The operant conditioning point of departure is the third major movement in this section. Clinically oriented adherents of the Skinnerian conceptualization have manipulated the gratifying and aversive consequences of emotionally associated behaviors such as tantrums, avoidances, and crying (see Chapter Fourteen, for example) and have reported excellent results. Traditionally, this group has concentrated on behavior, and avoided attempts to modify unobservable internal events because of a distrust of "mentalistic" concepts, but recently many users of operant techniques have become more interested in the modification of private events (Jacobs & Sachs, 1971). Included in this chapter will also be a consideration of some of the other social-learning concepts not yet discussed.

SYSTEMATIC EXPERIENTIAL LEARNING

In a recent article, Carkhuff (1971a) asserts that the training of clients and of the "significant others" in their environment, using systematic programs in interpersonal skills, is more effective than unstructured experiential learning. The dimensions of responsiveness in which training occurs include empathy and warmth, which fall within the purview of this chapter. Carkhuff summarizes evidence which suggests the benefit of training in groups of chronic neuropsychiatric patients, delinquent children, ghetto school children, etc. in socioemotional behaviors in the manner which had been previously developed, as described below, to train counselors.

Truax and Carkhuff have also demonstrated in a series of studies, some of which are reported in references already cited, the effectiveness in training change agents at various professional and non-professional levels. The method (described in Traux & Carkhuff, 1967) uses a combination of didactic and experiential learning in group situations in which tape-recorded models of how to be and not to be empathic or warm, for example, are presented. Trainees are first trained in using rating scales on these dimensions. Next they are required to make therapeutic responses to patient talk, and are given immediate feedback via the rating scales on the level of their responses. Role playing by trainees is then recorded and brought to class to be rated by other trainees on these same dimensions. Finally, tape-recorded interviews by trainees with real clients are rated by other class members in the same manner. Increases by such trainees in the empathic or warmth dimensions of their interactions with clients has recently been reported for inner-city lay personnel and hard-core unemployed (Carkhuff, 1971b) and medical corpsmen (Anthony & Wain, 1971). A somewhat similar kind of training program for priests and nuns (Shack, Walker, Sheridan, Egan & Lavigne, 1970), although perhaps using more laboratory-training methods, reports that when trained versus untrained trainers are compared as laboratory leaders, laboratory participants, naive judges and trainers of the trainers all rate the trained leaders as dealing in a more catalytic role with emotional process.

A final study in the Truax & Carkhuff conceptualization,

Deliberate Psychological Education (Mosher & Sprinthall, 1971), opens up tremendous potential. The authors trained 23 unselected high school students in the interpersonal skills referred to above in the context of a class in counseling, and obtained substantial increases in empathy. Other impressive, if unmeasurable, indications of the impact of training are two projects which have been initiated by the students. One group of students raised the funds to purchase a home and hire adults to act as houseparents for teenagers who could no longer live at home. A second group of students is establishing a student-run counseling center in the high school itself, which may be more psychologically accessible to high school students than one staffed by older adults.

Summary and Conclusions

The work of Truax, Carkhuff and colleagues may well deserve more space than has been allotted in this and the previous chapter. It is perhaps the only example of a set of concepts deriving from a psychotherapy context, as applied to groups, having been explored in a systematic, thorough and scientific fashion. This work springs from the research tradition of the Rogerian movement, and the training of its leaders is the research orientation of the Ph.D. degree in psychology. I would think it unlikely, otherwise, that individuals would even try to measure behavior as mushy as empathy, warmth and genuineness, or to be able to translate these terms into the language of reinforcement, as will be demonstrated later in this chapter.

However, as I have suggested elsewhere in this volume, the development of reliable and appropriate tools has a powerfully facilitative effect on research, and the application of the measurement of empathy to the study of treatment, education, and training, is an excellent demonstration of this principle.

As is always the case, more research can be prescribed, even in areas which have been well explored. The identification of additional dimensions of counselor effectiveness would be useful, and research is already under way on styles of confrontation, personal influence, etc. (Truax & Mitchell, 1971). Translation of the technology into forms which are suitable for delivery to normal parents and children as a technique for the prevention of maladjustment would have much social utility. Studies of those Ss who have difficulty benefiting from present training procedures and the development of more effective substitute measures for such Ss, would be desirable. Evaluations of the advantages and disadvantages of various models, feedback procedures and other components of the training program provide another set of useful research problems.

COGNITIVE AND BEHAVIOR REHEARSAL

Descriptions and Theory of Systematic Desensitization

The Systematic Desensitization technique of treatment, as developed by Wolpe (1958), has from its outset been primarily used for the treatment of anxiety and a variety of avoidance behaviors with which anxiety is presumably associated. The rationale for the treatment is as follows: systematic desensitization treatment is based on a psychological principle called counterconditioning, in which one prevents an undesirable response from occurring by causing a more desirable substitute to replace it.

Neurotic behavior often consists of avoiding various kinds of situations or actions. The neurotic behavior was developed historically because the neurotic individual experienced pain or fear in his encounters with these situations. The specifics of the historical events are ordinarily of no interest to the desensitizer. However, in the present, the neurotic individual becomes anxious when confronted with similar circumstances to those in which the neurotic behavior was learned, and he avoids such situations and actions in order to reduce his discomfort.

The treatment usually begins by training the patient in relaxation. Relaxation is presumed to be one of the classes of responses which is antagonistic or opposite to anxiety, so that it would be unlikely for it to be possible for a patient to be anxious and relaxed simultaneously. The environmental events which are associated with a specific fear and avoidance are analyzed by the therapist and patient and organized in a hierarchical order with respect to the amount of fear elicited by each event. For example, a patient who reported an inability to find a job because of fear might report a little fear when reading the classified ads, a greater amount of fear when calling for an appointment for an interview and the greatest amount of fear in the interview.

The goal of counterconditioning procedure would be to substitute relaxation for fear to each of these events, beginning with the least fearful event, and a process called cognitive rehearsal is ordinarily used for this purpose. In cognitive rehearsal, the patient, while in a deeply relaxed state, imagines himself making the fearful response, e.g., reading the classified ads. He is instructed to stop the rehearsal if he feels anxious while imagining the response, and to re-relax himself and try again in such circumstances. The practice is continued until the patient can imagine the action without experiencing fear. He then repeats the process with the next-most-feared item in the hierarchy, until he can imagine the entire sequence without fear. This anxiety reduction to the imagined sequence of events should generalize or transfer to the real sequence because the two series are similar to each other. The patient should therefore experience less anxiety in the real situations. He should, therefore, be less motivated to make the avoidance responses and have more freedom to behave in a more appropriate or effective manner.

Many therapists have reported the successful treatment of a variety of symptoms by means of Systematic Desensitization. An issue has arisen , however, with regard to why it is effective. As I have pointed out elsewhere in detail (Jacobs & Wolpin, 1971), a considerable body of literature exists which demonstrates that desensitization is effective when the relaxation component is omitted from the treatment, and also when the rehearsal of items does not proceed in a hierarchical manner. Avoidance responses of Ss decrease after treatment even when the Ss are made to feel more anxious during treatment instead of less anxious (Jacobs, Edelman & Wolpin, 1971). Studies also show that the success of treatment is markedly reduced if Ss treated by means of Systematic Desensitization are told that they are Ss in an experiment to study their responses, instead of being told that they are being treated to reduce fear and avoidance.

Finally, the relationship between verbal reports of fear and behavioral avoidance is not nearly as high as theory would lead one to believe. As the Jacobs, Edelman & Wolpin (1971) study showed, a fairly high relationship between fear and avoidance existed in habitual repressors, but not for other kinds of Ss.

These kinds of evidence suggest to me that the expectations and habits of the patients or Ss may be more important than the variables described in the theory. Indeed, it makes me raise the question of whether Systematic Desensitization is anything more than a very convincing and elaborate technology for persuading patients that treatment will be effective.

Early Research

The potential for simultaneous group cognitive rehearsal by individuals with similar problems was demonstrated early by impressive results reported by Lazarus (1961). The greater efficiency of such an approach is obvious. The even greater efficiency of using a standardized program applicable to groups was demonstrated much later (Nawas, Fishman & Pucel, 1970). However, in the decade between these two studies, relatively little research on group desensitization has been reported.

Paul (1969), in his careful review, describes only ten studies, including the original Lazarus (1961) study referred to earlier, and a second Lazarus study based on two groups of three Ss each, where all Ss were successfully treated for sexual problems. Paul's review also includes three experimental analogue studies by Rachman which are also based on such small numbers of Ss that the results are not worth reporting. Two additional studies by Paul & Shannon, and by Paul, compared group desensitization of Ss with public-speaking anxiety to results obtained from individual desensitization, insight-oriented psychotherapy, an attention-placebo group and a no-treatment control group. The authors reported that improvement from group desensitization was as significant as individual treatment on a number of specific and general self-report measures. There was also a significant increase in grade point for the group members over the treatment controls. The absence of specific behavioral indices of speech anxieties in this study is unfortunate. The second study referred to is a two-year followup of the Ss treated in the Paul & Shannon study, which reports maintenance of the specific and general gains made during group desensitization.

Paul also describes a study in 1966 by Katahn, Strenger and Cherry in which desensitization was performed with groups of test-anxious students. The students were also exposed to bibliotherapy (treatment by reading relevant books and literature) and general discussions of study skills, etc. and comparisons were made with 6 volunteer controls who could not participate because of schedule difficulties and with students who didn't wish to participate (22 nonvolunteer controls). The treated *S*s improved more in grade-point and decreased more on a Test Anxiety questionnaire than combined control groups, but a number of problems, including the characteristics of the controls and the use of the class instructor from which *S*s were selected as therapist, pose difficulties in interpretation of the findings.

Paul reports two additional studies of group desensitization. The first, Burnett and Ruan, reports success of the procedure with 25 of 100 hospital patients available for followup, but the confounding of desensitization with educational meetings, assertion training and physical therapies, as in the previous study, makes the results difficult to interpret. The final study described, Shannon and Wolf, was an analogue, using group treatment of college students who reported intense fear of snakes. Group desensitization with and without models were both reported to cause greater reductions in avoidance than no-treatment controls, but neither treatment group was superior to the other. Although Paul makes no summary evaluation of this group of studies, in addressing himself to the outcome issue he apparently includes these studies in the substantial support he sees for the effectiveness of Systematic Desensitization, and the probability that it is superior to other interventions. However, if one were to discard from these nine studies and a followup study those studies where the number of *S*s is too small; those studies where there was an opportunity for the therapist's preference or enthusiasm for desensitization to bias the results; those studies where the desensitization treatment was confounded with the use of other treatments, and those studies where no control group was used or where the control group selected may have consisted of *S*s less motivated to improve, there is little left to support any contentions about group desensitization.

Recent Research

Since Paul's review a number of other studies have examined the effect of manipulating some of the behavior rehearsal operations. Other studies have explored the effectiveness of behavior-rehearsal techniques in groups with different populations and different symptoms. A last group of studies has reopened the question of the superiority of behavior-rehearsal techniques to other treatment modalities.

Studies of the Variables

For some reason which I don't understand there has not been much study of some of the important behavior-rehearsal variables. Studies which vary the number of rehearsals or study the type and clarity of imagery or the personal characteristics of the patient are rare or absent in the literature. Notably absent are studies of the relationship between participants. Yet practitioners of the behavior-rehearsal methods recognize that such relationships are important. Carkhuff (1971a) reports, "Wolpe has conceded that as much as 60% of the effectiveness of the counter conditioning process may be due to nonspecific relationship factors [p. 126]." The first two studies in this section explore some of the relationship issues.

Donner & Guerney (1969) report on the use of automated group desensitization of test anxiety with college females and a followup five months later (Donner, 1970). Using therapist-present groups and therapist-absent groups of two to four Ss, and predetermined taped programs of eight sessions, both groups changed significantly more in grade-point than a matched waiting-list control group, with superior, but not significantly so, performance by the therapist-present treatment group. The authors report that the *most anxious* Ss during visualization improve in grade-point significantly more than the less anxious, a finding which contradicts the presumed theoretical basis of the reciprocal inhibition treatment, as reviewed briefly in the introduction of this section.

Donner in his follow up of Ss still attending school five months later reports that significantly more Ss in the therapist-present treatment condition continue to improve in gradepoint than in the therapist-absent group. Donner also explored the possibility of symptom substitution by interviews asking Ss to report positive and negative changes in other attitudes at the end of the semester. The treatment groups reported more positive change than the controls, and no Ss reported negative changes.

The finding of superiority for the therapist-present rehearsal condition is an interesting one. Donner suggests two explanations, both of which receive some support from post-treatment comments of the Ss. The first is that the therapist-present condition was more similar to the classroom-and-instructor anxiety-arousing situation which was the focus of treatment, and therefore, the practice of not being as anxious was closer to the real situation for the therapist-present group. Donner suggests as a second explanation that the therapist-present condition had motivational aspects such as inducing Ss to follow instructions more closely. For example, more Ss dozed in the therapist-absent condition.

Zupnick (1971), suggesting that group therapy can be conceptualized as individuals exposed to multiple peer models, examined, in an analogue study, the effects of models on snake-phobic college sophomores treated in group or individual settings. Confederate models were trained to perform at fearless-competent, peer-equal and fearful-incompetent levels. In individual treatment, the modeling behavior did not affect treatment. In the group situation Ss exposed to the peer-equal model were most affected, handling the snake more than controls or those exposed to the fearful-incompetent model. In a followup session three weeks later the Ss exposed to the fearless-competent group model performed better than the group controls or those exposed to fearful-incompetent models. The differences between followup and immediate results are not explained. Zupnick explains the results in terms of the initial disinhibiting effect on the fear-response of the model, the presence of coacting peers who could reinforce or praise emulations and the correct response cues provided by other Ss who handled the snake.

Zupnick's results support the possibility of increasing the effectiveness of desensitization by use of appropriate models. His explanations for the results reflect the increasing sophistication regarding group phenomena of those in the behavior-rehearsal tradition. Audiences have effects on performers, and performers have effects on audiences. Individuals who are doing things in groups play both roles, and it may be possible to mobilize both these effects to maximize change.

Steffy, Meichenbaum & Best (1970) studied the rehearsal process. The authors attempted to decrease cigarette smoking by aversive conditioning and compared an insight control discussion group to four groups which varied overtness of rehearsal and use of actual or imagined cigarettes. Ss' description of a high-probability smoking situation and of the sequence of their smoking responses was rehearsed overtly in two groups and covertly in the other two groups. For half of the Ss, refusal to smoke or putting out an actual cigarette, avoided or terminated shock. For the other half there was no actual cigarette present or smoking rehearsal before shock was terminated or avoided. The authors report that the covert verbalization–smoking rehearsal group decreased in frequency of smoking more than other groups, and remained significantly lower at a six-month followup. The authors speculate that the covert rehearsal may have permitted Ss to allow themselves to become more emotionally involved. Another effect of an audience may be operating.

The previous studies represent innovative approaches to the improvement of behavior rehearsal treatments. Self-instructions, models and relationships are shown to be variables which have an effect on the success of rehearsal treatments.

Attempts to identify the critical agents in group desensitization, an area of much research in individual desensitization, are seen in the next two studies.

Leon (1968) desensitized snake-phobic college students by cards to snake related material or nonsnake-related material and compared the results to a no-treatment control group. He reports that Ss desensitized to snake-related material exhibited significantly less fear after treatment whereas the other two groups showed no appreciable improvement.

Freeling & Shemberg (1970) assigned 30 high-test anxious undergraduates to desensitization, relaxation and imagery groups. Each group met for six sessions. Scores on the Test Anxiety Questionnaire decreased significantly more after treatment for Ss in the systematic desensitization group than for those in the imagery group but not than for those in the relaxation group. However, significantly more Ss in the systematic desensitization group decreased in reported test anxiety than in the other two groups. The only significant increase in task performance after treatment was for the imagery group, a finding contrary to expectation, which is not explained.

New Subject Populations

Three studies have tried group desensitization techniques using new subject populations, with mixed results. Kondas (1967) studies one small sample of public school children and another of undergraduates. Both were treated in groups by systematic desensitization, relaxation training and rehearsal of hierarchies without relaxation, for stage fright and examination anxiety. He reports that the systematic desensitization was highly effective in both studies in reducing reported fear and palmar sweating. Relaxation training was effective with the children but not the college students.

Sieveking (1969) studied group desensitization of speech anxiety in institutionalized adolescents, and reported that the results could not be unequivocally interpreted.

Kass (1969) examined a shortterm desensitization treatment for self-reported test-anxious adults returning to college after absences of several years. A group receiving two relaxation and four desensitization sessions was compared to a group receiving three sessions of didactic instruction in test-taking, and to a no-treatment control group. Kass reports the desensitization group superior after treatment in self-reported anxiety to the control group in a simulated and delayed real-test situation, and to the didactic group in the real situation. The desensitization group was also superior to the control on a heart rate measure, but skin resistance, actual test performance, semester completion and a number of other criteria did not differentiate between groups.

The ability of rehearsal techniques to reduce anxiety, these studies suggest, is a fairly general phenomenon. Decreases in self-reports of anxiety are the most consistent criteria of improvement observed. Other techniques, such as relaxation and instruction, are also sometimes effective.

Behavior Rehearsal and Other Treatments

In 1965 I directed a doctoral dissertation by Freda Dixon (described in Jacobs & Wolpin, 1971) which compared group systematic desensitization with group counseling of test-anxious college students. It was a thorough study which used changes in grade-point, in performance on an examination and in self-reports of fear, as criteria. The major shortcoming was the use of the same therapist who was the experimenter to run both conditions. We realized that this was a deficiency, and tried to provide some remedy by asking Ss in both conditions to rate the therapist on a large number of characteristics. The ratings of the two groups were not different. The results of the study were that both groups improved on all the criteria, with no substantial differences between the two treatments. Unfortunately, we never tried to publish the results, partly because studies which found no differences were not as readily accepted by scientific journals in those days as in the present.

Since that time, a number of studies have compared individual desensitization to other treatments, and have concluded as Paul does in my earlier reference that desensitization is probably superior to other treatments. I have examined these studies, and I am suspicious of this conclusion for reasons which I have given in detail in Jacobs & Wolpin (1961). However, the studies of desensitization in groups which I will report in this section reopen the superiority-of-treatment issue, since they suggest to me that there are a number of treatments which may be as effective as systematic desensitization.

A number of recent studies have compared rehearsal methods to other forms of treatment. Hedquist & Weinhold (1970) compared Lazarus's behavioral rehearsal technique to the social learning approach of Mainord in the treatment of socially anxious college students in groups. The behavioral rehearsal group utilized repeated trials of role-playing and feedback from other group members. The social learning group used four group rules of honesty, responsibility, helpfulness or feedback and action or commitment to carry through action plans. The criterion was the number of assertive responses listed in a diary report by group members, the validity of which was established by the investigators who checked a sample of the responses.

Both treatments were superior to a discussion group which met weekly to assist Ss to better understand their interpersonal behavior. A followup study using the same criteria six weeks after completion of treatment indicated no significant differences between the experimental groups, although the rates of assertive responses had all decreased substantially for the treatment groups. The trend was still in favor of the treatment over the control groups, with a slight superiority for the social learning treatment. The small number of Ss 40, also makes it unwise to attempt to generalize too much from this study.

Meichenbaum, Gilmore & Fedoravicius (1971) argue that all insight-oriented treatments are not the same, and dispute the implication of Paul's (1966) results that desensitization treatments are superior. Meichenbaum et al compared a desensitization group treatment of speech-anxious Ss to an Ellis-derived insight treatment designed to make Ss aware of the self-verbalizations which contributed to their maladaptive behavior on behavioral and self-reported measures. The best results were achieved by the insight and desensitization treatments, with no apparent superiority for either, except that the desensitization treatment worked significantly better for Ss with specific anxieties, and the insight significantly better for the more generally socially anxious.

Two publications by Laxer and associates reopen the issue of whether desensitization treatments are superior to just relaxation. Laxer, Quarter, Kooman & Walker (1969), in the first study, are among the few to include substantial numbers (approximately 30) in their control, relaxation and desensitization groups of high-anxious secondary school Ss who were treated in small groups of Ss two to four Ss. Scores on self-report measures of anxiety are lower after treatment for both experimental groups than for the control group. No appreciable differences exist between the experimental groups. The only significant differences were observed on a test of manifest anxiety, where the decrease in scores of the relaxation group exceeds that of the control group. No differences on grade achievement occur. A second study reported in the same article, which compared only a desensitization condition to a control, found significantly greater reductions in manifest anxiety for the desensitization than for the control groups, but no grade-point improvement.

A second study, Laxer & Wolker (1970), included, in addition to the treatments of the first study, a treatment in which simulated examinations were repeatedly presented without feedback to Ss, a relaxation simulation condition which paired simulated examinations with relaxation, and a placebo-attention control discussion group. The self-report of anxiety scores to two anxiety measures, and two measures of grade-point, were differentially affected by treatments, and both the relaxation alone and desensitization groups differed from the control group.

Systematic desensitization was compared to reactive inhibition therapy by Graff, MacLean & Loving (1971). Reactive inhibition therapy is an extinction procedure in which the client is asked to feel and experience his anxiety by attending to all the unpleasant emotions and bodily sensations which accompany it instead of avoiding the anxiety. Presumably, the effortfulness will reinforce the termination of anxiety.

Graff and colleagues collected 84 test-anxious college students and assigned them to a desensitization group, a reactive-inhibition group, a discussion-placebo group which discussed neutral topics and a waiting-list control group. All groups met 3 times per week for 11 meetings. Self-reports of test anxiety and general anxiety were lower after treatment in the experimental than the control groups, and in an 8-week followup, the reactive inhibition treatment was slightly superior, but not significantly so, to the desensitization treatment. However, the desensitization sessions had a 45–60-minute duration, whereas the inhibition group was more efficient because it met for only 15–25 minute sessions.

The use of the same trainers to lead both treatment groups makes one suspicious of the possibility of experimenter bias. The presence of only one group per condition, a shortcoming of many of these studies being reported, is also unfortunate.

It is of considerable interest that in none of the five most recent studies comparing group desensitization to a variety of other treatments is the group desensitization procedure superior. Clearly the announcement of its superiority is premature. It is also possible that the group situation introduces other variables into intervention which other treatments may use more effectively. Systematic desensitization, which still seems to be primarily geared to the parallel learning model, may not yet be making use of the audience, modeling and interaction effects which represent potential forces in group interventions.

Group Treatment of Depression and Anger

Although there are no reports of which I am aware of group rehearsal types of treatment of depression, Seitz (1971), in his review of behavior modification techniques for the treatment of depression, cites two individual cases, one treated successfully, a second with only moderate success. Group treatment would appear to be feasible.

Cautela (1971) suggests that covert negative reinforcement is particularly useful with depressive patients who cannot think of positive events in their lives to use to reinforce imagined adaptive responses. Covert negative reinforcement is based on the escape-conditioning paradigm, and involves rehearsing the termination of a noxious imagined scene followed by the response to be increased. Cautela reports some supportive experimental studies showing that judgments and attitudes in a college population are affected by procedures in which imagined escape from a noxious scene is paired with previously neutral or negative events. Cautela's procedures are easily adaptable for use in groups, although I know of no such research so far.

To my knowledge there have been no group attempts to decrease anger by cognitive rehearsal methods. That such attempts may be worth exploring is suggested by Herrell's report of success with a single case (1971).

Behavior rehearsal therapists have so far concentrated on eliminating the negative. Those interested in systematic experiential learning, as we have already seen, and the Skinnerians, as we will see in the next section, have emphasized accentuating the positive relatively more than behavioral rehearsal theorists. A little research exists on practicing positive emotions (Jacobs, 1971; Konrad & Jacobs, 1968), which will be referred to in the next section. In addition, we have some unpublished data (Jacobs, Roberts & Modecke, 1971) on the affective consequences of having students practice hierarchies of positive and neutral experiences. We have not yet analyzed formally the adjective checklist endorsements of participants in the study, but I have looked at the results, and I'm sure that those rehearsing positive experiences have reported feeling happier afterwards than those who rehearsed neutral experiences.

Summary and Conclusions

Clearly there has been an increase in recent years in the study of the application of rehearsal methods to the group treatment of emotion. Of particular importance may be the further exploration of the role of such social learning concepts as modeling, and such private events as covert instructions.

Although behavior rehearsal and counterconditioning methods seem to be effective in reducing anxiety, there is little evidence from the early group studies that systematic desensitization is superior to other treatments. The most recent studies are uniform in the finding that other treatment methods are at least as effective.

There is little systematic research so far on basic group variables such as size or composition of the group. Although there is agreement among behavior therapists that relationships are an important component of treatment, few studies have attempted to study such variables.

Group rehearsal methods have been effective recently in reducing anxiety in a variety of subject populations. Little study exists of group rehearsal methods for the reduction of other emotions, such as depression and anger, or for increasing the amount of positive emotion, although evidence from individual cases suggests it is feasible to do so.

OPERANT CONDITIONING AND SOCIAL LEARNING APPROACHES TO MODIFYING EMOTIONAL BEHAVIOR IN GROUPS

The pragmatic approach of the operant conditioning movement has focused primarily on increasing and decreasing the rate of responding for selected responses of individuals by manipulating the gratifying and aversive environmental consequences of the behavior. Special problems which occur in increasing the rate initially of exceptionally rare and infrequent responses of individuals will be treated as a separate issue in the first part of this section entitled elicitation. A third issue, that of insuring the durability of modified response after the termination of the so-called treatment method, will be treated in the final section.

The application of operant techniques to the solution of mental-health and educational problems is of fairly recent origin. However, in recent years, especially, a considerable amount of research has been directed towards work with children, and focused on two types of groups where little systematic successful research had been previously achieved: the family (see Chapter Fourteen) and the classroom (Fargo, Behrns & Nolen, 1971).

RESPONSE ELICITATION

Shaping

It is difficult to modify the frequency of occurrence of responses which occur very infrequently or not at all. One of the original Skinnerian solutions to this problem with infrahuman organisms is called *shaping*. The behavior in the organism's repertoire most closely approximating the desired behavior is positively reinforced when it is emitted by the organism, in order to increase its frequency. This reinforced behavior also is sometimes more and sometimes less similar to the desired behavior. By reinforcing the more similar, and not reinforcing the less, the desired behavior can often be arrived at by a method of successive approximations. The success of the method of training complex behavior sequences in animals is testified to by the many baseball-playing chickens in our zoos and circuses.

A number of studies suggest that affective responses in humans are shapable. For example, autistic children have been described as having a deficit in the emission of affectionate responses. Patterson (1969) even suggests that the affectionate overtures of the parents and other caretakers of autistic children may be extinguished because of the unavailability of reciprocal affection in the repertoires of the children. Lovaas has produced a film that depicts the manner in which he was able to shape a response in autistic children of embracing an adult for social approval by beginning by reinforcing the children for reaching around an adult for candy rewards.

These methods of successive approximations may also be applied to modifying the rate of responding. Jacobs & Golden (1970) is a typical example. Four multiproblem elementary-school children were observed to be out of their seats 78, 75, 68 and 51 percent of the time during five 15-minute observations of seatwork periods. The children were also observed to be behaving aggressively and distracting other class members when out of their seats. Contracts were arranged with the problem children whereby they would receive tokens, material rewards and social approval for remaining at their seats for very short periods of time. Half of the children being treated also earned material rewards for the other class members by their successes. It was observed that the reinforcements to the p ers of the children being treated elicited peer pressure toward fulfillment of the contract. The time periods of continuous at-seat behavior necessary to earn the tokens was gradually increased from one minute to eight minutes during 4–5 hours of treatment spread out over the next 4 weeks, until the children were remaining in their seats for 15-minute periods. Unobtrusive observations by a teacher's aide of two of the children, taken two weeks after the cessation of treatment, revealed that the children were still at their seats for over 90 percent of the time.

In the case above, shaping was used to gradually lengthen the duration of a response because the Ss may not have been able to sustain such responses for long periods of time at the initiation of treatment. It is probably advantageous when attempting to prolong the duration of responses in individuals to start with response-success criteria within the repertoire of the S. Such a strategy will insure the earning of rewards for the earlier responses, which are otherwise weak and easily extinguished. It may be that the frequent administration of tokens for these children also represents a "reminder" which is necessary because the children lack adequate covert self-instructional systems

These multiproblem children, it is our observation, rarely receive positive reinforcements from teachers for appropriate behavior and in addition are also ordinarily sociometrically unpopular, so that it is unlikely that substantial amounts of peer reinforcement is directed towards them. One would speculate that school is not a very gratifying environment to such children, and it would be surprising if they learned very much, or if they stayed in school any longer than absolutely necessary. Shaping more reinforceable responses in these children and reinforcing them for their approximations may also result in more complex and generalizable beneficent changes in their self-concept systems and in the interactions of these children with teachers.

Shaping may occur in a more complex manner in a laboratory group or traditional treatment group. Exercises like those in which secrets are written on cards and read anonymously to the group represent a somewhat unsystematic approach to shaping self-disclosure. A set of such exercises, graduated with respect to the element of risk-taking associated with each behavior, could be arranged, although I know of no such systematic approaches which have been employed or evaluated. The psychodrama movement has also employed complex and unsystematic shaping techniques for many years. The general format is one in which participants recieve feedback from observers regarding the appropriateness of their role portrayals, and then replay the roles.

The shaping approach of Truax, Carkhuff and colleagues described earlier has reported substantial success. Trainees were presented with taped models of effective counselor responses, such as empathy, and then required to respond to client statements in an empathic manner. The shaping consists of immediate feedback provided to trainees by observers by means of rating forms and comments. Sizable increases in empathic level of response after training have been reported.

Shaping responses, particularly in the original Skinnerian manner which was described first in this section, is a long and tedious process. Other methods of elicitation such as modeling are often more rapid, and therefore preferable.

Modeling

Modeling is a second eliciting procedure, based on the well-established information that, under certain circumstances, individuals will attempt to reproduce or copy the behavior of others. The extent of such imitation is determined by some of the attributes of the model, such as his status, and also determined by some of the attributes of the observer, such as his anxiety level. The extent of imitation is also determined by some of the relationships between observer and model characteristics such as relative age, although not too much data exists relative to this last issue. Bandura (1969) suggests that in such observational learning, the modeling stimuli induce perceptual responses in the observer which tend to endure as retrievable images or other symbolically represented or coded events.

Modeling provides a rapid method for the elicitation of novel or new responses as well as for rare or unusual responses. The process appears to include both informational and motivational components. The informational component provided by modeling enables the individual to rearrange components of complex responses which are ordinarily already available to him, in a new combination. For example, in copying a dance step, one could recall an image of the sequence and timing of the movements of the model's feet, or retrieve a verbal coding of the observed sequence in terms like left-right-together. Although all the component responses, e.g., foot movements, would ordinarily have been previously available, one may never have rearranged them before in exactly such sequence. Included in modeling is also a monitoring process in which one compares the emitted response to its representation in order to correct disparities.

A second informational component of the modeled behavior is related to its consequences when they are available to the observer. Such information may have motivational implications. Observing another individual handle a snake without being hurt may be reassuring or anxiety-reducing, for example. Observing the behavior of the model being rewarded may serve to direct or increase the incentive motivation of the observer. Observing hostility expressed with no consequent punishment may raise the probability of occurrence of aggressive responses of individuals which have been previously inhibited by fear. More directly, motivation-arousing consequences of modeled behavior are related to the desire for approval of observers of the imitation. In the Zupnick (1971) study, where models are shown to facilitate the extinction of snake-phobic responses in a group situation, he refers to the potential approving or disapproving effect on the performer of having others observing. I suspect that the presence of the model during the imitative performance would have a similar, although perhaps not as powerful, effect as the presence of a larger audience. The presence of an audience of other performers might also increase the competitiveness of participants.

Truax, Carkhuff and colleagues have been exploring the use of modeling in group treatment and training for a number of years. The process is called vicarious therapy pretraining or VTP. Patients are exposed before treatment to a model consisting of a 30-minute audiotape recording of "good patient therapy behavior." The tape illustrates how clients explore themselves and their feelings. A number of the early studies are summarized in

Truax & Carkhuff (1967), and the authors report significant changes in self-reports of symptomatology on the scales of the MMPI after group treatment in two studies of a population of mental-hospital inpatients, and for one study of outpatients. No success was achieved using VTP with a population of juvenile delinquents. One of the more recent studies (Truax & Wargo, 1969) showed reliable differences between 5 groups of outpatients treated in group therapy who had been exposed before treatment to VTP and five groups which had not. The differences reported were primarily on self-report instruments, and reflect changes in self-concept and on the neurotic symptomatology scales of the MMPI, which are related to subjective distress such as anxiety and depression.

A second set of studies (Glick, Jacobs, Deacon, Waldron & Lublin, 1966; Konrad & Jacobs, 1967, 1968) described in Jacobs & Sachs (1971) were directed at increasing the feelings of well-being of depressed and schizophrenic patients by a combination of modeling positive affective responses to the patient, and role-rehearsal by the patient with feedback and reinforcement from other group members. Groups of three or four including one patient and two or three student volunteers met weekly for six half-hour sessions. Parts from popular plays portraying the character experiencing positive emotions were modeled by the students, then rehearsed by the patients. A companionship group, which met with patients on the same number of occasions but where the interaction was unstructured, and a control group, which filled out the Jacobs' Survey of Mood and Affect (Jacobs 1971) on an equivalent number of occasions to that of the other two groups but was not otherwise treated, were included in the study. The role-playing group increased more in feelings of well-being and energy as judged by self-reports compared to the other two groups and maintained its superiority during an unstructured interaction a week after treatment with students different from the ones who had treated patients.

An application of modeling relevant to the personal-growth laboratory is a recent doctoral dissertation completed by Howard Bean here at West Virginia University (Bean, 1971). Using an analogue study, he demonstrated that a half hour of modeling interpersonal openness by group leaders for undergraduate volunteer Ss caused a profound increase in the rate of production of interpersonal openness by group members. The increased amount of self-disclosure by observers exposed to a model is much greater than that produced by instructions describing interpersonal openness and requesting that group members perform such responses. I suspect that increasing the persuasiveness of the instructions might produce better results.

Instructions, Sets, Prompts

Another elicitation strategy which is sometimes more efficient than shaping is the use of classes of verbal stimuli such as questions, requests, demands. These stimuli may be presented orally or in a written form to attempt to elicit selected classes of responses, including unusual responses or those which individuals have never emitted before. Most individuals are accustomed to complying with requests because performance is likely to result in social approval, and noncompliance to sometimes have aversive consequences. However, individuals have ordinarily also learned that complying may sometimes have more benefits for the stimulator than for themselves, and therefore often have a certain amount of wariness.

Instructions, which are complex requests, may identify the response components to be emitted and the order in which the components should appear. Sometimes instructions even describe the consequences of the requested response, e.g., that it will lead to some class of reinforcements. The responder will, of course, assign varying degrees of credibility to such predictions of consequences, depending on such aspects of the emitter as his status, etc. If the coding systems employed as the stimulus approximate those of the responder, the responder can retrieve the appropriate responses from the vast amount of information he has stored about responses and response components which he may never before have emitted. Such response information has been acquired by his opportunities to observe others, from the visual, auditory and symbolized representations of behaviors he has been exposed to from films, TV, radio, books, newspapers, conversations, etc. That is to say, an individual may be able to respond to the stimulus, "Pretend you are his father," even though he has never been a father, because he has stored varying amounts of information about father behavior.

A number of studies suggest the usefulness of instructions and questions in eliciting emotional responses in groups. Feldman (1971), for example, has just completed a study of the effect of instructions on the subsequent behavior in psychotherapy groups of newly admitted patients to an inpatient psychiatric service. Doctor or patient peers delivered special orientation messages to the new patients which described the behaviors which would enable the patients to benefit from group treatment. Feldman found that orientation by a doctor was more effective than that by another patient or than no orientation when she counted the number of emotional responses such as those involving personal comments and feedback responses in first group therapy sessions. The doctor-oriented group was still superior, but no longer significantly so by the second day of treatment. Feldman suggests that emitted responses may need to be reinforced in order to be maintained.

Liberman (1970a), in a study to be discussed in more detail later, reported that the use by a therapist of questions, comments and invitations to respond (prompts) was successful in increasing group cohesiveness.

Moore (1971), in another analogue study recently completed here, found that videotape models of self-disclosure, written descriptions of self-disclosure and instructions to self-disclosure were all superior to a control condition in the numbers of self-disclosing statements emitted in small groups after exposure to the experimental stimuli. Although the videotape model elicited the most self-disclosure, the results were not reliably superior to those of the other conditions. Bean, in the study reported earlier (1971), did find modeling to be significantly superior to instructions in eliciting self-disclosure. However, the persuasiveness of his instructions did not appear to be high. Bean also used a live model, whose modeling as a presentation of behavior may be confounded with the interactional nature of the modeling as a response to the behavior of other group members.

It is clear that there is still much to learn about the principles of eliciting emotional responses in groups. Instructions, models and shaping have all shown promise. The informational and motivational components of both models and instructions need further exploration in order to increase the effectiveness of elicitation.

INCREASING RESPONSE STRENGTH

The previous sections have already indicated that the frequency of responses is increased if the responses are followed by a variety of materials, activities or reactions from others that are gratifying. However, the avoidance of termination of noxious stimulation may also increase the frequency of responses which immediately precede such events. Both of these methods have been used to increase the frequency of emotional responses in group situations.

One of the earliest studies by Ullman, Krasner & Collins (1961) used pictures as stimuli, and reinforced group-therapy patients for responding with emotional words. One group of Ss was reinforced by the E with head nods and approving "Hmm-mms"; a second group by loud clicks; and a third group received no reinforcement. The scores of patients reinforced by means of social approval increased slightly but significantly on a scale measuring adequacy in interpersonal relations in group therapy sessions as rated by group leaders, whereas the scores of patients in the other two conditions did not.

Oakes (1962) systematically reinforced each of the 12 kinds of responses in Bale's group observation system (see Chapter Twelve for a fuller description of the categories) which were emitted by discussion-group Ss who were informed that they were participants in an experiment on psychological insight and that a light would flash each time an insightful statement occurred. Significant increases occurred only for Category Number Five, "giving opinions, evaluation, analysis, expresses feeling, wish." However, the results should be interpreted with caution because of the large number of comparisons performed in the analysis.

The Jacobs studies referred to earlier in which patients practiced feeling happier (Jacobs, 1971), a study of Hawkins described in Patterson (1969), and a recent study by Betz (1969), used combinations of modeling and reinforcement to increase emotional responses in group participants. Hawkins compared three therapy groups of schizophrenic patients. All groups had a therapist who was programmed to reinforce affective responses produced by group members. One group also had patient models who frequently made affective responses, another had patient models who avoided affective material and the third group had no models. The largest increase in the production of affective responses occurred in the group which had both models who produced frequent affective responses and the reinforcing therapist. Betz 1969), in a study interpretable in modeling and reinforcement terms, compared counseling trainees exposed to different kinds of experiences in groups as part of a practicum experience. The leader of affective counseling groups responded to and encouraged the members' expression of feelings. In cognitive groups, the leader focused on content rather than feelings. Judgments of samples of typescripts showed that the two different treatments were achieved. Comparison of typescripts of individual counseling sessions by the participants revealed that the counselors receiving the affective group treatment significantly increased in ability to respond to clients' affect after their group counseling experience.

Two additional studies, similar to the preceding in their general approach to reinforcement, are also relevant. The first (Warner & Hansen, 1970) studied two model-reinforcement groups and two verbal-reinforcement groups in which the counselor tried to keep the discussion on the feelings of alienation of a group of high school students selected on the basis of high amounts of alienation. He also reinforced verbally all student responses which suggested positive attitudes toward their position in the social structure. In addition, two male and two female Ss selected on the basis of high overall adjustment to society, participated in the model-reinforcement groups, with neither the models nor other group members being aware that the models had been selected as models. In a placebo group, the counselor made no attempts to reinforce or direct the discussion. A non-discussion control group was also included.

A retest of the scale of alienation to participants after six sessions revealed that the Ss in the two experimental conditions, although not differing from each other after treatment, improved more than the Ss in both control groups.

In a followup study six months after treatment, Warner (1971) obtained ratings from two teachers for each *S* of a sample of 84 Ss who had participated in the experiment. The teachers apparently had no knowledge of which Ss had participated in which experimental conditions. Although the reliability of the teachers' ratings was low, the behavior ratings of the students who had participated in the experimental groups were superior to those in the control groups.

A large number of studies of family groups, reported in Chapter Fourteen, describe the use of reinforcement to modify emotional behaviors in children.

Saslow (1965) used two kinds of reinforcement to reward a depressed patient for making comments, including self-references, to tape-recordings of group psychotherapy sessions. The patient was asked to listen and stop the tape to comment any time he wished. Saslow termed this positive free reinforcement. In what Saslow called a positive forced reinforcement condition, the group psychotherapy tape was played for two-minute segments which included a remark by the patient. He was rewarded by the playing of the next segment if his response to the tape segment included a self-reference. Both conditions produced marked increases in the amount of time this patient spent talking about himself in subsequent group-therapy sessions. However, an aversive treatment condition, in which the tape segments were repeated if no personal reference by the patient occurred, which came between the two positive conditions, makes it difficult to estimate the relative effectiveness of the various conditions of hearing tape segments as a reinforcer. Possible serial-order effects make relative comparisons between the conditions unwise.

Lewinsohn & Atwood (1969), defining depression as a reaction to an absence or decrease of reinforcements, have also worked within an operant framework with a depressed patient and the remainder of her family. Counseling with both the patient and other family members seemed to increase the amount of reinforcement in the patient's environment, and a concomitant decrease in depression was observed.

The studies by Liberman (1970a, 1970b) have been recently directed to the reinforcement issue. In the first, the group therapist reinforced by social approval and prompted patient cohesiveness responses which were defined as those response categories related to intimacy, solidarity or affection. The results were compared to those of a second group of outpatients where the therapist sustained a more traditional group-centered approach. An elaborate analysis of ratings by observers during sessions and a variety of self-reports from patients were obtained. The difficulty in preventing the biases of observers from contaminating ratings in such designs illuminates one of the many difficulties of group research. Liberman showed that both groups increased over time in the amount of positive affect expressed by group members. The increase was significantly greater for the group in which the therapist was programmed to prompt and reinforce cohesive behavior. Liberman's results also suggest that a greater-than-chance number of cohesive responses by group members followed prompts and reinforcements by the therapist, regardless of whether the therapist was programmed or not. Liberman asserts that the therapist behavior systematically influences the behavior of group members, regardless of whether or not his behavior is a consequence of a deliberate strategy, or even whether he is aware of the contingencies of his behavior.

Liberman shows that the therapist maximizes the impact of his acknowledgments or reinforcements if (1)) he responds as soon after the target behavior as possible, (2) he keeps his interventions as unique as possible and (3) he speaks directly to the patient rather than about him.

An analysis of the sociometric responses of patients in Liberman's study showed a greater increase in liking for other patients in the experimental group than in the control group. Two measures of symptomatology, based on patients' self-reports, revealed that the patients in the experimental group obtained more rapid relief of complaints than patients in the comparison group. For one measure, the superiority persisted after a year followup.

A second report (Liberman, 1970b) examined the effect of reinforcing and prompting hostility to the therapist. He found that neither the therapist who had been programmed to reinforce and prompt hostility systematically, nor his more traditional therapist, actually prompted or reinforced more than a very small proportion of the hostile responses.

Examination of both groups suggested that reinforcing hostility to the therapist was much more effective than prompting hostility to the therapist; that reinforcement given immediately following the target behavior led to further expression of hostility a much higher proportion of the time than if comments by other speakers were allowed to intervene before the reinforcement was made; but there was no relationship between the expression of hostility to the therapist by patients and improvements in dominance, independence or symptomatology.

Liberman also concludes that he could find no evidence that hostility to the therapist related in either a positive or inverse manner to hostility to other patients or to cohesiveness. He suggests that hostility is not an affect which is dammed up in a reservoir, because he observed that the higher level of cohesiveness in the experimental group did not decrease the frequency of angry feelings that patients expressed towards each other. He concludes that the expression of affects such as affection and hostility are controlled by the environmental consequences, and can be increased or decreased by environmental stimuli.

Combining reinforcement techniques with systems approaches and social psychology concepts leads to intriguing strategies. For example, we have been exploring the value of using a token system to encourage some typically emotionally inhibited adolescent males in a psychotherapy group to self-disclose more. Self-disclosure statements earn tokens which are exchangeable for donated phonograph records and tickets to athletic events. We have also collected sociometric ratings of the likes and dislikes of the pupils in elementary school classrooms towards the other pupils with the goal of identifying the social isolates and then of developing a classroom community program of mutual assistance, using material and social rewards as reinforcements for helping behaviors and for constructive social interaction.

A final positive reinforcement study is that of Truax (1968), in which excerpts from tape recordings of 30 clients participating in group therapy with four different therapists were analyzed. Patients receiving the highest levels of reinforcement (empathy, warmth and genuineness) for self-exploration showed greater overall self-exploration, and also significantly better outcome based on a complex criterion. The two patients for each of the four therapists receiving the highest level of reinforcement were compared to the two receiving the lowest amount. This yielded even greater differences in outcome than the overall comparison. Additional information on therapist reinforcement is provided (Truax & Mitchell, 1971). An analysis of individual therapy protocols revealed that three therapist reinforcers (empathy, warmth and directiveness) were dispensed very selectively with regard to nine categories of patient behaviors. Four or five classes of patient behavior which elicited therapist reinforcers increased significantly over time, whereas of the four classes of patient behavior which the therapist did not reinforce, three categories neither increased nor decreased.

The Liberman studies and the Truax studies suggest that therapists selectively administer reinforcements, whether they intend to do so or not, which increase the frequency of certain patient behaviors. The hypothesis that superior interventions are a consequence of the therapist's ignorance of the effects of his behavior (because he might lose his sensitivity and spontaneity if he knew he was reinforcing patients, as is sometimes argued) is a testable one, but the hypothesis doesn't sound too plausible. Other positive-reinforcement studies provide substantial evidence that positive reinforcement effects response frequency. More research on the common varieties of social responses which are reinforcers would be valuable. Information regarding the amount of response change accomplished by administering differing amounts of various reinforcers to different types of Ss, and the role of the characteristics of the reinforcement-deliverer, might add to the effective use of reinforcing techniques.

Escape from or avoidance of aversive stimulation has also been shown by the infrahuman literature to represent a powerful source of reinforcement. Miller (1948), in a study referred to earlier, demonstrated that exposure to a few aversive, but not dangerous, shocks often set in motion hundreds of avoidance responses in infrahuman organisms. Such techniques have not often been used in groups. Also the frequent use of group commitment to insure that out-of-group behavior of members is consumated (see Chapter Seven, for example) carries the implication that failure to fulfill commitments may meet with group disapproval. Such anticipations may motivate contract fulfillment by group members. The Steffy, Meichenbaum & Best study, reported earlier in the section on behavior rehearsal techniques, used escape or avoidance of painful shocks in the group situation to promote refusal to smoke or the termination of smoking by group members, with temporary success.

DECREASING RESPONSE STRENGTH

Extinction (not providing reinforcement contingent on response) and punishment (providing aversive reinforcement as a consequence of undesirable responses) are the two major techniques for decreasing response strength. Patterson (1969), in a discussion of what he calls the irrational social system, contends that the social environment provides reinforcement for much deviant behavior. His own data reveals that peers of delinquents, for example, reinforce them, by verbal approval and other reinforcers, for making antiauthority statements at least 70 percent of the time. There is much base rate and observational data of families and classrooms which show beyond a doubt that parents and teachers ordinarily pay more attention to the behavior to which they object, than to samples of the behavior which might be suitable replacements. Attention from adults is a powerful reinforcer for children, and group leaders are unknowingly reinforcing the behavior which they would prefer to eradicate.

In order to decrease the occurrence of undesirable behavior it is necessary to interfere with any positive contingencies which have been associated with the undesirable behavior. The problem of peer reinforcement was solved by Carlson, Arnold, Becker & Madsen (1968) by providing candy reinforcements for class members for not turning around to watch a girl who was getting a lot of attention by throwing tantrums in the classroom. Teachers and parents are frequently advised not to attend to chronic emotional behavior, such as excessive crying, as an extinction procedure.

Ordinarily, when extinction or aversive methods are being used to reduce the frequency of undesirable responses, a process of reinforcing the more desirable replacement behavior when it occurs, is simultaneously initiated. Observations frequently reveal that teachers or parents are not reinforcing desirable behaviors which are intermittently occurring.

I'm not aware of any studies of treatment groups which have attempted to use extinction techniques except of Graff, MacLean & Loving (1971), discussed earlier in the behavior-rehearsal section. Also, the differential use of reinforcers by therapists for different patient response classes, as reported earlier by Truax (1968), suggests that somewhat unsystematic extinction processes occur in treatment and laboratory groups.

Punishment, or providing aversive reinforcement, also inhibits undesirable behavior. The time-out period, in which a child emitting undesirable responses is removed from the classroom or family group to an unstimulating environment, probably has aversive qualities. It also has the advantage of removing the child from potential reinforcements for deviant behavior, from peers, for example. The withdrawal of reinforcements for deviant behavior, in token systems with children, is also clearly aversive, and also effective in inhibiting responses. The Carlson et al. (1968) study referred to earlier, removed reinforcements from peers who attended to the tantrums of the child who was the focus of treatment.

The Steffy, Meichenbaum & Best smoking study referred to earlier associated tactual elective shocks with smoking behavior, and, as frequently occurs in such uses of aversive stimuli, allowed the performance of appropriate behavior to avoid the punishment. Saslow, as reported earlier, replayed therapy-group tape segments over to a depressed patient when he did not make self-reference statements, and reports not only that the patient showed marked discomfort during the repeats of the tape, but also that self-reference statements in group therapy increased markedly after "forced negative reinforcement" procedure was used with the patient. The Lewinsohn & Weinstein manuscript reported in Seitz (1971) may have also used negative feedback systematically as an aversive contingency for certain behavior classes. Depressive patients in group psychotherapy were given feedback by raters on the consequences of their responses. As will be shown in the next chapter, negative feedback about behavior is clearly aversive in a laboratory training, and should inhibit the behaviors to which it is referred.

There does not seem to be as much research on the use of aversive stimuli to inhibit undesirable responses as on the use of extinction, or on the use of positive reinforcements. This is possibly attributable to a general repugnance to the production of pain in others by those in the social helping professions and sciences. The semantic confusions, and values about hostility and punishment, as well as potentially undesirable side-effects of the use of aversive stimuli, all probably contribute to the reluctance of interveners to use punishment extensively except in mild degrees and with euphemistically described operations. Baer (1971) suggests that "a small number of brief painful experiences is a reasonable exchange for the interminable pain of a lifelong maladjustment [p. 36]."

STABILIZATION AND MAINTENANCE OF EMOTIONAL BEHAVIOR

All programs designed for the modification of behavior have been concerned with the issue of insuring the persistence and generality of the modified behavior after the termination of the program. Such problems underlie the preoccupation of the laboratory movement with "reentry" problems, the apprehension regarding loss of stimulus control of those who work in the classrooms and the clamor for followup studies on patients in group psychotherapy. One variable related to stabilization is the length of time of treatment. Most past strategies of intervention have been based on an intrapsychic treatment and have therefore pursued the goal of achieving more or less permanent changes in covert and sometimes overt response systems of the individual during a period of treatment, the length of which was more or less unspecified. Under such circumstances the learning of appropriate responses and extinction or eradication of undesirable responses had to be very strongly established. It was expected by the therapist and the patient that many learning and/or unlearning trials would be necessary to achieve the goal.

The training laboratory intervention, which was also a one-shot personal-change experience, faced the same problem. Schein & Bennis (1967), for example, speculate that two-week-long training laboratories are better for all phases of the learning experience. A caution is that the longer laboratories might cause more difficulty for the trainee in attempting to integrate new responses into ongoing relationships. Gibb (1971) estimates that from 50 to 200 hours are necessary to produce the changes necessary for growth. Whether the differences exist between the length of time necessary to produce emotional change and those necessary to change other response systems, has not been explored. However, a number of authors, Corsini (1970) and

Stoller (1970) for example, believe that a very rapid change may occur in a sufficiently intense emotional climate. The large body of literature reviewed by Goldstein (1968) suggests that the expectations of the therapist may have considerable effect upon a number of the dimensions of attitude change in patients.

Interventions contracted for the correction of maladaptive behavior are ordinarily expected to eventually terminate. The same expectations commonly exist in training oriented interventions, although, as I have pointed out in an earlier chapter, such expectations may not always be plausible or necessary. Termination of the intervention also usually makes it impossible for the intervener to continue the schedules of reinforcement which he has constructed to maintain high levels of adaptive responses. In view of previously presented evidence that the typical social evnironment is not likely to continue his schedule, and, as a matter of fact, is more likely to reinforce maladaptive responses, what strategies does he have available to him? At least five or six possibilities seem promising, aside from that of never terminating, or planning a termination which includes a series of intermittent contacts with the intervener in order to provide additional reinforcements. Such other strategies include achieving high response strength, training in self-reinforcement, training in general reinforcement tactics, training in reinforcement eliciting classes of response and modifying the environment.

High Response Strength

A substantial body of literature exists in the field of human and animal learning to the effect that repetition or practice of responses makes such responses more habitual. The effects of frequency of practice of affective responses has not, to my knowledge, been studied as a variable in group situations. However, if there is any validity to the contention that brief periods in treatment, or in training laboratories, are not as effective as longer periods of exposure, it is conceivable that additional practice of various emotion-related responses may contribute to greater efficiency of intervention. A considerable amount of evidence also exists—for example, Ferster & Skinner

(1957), which demonstrates that partial, or intermittent reinforcement of responses results in greater resistance to extinction of responses—although I am not aware of any group studies that have attempted to manipulate this. Certainly the persistence of slot-machine players and fishermen suggests that under appropriate conditions very little reinforcement is necessary to maintain high rates of response in humans. Liberman (1970a), in his paper reported earlier, describes the nature of the reinforcement for cohesiveness as intermittent, and speculates that this had apparently had little deleterious effect on the learning of cohesive responses. Intermittent reinforcement is commonly used deliberately to maximize resistance to extinction when operant techniques are employed with children.

A second technique which might increase the response strength of avoidance responses is suggested by the work of Stampfl and Levis (Stampfl, 1965). These authors assert that when a serial order of stimuli is terminated by an aversive stimuli, tremendously persistent avoidance responses may be elicited by these stimuli. Extinction of avoidance to those stimuli originally temporally closer to the aversive condition allows the occurrence of more distal stimuli, which seem to rearouse anxiety and avoidance to the extinguished stimuli.

An example may make this process clearer. An animal is placed in a compartment from which he can escape easily. A buzzer sounds, and a light flashes ten seconds later, which is followed immediately by a mild shock. The animal will immediately escape from the compartment, and will probably continue to do so many times whenever the light flashes. However, if he is never shocked again, his escape will become slower. Eventually he will remain in the compartment after the light has flashed. If the buzzer is now sounded, the escape response to the light will be reinstated for an additional number of trials. However, I know of no studies employing such techniques systematically to increase response persistence in humans.

All of these interventions are based on the hope of the intervener that he can produce durable enough behavior change to insure its persistence after the return of the intervenee to a meagerly, if not perversely, reinforcing environment.

Training in Self-Reinforcement

The capacity of social training to endow humans with extremely persistent systems for aversively stimulating themselves, such as the constant devaluations of their performances by some individuals, needs little documentation (Chapter Six, for example). Such examples raise the question of whether it may also be possible to train people in persistent techniques for positively stimulating or reinforcing their own behavior. Recently, research has been addressed to the general issue of self regulatory behavior, and as Kanfer (1971) reports, there is evidence that self-reinforcement responses are trainable and manipulable and have motivational properties at least as potent as the reinforcements administered externally.

Systematic training in self-reinforcement might also increase the stability of interventions after their termination, by requiring less reinforcement from the environment for response-persistence. In addition, since an important aspect of such self-regulation is based on evaluations of one's performance and its environmental consequences the training programs such as those used by Ellis (in his chapter earlier in this book) may also be useful in modifying the evaluated magnitude and quality of the social reinforcements being received by individuals from their environment. However, it may be necessary in both strategies, discussed so far, to provide additional external reinforcement to maintain appropriate responses or self-reinforcing responses.

Training in Principles of Getting Reinforcements for Appropriate Behavior

A third strategy is derivable from the model proposed in Chapter Three, or the training of parents as behavior modifiers described in Chapter Fourteen. Individuals can be trained systematically to monitor their responses and to determine when such responses elicit gratification or aversive stimulation from the social environment. Such training enables the individual to negotiate with his social environment with respect to which of his responses are reinforced. Such training may also enable the individual to change his environment if it only reinforces ultimately self-defeating responses or those responses likely to endanger his general objective.

Training in Specific Reinforcement-Eliciting Responses

Training in interpersonal skills, as practiced by the Truax & Carkhuff group, may be another approach, based on the establishment in the individual of response repertoires which are generally reinforceable from the environment. Training an individual to emit more empathic responses (Truax & Carkhuff, 1967), provides him with a generalized behavioral reinforcer which increases the frequency of occurrence of a variety of classes or responses in those with whom he interacts. However, empathic responses also increase interpersonal exploration, self-disclosure or intimacy in others (Truax & Mitchell, 1971), and therefore may reinforce the emitter of the empathy to maintain a high level of empathic responses. Similarly, as Truax and Mitchell point out in their notion ofreciprocal affect, warmth or acceptance from the therapist may elicit warmth from clients. Since warmth has also been shown to have the property of a generalized reinforcer, training clients to emit more warmth towards others will also elicit more warmth from others to reinforce the emission of warmth from the client. Truax also reports some interesting evidence supporting the analysis above, which suggests that the therapist use of such reinforcers as warmth or empathy may be somewhat determined or manipulated by the behavior of clients. This would lead one to believe that such ordinarily reinforcing responses may also decrease in frequency when they are not reinforced by other individuals.

If such training of emotional interpersonal skills actually does produce responses which ordinarily elicit their own reinforcement from the environment, this training has the advantage, compared to other kinds of training, of building in automatically self-maintaining responses.

Modifying the Environment

A fifth commonly used strategy is to try to work to modify the behavior of an entire system or subsystem. Family therapy, conjoint therapy, a laboratory with the executives of a particular business organization, represent common examples of this systems approach which are already in use. In the classroom situation, Patterson (1969) reports reinforcing an isolated child for approaching other children, and also reinforcing the other children in the classroom for making overtures to the isolated child. In some unreported research we have conducted here, we have some evidence to suggest that reinforcing problem children in classroom for appropriate behavior, and also allowing them to win rewards and dispense them to their classmates for such behavior, may improve the sociometric status in the classroom of the problem children.

An alternative strategy that suggests itself under circumstances where members of the postintervention systems are absent or unavailable, as when one is treating unrelated adults would be for the leader or trainer to attempt to produce a system to maintain the changes achieved by the intervention. A special effort might be made to produce cohesiveness between group members who have an opportunity for postintervention interactions. Interventions could be designed to assist members to become adept at mutually reinforcing each other's expressions of intimacy or affection or solidarity, and encouraging them to continue postintervention interactions. The benefits of chaining responses might be invoked by training individuals to reinforce each other for reinforcements of selected responses. In a classroom situation, for example, we have recently started to explore the consequences of reinforcing a somewhat isolated child every time he verbally reinforces another problem child for performing a criterion response. The production of programs to produce social systems which monitor and reinforce selected aspects of the social environment has intriguing possibilities.

SUMMARY AND CONCLUSIONS

Learning and behavior theory strategies have led to a refreshing and hopefully more productive specification of the hypotheses in recent research on emotions in groups. More manipulative and less descriptive research also seems to characterize the contemporary studies, as the emphasis shifts from such questions as "What happens to emotions in group therapy?" to more specific questions, such as "Will reinforcing patients for cohesive responses towards each other affect group cohesiveness?"

An impressive amount of cross-fertilization with regard to concepts is also occurring between those researchers who study psychotherapy and those who study training and education. Reinforcement, cohesiveness, modeling and feedback are terms bandied about in all intervention systems.

A shift in emphasis of the learning and training-oriented studies from conceiving groups as convenient and more efficient systems for parallel training to attempts to exploit and study the relationships between group members had led to interesting results in the studies of the classroom and family.

REFERENCES

Anthony, W. & Wain, H. An investigation of the outcome of empathy training for medical corpsmen. *Psychological Aspects of Disability*, 1971, **18**, 86–88.

Bandura, A. *Principles of behavior modification.* New York: Holt, Rinehart & Winston, 1969.

Baer, D. M. Let's take another look at punishment. *Psychology Today*, 1971, **5**, 32–37.

Bean, H. B. The effects of a role-mode and instructions on group interpersonal openness and cohesiveness. Unpublished doctoral dissertation, West Virginia University, 1971.

Betz, R. Effects of group counseling as an adjunct practicum experience. *Journal of Counseling Psychology*, 1969, **16**, 522–528.

Carkhuff, R. Training as a systematic experiential learning preference mode of treatment. *Journal of Counseling Psychology*, 1971a, **18**, 123–131.

Carkhuff, R. Principles of social action in training for new careers in human sciences. *Journal of Counseling Psychology*, 1971b, **18**, 147–151.

Carlson, C., Arnold, C., Becker, W. & Madsen, C. The elimination of tantrum behavior of a child in an elementary classroom. *Behavioral Research and Therapy*, 1968, **6**, 117–119.

Cautela, J. Covert conditioning. In A. Jacobs & L. Sachs (Eds.), *The psychology of private events.* New York: Academic Press, 1971. Pp. 109–130.

Corsini, R. J. Immediate therapy in groups. In G. M. Gazda (Ed.),

Innovations to group psychotherapy. Springfield, Ill.: Charles C Thomas, 1968. Pp. 11–41.

Donner, L. Automated group desensitization. A follow-up report. *Journal of Behavioral Research and Therapy*, 1970, **8**, 241–247.

Donner, L. & Guerney, B. Automated group desensitization of test anxiety. *Journal of Behavior Research and Therapy*, 1969, **7**, 1–13.

Fargo, G., Behrns, C. & Nolen, P. *Behavior modification in the classroom*. Belmont, Calif.: Wadsworth, 1971.

Feldman, J. B. The effects of patient vs. physician orientation of new hospital admissions on values and group verbal behavior. Unpublished masters' theses, West Virginia University, 1971.

Ferster, C. & Skinner, B. F. *Schedules of reinforcement*. New York: Appleton-Century-Crofts, 1957.

Freeling, N. & Shemberg, K. The alleviation of test anxiety by systematic desensitization. *Journal of Behavioral Research and Therapy*, 1970, **8**, 293–299.

Gibb, J. R. The effects of human relations training. In A. E. Bergin & S. L. Garfield (Eds), *Handbook of psychotherapy and behavior change:* an *empirical analysis*. New York: John Wiley — Sons, 1971. Pp. 839–857.

Glick, J., Jacobs, A., Deacon, S., Waldron, R. & Lublin, S. Mood modification in mental hospital patients by undergraduate students. Paper read at the Western Psychological Association Convention, 1966.

Goldstein, A. P. *Therapist-patient expectancies in psychotherapy*. New York: Pergamon, 1962.

Goldstein, A. P., Heller, K. & Sechrest, L. B. *Psychotherapy and the psychology of behavior change*. New York: John Wiley & Sons, 1966.

Graff, R. W., MacLean, G. D. & Loving, A. Group reactive inhibition and reciprocal inhibitions therapies with anxious college students. *Journal of Counseling Psychology*, 1971, **18**, 431–436.

Hedquist, F. & Weinhold, B. Behavioral group counseling with socially anxious and unassertive college students. *Counseling Psychologist*, 1970, **17**, 237–242.

Herrell, J. Use of systematic desensitization to eliminate inappropriate anger. *Proceedings of the 79th Annual Convention of the American Psychological Association, 1971, 431–432.*

Jacobs, A. Mood-emotion-affect. In A. Jacobs & L. Sachs (Eds.), *The psychology of private events*. New York: Academic Press, 1971. Pp. 131–163.

Jacobs, A., Edelman, M. & Wolpin, M. Effects of differential anxiety level and the repression-sensitization dimension in desensitization therapy. *Proceedings of the 79th Annual Convention of the American Psychological Association, 1971*, 427–428.

Jacobs, A. & Golden, F. Report to Cassville School. Unpublished manuscript, 1970.

Jacobs, A., Roberts, K. & Modecke, S. Cognitive rehearsal of positive experiences and emotion. Unpublished research, West Virginia University, 1971.

Jacobs, A. & Sachs, L. (Eds.) *The psychology of private events.* New York: Academic Press, 1971.

Jacobs, A. & Wolpin, M. A second look at systematic desensitization. In A. Jacobs & L. Sachs (Eds.), *The psychology of private events.* New York: Academic Press, 1971.

Kanfer, F. H. The maintenance of behavior by self generated stimuli and reinforcement. In A. Jacobs & L. Sachs (Eds.), *The psychology of private events.* New York: Academic Press, 1971.

Kass, E. L. The effect of short-term group desensitization on test anxiety. *Dissertation Abstracts International,* 1970, **30,** 3729A.

Kondas, O. Reduction of examination anxiety and "stage fright" by group desensitization and relaxation. *Journal of Behavioral Research and Therapy,* 1967, **5,** 275–281.

Konrad, W. & Jacobs, A. Interaction of college students with schizophrenics and mood change. unpublished manuscript, 1967.

Konrad, W. & Jacobs, A. A social therapy program with schizophrenics to change mood and social responsiveness. paper presented at the California State Psychological Convention, 1968.

Laxer, R., Quarter, J., Kooman, A. & Walker, K. Systematic desensitization and relaxation of high test-anxious secondary school students. *Journal of Counseling Psychologist,* 1969, **16,** 446–451.

Laxer, R. & Walker, K. Counterconditioning versus relaxation in the desensitization of test anxiety. *Journal of Counseling Psychology,* 1970, **17,** 431–436.

Lazarus, A. Group therapy of phobic disorders by systematic desensitization. *Journal of Abnormal and Social Psychology,* 1961, **63,** 504–510.

Leon, H. Reciprocal inhibition: An evaluation of group procedures with "normal" snake phobic subjects. *Diss. abs.,* 1968, **28** (9-B), 3878–3879.

Lewinsohn, P. & Atwood, G. Depression, a clinical research approach. *Psychotherapy: Theory, Research and Practice,* 1969, **6,** 166–171.

Liberman, R. A behavioral approach to group dynamics: I. Reinforcement and prompting of cohesiveness in group therapy. *Behavior Therapy,* 1970a, **1,** 141–175.

Liberman, R. A behavioral approach to group dynamics: II. Reinforcing and prompting hostility to the therapist in group therapy. *Behavior Therapy,* 1970b, **1,** 312–327.

Meichenbaum, D. D., Gilmore, B. & Fedoravicius, A. Group insight versus group desensitization in treating speech anxiety. *Journal of*

Consulting and Clinical Psychology, 1971, **36,** 410–421.

Moore, D. The effects of different modes of presenting a model of self disclosing behavior. unpublished masters' thesis, West Virginia University, 1971.

Mosher, A. and Sprinthall, N. A. Deliberate psychological education. *The Counseling Psychologist,* 1971, **2,** 3–82.

Nawas, M., Fishman, S. & Pucel, J. A standard desensitization program applicable to group and individual treatments. *Behavioral Research and Therapy,* 1970, **4,** 49–56.

Oakes, W. F. Reinforcement of Bales' categories in group discussion. *Psychological Reports,* 1962, **11,** 425–435.

Patterson, G. R. Behavioral techniques based on social learning: An additional base for developing behavior modification techniques. In C. M. Franks (Ed.), *Behavior therapy: Appraisal and status.* New York: McGraw-Hill, 1969. Pp. 341–374.

Paul, G. Outcome of systematic desensitization II: Controlled investigations of individual treatment, technique variations, and current status. In C. M. Franks (Ed.), *Behavior therapy: Appraisal and status.* New York: McGraw-Hill, 1969. Pp. 29–62.

Saslow, G. A case history of attempted behavior manipulation in a psychiatric ward. In L. Krasner & L. Ullman (Eds.), *Research in behavior New York: Holt, Rinehart & Winston, 1965.*

Schein, E. H. & Bennis, W. G. *Personal and organizational change through group methods.* New York: John Wiley & Sons, 1967.

Seitz, F. C. Behavior modification techniques for treating depression. *Psychotherapy: Theory, Research, and Practice,* 1971, **8**(3), 181–184.

Shack, J., Walker, K., Sheridan, K., Egan, G. & Lavigne, J. A training program for small group leaders: II. Evaluation. Unpublished manuscript, 1970.

Sieveking, N. A. Systematic desensitization in groups with institutionalized adolescents. *Dissert. Ab. Internat.,* 1970, **30,** 4383B.

Stampfl, T. G. Implosive therapy: The theory the subhuman analogue, the strategy and the technique: I. Battle Creek: Veterans Administration Bulletin, 1965.

Steffy, R., Meichenbaum, D. & Best, J. Aversive and cognitive factors in the modification of smoking behavior. *Behavioral Research and Therapy,* 1970, **8,** 115–125.

Stoller, F. H. Marathon group therapy. In G. M. Gazda (Ed.), *Innovations to group psychotherapy.* Springfield, ill.: charles C Thomas, 1968. Pp. 42–95.

Truax, C. Therapist interpersonal reinforcement of client self exploration and therapeutic outcome in group psychotherapy. *Journal of Counseling Psychology,* 1968, **15,** 225–231.

Truax, C. & Carkhuff, R. *Toward effective counseling and psychotherapy: Training and practice.* Chicago: Aldine, 1967.

Truax, C. B. & Mitchell, K. M. Research on certain therapist interpersonal skills in relation to process and outcome. In A. E. Bergen & S. L. Garfield (Eds.), *Handbook of psychotherapy and behavior change: An empirical analysis.* New York: John Wiley & Sons, 1971. Pp. 299–344.

Truax, C. & Wargo, D. Effects of vicarious therapy pre training and alternate sessions on outcome in group psychotherapy with outpatients. *Journal of Consulting and Clinical Psychology,* 1969, **33,** 440–447.

Ullman, L., Krasner, L. & Collins, B. Modification of behavior through verbal conditioning: Effects in group psychotherapy. *Journal of Abnormal Soc. Psych.,* 1961, **62** (1), 128–132.

Warner, R. Alienated students: Six months after receiving behavioral treatment. *Journal of Counseling Psychology,* 1971, **18,** 426–430.

Warner, R. & Hansen, J. Verbal-reinforcement and modeling-reinforcement group counseling with alienated students. *Journal of Counseling Psychology,* 1970, **17,** 168–172.

Wolpe, J. *Psychotherapy based by reciprocal inhibition.* Stanford: Stanford University Press, 1958.

Zupnick, S. Effects of varying degrees of a peer model's performance on extinction of a phobic response in an individual or group setting. *Proceedings of the 79th Annual Convention of the American Psychological Association,* 1971, 433–434.

17. The Use of Feedback in Groups

Alfred Jacobs

Many authors contend that feedback is one of the most important processes which occur in group interventions. Yet a surprisingly small amount of knowledge exists regarding the most effective manner of delivery of feedback. The major problem arises from the fact that neither the delivery nor the reception of feedback is solely an objective transfer of information, but both arouse strong emotions.

Research by the author and colleagues examine this problem in more detail. Feedback describing the personal assets of group members is reacted to by the recipients with feelings of well-being and energy, whereas feedback which identifies deficiencies arouses anxiety and depression. Moreover, the positive feedback is rated by recipients as more believable than the negative in two studies. The informational value of negative feedback, is, therefore, less than the informational value of positive feedback. The determinants of both the hedonic and informational aspects of feedback need further study.

The literature on delivery of verbal feedback is somewhat sparse and the results sometimes inconsistent from study to study. However, it does seem clear that providing opportunities for group members to deliver more feedback than would usually occur spontaneously leads to superior outcomes.

Videotape reproduction of behavior, highly acclaimed by practitioners as a medium for the delivery of feedback, has been evaluated in a number of recent studies. The results reported are not of such a nature as to engender a high level of enthusiasm. However, naive experimental designs and an unsophisticated approach to the use of videotape feedback may account for some of the poor findings. There is a need for more good research on the use of videotape, as well as in a number of the other important dimensions of feedback delivery which are described in this chapter.

INTRODUCTION

I will consider in this chapter some of the issues and knowledge surrounding the use of feedback in groups. The term *feedback* was originally coined by the physicist, Wiener (1948), who defined it as the alteration of a systems' input via its own output, by means of a closed system feedback loop. Wiener conceptualized learning itself as primarily a feedback phenomenon. It is probably no accident that Lewin, who was teaching at MIT at the time, and therefore was exposed to wiener's work, introduced the term into social science as a shorthand term for messages describing deviations from a desired goal.

The role of feedback in learning, particularly motor learning, has been extensively studies (Bilodeau, 1961). Most of the material is not directly relevant to the topic of this paper, which will primarily be addressed to the problem of using feedback in groups designed for social intervention. The chapter is organized in the following manner: first, a general discussion of feedback as a methodology for providing information to group members; second, a review of recent research studying the use of verbal feedback in groups; third, the use of auditory and especially visual reproductions of behavior which have been widely acclaimed as resources for providing feedback. The paper will conclude with a discussion of some of our own recently completed research on sequence and valence of feedback in analogue and microlab groups.

THE NATURE OF FEEDBACK IN GROUP INTERVENTIONS

Individuals who are interacting with others in social systems divide their attention among a number of activities. At times individuals attend primarily to the responses which they themselves are emitting; at other times individuals are attending to the responses of others in the system. At still other periods, the individuals scan verbal and nonverbal responses of other members of the system in order to determine the evaluative responses of these others to the messages and stimuli which have been emitted. An important distinction which I make between such general information acquisition which ordinarily occurs in social systems, and the process that has been called feedback, is that I prefer to emphasize that aspect of feedback in which one member of a system provides information deliberately rather than accidentally, unknowingly, or unwillingly. By this I mean that the individual delivering the feedback is motivated to provide information which he believes is otherwise unavailable to the other.

The definition of feedback presented by Benne, Bradford & Lippitt (1964, pp. 15–44) includes many of the elements which would be agreed on by most users of the term: "Feedback, as used here, signifies verbal and nonverbal responses from others to a unit of behavior provided as close in time to the behavior as possible, and capable of being perceived and utilized by the individual initiating the behavior."

The term *feedback* has been applied, in the literature on groups, to a variety of different operations. It is probably wisest to assume, in the absence of other information, that these operations may differ in a number of important dimensions, including that of effectiveness. Examples may better illustrate the diversity of information which is delivered to group members and called feedback. An individual delivering verbal feedback to another might identify some overt behavior which was emitted by the person receiving feedback, or he might comment on his own reactions to that person. The feedback-giver may also identify behaviors of other group members which seem to be responses to the behavior of the feedback receiver. Examples of each of these might be comments like:

(1) I notice you haven't said much today.
(2) I noticed that I turned away each time you began to talk.
(3) John whispered something to Mary when you said that.

These three types of feedback would probably be differentially valuable to individuals who habitually ignore either their own responses or the responses of other system members.

Another way of delivering information regarding the overt responses of system members is by imitating the responses. In one technique, called *mirroring,* the behavior of a group member is imitated for him by another so that he has an opportunity to observe it. This technique is often used by those who do psychodrama. However, the effectiveness of imitation depends partly on the ability of the imitator to accurately reproduce behavior. Technical devices for reproducing overt behavior are also now available, with audiotape reproduction having the particular advantage of being able to reproduce voice quality and timing more accurately than imitators. videotape reproduction has the advantage of being able to present visually to the individual his own facial responses, which are ordinarily unavailable to him, as well as his own nonverbal responses which are typically not in the focus of the individual's attention.

The accuracy and exactness of verbal feedback is also potentially increasable by using raters to count the frequency of various kinds of interactions, as Seitz (1971) reports was done by Lewinsohn and Weinstein in their unpublished work with depressive patients, or as described in Chapter Thirteen. Few studies of the effectiveness of this manner of delivering feedback exist.

A second class of feedback attempts to provide information about the covert responses of system participants. The deliverer of feedback may supply information which is otherwise unavailable because it may not have other public manifestations; for example, that he is bored by what is being said. Feedback referring to the covert responses of persons other than the giver of feedback, is of course inferential. inferential feedback may be useful to the recipient. For example, he may be informed that his facial expression is one which he typically has assumed in the past when he had said he was angry, or when he had acted aggressively, or is similar to that observed in others who say that they are angry. Most writers, Stoller (1968), for example, believe that feedback is more useful when it describes overt responses, than when it is inferential.

Inferential feedback is ordinarily based on assumed relationships between observed behavior and personality variables, or may involve speculation regarding the historical determinants of behavior. An example of the first would be something like "You must be guilty about that because you are protesting an inordinate amount," and of the second, "You probably didn't get along well with your sister because you argue a lot with female group members." material referred to in the previous chapter (Truax & Mitchell, 1971) suggests that it is possible to train individuals)empathy training) to become more adept at identifying from verbalizations the covert feeling responses of others.

Argyris (1968) suggests that the individual who has had to survive by becoming relatively closed may not be amenable to change by feedback which can be directly verified by self and others. Closed individuals, he argues, may distort verifiable information. It may be necessary for such an individual to explore his history to learn how he developed into a closed system, and to be presented by others with hypotheses about himself which he is unable to generate himself.

Another class of ordinarily covert responses are those internal body changes which are often associated with emotional states. These internal states may be inferred by others with varying amounts of reliability by identifying nonverbal, but overt manifestations, such as blushing or tremors. It is also often true that the individual within whom the response is occurring is not likely to be able to make accurate estimates of the response magnitude, particularly for responses of small magnitude. Improved instrumentation now makes it possible to increase the accuracy of such information if one desires it.

The two major properties of feedback are its informational and its hedonic components. The informational aspect, as has been suggested earlier, provides for individuals the data which enables them to redirect or modify responses. The hedonic quality of the feedback determines its motivational aspects. The recipient of information which refers to his social performance ordinarily also perceives such information as either including (or as primarily) an evaluation of social competence. He is, therefore, likely to respond to messages of competence or superiority as beneficent, and to those of competence as noxious.

Hedonically positive feedback, being a general reinforcer, is likely to increase the occurrence of the responses to which it refers, as well as to arouse incentive motivation in its recipient and in other observers of such feedback. Positive feedback is also likely to identify the feedbacker, the group and the process as events which are associated with gratifications.

Negative feedback, on the other hand, is likely to engage the habitual responses of its recipient to aversive stimulation. Such habitual responses to noxious events may often include classes of covert self-devaluative responses (see Chapter Six) which interfere with and disrupt the reception of information. It is also common for organisms to attempt to escape from and to avoid aversive stimulation. Humans possess complex processes for this latter purpose, such as decreasing the aversiveness of evaluations by denying that the evaluations are accurate. Aggressive responses are also frequently evoked in Ss who are aversively stimulated. These tendencies to avoid and or attack, which are aroused by the delivery of negative feedback, also probably become associated to the conveyor of feedback, the group setting and the group process in such a manner as to not facilitate the dispensation of information.

On the basis of such reasoning, Argyris (1968) and Bach in Chapter Seven, conclude that feedback should be minimally evaluative and maximally informative. Others have suggested that the threatening implications of negative evaluations may be reduced by very clear and specific delimitation of the behavior being identified, in order to prevent the receiver of feedback from overgeneralizing the implied criticism. Still others have speculated that the identification for the recipient of negative feedback of behavior which may be suitable for the replacement of the undesirable responses is also threat-reducing. Both hypotheses are plausible, but among the many interesting but unproven assertions which exist with regard to the manner in which feedback may be most effectively delivered.

On the other hand, aversive stimulation also has the property of inhibiting habitual responses, thereby making it more likely that individuals may display less habitual and hopefully more appropriate or effective behavior. It is also true that the escape from or avoidance of aversive stimulation is a powerful reinforcer, and therefore, provides high motivation for group members to replace disapproved-of responses by behavior which does not elicit group disapproval. Stoller (1968a) focuses on these functions of the discrepant feedback which individuals receive at the beginning of marathon groups.

The evidence which I will report in more detail later suggests rather strongly that the recipients of negative feedback report that it is less credible than positive feedback. It is not plausible that individuals will be affected as strongly by information of dubious credibility, and it would therefore seem appropriate to study strategies by which the credibility of negative feedback might be increased. The reproduction by mechanical devices of the behavior to which the feedback refers might increase its credibility. Other techniques of more accurate recording or measurement might serve a similar purpose.

We have also attempted to increase the credibility of feedback in our research by requiring those delivering feedback to select the information from a standard list of alternatives. Such a procedure allows the recipient to determine how much consensus exists among the group members regarding the existence of the behavior to which the feedback refers. Particularly when the deliverers of feedback are reporting their otherwise private reactions, where the authenticity is basically unverifiable, the issue of consensus may become more crucial than that of accuracy. Under such circumstances, the accuracy of the perceptions of the individual's behavior by other group members may not be of as much concern as the information to the feedback recipient that he is creating, by his behavior, some nomothetic consistency in private responses of others—for example, that he is boring *most* of his listeners. The problem may then be translated into whether or not the group member desires to have this effect on others. What behaviors might he employ to produce less of this response in others if he does not wish to have this effect, and how might he produce more desirable responses in group members? The same reasoning may be applied to an idiopathic private response aroused in a deliverer of feedback. The recipient of the feedback may here also need to determine whether he wishes to produce the described effect or some other in the feedback deliverer.

Very little systematic study has been devoted to the improvement of feedback delivery in group situations. In the next section I would like to examine some of the evidence which has been collected regarding the use of verbal feedback in groups.

VERBAL FEEDBACK IN GROUPS

There are two reviews which bring us up to date on the research on the use of feedback in T-groups. The first, by Dorothy Stock (1964), reports an early study by Lippit in which personal counseling interviews were used to communicate how individuals were perceived by the group members, and the ways in which they would like each other to change. This procedure produced more change than one in which members did not receive such feedback. Stock reviews a number of studies by Gibb, in one of which he concludes that feeling-oriented positive feedback results in the greatest efficiency, least defensiveness and the greatest spread in participation, and, in another, that role-playing plus feedback resulted in more change than either alone or neither. Stock also cites a study by Miles which reports findings which appear contradictory to those of Gibb—that strong negative feedback was most effective in inducing change. The Miles study used a small number of Ss.

Campbell & Dunnette in their review (1968) evaluate the research summarized by Stock as providing evidence that additional feedback, over and beyond what ordinarily occurs in the T-group, is valuable. Experimental procedures which introduce additional feedback into the T-group improved performance. Campbell & Dunnette draw the same conclusion from a more recent study by French, Sherwood & Bradford in which being rated on personality scales by all the group members, being told the results of the rating, and discussing it with other group members was compared to other experimental conditions which omitted discussion of the rating and feedback of the rating. The feedback and discussion conditions produced greater changes in the self-rating of the subjects than the other conditions. I am somewhat skeptical of the value of self-ratings of behavior change in such a situation where differential amounts of social pressure for changing, or perceiving oneself as changing may have been induced by experimental conditions.

Campbell & Dunnette are somewhat critical of the unpublished Gibb study which concludes that feeling-oriented positive feedback is superior, pointing out that the conclusions are derived somewhat indirectly and by implication from the results.

Campbell & Dunnette conclude, "It is imperative that the

relative contributions of the various technological elements in the T-group method be more fully understood . . . questions concerning the optimal procedures for giving feedback, for enhancing feelings of psychological safety, and for stimulating individuals to trying of behavior should also be investigated [p. 100]."

A number of more recent studies have attacked the problem of evaluating the effectiveness of feedback. Two studies by Kolb, Winter & Berlew, (1968) investigated the manner in which graduate students selected personal change goals and worked to achieve them during group meetings. Ss who were in groups where exchange of feedback about the progress towards the personal change goals was encouraged reported significantly more change than did Ss in groups where the projects were not discussed. A second experiment, in which all Ss were encouraged to discuss the projects, revealed that the amount of discussion of an individual's project during the second half of the semester was significantly related both to self-perceived change and to group leaders' ratings of change.

In a second paper Myers, Goldberg & Welch (1968) found that Ss in experimental groups who filled out sociometric questionnaires describing each other and received feedback on the ratings from other group members showed a significantly greater increase in sensitivity during a three-day period than control subjects who were not exposed to the sociometric procedure. However, as the authors point out, since raters in the experimental condition had an opportunity to see the ratings of others, it is conceivable that the significant reduction in discrepancy scores may be attributable to conformity to group norms.

A final study by Kolb & Boyatis (1970) is on the dynamics of the helping relationship. Effective helpers in the T-group situation were defined as those who attempt to help others where others saw this help as significant and important to them. Two comparison groups consisted of ineffective helpers (who attempt to give others help but these others do not regard the help as important), and nonhelpers (who do not attempt to help). The definitions were based on the number of times each member of the group had been mentioned as a giver of significant feedback, and on the total number of times the member indicated that he had given feedback to other group members. The highest and lowest *Ss* on each of these two dimensions were selected to construct the three groups.

The authors conclude that effective helpers are moderately motivated in terms of their need for achievement, power and affiliation, while ineffective helpers are high in power and achievement needs and low on need affiliation. When types of feedback given by effective and ineffective helpers were compared, the effective helpers gave more positive feedback and less negative feedback than the ineffective helpers. As the authors point out, they can conclude only that more positive feedback was heard from effective helpers.

It is difficult to dispute Campbell & Dunnette's low evaluation of the scope of our knowledge of these variables of feedback, which so many writers allege is one of the most important of group processes. Many information gaps exist with regard to the feedback process itself, and the characteristics of the deliverers and recipients.

Little is known of the effects of differing amounts or sequences of feedback. The language of delivery has been little studied and the most effective timing of delivery is not known. Whether differences exist between public versus anonymous delivery is also unknown.

As is evident from the literature reviewed, the research on feedback does not address itself to a number of other important issues. Among these are such questions as refer to the most effective ways to get people to give feedback to others in groups; how may one facilitate its accuracy or its reception? What are the relationships between feedback and the increases or decreases of the behavior associated with it? Very little, if any, research has been done on closing the feedback loop; that is, insuring that the feedback is received. Little analysis exists with regard to individual differences in resistance to feedback reception or the most effective ways to deal with such differences. The Kolb & Boyatis article quoted earlier has made a beginning in the identification of individuals who give effective feedback. There are undoubtedly other characteristics, such as the amount of individual attractiveness, the accuracy of previous feedback and role and status in the group, which should play a part. The amount of consensus among members giving the feedback may also be an important variable. The valence and the sequence of feedback are as we will show later, also important variables. Other interactions which lead to cohesiveness of the group may also affect the acceptance of feedback.

TECHNOLOGICAL ADVANCES IN FEEDBACK

Technological advances such as those of audio or videotape, which have been with us for some years, make it possible to rapidly provide auditory or visual reproductions to individuals of the behavior which they emit. However, a recent Bailey & Sowder review (1970) revealed that there existed little in the way of good empirical evaluations to review.

I am particularly surprised at the paucity of systematic study of the use of tape recorders, which have been easily available for at least 25 years. It has been common to use tape recordings in training or supervision of treatment sessions, although, in my own experience, it is more difficult to supervise group than individual interventions because of difficulty in maintaining the identification of group participants at first. The only systematic study Bailey & Sowder discuss on the use of audiotape feedback is the following recent study by Bailey himself.

Bailey (1970) studied three groups of prison inmates, one of which heard alternate audio replays of therapy sessions, a second, which met and was recorded the same number of times but did not hear the replays and a control group. No differences were observed in self-concept measures. Bailey reports that the patients in the replay group were more verbally productive during sessions than the nonreplay group but his statistics are inappropriate. He concludes that some patients may have improved and some deteriorated because of treatment, but presents no evidence on which to base his conclusion.

Interestingly enough, somewhat more research exists on the use of videotape, but much of it is poorly designed. In additon, of course, there exists a large amount of literature of a more anecdotal nature (Stoller, 1968b; Berger, 1970) on which the effectiveness of videotape feedback is alleged.

A study by Boyd & Sisney (1967) which reports a marked decrease in the pathology level of a group exposed to one videotape confrontation has a number of methodological problems which are pointed out by the authors themselves. More recently Danet (1969) studied two university student groups which met weekly for ten 50-minute sessions. The composition of two groups may not have been initially comparable. Ten-minute segments were extracted from a previous meeting for playback at the beginning of the following session to the E Ss. Frequency of participation data was interpreted by the author as revealing that the control group was a well defined group with a stable pattern of interactions whereas no pattern was apparent in the experimental group. Danet hypothesizes that the videotape playback provided in the study had a disrupting influence. Because of the small members of Ss, I find it difficult to separate this study from the anecdotal reports which fill the videotape literature. Braucht (1970), using elaborate measures of change in self-concept had patients who were involved in group therapy watch a videotape of preceding sessions, while a part of the group, serving as control, filled out ratings. Braucht found no increases in self esteem for experimental subjects, but significant increases in the variability of self-esteem scores of the subjects in the videotape treatment conditions. however, patients increased in the accuracy of their self perception after exposure to videotape recordings. Braucht further reports that patients who have been under hospital care the longest or who are psychotic, gain most from the videotape confrontation.

Robinson & Jacobs (1970) used Focused Videotape Feedback with groups of hospitalized patients. (In the Focused Feedback technique, the group leader selects for replay segments of videotape which contain reproductions of specific behaviors or interactions which he believes may be particularly meaningful for a specific group member or combination of members to observe. The leader replays the videotape, identifying for the viewer the specific aspects of the behavior towards which attention should be directed.) Videotape groups met in a feedback session immediately following each regular group therapy session. The cotherapist replayed videotaped excerpts from the group therapy session, and made positive or negative comments to the patients about the behavior which had been selected for viewing. Control groups were also videotaped, but the following session consisted of a discussion of the previous group therapy session by the therapist in which he also tried to deliver feedback without the use of the videotaped reproductions. The feedback comments of the therapist were tabulated, and raters rated the beginning and ending sessions of both groups for instances of the patient behavior referred to in the feedback. The videotape groups showed more of the adaptive behavior referred to in the therapist's feedback comments and less of the maladaptive behavior after exposure to the feedback than was the case for the control groups. However, a rating scale used by patients to estimate improvement in the behavior about which feedback had been given, showed no difference between the groups.

We have here another example of this very common finding which I have referred to in an earlier chapter, which is that self-report measures of improvement are often unrelated to ratings of improvement by others, or to other criteria of change. In this instance we have raters identifying significant increases in adjustive behavior, but no apparent awareness of changes in the self reports of the patients. I was surprised at the extent of resistance to the acceptance of this finding in some of my colleagues, who were so strongly committed to the position that insight must precede change, that they insisted that the change must be trivial if the patients had little or no awareness of it. It might have been more plausible for those suspicious of the results to argue that the patients may have been reluctant to admit changes which may have exposed them to the dangers of discharge from the hospital which was serving as a temporary refuge. A body of literature on impression management (Braginsky, Holzberg, Ridley and Braginsky, 1968) suggests that the "crazy behavior" of patients may serve such purposes. However, as has been shown in the previous chapter, most individuals do not keep accurate records on the frequency of much of their behavior, and that it is therefore quite plausible for behavior change to occur without much if any awareness. Certainly some of the maladaptive behavior changes of therapists and teachers towards particular group members are not accompanied by insight or awareness; otherwise such behavior would be less likely to occur.

Humm (1970) used immediate videotape replay in two groups of counseled high school students and two control groups of counseled students. Videotapes of the sessions were judged, using the Hill Interaction Matrix (see Chapter Thirteen), a group rating system. Relative changes in perceptions of self and others were measured by means of self rating scales. Problems of potential counselor bias, Hawthorne effects and biasing by loss of subjects for post-test are possible. However, in any case, the results suggested that videotape replay had no effect, or may even have made things worse.

A group of 48 administrators and counselors who volunteered as participants in a human relations training laboratory were assigned by Anderson, Hummel & Gibson (1970) to four T-groups which met for six three-hour sessions. Two groups were videotaped for the first half of three sessions, and observed and discussed a playback of selected portions of the videotape during the second half of the session. Criterion measures included a personality research questionnaire and three interpersonal questionnaires which were administered one week and again four months after the laboratory. The videotape excerpts which were played back were selected on the basis of significant periods of interaction, or lack of such, as flights from work. The data of 40 of the 48 Ss was available for analysis and revealed no significant differences for the videotape conditions. Clinical observations by the trainers were that the videotape did not elicit anxiety or hostility, but impatience for the interruption was observed.

Martin (1971) replayed random segments of videotapes of previous T-group sessions to three groups after five sessions were completed. He hypothesized that there would be decreases in the variance of group output if the videotape increased democratic and cooperative group interaction because everyone would have a more equal share of the time. This is a somewhat narrow definition of democracy. He did not find that group variances of verbal output decreased, and, in fact, a significant increase was observed in one group. He concludes that his results are consistent with earlier reports that videotape may have disrupting and negative effects on groups. Martin did not select sections of videotape that would have some particular effect on the group or its members. Neither did he point out to members what he was attempting to achieve, which may have weakened the effectiveness of the intervention. In modeling terms, he presented a model of what the group had been doing up to that point, and they followed the model—they even got better at it. The assumption that equal participation is desirable assumes that the amount of member participation previous to the introduction of videotape was undesirably disproportionate, whereas there is no basis presented for such an assumption.

The high level of interest and availability of videotape equipment will undoubtedly combine to produce a flood of videotape research in the near future. Two recent dissertations represent a sample of what may be to come.

Schloss (1969) composed four groups from freshman college student volunteers, and compared real-self and ideal-self descriptions (Ss are asked to order a set of standard statements in such a manner as to indicate which statements are most descriptive and which least descriptive of their actual behavior. The same technique is used by Ss to describe how they would like to be.) after eight weeks of counseling. A no-treatment control group was compared with a group required to listen to audiotaped playback of sessions, one required to view and hear videotape playbacks and a counselling group which did not receive playback. Although it is difficult to determine from the abstract, it sounds like the complete sessions were replayed, which could be quite boring. Discrepancies between ideal and real descriptions decreased only for the group which received only group counseling without feedback.

Such decreases in the discrepancy between one's ideal behavior and actual behavior are often used as criteria of improvement because the experimenters attribute the decrease to the lowering of unrealistic ideals as a consequence of greater self-acceptance, or to changes in one's actual behavior after treatment so that one's behavior more closely approximates the ideal. However, increased discrepancies between real and ideal behavior may also result from successful interventions, and may make an evaluation of the effectiveness of treatment difficult. Defensive individuals, for example, are likely to exaggerate the quality of their adjustment, so that the discrepancy between real and ideal before treatment is small. Increases in the discrepancy may reflect progress for such patients, and indicate that they have less need to deny or distort their shortcomings. Asocial individuals who internalize more culturally appropriate value-systems during treatment may also have larger discrepancies between real-self and ideal-self after successful treatment than before. Therefore, decreases in discrepancies for these last two classes of patients may reflect the fact that an intervention has made them more defensive, or supported their rationalizations about socially unacceptable behavior.

Miller (1969) compared immediate and delayed (two days after the session) audiotaped and videotaped counseling sessions to no-playback groups. Six *S*s drawn from a college freshman population composed each group. Videotape feedback decreased self-ideal discrepancies more than audio playback, or no playback. Nelson & Shardlow (1970) studied three groups of nine schizophrenic patients each. Two groups met for five months on a semiweekly schedule. The videotape group saw a playback each week of its earlier session, whereas the treatment group did not. A third group served as a no treatment control. Ratings by nurses and self reports on the MMPI measures of amount of psychiatric symptoms served as the major criteria. Two MMPI differences were reliable, but not interpretable in terms of superiority of the videotape treatment. Nurses ratings did not differentiate the treatments. The authors present a number of possible explanations for the lack of superiority of the videotape treatment.

The high acclaim videotape has received from practitioners has not been matched by the results of the experimental evaluations. I would tally the studies reviewed here as four which show positive results and six that show negative or no results. I think there are a number of possible explanations. The poor results achieved by some of the users of video-tape feedback may be caused by the manner in which the feedback was delivered to the participants. Stoller's (1968) suggestion that, for most groups, it is more effective to focus the videotape replay, is an excellent one. By focussed, Stoller means that segments should be purposefully rather than randomly selected for videotape replay, and that the therapist or trainer must identify for the participants those aspects of the behavior to which he wants the group or individual to attend and why. Individuals vary widely both in their ability to observe behavior, and in the categories for observation which are selected by them, as anyone who has tried to train observers of even simple behavior will testify. Therefore, the manipulator of the feedback has no basis to believe that observers will attend to that aspect which he wants to use to convey information, unless he clearly identifies the informational aspects.

The tactic of replaying the whole session is ordinarily a poor one. As its best it represents a boring or mildly aversive period of time, which may very well be frustrating to many participants in treatment. The tactic of replaying random segments of sessions, or even of selected segments at inappropriate times, it might be anticipated, could be disruptive, of ongoing important activities.

Less negative methods for the delivery of videotape feedback exist. In instant replay, for example, the leader or other participants ordinarily request a replay of a brief segment of the interaction recorded immediately prior to the request. Such feedback is usually much more relevant to what is going on in the group at the time, and, therefore also more interesting. However, a more general issue raised by some of these studies relates to whether one can do meaningful research on group interventions without some sophistication regarding the kinds of events which occur in groups, or without undertaking substantial pilot studies to "work out the bugs" in a study, or both.

Other studies selected poor criteria to demonstrate the effects of videotape feedback. I believe that the general self-concept criterion which has been used frequently to evaluate the effectiveness of videotape, represents a very natural but unfortunate choice for a number of reasons. Statistically, the use of discrepancy scores is undesirable because of the contributions of the unreliability of both measures to the difference score. I have earlier discussed the overly simplistic notion that decreases in discrepancies between real and ideal self concept are necessarily a criterion of the effectiveness of treatment. In addition, I believe that the kinds of behaviors which are most useful to identify by videotape feedback are rather specific, visible and frequency of nonverbal aspects of interaction, which may not be related to the more general self-concept categories.

Since Ss do not usually keep accurate tallies of such behaviors, it is ordinarily difficult for them to report changes in frequencies, no less to relate combinations of such changes to general self-perceptions. Margo Robinson and myself (Robinson & Jacobs, 1966) did a study of self-concept changes as a function of videotape feedback with hospitalized schizophrenic patients as a pilot before the study reported earlier in this chapter, and found no results, which may also explain my bias. We then worked out the technique we used in the second study, that of deriving our criteria of change from that behavior of patients which was identified in the feedback. This seemed to us to make more sense, because there would be no particular reason to expect that videotape feedback would change unidentified pathology.

A third set of problems is related to the control groups used in videotape playback research and the questions presented by various selections of control groups. Although I agree in general with Bailey and Sowder's (1970) assertion that it is essential to eventually determine whether videotape playback treatment is superior to no treatment, I believe enough evidence has accumulated to suggest that there do exist group treatments which are reliably effective in reducing subjective distress (for example, see preceding chapters). The demonstration that videotape feedback is superior to a proven method is a legitimate enterprise. However, whether one hour of treatment plus one hour of videotape playback is superior to two hours of treatment, which is the design of several studies reported earlier, is another question, and perhaps a different one from comparing one hour of treatment plus one of videotape playback to one hour of treatment and one of feedback in another modality.

Perhaps a more meaningful answer can be obtained by selecting a specific category of behavior, aggression, for example, and a specific treatment (Bach's fight training, as described in Chapter Seven), and determining whether replaying videotape excerpts is more beneficial than not, using appropriate criteria for change. Analogue studies may also be useful in attempting to explore the value of videotape playback, again because one is able to direct analogue studies more specifically. Using naturalistic studies, such as typical agency service delivery system evaluations, to attempt to establish validity for videotape playback is an extremely ambitious undertaking. Group intervention research poses tremendous difficulties of potential trainer bias, rater bias and the necessity for using groups within treatment designs with several groups assigned to each condition in order to attempt to randomize some of these effects. To add the potential Hawthorne effect of videotape on participants, trainers, and raters, by which I mean to indicate the increase in expectation of success when any new and dramatic element is introduced into an intervention, perhaps complicates naturalistic group research beyond accomplishment.

Other technological improvements such as the small portable

instruments for measuring and transmitting displays of internal ordinarily less controllable responses—for example, heart rate, blood pressure or amount of perspiration—may also eventually play a role in increasing the amount of information available to patients in groups, and add to the nonverbal feedback and information which is available.

SEQUENCE AND VALENCE OF FEEDBACK RESEARCH

I would like to describe in this concluding section some of our research here at West Virginia University on group processes where we have been particularly concerned with the effects or order of delivery sequence of positive and negative feedback. Todd Schaible (Schaible, 1970; Schaible & Jacobs, 1971a) studied the effect of sequence and valence of feedback on whether *S*s believed the feedback, whether they found it desirable and whether the feedback increased their liking for other group members and the group meetings. Schaible hypothesized from the writings of the self theorists (Rogers, 1951) that individuals are more receptive to positive self enhancement than to information or feedback which threatens the self-image, and from the cognitive dissonance theorists that individuals will be predisposed to ward off information which would disconfirm a positive conception of the self. Schaible conducted an experimental paradigm of a group feedback situation under the guise of a further standardization of a personality test.

*S*s were formed in four member groups and were presented with pseudofeedback which consisted of two adjectives purported to be the results of the previously taken personality questionnaire. The pseudo-feedback items consisted of descriptive adjectives like intelligent, uncooperative, farsighted and scheming. The feedback given was identical for all *S*s within the group, and had no relationship to the actual results achieved on the personality questionnaire. The true results achieved on the tests were conveyed to *S*s at the close of the hour-long session. The ordering of the presentation of positive and negative feedback was varied in different groups. Four groups were formed. Initial positive feedback was followed either by further positive or negative feedback in two groups; initial negative feedback was followed by further negative feedback or positive feedback in the second two groups. The social desirability value of feedback items had been determined by previous pilot studies. Two levels of intensity of social desirability were composed for both negative and positive feedback items, which were designated as weak or strong feedback.

The dependent measures consisted of self-reports of believability as accurate, desirability of feedback and of feelings of group cohesiveness, and were analyzed by means of analysis of variance techniques. Schaible's results suggest that both strong and weak initial positive feedback were responded to as more acceptable and desirable than when negative feedback was given. The effect was most marked for the strong positive and strong negative feedback. He also found that weak positive and weak negative second feedback were more readily endorsed as acceptable and desirable when preceeded by positive initial feedback than by negative. Weak positive initial feedback increased the acceptability-desirability of strong positive and strong negative second feedback at almost significant levels. Measurements of group cohesion showed that a significantly greater number of Ss who received positive initial feedback had developed strong feelings of cohesiveness, compared to those who had received negative initial feedback.

We then decided that we would try to check out Schaible's results in a sensitivity training laboratory situation (Jacobs, Jacobs, Gatz, & Schaible, 1973). The Ss were 45 student volunteers from a class in personality. Twelve graduate students in clinical psychology served as trainers in a very tightly scheduled laboratory program. The design of the program forced the participants to interact in typical group exercises. Following each exercise, participants had an opportunity to give each other feedback. The first feedback session followed NASA, a group problem-solving activity (Pfeiffer & Jones, 1969). Each group member was required to rate each of the other group members from a list of 20 behavioral descriptions of individual functions in a group of the type suggested by Morton (1967) (e.g., acting bossy, offering positive opinions). The second feedback occasion was designed around an exercise constructed by the authors where group members had to ask each other and answer intimate questions concerning their self-perceptions and personal beliefs on several controversial issues. Members were then required to rate other members on a list of descriptions based on suggestions from Gordman (1969) including the amount of empathy and warmth displayed by each group member.

Three conditions were set up. In the first condition, Ss used the descriptions on the first list to give each other two items of positive feedback and the second list to give each other two items of negative. The negative feedback was defined as identifying to the recipient two items of behavior on which the transmitter of the feedback believed that the recipient would benefit from improvement in the identified attributes. Positive feedback was defined as outstanding or especially good behaviors. In the second condition, the first list was used for negative feedback, and the second list for positive, and in a third condition, one positive and one negative feedback item was given after each exercise.

We thereby confounded feedback conditions with both time at which feedback was administered and with the differences in the two lists. We have since checked the average social desirability values of items in both lists and found no reliable differences between them.

The feedback delivery was massed in a manner somewhat similar to the strength bombardment exercise used in training laboratories. That is, each individual received feedback consecutively from all the members of his subgroup. We split up each group into two subgroups for feedback in order to save time, to avoid adaptation by recipients to the feedback and to reduce boredom in the group.

We had a "dry run" with the trainers in which they served as group members and practiced with the materials before undertaking the actual experimental mental laboratory with students. I would like to make some incidental observations based on watching the trainers go through this dry run laboratory, and using such exercises with a number of other populations since then. The first is that the process of organizing the feedback to one individual with the bombardment technique makes certain aspects of the feedback process very salient. It highlights the difficulties encountered by most people when they are required to deliver negative feedback. Qualifications, denials and attempts to dilute the negative feedback were very apparent in this group of trainers. The negative feedback seemed to far outweigh the positive and created a high level of tension, even though half of the group members were quite sophisticated in group process, and insisted that this was only a rehearsal. When giving mixed feedback most individuals try to preface their negative feedback with positive. Also we observed what seemed to be a curvilinear or adaptation effect. The painful impact of negative feedback, particularly when members agree on the nature of the feedback, seems to reach its peak after three or four repetitions and then becomes less noxious. The positive feedback seemed to affect the trainers less, seemed to lack authenticity and, as one of the group members put it, "sounded like reading a graduation book."

From eyeballing the responses on the affect adjective checklist filled out by the trainers, it seemed that those trainers who were most profoundly affected emotionally by the feedback had received and remembered at least one very negative feedback item which they believed to be accurate. However, it seemed clear from examining the responses of the trainers to the Jacobs adjective checklist, that this artificial and practice situation had aroused intensive emotional reaction in all, for all the frequent references by the trainers to the artificiality of the situation and the feedback. The overall rating of the value of the dry-run laboratory by the trainers was substantially lower than that of any of the laboratory groups we later ran, and those trainers who had had the least amount of experience in groups seemed to feel that they got the most out of the dry run laboratory. Previous group experience may be an important determinant of laboratory evaluation, and what appears to the experienced trainers as unprofitable for themselves may be evaluated as quite profitable by those without previous laboratory experience. The trainers were frustrated and complained about the amount of structure; the student laboratory participants complained, but to a lesser degree, about having too many forms to fill out. Participants giving positive feedback complained less about forms and structure than those giving negative feedback. It is of interest to note that both the trainers in their practice session and the student participants assigned substantial value to the laboratory experience on an evaluation form in spite of the complaints.

To get on to the analysis of the laboratory data, an affect adjective checklist (Jacobs, 1971) was given after each occasion on which feedback was delivered to group members. It was clear that the negative or positive value of the feedback had a statistically profound effect on the emotional reactions of participants. Feelings of well-being were much higher after positive tha fter negative feedback, with the reactions to the mixed feedback condition being intermediate. Lack of energy ratings occurred in a pattern which was opposite to that shown for feelings of well-being. Reports of lack of energy were higher after negative and lower after positive feedback. Anxiety appeared to be more severe following negative feedback, particularly when negative feedback was given first. The pattern for reports of depression was similar to that observed for reports of anxiety.

As we had found in Schaible's study, positive feedback was rated by Ss as much more credible and desirable than the negative feedback. However, contrary to the results of Schaible's study, Ss to whom negative feedback was delivered first and positive feedback second reported that the feedback, on the average, was more acceptable and desirable as compared with Ss in the other two conditions. Ratings of group cohesiveness also increased most in the negative feedback first, positive feedback second condition, although the results are not as significant as one might desire. Ratings of amount of group cohesiveness decreased over the day for Ss in the remaining two conditions. Ss receiving a positive and negative feedback sequence or a negative and positive feedback sequence reported at the end of the day that the laboratory had been significantly more valuable to them than Ss to whom mixed feedback was delivered on both occasions. A content analysis format from Schein & Bennis (1967) that I adapted for self-report was used to measure laboratory value. Although there were two groups of Ss in each condition, none of the differences between these groups in all the analyses were significant. Neither were overall ratings of trainers by Ss significantly different for any conditions or groups at the end of the day. The importance of trainer and group uniqueness-variables in highly structured laboratory sessions may be somewhat overestimated generally. I might add, parenthetically, to illustrate one of the difficulties of studying laboratory training, that we estimated the cost of planning and conducting the research if all participants had been paid typical hourly rates, at over $10,000.

To summarize our findings with respect to order and valence of feedback, we found that when we moved from the test tube into the factory, the results were reversed from those obtained in the first Schaible study. However, as in the previous study, recipients of feedback of negative or critical nature rated it as less credible and less desirable than feedback describing positive social attributes. This phenomenon, which we have named "the credibility gap," we now have evidence is a highly consistent and reliable phenomenon. As our later studies show, positive feedback is rated as more credible and desirable than negative feedback when the feedback is selected by the deliverer from a variety of different lists of descriptions; whether the feedback consists of statements describing the emotions of the deliverer, the behavior of the recipient or a mixture of both; when the feedback is delivered by all the group members, or one group member or the group leader; when the feedback is delivered publicly as in a confrontation, or anonymously; when the feedback is not derived from a list at all but constructed spontaneously by the deliverer and when the deliverers and recipients of unstructured feedback consist of individuals who know each other only briefly (one hour) as well as when the deliverers and recipients of unstructured feedback have worked together intensively for six weeks as members of a group treatment team in group psychotherapy.

The significantly opposite results we had obtained in two studies which examined the effects on credibility of delivering different sequences of positive and negative feedback led us to design a third study (Schaible & Jacobs, b, submitted for publication). We again recruited undergraduate volunteers for a group experience, and exposed them to two exercises designed to generate information about each other. In this case, the one exercise required the group members to arrive at a consensus with respect to controversial issues, and the second exercise required the group members to arrive at a consensus where insufficient evidence was provided to reach a decision. Group members selected two items of feedback from lists of behavioral descriptions, balanced for social desirability ratings, to deliver to one other member. The feedback was designed to identify behavior either enhancing (positive feedback) or hindering (negative feedback) the recipients' interpersonal effectiveness. In one condition group members selected two items of positive feedback to be delivered after the first consensus exercise to one other group member, and two items of negative feedback to be delivered after the second consensus exercise to the same group member; whereas, the order was reversed in the second condition. Two other conditions of feedback delivery were included in the experimental design in order to determine whether feedback delivered at the beginning of the experiment was rated differently by recipients than feedback delivered after a longer period of group interaction. In the first of these additional conditions, group members selected two items of positive feedback describing one other group member after the first exercise but did not deliver them; however, they did deliver two items of negative feedback to the same group member after the second exercise. In the last condition, Ss selected two items of negative feedback after the first exercise but did not deliver them, and then selected two items of positive feedback after the second exercise and delivered them. Schaible's original results with respect to the superiority of delivering positive feedback before negative were corroborated in the second study.

We again found strong evidence for "the credibility gap." We also again found a sequence effect. Negative feedback was rated by participants as significantly more credible and desirable when it followed positive feedback than when it preceded it; and positive feedback was rated as less credible and less desirable when it followed negative feedback than when it preceded it. However, we also found that the negative feedback delivered after the second consensus exercise (which had not been preceeded by the delivery of other feedback) received essentially similar ratings of credibility and desirability to the negative feedback delivered earlier in the session as first feedback after the first consensus exercise. A similar relationship was observed between the ratings of positive feedback delivered as first feedback later in the experimental session when compared with positive feedback given as first feedback earlier in the session. In other words, the ratings of positive and negative feedback delivered after one half hour of interaction were very similar to the ratings obtained after over an hour of interaction. We also found the positive-negative sequence to lead to significantly higher ratings of group cohesiveness among group members than the reverse sequence, as Schaible had reported in the first study.

We have some hunches to account for the differences between these three sequence studies. The Jacobs, Jacobs, Gatz & Schaible study was designed to simulate the flow of events which might occur in an actual group treatment situation. Ss started with a warmup exercise, proceeded to a relatively neutral consensus exercise and then to a self-disclosure exercise which involved more risk-taking as well as the delivery to Ss of more affectively toned feedback. Negative emotional feedback is rated by its recipients as the least credible and the least desirable feedback, as some of our research which will be referred to later discloses. An examination of the results of the Jacobs, Jacobs, Gatz & Schaible study shows that the inferiority of the positive-negative sequence of valence to the negative-positive sequence is attributable primarily to the decrease in the credibility and desirability of the ratings of negative affective feedback delivered after the self-disclosure exercise. In contrast, the differences in credibility and desirability ratings of the second feedback in Schaible and Jacobs (b) which used less affective exercises and feedback lists, are very small and nonsignificant. On the other hand, the largest differences in credibility and desirability ratings between positive and negative feedback in Schaible & Jacobs (1970) and Schaible & Jacobs (1970a) occur on the occasion of the delivery of first feedback, where Ss rated all the feedback delivered, whereas these differences are minimal in Jacobs, Jacobs, Gatz & Schaible, where Ss selected two items for rating from the pool of feedback delivered to them. We are suspicious that these differences in the methodology may partially account for the disparity in the results of three studies.

In summary, two of the three V-O studies on valence and order of feedback suggest that the believability or accuracy of verbal feedback delivered in group situations is significantly enhanced if the positive feedback is delivered before the negative. In addition, feedback that would be ordinarily rated as highly undesirable becomes less undesirable when preceded by positive feedback, and feedback that would ordinarily be rated as highly desirable becomes somewhat less desirable when preceded by negative feedback.

These results are predictable from dissonance or balance theories in social psychology. Such theories suggest that when the recipient rates positive feedback as credible, he is simultaneously defining the deliverer as a reliable source of this desirable information. Dissonance, or conflict, is aroused in the recipient when the same source subsequently delivers undesirable information or negative feedback, since if the recipient were to completely reject this undesirable information as true, the recipient would also have to question the accuracy of the observer who had previously delivered desirable or flattering information. Our data suggests that the recipient compromises, and decides that the negative feedback is not really so bad, and its deliverer not nearly so inaccurate, as might have been the case if the negative feedback had not been previously preceded by positive. A similar train of reasoning can be followed to explain the effect of first delivering negative feedback, and then positive.

Both Schaible and Jacobs' studies also suggest that participants rate group cohesiveness as significantly higher if the order of delivery of feedback is positive valenced feedback-first. Cohesiveness has been asserted by a number of sources to be an important attribute of groups, because it has been shown to be related to improved attendance, to the ability of members to influence each other, and to other desirable characteristics of groups designed to change behavior. If our results are generalizable to such longer and more complex attempts to change the behavior of individuals by group intervention techniques as psychotherapy and growth groups, one might speculate that setting ground rules which limited early feedback between group members to statements of positive valence, or encouraged members to deliver such statements to each other, would increase the attraction between group members as well as facilitating the acceptance of later feedback.

The Jacobs, Jacobs, Gatz & Schaible (1973), on the other hand, suggests to us that there may be combinations of group experiences, procedures and/or types of negative feedback, which have such a profound influence as to overpower the advantages in facilitating group processes gained by the initial delivery of positive feedback.

These three quasi-naturalistic studies discussed so far also raise some general issues regarding research and intervention, to which we may attend at this point. We believe that we have developed a viable technology for the study of social interaction in groups. The major elements of this technology consist of the use of volunteer college students, who are curious about group process, and motivated towards self-knowledge, the use of series of structured exercises to facilitate rapidity of involvement, control over the effect of Ss on each other by the use of group instructions and structured materials which constrain the response repertoire of Ss, simple but effective self-report rating scales to measure responses of the Ss. Participants become highly involved over the first two hours of the experience, and our data suggests that the feedback the Ss deliver, although derived from items on lists, is responded to by recipients as highly accurate. The average accuracy ratings for positive feedback in most of our studies are greater than 7 on a 9-point scale, and over 70 percent of the ratings are 7, 8 and 9. Even for the negative feedback, which is ordinarily rated as less accurate, the average rating is about at the midpoint of the scale, or between 4 and 5. Participants respond to a laboratory evaluation scale, administered at the end of the session, in such a manner as to make us believe that Ss perceive substantial change in themselves on a wide variety of items. Large amounts of data can be collected in relatively brief periods of time, and evidence can be accumulated with regard to a wide scope of questions. Psychological research in the past has often followed a development of instruments and technologies; for example, the pattern analysis studies on the WAIS after World War II, the large output of MMPI studies after its publication, the increase in studies on desensitization after the development of the Lang and Lazowick technology.

The second issue which I would like to raise at this point refers to whether these microlabs have value as techniques of intervention. I have recently started to believe that even the one-or two-hour microlab is a useful vehicle for social learning. Students who are involved in microlabs see them as valuable, according to our studies. I have had personal learning experiences about myself and others in these brief microlabs which made a more profound impression on me than similar periods of exposure to traditional classes or traditional individual or group psychotherapy. However, it is my impression that there may be points of diminishing return in these short episodes of experiential learning to individuals who have already had large amounts of T-group or sensitivity-group experience, although even our advanced graduate students in dry runs, conducted to familiarize trainees with the exercises to be used, often react to microlabs as real experiences, rather than as going through the motions.

Our successes in the study of feedback by means of the technology we had developed encouraged us to design another series of studies on feedback. These new studies were more concerned with valence and type of feedback (the V-T studies) as contrasted to the ones we have already described, which fall into the class of valence-order studies or V-O studies, and also to explore other criterion variables in the situation.

We used generally similar procedures as in previous studies, consisting of combinations of warmup exercises to stimulate interaction, consensus exercises where groups had to come to agreement on complex decisions and self-disclosure exercises to encourage risk-taking and to make available to participants other varieties of information about each other. Participants selected items of feedback from lists made available to them which constrained the valence and type of feedback that they were able to deliver to each other, after the conclusion of these exercises, and each member, in turn, was the recipient of the feedback delivered to him by all of the group members. Each recipient, as he received feedback from each person, rated the item on nine-point scales for its accuracy, its desirability and what we called *impact,* that is, whether the feedback affected him weakly or strongly. More complex measurement of group cohesion and lab evaluation were also obtained from Ss, as in the previous studies.

Three types of feedback were examined in the first study (Jacobs, Jacobs, Cavior & Feldman, in press). The first type of feedback we called behavioral, and the category consisted of descriptions of the behavior of recipients. Positive behavioral feedback consisted of good or outstanding behaviors of the recipients such as behaving in a friendly manner or being attentive, and negative behavioral feedback consisted of behaviors which the deliverer thought the recipient should improve, for example, if he were unattentive or unfriendly. Emotional feedback consisted of the delivery of a statement describing the feelings of the deliverer about the recipient. Positive emotional statements included those such as "I like you" or "I was pleased," and negative statements would consist of selections from a list including such alternatives as displeased or disliked. Each of the lists consisted of 14 items, and the lists of negatively valenced items were antonyms of the positively valenced items. A third type of feedback was a combination of behavioral and emotional, which, in the case of positive feedback, consisted of such statements as "You were attentive" and "I liked you"; in the case of negative emotional feedback, "You were inattentive" and "I was displeased."

Each *S* delivered two items of feedback to each of the other group members. The feedback consisted of either of two emotional items (pure emotional feedback), two behavioral items (pure behavioral feedback) or one of each (mixed behavioral emotional feedback) and where the valence and type of the feedback was controlled by the lists available so that each individual received all positive or all negative items identical in type to that recieved by other members of his group. This procedure resulted in six experimental conditions, and, in view of the fact that our previous research had not shown very much difference between groups assigned to the same condition or evaluations of different trainers, we assigned one group of eight subjects to each condition.

Again we found valence to be a highly significant determinant, with the positive feedback being more believable than the negative. We found the valence-by-type relationship also to be highly significant. Emotional feedback was the most believable type of feedback when it was positive (I like you); and the least believable of all kinds of feedback when it was negative (I dislike you). We found an interesting mirrorlike effect with positive behavioral emotional feedback being next most believable, and pure positive behavioral feedback being next in credibility. Therefore, all feedback of positive valence was superior to all feedback of negative valence, regardless of type. The most believable of the negatively valenced feedback was the pure behavioral, next the negative behavioral emotional and poorest, as has been mentioned before, the pure emotional feedback. Therefore, in terms of the two items of feedback delivered, the order of credibility was positive EE, positive BE, positive BB, negative BB, negative BE, and negative EE.

A further analysis of these credibility scores revealed to us what we called a potentiating effect. That is, we compared statistically, the believability of pure and mixed emotional feedback, and of pure and mixed behavioral feedback. We found that the behavioral feedback in the mixed positive behavioral emotional condition was more believable than pure behavioral feedback, and that the behavioral feedback in the mixed negative condition was less believable than the pure negative behavioral feedback, whereas we found no significant differences between the emotional component of mixed feedback and of pure feedback. The addition of a positive emotional reaction (I like you) to a positive behavioral observation (You are attentive) increases the believability of the behavioral item. On the other hand, coupling a negative emotional observation (I dislike you) with a negative behavioral observation (You are inattentive) decreased the believability of the negative behavioral feedback. These results led us to the conclusion that we had discovered a potentially powerful lever for modifying the credibility of feedback.

We also found in this first VT study that positive feedback was responded to as significantly more desirable than negative, as effecting individuals significantly more strongly than negative and as leading to significantly greater amounts of feelings of group cohesiveness than negative. Clearly our data suggest that, in the absence of other considerations, positive feedback has marked advantages over negative. The type of feedback was also a significant determiner of various kinds of ratings by the participants. Behavioral feedback was reacted to as having more effect on Ss than either behavioral emotional or pure emotional. Pure emotional and pure behavioral feedback lead to significantly greater amounts of group cohesiveness than mixed feedback, and Ssreceiving pure behavioral feedback evaluated the laboratory as substantially and significantly more valuable than those receiving the other two types of feedback. Therefore, behavioral feedback has advantages over the other two varieties, and pure feedback tends to be more effective than mixed feedback.

The second of our valence-type studies (Jacobs, Jacobs, Cavior & Burke, in press) of feedback is identical in procedure to the previous study except that the feedback was delivered anonymously instead of publicly. It is common practice when evaluative information is delivered by individuals to others that the identity of the deliverer is not revealed. Evaluations of faculty by students, or articles by journal reviewers, adhere to this practice. It is argued that evaluators are uncomfortable about delivering negative information to others, and there is as a matter of fact information to support this contention (Tesser, Rosen & Tesser, 1971). It may, therefore, facilitate the delivery of negative feedback for the deliverer to be anonymous. Does it also facilitate the acceptance of feedback?

The delivery of feedback in groups is ordinarily open and confrontative. As we have shown in the previous study, under such circumstances positive emotional feedback, which refers to the feelings of the deliverer, is more believable than positive behavioral feedback, and negative emotional feedback is less believable than negative behavioral feedback. There is no reason intrinsic to the information contained in such categories of statements which we have classified as emotional that should lead the recipients to rate emotional information as more or less accurate than evaluative statements of observers regarding the social competence of the individual's interactions with others in the group (behavioral feedback). If anything, observations regarding his behavior may be more useful to the recipient than statements of the emotional responses of others, since his own behavior may be more amenable to change than the emotional reactions of others.

Our earlier discussion of the Jacobs, Jacobs, Gatz & Schaible data presents support for the existence of emotional responses to the reception of feedback. We suspect that these emotional reactions, in combination with the informative component of feedback, mediate the ratings of accuracy. If the intensity of the emotional reaction mediating the accuracy responses has most to do with being liked or disliked by others, it is plausible to expect that the emotional reaction will be most intense in such situations where the deliverer visibly and identifiably emits the stimulus, and less so in situations where he does not emit the stimulus visibly or identifiably. What we are suggesting is that the anonymous delivery of feedback may detoxify it from some of its negative emotional qualities, and perhaps its positive emotional effect as well.

In the second study, therefore, group members, after going through the same procedures of interaction, selected the feedback for the other participants without knowledge that they would not deliver it, in order to insure that the feedback to be selected was similar in the two studies. The group member then passed the feedback selections to the group leader, who delivered all of the feedback from the group in a standard manner to each group member in turn. The criterion measures were ratings identical to those used in the first study.

However, the anonymous delivery of feedback did not affect the relationship between valence and credibility. The positive feedback was still rated as more accurate than the negative. Positive feedback was also rated as significantly more desirable, and was reacted to significantly more strongly than was the negative.

The anonymous delivery of feedback, on the other hand, did lead to different results with respect to the valence-by-type interaction in the credibility ratings, as compared to public feedback delivery. Significant differences in credibility ratings are produced again by the six experimental conditions, as in the previous study. The order from most to least believable of the feedback is now pure positive behavioral, mixed positive behavioral emotional, pure positive emotional, pure negative emotional, pure behavioral negative and finally mixed negative behavioral emotional. Therefore, the pure emotional feedback, which was the most believable of the positive types of feedback when delivered publicly, now becomes the least believable of positive feedback, and the pure negative emotional feedback, which was the least believable of negative feedbacks when delivered publicly, becomes the most believable negative feedback. The differences between positive and negative emotional feedback are no longer significant.

The anonymous delivery of feedback appears also to dissipate the significance of the relationship between valence and cohesiveness, and type of feedback and cohesiveness, observed under conditions of public delivery. Instead, the type-by-valence interaction becomes significant with positive emotional feedback leading to the most group cohesiveness, but also with positive feedback being in general related to more cohesiveness than negative feedback. Finally, Ss receiving behavioral feedback still rate the laboratory experience as significantly and substantially more valuable than those receiving the two other kinds of feedback.

Thus in both these V-T studies, positively valenced feedback is more believable, more desirable and of greater impact than negatively valenced, and behavioral feedback is rated as more effective than mixed or emotional. However, feedback consisting of the feelings of the deliverer are modified considerably with regard to believability by knowledge or lack of knowledge of the deliverers' identity. Group cohesiveness also seems to be affected in a rather complex manner by knowledge of the deliverer, except that positive emotional feedback is still an important ingredient in the feelings of members about each other.

A third type-study (Feldman, in preparation) follows from the results of the previous two studies, in which the data suggest that the believability of behavioral information may be modified by pairing it with statements referreing to the emotional reaction of the deliverer. In addition, some of our exploration of operant styles of intervention with children had led us to suspect that substantial behavior change can be accomplished by reinforcing or delivering social approval for socially desirable behavior, even though such behaviors occurred infrequently, rather than treating socially undesirable alternatives aversively. Feldman attempted to use both of these principles to increase the credibility of feedback. He paired behavioral feedback with positive emotional feedback and also identified the occurrence of the desirable behavior rather than commenting on its absence.

In the Feldman study, volunteers went through an hour of exercises similar to those described earlier, then selected feedback from lists of statements designed to identify behavior categories in which the recipient might improve. In one condition, deliverers selected items from what was called a negative behavior list consisting of items such as "I think you appeared unwilling to accept information." The second list was called a conditional positive emotional behavior list and consisted of a positive statement paired with an identification of the behavior to be increased, such as "I like it when you appear willing to accept information."

We were also interested in studying delivery style, and therefore feedback was delivered in either an affective manner, in which the deliverer walked up to the subject, looked him in the eye, etc., or an objective manner in which he remained in his seat, avoided eye contact, etc. The design of the study included two conditions of delivery style, affective or objective, as well as two types of feedback, negative behavioral or conditional positive emotional behavioral. Several groups of Ss were assigned to each of the four sets of experimental variations generated by the design.

Several additional criterion ratings were included, in addition to the ones described earlier. The feedback selectors rated the difficulty of selection of each item, and the recipients rated their intention to change or modify the behavior identified. Ss also rated the warmth of the trainer-deliverers.

Highly significant results were again obtained. The conditional positive emotional behavioral feedback was rated as significantly more credible, significantly more desirable, having significantly greater impact and leading to significantly greater intention to change behavior. All these results were significantly beyond the .0001 level. The negative behavioral feedback also led to significantly less cohesion, and to a significantly poorer evaluation of the laboratory experience. However, the differences in delivery style did not lead to any significant differences in the criterion variables, although the participants rated the affective deliverers as significantly more warm.

At this point it seems clear to us that the delivery of information in groups is powerfully affected by whether the information is positive or negative. Positive information is almost inevitably rated as more accurate, having more impact, being more desirable and leading to more group cohesiveness. When it precedes negative information it seems more likely to make the negative information more believable, more desirable and giving rise to greater group cohesiveness than when the reverse sequence occurs. Positive and negative emotional information referring to the feelings of the deliverer appear to be particularly powerful when delivered publicly, give rise to extreme ratings of believability and even seem to have the power to increase the believability of behavioral feedback when associated with it. Positive emotional feedback seems to be particularly strongly associated with ratings of group cohesiveness. However, Ss to whom behavioral feedback is delivered in groups, report that the groups are more valuable than when other types of feedback are delivered. Finally, information feedback statements can be constructed regarding behavior to be improved, consisting of pairs of positive emotional statements and identification of instances of the desirable behavior. Such statements are more easily selected for delivery, and lead as well to ratings of greater believability, desirability, impact and intention to change as compared with the delivery of descriptions of the undesirable behavior.

Four additional studies have been planned at this point. Some are simple mopup studies, and others emphasize the exploration of new areas within the context of the same technology. For example, one is a study which examines valence, order and type in one design. A second study plans to examine some of the hunches we have about the differences between our three studies of valence and order. A third study plans to use unstructured feedback delivery to construct structured lists for the study of the effect of valence on some of the criterion measures, in order to determine if the delivery of structured feedback is any different than that of unstructured. A final study plans to explore the valence dimension, using Leary's categories of response identification, in order to further refine the positive and negative dimension, and in addition, to explore the relationship which may exist between the type of feedback delivered to individuals and the type of feedback the recipient delivers back in return. Clearly there are a multitude of unexplored variables. We have done little so far with trainer style, with content of group exercises and with the length of groups, and although we have collected considerable data on the delivery and reception of feedback with respect to attractiveness of deliverer and recipient, and also personality measures, we have not yet analyzed most of this material.

Let me refer to two other studies of information delivery to individuals which we completed some time ago, in order to illustrate some of the complexities of the feedback problem. The first (Jacobs & Maas, 1969) required college students who had requested educational counseling to estimate their standing on tests of aptitude before and after their actual performances on such tests were reported to them. Those students who had underestimated their performance (in other words, were informed that they were more competent than they had suspected) increased their estimates of ability more on the post-test than those who had overestimated their ability lowered their estimates on the post-tests. Such results seem to be corroborative of those we obtain when we examine positive and negative feedback in groups.

In a second study (Jacobs & Deacon, 1969), we reported back to diabetic patients whether their responses to items of information about self care were incorrect or correct. Psychologists generally believe that telling individuals that they are incorrect arouses a negative or aversive state, and we expected that the Ss in our study would not learn the correct answers to the initially incorrect items as well as to the initially correct ones. We did not find this to be the case. Although our feedback technique was highly superior to ordinary hospital methods of teaching self-care, patients learned the correct answers as well when their initial answer was incorrect as when it was correct. It is clear from this second study that being told that you are incorrect, or have a deficiency of information, is sometimes not as important to the feedback recipient as the opportunity to correct the situation.

CONCLUSION

In conclusion, a number of authors contend that feedback is a very important mechanism by means of which groups modify the behavior of group members. Feedback contains both informational and motivational attributes. The motivational aspects of negative feedback may sometimes interfere with the reception of its informational components.

The research on verbal feedback suggests that experimental operations which provide for more feedback exchange among members than ordinarily occurs spontaneously in groups will lead to superior outcomes. Evidence with regard to a number of important dimensions of feedback delivery and reception is meager and sometimes contradictory.

There has been surprisingly little research on the use of the mechanical reproduction of verbal behavior for the purposes of providing feedback. However, a rapidly growing literature is appearing with regard to the use of visual reproduction of behavior to provide feedback. The majority of the evaluations of videotape feedback, which have been published recently, do not support its effectiveness, and some writers even speculate that videotape feedback may be disruptive to the achievement of group objectives. It should be noted, however, that some of these studies have been poorly designed and have used criteria of effectiveness whose appropriateness is disputable. In other studies, the technique of videotape feedback used is unsophisticated and could understandably arouse boredom or frustration. It seems reasonable to wait for further evidence for a fair evaluation of videotape feedback as an intervention technique.

Our own research on the valence and order, and valence and type, of feedback has yielded promising results. The "credibility gap"—that Ss rate positive feedback as more accurate than negative—seems to be a very general phenomenon. Positive feedback also seems generally to be rated by its recipients as more desirable, as affecting them more and perhaps as leading to greater intention to change, than negative feedback. Ss receiving behavioral feedback value the laboratory experience more. Emotional feedback delivered publicly seems to have a potentiating effect, which can be used to increase the believability of behavioral feedback with which it is associated. Finally, positive feedback, particularly if emotional, seems to be highly related to group cohesiveness.

REFERENCES

Anderson, A., Hummel, T. & Gibson, D. An experimental assessment of videotape feedback and two orientation procedures in a human relations training laboratory. *Journal of Comparative Group Studies*, 1970, **1**, 156–176.

Argyris, C. Conditions for competence acquisition and therapy. *Journal of Applied Behavioral Science*, 1968, **4**, 147–177.

Bailey, K. Audiotape self confrontation in group psychotherapy. *Psychological Reports*, 1970, **27**, 439–444.

Bailey, K.E. & Sowder, C.D. Audio tape and video tape self confrontation and psychotherapy. *Psychological Bulletin*, 1970, **74**, (2), 127–137.

Benne, K.D., Bradford, L.P. & Lippitt, R. The laboratory method. In L.P. Bradford, J.R. Gibb & K.D. Benne (Eds.), *T-Group theory and laboratory method.* New York: John Wiley Sons, 1964. Pp. 15–44.

Berger, M.M. (Ed.) *Videotape Techniques in Psych'atric Training and Treatment.* New York: Brunner/Mazel, 1970.

Bilodeau, E.A. & Bilodeau, I.M. Motor skills learning. *Annual Review of Psychology*, 1961, **12**, 243–280.

Boyd, H. & Sisney, U. Immediate self image confrontation and changes in self concepts. *Journal of Consulting Psychology*, 1967, **31**, 291–296.

Braginsky, B.M., Holzberg, J.D., Ridley, D. & Braginsky, D.D. Patient styles of adaptation to a mental hospital. *Journal of Personality*, 1968, **36**, 283–298.

Braucht, G. Immediate effects of self confrontation on the self concept. *Journal of Consulting and Clinical Psychology*, 1970, **35** (1), 95–101.

Campbell, J.P. & Dunnette, M.D. Effectiveness of T-group experiences in managerial training and development. *Psychological Bulletin*, 1968, **70**, 73–104.

Danet, B. The impact of audio-visual feedback on group psychotherapy. *Journal of Consulting and Clinical Psychology*, 1969, **33**, 632.

Feldman, G. Negative behavioral and positive emotional conditional behavioral feedback in groups. Ph.D. dissertation, in preparation.

Gordman, G. An experiment with companionship therapy. In B.G. Guerney (Ed.), *Psychotherapeutic Agents.* New York: Holt, Rinehart & Winston, 1969. Pp. 121–128.

Humm, S. Use of focused videotape feedback in high school counseling. *Journal of Comparative Group Studies*, 1970, **1**, 101–127.

Jacobs, A. Mood, emotion, affect. In A. Jacobs, & L. Sachs, (Eds.), *The psychology of private events.* New York: Academic Press, 1971. Pp. 131–163.

Jacobs, A. & Deacon, S. Effects of feedback on communication of medical prescription to diabetic patients. *Proceedings of the 77th Annual Convention of the American Psychological Association*, 1969, 767–768.

Jacobs, A., Jacobs, M., Cavior, N. & Burke, J. Anonymous feedback: The credibility and desirability of structured emotional and behaviroal feedback delivered in groups. *Journal of Counseling Psychology.* In press.

Jacobs, A. & Maas, J. Changes in self estimates of psychological attributes as a function of the direction of discrepancies between initial estimates and reported test scores. *Psychological Reports*, 1969, **25**, 359–362.

Jacobs, M., Jacobs, A., Cavior, N. & Feldman, G. Feedback II: The credibility gap: Delivery of positive and negative emotional and behavioral feedback in groups. *Journal of Consulting and Clinical Psychology*, in press.

Jacobs, M., Jacobs, A., Gatz, M. & Schaible, T. The credibility and desirability of positive and negative structural feedback in groups. *Journal of Consulling and Clinical Psychology*, 1973, **40**, 244–252.

Kolb, D.A. & Boyatis, R.E. On the dynamics of the helping relationship. *Journal of Applied Behavioral Science*, 1970, **6**, 267–289.

Kolb, D.A., Winter, S.K. & Berlew, D.E. Self directed change: Two studies. *Journal of Applied Behavioral Science*, 1968, **4**, 453–471.

Martin, R. Videotape self-confrontation in T groups. *Journal of Counseling Psychology*, 1971, **18**, 341–347.

Miller, D. The effects of immediate and delayed audiotape and videotape playback of group counseling. *Dissertation Abstracts International*, 1970, B 30, No. 8, 3872 B.

Morton, R.B. The patient training laboratory: An adaptation of the instrumented training laboratory. In E.H. Schein, & W.G. Bennis (Eds.), *Personal and organizational change through group methods.* New York: John Wiley & Sons, 1967. Pp. 114–151.

Myers, G.E., Myers, M.T., Goldberg, A. & Welch, C.E. Effect of feedback on interpersonal sensitivity in laboratory training groups. *Journal of Applied Behavioral Science*, 1969, **5** (2), 175–185.

Nelson, C. & Shardlow, G. A "pilot" investigation of videotape technique in group psychotherapy of hospitalized chronic schizophrenic patients. *Newsletter for Research in Psychology*, 1970, **12**, 55–58.

Pfeiffer, J.W. & Jones, J.E. *A handbook of structured experiences for human relations training.* Vol. I. Iowa City: University Associates Press, 1969.

Robinson, M. & Jacobs, A. The effect of focussed videotape feedback in group psychotherapy with mental hospital patients. *Psychotherapy: Theory, Research, and Practice*, 1970, **7**(3), 169–172.

Robinson, M. & Jacobs, A. Changes in self concept with videotape feedback. Unpublished manuscript (1966).

Rogers, C. *Client Centered Therapy*. Boston: Houghton Mifflin, 1951.

Schaible, T.D. Group cohesion, feedback acceptance and desirability: Functions of the sequence and valence of feedback. Unpublished masters thesis, West Virginia University, 1970.

Schaible, T. & Jacobs, A. The sequence and valence of feedback in groups. In preparation. a

Schaible, T. & Jacobs, A. Feedback III: Sequence effects: Enhancement of feedback acceptance and group attractiveness by manipulation of the sequence and valence of feedback. Submitted for publication. b

Schein, E.H. & Bennis, W.G. *Personal organizational change through group methods*. New York: John Wiley & Sons, 1967.

Schloss, J.J. The effect of video and audio playback in groups counselling on personality change. *Dissertation Abstracts International,* 1970, **30,** 3284A.

Seitz, F.C. Behavior modification techniques for treating depression. *Psychotherapy: Theory, Research, and Practice,* 1971, **8** (3), 181–184.

Stock, D. A survey of research on T groups. In L.P. Bradford, J.R. Gibb, & K.D. Benne (Eds.), *T-group theory and laboratory method: Innovation in re-education.* New York, London, Sidney: John Wiley & Sons, 1964. Pp. 395–441.

Stoller, F.H. Marathon group therapy. In G.M. Gazda (Ed.), *Innovations to group psychotherapy.* Springfield, Ill.: Charles C Thomas, 1968a. Pp. 42–95.

Stoller, F.H. Focussed feedback with videotape: Extending the group's functions. In G.M. Gazda (Ed.). *Innovations to group psychotherapy.* Springfield, Ill.: Charles C Thomas, 1968b. Pp. 207–255.

Tesser, A., Rosen, S. & Tesser, M. On the reluctance to communicate undesirable messages (the mum effect): A field study. *Psychological Reports,* 1971, **29,** 651–654.

Truax, C.B. & Mitchell, K.M. Research on certain therapist interpersonal skills in relation to process and outcome. In A.E. Bergen & S.L. Gafield, (Eds.), *Handbook of psychotherapy and behavior change: An empirical analysis.* New York, London, Sidney, Toronto: John Wiley & Sons, 1971. Pp. 299–344.

Wiener, N. *Cybernetics or control and communication in the animal and in the machine.* New York: John Wiley & Sons, 1948.

Name Index

Subject Index

Lewis and Clark College - Watzek Library
HM134 .J33 wmain
Jacobs, Alfred/The group as agent of cha
3 5209 00419 2312